In Memory of
Coretta Scott King
1927-2006

WTJacobs Photography

Serving: GA, TN, SC, AL, MS, LA & MO

www.rollsroycemotorcarsatlanta.com

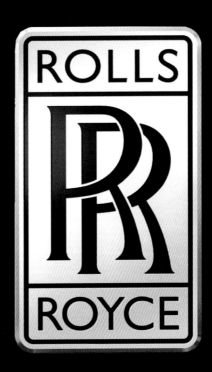

Rolls-Royce Motor Cars Atlanta

3040 Piedmont Road
Atlanta, Georgia 30305
1-877-GA ROLLS
(1-877-427-6557)

Gregory Williams

Showroom: 404-237-6200
Mobile: 404-771-2799

Email: gwilliams@hennessy-auto.com

Photo from the 2006 Edition Unveiling Reception

Photos from the 2006 Edition Book Signing hosted by Barnes & Noble Booksellers at Camp Creek Marketplace.

Celebrating African-American Achievements

WHO'S WHO
IN BLACK
Atlanta®

THE NINTH EDITION

Who's Who In Black Atlanta®
is a registered trademark of
Briscoe Media Group, LLC

Purchase additional copies online @
www.whoswhopublishing.com

Corporate Headquarters
Who's Who Publishing Co., LLC
1650 Lake Shore Drive, Suite 250
Columbus, Ohio 43204

All Credit Cards Accepted
*Inquiries for bulk purchases for youth
groups, schools, churches, civic or
professional organizations, please call
our office for volume discounts.*

Corporate Headquarters
(614) 481-7300

**Copyright © 2006 by C. Sunny Martin,
Briscoe Media Group, LLC**

Library of Congress Control Number: 2006937384

Photo Credits
Denise Gray Photography
C. Sunny Martin

**ISBN # 1-933879-11-4 Hardback
$50.00 each-U.S. Hardback
Commemorative Edition**

**ISBN # 1-933879-10-6 Paperback
$34.95 each-U.S. Paperback**

together,
we soar to new heights

©2006 Delta Air Lines, Inc.

▲Delta
delta.com

We recognize and take pride in the diversity of employees, customers and communities we serve globally.
We embrace the sense of global inclusion that makes Delta a truly uplifting place to work.

MEET THE TEAM

C. Sunny Martin
Founder & CEO

WHO'S who
PUBLISHING CO., LLC

Ernie Sullivan
Senior Partner

Paula Gray
VP Customer Care

Melanie Diggs
Executive Editor

Yolanda Reynolds
Atlanta Publisher
Office: (770) 968-5280

Aaron Leslie
Production Manager

Christina Llewellyn
Graphic Designer

Carter Womack
Regional VP

Tamara Allen
Senior Editor

Nathan Wylder
Senior Editor

Elizabeth Harris
Graphic Designer

Monica Cabbler
Sr. Account Manager

Tina Berry
Executive Assistant

Sarah Waite
Webmaster

Adam DeDent
Copy Editor

Virginia Parham
Account Manager

Jeanne Goshe
Copy Editor

Erica Bowshier
Comptroller

Eric Jefferson
Graphic Designer

CORPORATE OFFICE
1650 Lake Shore Drive, Suite 250 • Columbus, Ohio 43204 • (614) 481-7300
Visit Our Web Site - www.whoswhopublishing.com

Delivering an
Exceptional Ownership Experience

HENNESSY
AUTOMOBILE COMPANIES

WHO'S who

7

I believe in getting more out of life.

My time is precious. Every moment counts. That's why I chose Kaiser Permanente. My doctor is close to home, so when I go for a checkup, I can visit the lab and pharmacy, too—all in one trip. Back home, I can go online and order refills, request routine appointments, get health advice, e-mail my doctor, and more. It's that easy. This way, I have more time to spend on what matters most—life.

For more information about Kaiser Permanente, call **(404) 364-7105**.

Our 12 medical centers are convenient no matter where you live:

Alpharetta	Glenlake
Brookwood at Peachtree	Gwinnett
Cascade	Henry Towne Center
Crescent Center	Panola
Cumberland	Southwood
Forsyth	Townpark

www.kp.org   KAISER PERMANENTE® thrive

Kaiser Foundation Health Plan of Georgia, Inc.
Nine Piedmont Center, 3495 Piedmont Road, Atlanta GA 30305 (404) 364-7000

CONTENTS

Business

Social

Leisure

Meetings

Conventions

Events

Occasions

Accommodations

Function Facilities

Catering

FOR ALL OF YOUR HOSPITALITY NEEDS,
FEEL THE HYATT TOUCH.®

DIVERSITY, DILIGENCE AND DEDICATION.

UNDERSTANDING THE SPECIAL NEEDS OF TRAVELERS IS OUR HERITAGE.

Since 1967, millions of people have experienced our superior level of hospitality. They've traveled from across the globe, across the country, and even from across the street. We're pleased to welcome them time after time. We're even more pleased to know the reason they return is because we understand and have been diligent and dedicated to serving their diverse personal needs. That's because we also come from across the globe, the country, and even from across the street. The staff of Hyatt Regency Atlanta is a collection of people from the same cultures, with similar histories, traditions and dreams of the many guests we have the privilege to serve. In all of our years of success, this common bond of diversity with our clients has been our greatest business asset. We invite you to experience the hospitality excellence that comes from the diversity, diligence and dedication of Hyatt Regency Atlanta. This is not your typical hotel story. This is the Hyatt Touch.™ For information, call 404 577 1234 or visit **hyattregencyatlanta.com**.

HYATT
REGENCY
ATLANTA ®
ON PEACHTREE STREET

DIVERSITY ISN'T AN OBLIGATION IT'S A CELEBRATION.

We at WaMu believe that when diversity is understood and embraced, it opens up an environment where opportunities are limitless. We proudly support "Who's Who" in Black Atlanta's commitment to providing a diversified community that benefits everyone. For more information about our community support and our commitment to our diverse communities, visit wamu.com.

 WaMu

In real estate as in pro sports, sometimes the biggest opponent is the clock.

Some would say the luxury home market in Atlanta is highly competitive. DeShawn Snow, president of EDJ Realty, would agree. However, as the wife of NBA pro Eric Snow, competition is like a member of the family.

"I deal with a lot of players families and they all have very specific needs and very little time to fill them. What I offer is *Red Carpet Service* to clients who are often going through some very quick relocations. Time is of the essence, and I take that seriously."

We invite you to explore the personalized service of working with EDJ. Experience our impeccable service and magnificent amenities. We offer a full service concierge, access to our corporate condo...your "Home Away From Home", DSF and the EDJ Insider.

View www.edjrealty.com to learn more about EDJ amenities, exclusive communities, and properties.

EDJ Realty, LLC is recognized by Who's Who in Luxury Real Estate.

e dj Realty LLC
Exceptional Service for Exquisite Living

E-mail: dsnow@edjrealty.com

11539 Park Woods Circle, Suite 401, Alpheretta, GA 30005

Ph: (770) 754 5070

Equal housing opportunity.

ANDREW YOUNG

To the Honorees of Who's Who in Black Atlanta,

On behalf of my wife Carolyn and I we applaud the accomplishments of the honorees in the 2006 edition of Who's Who in Black Atlanta, especially the featured personality, our own, the Honorable Shirley Clarke Franklin.

Mayor Shirley Franklin is an outstanding individual and currently serves as the Mayor of an historical and diverse City. Mayor Franklin has consistently proven her abilities over the years with both the Jackson and Young administrations. She served during the Young years as Chief Executive Officer serving faithfully in the day-to-day operations while I traveled abroad and also served the late Mayor Maynard H. Jackson term of office in the post of Commissioner of Arts and Recreation bringing first class exhibitions and fine art to our awareness.

Atlanta is tremendously blessed to have a lady of Mayor Franklin's caliber that we can depend on to steer this City on to higher levels. During the Olympics she coordinated and worked with Community Development as we staged the Centennial Olympic Games bringing to Atlanta a multicultural experience from all areas of the World.

Recently, it is through Mayor Franklin's leadership that the City of Atlanta successfully completed the 5th runway at Atlanta Hartsfield-Jackson International airport on time and within budget. Our Atlanta airport is the second busiest international airport and serves as home to both Delta and Air Tran airlines, as well as a welcoming to many international and domestic carriers.

Atlanta is privileged to have all of those represented today who are included in this edition and we send our love to all persons featured in this publication and best regards to their families, friends, employers and well wishers. Thank you, the editors and staff of Who's Who for taking a moment to bring to our attention the shinning stars of our great and beautiful City.

Peace & Blessings,

[signature]

Congress of the United States
House of Representatives
Washington, DC 20515–1005

Dear Friends:

As Georgia's Fifth Congressional District Representative, I am pleased to commend Who's Who Publishing Company on the 2007 edition of Who's Who in Black Atlanta. This edition will highlight and acknowledge Atlanta's most accomplished women.

I would like to congratulate Mayor Shirley Franklin and the other honorees being recognized in the 2007 publication. I applaud the achievements of our great Mayor because she has truly helped to build the "Beloved Community." Her hard work and dedication to the City of Atlanta will not go unnoticed.

I would like to take this opportunity to wish you much success and to again thank Mayor Franklin and the "Powerhouse Women" for their dedicated services to the city of Atlanta. We appreciate the work that you have done in our community.

Sincerely,

John Lewis

John Lewis
Member of Congress

THIS BOOK WAS MADE POSSIBLE BY THE GENEROUS SUPPORT OF OUR

SPONSORS

PLATINUM SPONSORS

DIAMOND SPONSORS

EMERALD SPONSORS

UNVEILING RECEPTION SPONSORS

PINK PAGES SPONSORS

Thanks to **you,**

Mavis has a new confidant who understands her situation, and this one doesn't even need to be walked.

WELLPOINT.

WellPoint is proud to support Who's Who in Black Atlanta.

DiversityInc® top50 Companies FOR DIVERSITY 2006

At WellPoint, you can be addressing tomorrow's health care issues, today. Significant issues, like putting the control of people's health and wellness back into their own hands. In Mavis' case, she had been injured in an automobile accident resulting in a long hospital stay and months of recovery. Luckily, with her trusted WellPoint nurse case manager readily on hand, she knew that she could call someone who could help her to navigate the process and get the care she truly needed. Someone who was well versed in these situations. Someone who could explain things easily. Someone out to make a difference. Someone like you.

Better health care, thanks to you.

Visit us online at **wellpoint.com/careers**

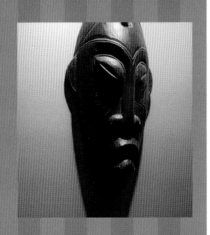
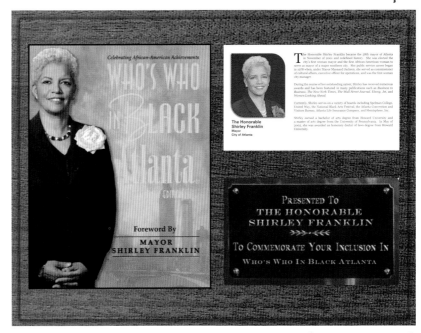

BRUSH
WITH GREATNESS

INTRODUCING
superFULL

Say bye-bye to bristles! Our revolutionary new Clean-Build Brush covers corner-to-corner, root-to-tip, for lashes that are super thick, super separated and superFULL.

DON'T BRISTLE. CALL YOUR AVON REPRESENTATIVE 1 800 FOR AVON OR VISIT US AT AVON.COM

OLD BRISTLE BRUSH

NEW superFULL BRUSH

UP TO
5X
FULLER
WITHOUT
CLUMPS

superFULL mascara
AVON

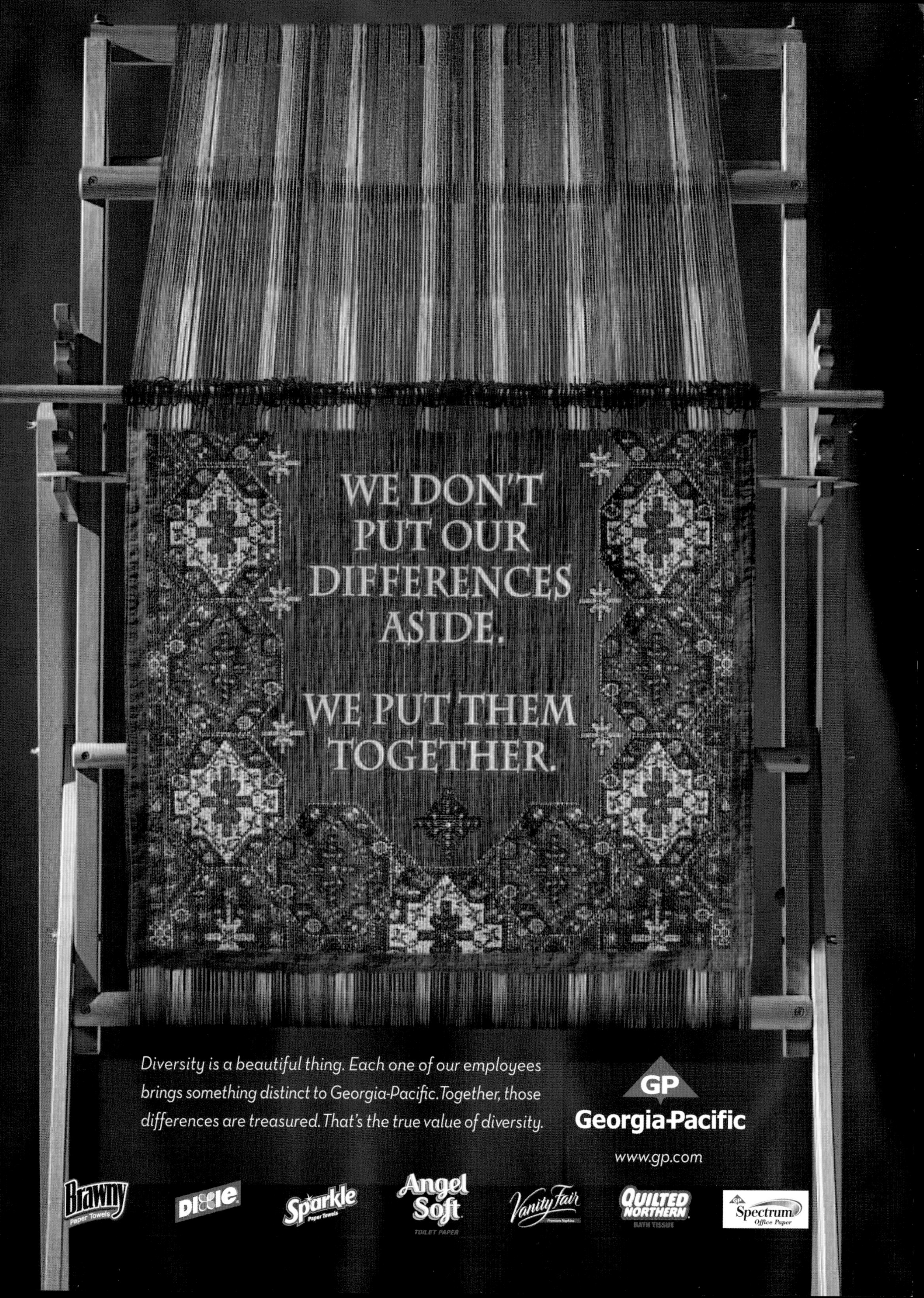

WE DON'T
PUT OUR
DIFFERENCES
ASIDE.
WE PUT THEM
TOGETHER.
Diversity is a beautiful thing. Each one of our employees brings something distinct to Georgia-Pacific. Together, those differences are treasured. That's the true value of diversity.
GP
Georgia-Pacific
www.gp.com
Brawny Paper Towels
Dixie
Sparkle Paper Towels
Angel Soft TOILET PAPER
Vanity Fair
QUILTED NORTHERN BATH TISSUE
Spectrum Office Paper

Bring out the best in everyone,
and you can achieve great things.

The men and women of Lockheed Martin are involved in some of the most important projects in the world. Though naturally diverse, our team shares a common goal: mission success. Our differences make us stronger because we can draw on the widest possible range of unique perspectives. Resulting in innovative solutions to complex challenges. Lockheed Martin. One company. One team.

www.lockheedmartin.com

LOCKHEED MARTIN
We never forget who we're working for™

Nine different people. Nine paths to success. One company that thrives on diversity.

WHAT CAN BROWN DO FOR YOU?

"I have a dream that one day

this nation will rise up and live out

the true meaning of its creed –

'We hold these truths to be self-evident,

that all men are created equal.'"

– Martin Luther King, Jr.

She kept the dream alive.

And it still lives.

Coretta Scott King

April 27, 1927 – January 30, 2006

The men and women of Lockheed Martin honor her life
and her contribution to the advancement of freedom for all.

Foreword

By The Honorable
Mayor Shirley Franklin

"Next to God we are indebted to women, first for life itself, and then for making it worth living."
Mary McLeod Bethune

While I am not sure if we make life worth living, we clearly are making it more exciting for other women.

I want to thank Sunny Martin and the ***Who's Who In Black Atlanta***® team for highlighting the varied contributions of Atlanta's African-American women in this special issue. I am proud and honored to have been included among so many great women and men in our community.

Atlanta has a rich history of women who have broken barriers and shattered myths. It is often said that we stand on the shoulders of others. I would add that we also hold on to the skirts of women who have paved the way for women like me.

Just as this book pays honor to the many achievements of those in our community, it is important to remember and honor Atlanta women as an invaluable resource, and this directory does that.

The most profound reason I had for running for office was that I could not look another young girl or woman in the face and honestly tell her she could do anything she wanted to, if I did not at least try to run and win as Atlanta's first woman mayor. I owed that to my daughters and all the women who

sacrificed so I might have broader opportunities as a black woman.

This includes women like Coretta King, Shirley Chisholm, Rosa Parks, Mary McLeod Bethune and other Atlanta women such as: Ella Baker, the executive director of the SCLC and organizer of the SNCC in the 1950s; Evelyn Gibson Lowery, founder and chairwoman of the SCLC's Women's Organizational Movement for Equality Now (SCLC/W.O.M.E.N.); Dorothy Bolton, domestic union leader; Grace Hamilton, the first African-American woman to serve in the Georgia legislature (1966-1984); Emma Darnell, the first African-American woman to head a division of Atlanta's city government; Justice Leah Ward Sears, the first female chief justice and the youngest person ever to serve on the Georgia Supreme Court; Johnnetta B. Cole, the first African-American woman to serve as president of Spelman College and to serve as chair of the board of United Way of America; Monica (Kaufman) Pearson, the first African-American and woman to become news anchor in the Atlanta market; and Carol Long Banks, the first African-American woman to serve on the City of Atlanta's board of alderman.

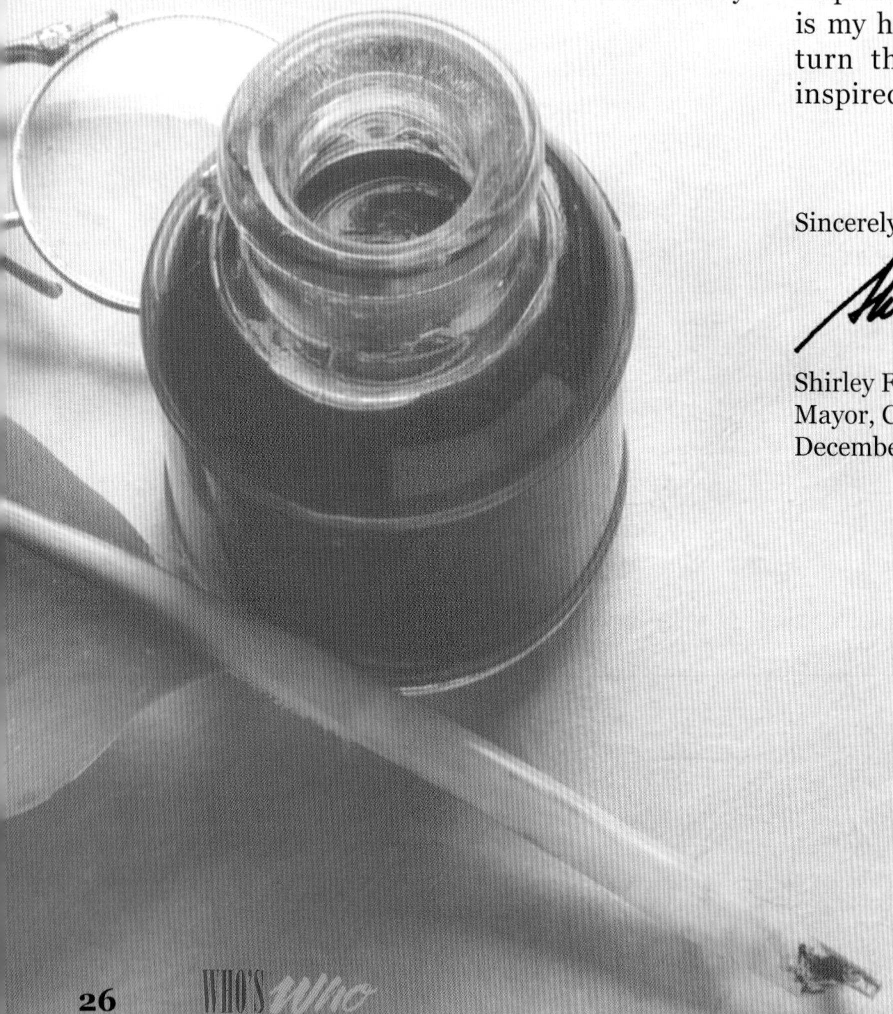

African-American women in Atlanta continue to inspire, encourage, and support a new era of dynamic leadership. I point to contributions from Juanita Abernathy, touching countless lives throughout the world with her message of hope, empowerment and justice; Myrtle Davis, co-executive director of Leadership Atlanta for ten years and a 12-year veteran of the Atlanta City Council; Ingrid Saunders Jones, senior vice president of The Coca-Cola Company and chair of the Coca-Cola Foundation; and Pearl Cleage, acclaimed playwright, poet and journalist.

The lives of these women and so many others have inspired and encouraged me through the years. It is my hope that the many young women who turn the pages of this issue will be equally inspired.

Sincerely,

Shirley Franklin

Shirley Franklin
Mayor, City of Atlanta
December 14, 2006

Moving Forward

With one of the most sophisticated communications networks in the world, nobody offers more services and options than BellSouth. From long distance to cutting-edge calling features to data services, and FastAccess® internet service, we offer everything you need for complete communications.

The diversity of our clients' financial needs calls for diverse solutions.

No two clients' financial needs are alike. That's why we strive for diversity of thinking and backgrounds among our associates. Different perspectives allow for greater creativity and collaboration, which enables us to create innovative solutions that serve all our clients. If you're looking for more than standard issue service and ideas, stop by any of our 1,700 offices, visit us online at suntrust.com, or call us at 800.SUNTRUST.

SUNTRUST
Seeing beyond money

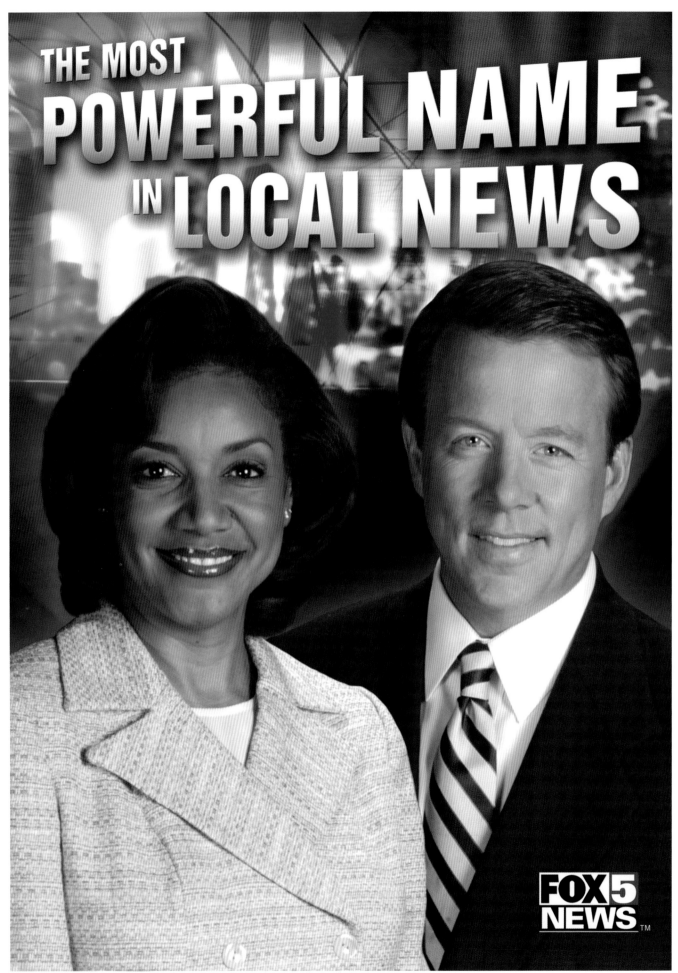

THE MOST POWERFUL NAME IN LOCAL NEWS

FOX 5 NEWS ™

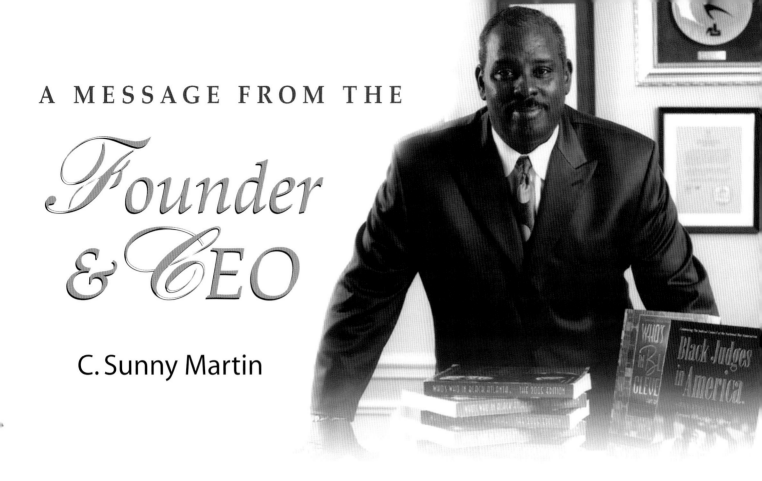

A MESSAGE FROM THE

Founder & CEO

C. Sunny Martin

Sometimes a brother just needs to get out of the way!

Each year we have the daunting task to deliberate on how we can outdo the previous year's edition and make it more appealing, more inclusive and more exciting for our loyal Atlanta readers.

I bet it was not two days after last year's unveiling reception that Yolanda mentioned to me that she wanted to do a special edition of **Who's Who In Black Atlanta**® that would feature a salute to Atlanta's Female Powerhouses. While I liked the idea, I mentioned to Yolanda that I didn't want to alienate the men by leaving them out of the publication.

So "The Queen of Hype," as Yolanda is affectionately called by some of her close friends and clients, worked it out! Alas, "The Pink Pages."

Atlanta is blessed to have so many powerful sisters on every level of leadership you can imagine. They represent corporate interests, they lead entrepreneurial ventures, they are represented in the media, and they lead educational institutions, churches and civic organizations throughout the metropolitan area. They are simply everywhere! In all sincerity, you really would be hard-pressed to find another American city that has so many African-American women in such key positions.

I am especially proud to feature Atlanta Mayor Shirley Franklin on this year's cover, proudly representing the sisterhood. In 1991 Shirley Franklin was featured in our very first publication on page 44. Her title was executive officer for operations in the late Mayor Maynard Jackson's administration. Today, she has risen to be lauded as one of the best mayors in the world. It doesn't get any better than that.

Sisters we salute you, we honor you in this very special edition, and we thank you for the leadership, love and compassion that you have showered upon the entire Atlanta community.

Finally, we are most proud of the footprints you have left for our young daughters to follow. May God continue to bless you all!

Criteria for Inclusion

Who's Who In Black Atlanta is an opportunity for us to afford a measure of recognition to the men and women who have made their mark in their specific occupations, professions, or in service to others in the Atlanta community.

A sincere effort was made to include those whose positions or accomplishments in their chosen fields are significant and whose contributions to community affairs, whether citywide or on the neighborhood level, have improved the quality of life for all of us.

The names of those brief biographies included in this edition were compiled from customary sources of information. Lists of a wide variety were consulted and every effort was made to reach all whose stature or civic activities merited their inclusion.

In today's mobile society, no such publication could ever claim to be complete; some who should be included could not be reached or chose not to respond, and for that we offer our apologies. Constraints of time, space and awareness are thus responsible for other omissions, and not a lack of good intentions on the part of the publisher. Our goal was to document the accomplishments of many people from various occupational disciplines.

An invitation to participate in the publication was extended at the discretion of the publisher. Biographies were invited to contribute personal and professional data, with only the information freely submitted to be included. The editors have made a sincere effort to present an accurate distillation of the data, and to catch errors whenever possible. However, the publisher cannot assume any responsibility for the accuracy of the information submitted.

There was no charge for inclusion in this publication and inclusion was not guaranteed; an annual update is planned. Comments and other concerns should be addressed to:

C. Sunny Martin, CEO
Who's Who Publishing Co., LLC
1650 Lake Shore Drive, Suite 250
Columbus, Ohio 43204
Phone: (614) 481-7300

E-Mail: sunny@whoswhopublishing.com
www.whoswhopublishing.com

A MESSAGE FROM THE

Atlanta Publisher

Yolanda Reynolds

"Therefore if any man be in Christ, he is a new creature: old things are passed away; behold, all things are become new." 2 Corinthians 5:17 KJV

The old is gone and the new is here. In this new season I thank my Lord and Savior Jesus Christ for His word in my life. It is a blessing to know that through Him I have triumphed. I am a new woman.

Reminiscing on Chaka Khan's "I'm Every Woman," this issue is about women and their contributions to our families and society. For this reason, I am honored to salute the Honorable Mayor Shirley Franklin who always makes us Atlantans proud. This book is a special tribute to her and the women in the ATL who MAKE IT HAPPEN!

I am thrilled about the Pink Pages, which features 37 of Atlanta's Female Powerhouses. We all know that Atlanta has many female powerhouses and in previous editions we featured notables such as **Monica (Kaufman) Pearson, the Honorable Leah Ward Sears, Beverly Dabney, Valencia Adams, Janis Ware** and several others in our Interesting Personalities section. These women are all committed to excellence, service and the betterment of Atlanta. Additionally, I applaud the efforts of the Pink Pages sponsors, 16 women business owners who came together in May to assist in making the Pink Pages section a reality. Moreover, without the support of our advertisers and supporters, this edition would not be possible. Thank you.

In all that you will read in this edition, I must offer my deepest thanks to our founder and CEO, C. Sunny Martin. Without hesitation, he allowed me the creativity to fashion this salute to women. His belief in me that I can carry out his dreams for the Atlanta publication encourages me and ignites the passion I feel to make him and those in my community proud of what we accomplish.

I also extend special thanks to the Columbus staff whose tireless efforts make these pages come alive. And certainly without my Atlanta team, Monica, my assistant Julietta, Alonia, Denise, Jeanette, Jacquee, Earnestine, Karen and Tyler (the girls team!), I could not have pulled this together. To my sons Ashton Sinclair and Wildon Chandler Reynolds, you are my stars and the loves of my life.

Finally, I dedicate this book to the women who help to shape and mold my life, my mother, Mary Wilson, and my deceased grandmothers, Margaret Wilson and Elizabeth Clark.

Congratulations to all the women who make it happen in the ATL! Enjoy!

Yolanda Reynolds

THIS IS BEER

I think new and different are worth the price of admission.

Louis Delsarte

Louis Delsarte Printmaking Studio

659 Auburn Avenue | Suite 136 | Atlanta, Georgia 30312 | (404) 581-0778

www.delsarte.com

Soft Lines!
Caribbean Colors!
Expressed Romanticism!
Historical Reflections!

And a *brilliant lust for life* is the embodiment in the art of Louis Delsarte. Described as a figurative painter, Louis Delsarte emerged onto the art scene more than thirty-five years ago as a painter. Using texture and abstraction and water-colors, paints, and mixed media, Louis Delsarte has created works of art that are unique to his own style and to his own experiences and imagination.

Eric Key
Executive Director, The Kansas African
American Museum, Inc., Wichita, Kansas

LOUIS DELSARTE is a profound figurative expressionist from New York City. He received his B.A in Fine Arts from Pratt Institute and his M.F.A. from the University of Arizona. Delsarte has taught painting and drawing at numerous institutions including Howard University in Washington, D.C., Pima College in Tucson, Arizona, Morris Brown College and Spelman College in Atlanta, Georgia. Currently, he is a teaching art and humanities at Morehouse College in Atlanta, Georgia.

The voices of the ancestors speak through me. My work is an interpretation of our communication. This spirit stirs a creative energy in me that moves with joy and passion and sees through the uninhibited vision of a child."

Delsarte's work can be found in numerous collections including the Studio Museum of Harlem in New York City, the Corcoran Museum of Art in Washington, D.C., the High Museum of Art and the Hammonds House Museum in Atlanta, the National Gallery of Art in Bermuda, and the Paul Jones Collection at the University of Delaware.

Delsarte has executed several important mural projects including *Transitions* for the New York Metropolitan Transit Authority and *The Spirit of Harlem* for Norfolk Bank on 125th Street in New York City. Delsarte is also known for his intense printmaking abilities and has been commissioned by Towson University in Towson, Maryland, New York University in New York City and the National Black Arts Festival Collector's Guild in Atlanta, Georgia.

Delsarte's image, *Selma to Montgomery*, was selected by the United States Postal Service as the selvage in the series of stamps, *To Form A More Perfect Union*, created to celebrate the struggle of African Americans in their search for equality in the United States of America. Delsarte's image of Dr. Martin Luther King evokes bittersweet memories of the civil rights struggle and is an inspiring reminder that we have a great deal to overcome.

The artist states, "I am inspired by memories from the past. The souls of loved ones are an integral part of my dreams and visions.

Delsarte on Women and World Peace

In 2003 Delsarte worked with Master Printmaker Lou Stovall in Washington, D.C. to create *The Letter*, a hand-pulled silkscreen for the National Black Arts Festival. He states, "*The Letter* was created during the Crown Heights riots in New York City in homage to my mother who was a great communicator. Oftentimes, she would sit by the window to read letters and correspond with family and friends. The riots represented the chaos and disorder that continues to plague our society. She was gravely concerned about world peace. Since the creation of e-mail, handwritten letters have become obsolete. Women of the world are capable of restoring peace and hope to our society. *The Letter* is an offering of my hope for the future." *Louis Delsarte.*

Images left to right: *Tempest* and *Reunion Revisited*
Artist photo by Denise Gray Photography, layout by Zakkee & Associates

Hartsfield-Jackson Atlanta International Airport

Keeping You Connected...

Our state-of-the-art **Wi-Fi System** keeps you connected in all 5.8 million square feet of the airport, even in our underground trains. Check your e-mail, surf the net, download your favorite music or send those vacation photos to mom.

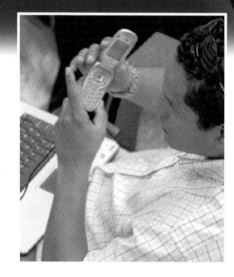

Don't miss a call. Hartsfield-Jackson's new **DAS** (Distributed Antenna System) will keep you talking, uninterrupted, from our front door to your flight.

...to Your World

Missing your flight won't be a problem with Hartsfield-Jackson's **Trak-a-Flight** and **Trak-a-Line** services. Get timely updates on the status of your flight and security line wait times sent directly to your PDA, mobile phone, pager and laptop. From curbside to airside, Hartsfield-Jackson has got you covered.

For more information on connectivity, logon to our **Web site** at www.atlanta-airport.com.

- MAYOR -
SHIRLEY FRANKLIN

QUINTESSENTIALLY
Redefining
ATLANTA

By Maynard Eaton

"*E*VERY GOOD ELECTED OFFICIAL
LISTENS TO THE ELECTORATE
AND EVERY SUCCESSFUL ELECTED
LEADER ALSO LEADS.
BUT, THERE IS A BALANCE.
THE LISTENING LEADS
YOU TO DIALOGUE,
WHICH CAN THEN
LEAD YOU TO THE
FORMULATION OF
PUBLIC POLICY
OR ADVOCACY."

- MAYORAL CANDIDATE
SHIRLEY FRANKLIN,
2000 INTERVIEW

After just five years in office, Atlanta's first female mayor has gone from rave reviews as our so-called "Sewer Mayor," to international acclaim as a polished and preeminent political superstar. Thus far, Shirley Franklin has surprisingly amassed the sort of power, popularity, prestige and honor roll report card grades—in her relentless and remarkable reversal and enhancement of Atlanta's image and fortunes—that she is routinely likened to the legendary political icon, Maynard Jackson, arguably the best mayor in Atlanta's history.

"I couldn't even imagine that," Shirley Franklin bristles at any comparison to Jackson's greatness. "I think I have management and administration skills which may be somewhat unusual among urban mayors."

Father Eugene, Mother Ruth and Mayor Franklin as a child.

Receiving the Profile in Courage award from Senator Edward Kennedy & Caroline B. Kennedy

Her stellar leadership has garnered features in *The New York Times, The Wall Street Journal, Fortune, Ebony, Black Enterprise* and numerous local and national publications. In 2005 *Time* named her one of the top five mayors in the country; she is ranked among the top ten mayors in the world by the World Mayor Internet organization; and was named one of "America's

Mayor Franklin and her father, Judge Eugene Clarke, share a smile.

Best Leaders" by *U.S. News & World Report* and the Center for Public Leadership at Harvard University's Kennedy School of Government. In 2005 *Esquire* named her one of the best and brightest and *American City and County* named her Municipal Leader of the Year. Likewise, Franklin is a recipient of the 2005 John F. Kennedy Profile in Courage Award.

Born and raised in Philadelphia, Pennsylvania, Franklin received a bachelor of arts degree in sociology from Howard University, and earned her master of arts degree in sociology from the University of Pennsylvania.

"Mayor Franklin and I are not friends but I gladly give her nothing but A's," says City Hall insider and political gadfly Dave Walker. "She deserves it; there's nothing to fight about. She has that leadership gene. She may be the best we've ever had."

"By every measure I can think of, she is a primetime politician; every much as important and impactful in her political milieu as the legendary Congresswoman Shirley Chisholm was in hers," believes Jim Welcome, publisher of *The NEWSMAKERS Journal*.

The respect Franklin engenders for her stellar stewardship is said to be comparable in many ways to the iconic imprint and impact Jackson made as our first black mayor.

"Jackson was probably the very best mayor one could have had for that particular era, and Franklin is the right mayor for this time. She's extremely good," opines Clark Atlanta University political scientist William Boone. "She's redefined Atlanta as the leader of southern cities and the prominence and prestige of being mayor of Atlanta. When she came in as mayor she faced some very tough issues. The plaudits she gets are well deserved. History will surely be kind to her."

"She's been an outstanding mayor," says civil rights icon Rev. Joseph Lowery. "She's been a strong leader. She bit the bullet, did what she had to do and came out triumphant. She's a woman of great integrity. She has been a breath of fresh air in government. She's astute and she's not bad to look at either."

"I compare her more with Maynard [Jackson] than any of our previous mayors," adds Marie Cowser, a perceptive and passionate 4th Ward community advocate. "They both had an 'I'm rolling up my sleeves and I'm taking charge persona, and I'll take the hits as they come.' She'll be remembered as one of Atlanta's very best because she took charge when everything was unraveling at the seams and made good things happen. She was what the doctor ordered at that moment."

The mayor's achievements have been so significant in the shaping of Atlanta's resurgence, that if the city charter did not prohibit her from seeking a third term and she could run for reelection again, political pundits believe Franklin's margin of victory would

likely be record setting.

"She will be recorded in history as an extremely successful female mayor," adds community activist Peggy Harper. "She stepped into a situation that was absolutely horrible. [Former Mayor] Bill Campbell left it in a damn mess and she cleaned it up! She's repaired bridges that Bill burned. History is going to be very favorable with her. If she were eligible for a third term, she would be elected hands down."

As Franklin shared during her campaign, she has listened, dialogued and lead. And, yes, the 61-year-old mayor's record reflects that she is as good as promised.

"She is a good listener," concedes her confidant and two-time campaign captain, Georgia State Senator Kasim Reed, a preeminent politician and powerbroker. "But what people really did not have an appreciation of is how good a closer she is. She

Mayor Franklin and staff stuff book bags for displaced students of the Katrina evacuation at the Atlanta Food Bank.

can close the deal. At the end of the day, she gets "it" done. The *it* can be the water and sewer funding. The *it* can be expanding the size of the police force. The *it* can be the city being the safest it has been in a decade. The *it* can be the Martin Luther King papers. Once she focuses on *it* she has the capability to get it done, and she has the capability to attract people with talent to help her."

Franklin says with pride that the hardest and single-most important achievement of her administration has been funding her ballyhooed $3.9 billion Clean Water Atlanta project to revamp the city's crumbling water and sewer system – a long overdue, politically dicey project that previous mayors ignored. Sewers will be her signature, she is convinced, and she says she is cool with that.

"It was a very sexy project," she smiles. "The public and elected officials, and nobody else likes to talk about sewers; but we had to make sewers interesting. We needed to make them essential. We had to sell it. We had to sell their importance. We had to sell the plan. We had to sell financing it. We did some heavy lifting. That was a hard project."

"I'm still the Sewer Mayor," she continues. "People still talk to me about water and sewers. I'm asked about sewers wherever I go. They ask me about the clean water campaign – why did I do it; how did we do it? Once we overcame the challenges associated with understanding the water infrastructure, it became easier to talk about other things. When people look back at this era, they'll say she fixed the sewers."

The impact and import of her fixing the sewers has far reaching consequences. In effect, her Clean Water Atlanta campaign has fueled the city's future health and development.

"The Sewer Mayor means that people who live in the City of Atlanta pay an affordable water bill, rather than having a water bill. If it were not for her work, the water bill would have doubled or even tripled and been one of the four largest bills that we all pay," says Senator Reed. "Being the Sewer Mayor is the reason you have $2 million of investments in construction in the city's urban center. If you weren't the Sewer Mayor and hadn't addressed those sewer issues, then the condominiums you see lining

the streets in various parts of our community, and the new homes you see throughout our city would not have been able to be built. They literally would not have had access to water because we would have been in violation of the federal consent decree. It's important that you take a broader view when you talk about the Sewer Mayor," says Reed.

Franklin's footprint has been her imaginative, even ingenious capacity to devise answers to seemingly unsolvable problems, like Atlanta's endemic water and sewer crises, the alarming crime rate, and the dire budget deficit, coupled with the culture of City Hall corruption. She faced and fought from her first day in office. She has been tested by fire, and now may well be Atlanta's quintessential mayor.

"I believe she is the best mayor in America," opines Reed. "Where she will rank among the mayors of Atlanta, I will leave that to other people, but I will tell you, she is certainly among the best by any standard you want to discuss."

"I BELIEVE SHE IS THE BEST MAYOR IN AMERICA."

"Mayor Franklin has done a great job in cleaning up the corruption in City Hall; she's done a great job in repairing the city's long-neglected infrastructure, and definitely done a great job in mending with the business community," adds Muslim minister and political activist Steven Muhammad. "That's why she will go down in history as one of the greatest mayors of Atlanta. She was able to put Atlanta back on track and engineer Atlanta for dynamic future growth."

Her charisma and experience, as the ace aide to both Mayors Maynard Jackson and Andrew Young, have proved to be the antidote to those dicey dilemmas that ignited her passion, perspective and panache, and fueled her visionary and robust initiatives. This includes triggering an economic empowerment engine, now known as the Beltline; a bold branding campaign for Atlanta; tackling the city's horrific homeless problem and making it a regional concern; selling the business community on securing the treasured Martin Luther King Jr. papers; promoting and promising to establish an Atlanta civil rights museum; and perhaps most significantly, raising funds for every eligible Atlanta high school senior, who doesn't do drugs and doesn't go to jail, to pursue a post-secondary education.

"Who does that and then actually goes out and raises the money?" asks Reed, who Franklin courageously tapped as a relatively unknown, 30-year-old to run her first $4.5 million campaign. "I think that is going to be the signature achievement of her administration. When you look at the number of kids that are now going to school because of her work, how many times is she going to see those young people? It's powerful, but it doesn't get as much attention as many of the other things that she has done."

That program, arguably Franklin's favorite, is called Next Step...The Atlanta Promise. She is a motherly figure, who meets with each student reaching for new heights toward their future. Franklin is not only a savvy politico and an expert city hall administrator, she is also a socially conscious and righteous rainmaker for an array of initiatives—all in the spirit of her mentor Mayor Jackson.

Many of her friends and supporters are clamoring for her to seek higher office once she leaves City Hall. Franklin says she has no interest in running for the U.S. Senate or the Georgia governor's office.

"I'm not saying for sure, but I'm saying very close to sure," she shares of running for another political seat. "I'm not trying to go anyplace else in this job. I'm not trying to build a political career for the next position. I like this job. This is the job I knew the most about. I'm not necessarily looking to parlay it into another political position, whether it's elected or appointed."

A southwest Atlanta resident for more than 30 years, Mayor Franklin has three adult children.

Mayor Franklin with mother and daughter, Kali Franklin, after her keynote address of the Hungry Club at Butler Street YMCA.

15 Financial Myths: Your Guide

You have a unique vision of what you want in life. You're already on the path towards where you want to be. But if you're like most people, you also have some misconceptions about money.

AXA Advisors has compiled the most common myths about investing, retirement, insurance, and estate planning. And countered them with the truths we've learned from helping more than three million individual and business clients with planning strategies.

Jane "Kim" Batten *Registered Representative* jane.batten@axa-advisors.com	3348 Peachtree Road Suite 800 Atlanta, GA 30326 Tel. (404) 760-2362

AXA
FINANCIAL
PROTECTION

Be Life Confident

www.AXAonline.com

Darryl Ford
Owner/General Manager

STONE MOUNTAIN

Jeep CHRYSLER DODGE

NewellRubbermaid™
Brands That Matter

Proud Sponsors of Who's Who in Black Atlanta

Newell Rubbermaid is a consumer and commercial products company that touches the lives of people where they work, live and play. Our brands matter to consumers around the world by making daily lives more convenient and comfortable. Known for innovation and quality, we offer a range of products, including infant car seats, storage solutions, gourmet cookware, writing instruments, tools and torches.

At Newell Rubbermaid, we value the diversity of our employees. We strive to create and foster a supportive and understanding environment in which all individuals can contribute to their maximum potential, regardless of their differences. We are committed to employing the *best* people to do the *best* job possible.

Quick Facts

» Headquartered in Atlanta, GA with offices worldwide
» Annual sales of $5.7 billion
» Over 100 years in business
» 26,000 employees worldwide
» Five global business segments:
  » Office Products
  » Home & Family
  » Tools & Hardware
  » Cleaning & Organization
  » Home Fashions

Explore career opportunities in:

Engineering | Marketing | Operations & Supply Chain | Sales | Finance

For more information or to apply online, visit:
www.newellrubbermaid.com

Sharpie. | IRWIN. | Goody | Rubbermaid | GRACO | Calphalon | WATERMAN

LENOX | PAPER:MATE | LEVOLOR | PARKER | DYMO | Amerock

Have we met?
We should

We're a global market leader in automotive systems and facility management and controls. We meet every day in different ways, in more than 50 countries around the world. In cars with innovative interiors and electronics. In buildings that are safe and comfortable. And in communities where we're investing to build the next generation of leaders.

We want to hire and work with smart, talented people who can bring us diverse perspectives and capabilities. If that describes you or your company, it's time we're introduced.

You know us ... we are Johnson Controls.

www.johnsoncontrols.com

CORPORATION OF THE YEAR

Delta
delta.com

L isa Abraham-Brown is director of human resources at Delta Air Lines. She leads the global human resource strategy for Delta's largest division, airport customer service, which includes more than 15,000 employees worldwide. In her role, she is responsible for leading the people strategy surrounding Delta's cultural transformation.

An experienced and proven HR professional, Lisa joined Delta Technology in 1999 as a human resource consultant. In 2003 she became a human resource manager in in-flight service. Lisa was promoted to general manager of human resources in reservation sales and customer care in 2004, and to her current position in 2006. With each position, her scope of responsibility has increased. Lisa has demonstrated an impressive depth of business knowledge, a strong drive for results, and effective relationship-building skills with her clients, team and constituents.

Prior to Delta, Lisa held various human resource and leadership positions at Prudential, Bank of Atlanta, Concessions International and Florist Transworld Delivery (FTD).

Lisa holds a bachelor's degree in human resources from Michigan State University and a master of business administration degree from Kennesaw State University.

Lisa Abraham-Brown
Director, Human Resources
Delta Air Lines, Inc.

S hirley W. Bridges is chief information officer for Delta Air Lines and serves as president and chief executive officer for Delta Technology, Delta's wholly-owned subsidiary in Atlanta.

Bridges is responsible for managing the day-to-day operation of Delta Technology, which is comprised of approximately 1,500 employees. These employees oversee all of the airline's information technology solutions, development and support.

Most recently, Bridges served as the chief operating officer of Delta Technology. Her responsibilities included oversight of critical business processes, maintenance and operation of systems and existing architecture, and production of corporate report cards.

Bridges has more than 30 years of project management and information technology experience. She joined Delta's IT department in 1990 as a senior project manager.

Bridges received her bachelor's degree in mathematics from Clark Atlanta University and her master's degree in project management from George Washington University. She resides in Fayetteville, Georgia.

Shirley W. Bridges
Chief Information Officer
Delta Air Lines, Inc.

Cherie Caldwell is managing director of global diversity, talent acquisition and retention at Delta Air Lines, the fastest-growing international passenger airline carrier.

Caldwell is accountable for building global strategies and implementing programs to optimize the hiring and retention of critical and diverse talent. This includes oversight of diversity strategies that expand Delta's visibility and reach into targeted communities, as well as the creation of a compelling employee value proposition that positions Delta as a sought-after and preferred employer.

Previously, Caldwell developed and implemented human resources strategies to enhance operational effectiveness for the more than 35,000 employees of the in-flight, reservations, and airport customer service divisions.

Before joining Delta in 2002, Caldwell served as vice president of human resources of a leading B2B company in the forest products industry. Her background includes various senior human resources roles at Fortune 500 companies, spanning multiple industries including transportation, retail, consumer products, manufacturing, financial services and energy.

Caldwell graduated with honors from the University of Maryland where she majored in human resources management. She currently holds a professional SPHR certification.

Cherie Caldwell
Managing Director of Global Diversity,
Talent Acquisition & Retention
Delta Air Lines, Inc.

Gary Donaldson serves as vice president of airline commercial systems at Delta Technology, the wholly-owned information technology subsidiary of Delta Air Lines. In this role, Donaldson is responsible for the commercial systems portfolio, which includes airline scheduling and network analysis systems, revenue management, revenue accounting and recognition, sales force automation, electronic ticketing and reservations. It also includes SkyMiles, eMarketing, integrated communications (DeltaNet), alliances, business intelligence and Delta.com.

Previously, Donaldson served as director of finance and executive services where he was responsible for providing the technology support to the corporate offices of finance, security, legal, communications, property and facilities, and supply chain management.

Donaldson joined Delta Technology in 1997. He holds a bachelor's degree in computer science from the University of Southern Mississippi and a master's degree in management from Pepperdine University.

Prior to joining Delta Technology, Donaldson served 22 years with the U.S. Army in a variety of command and staff information technology positions worldwide.

Gary Donaldson
Vice President
Airline Commercial Systems
Delta Technology, LLC

Sandy Palmer Gordon
Managing Director, Flight Attendants
Delta Air Lines, Inc.

Sandy Palmer Gordon is managing director of flight attendants for Delta Air Lines, the fastest- growing international airline. In this position, she is responsible for managing the day-to-day customer service performance of the Delta flight attendants.

A 16-year Delta veteran, Sandy began her career as a flight attendant. She has held numerous leadership positions, specifically within the in-flight services department. Prior to her current position, Sandy served as director of customer service of Song and played a key role during its startup, which led the way for many of Delta's new innovative customer products.

Previously, Sandy served as general manager of in-flight scheduling where she was responsible for managing the daily scheduling logistics of more than 18,000 flight attendants. In this role, she was the recipient of the REACH Award, recognizing her decisive and effective leadership during the 9/11 tragedy.

A native of Atlanta, Sandy received her bachelor of science degree in finance from Hampton University in 1990. Today she resides in Fairburn, Georgia with her husband and their two children.

Esther L. Hammond
Director
Equal Opportunity & Compliance
Delta Air Lines, Inc.

Esther L. Hammond is director of equal opportunity and compliance at Delta Air Lines. Esther spent the first 17 years of her career with Delta in Chicago, Illinois, relocating to Atlanta in 1995. In her current role, Esther is responsible for Delta's affirmative action plans, OFCCP audits, substance testing programs, criminal history record checks and employee networking groups.

Esther sits on the board of directors for the Delta Community Credit Union and the Jesse Draper Boys & Girls Club.

Esther holds a bachelor of science degree. She will receive her master of science degree in organization/management with a concentration in human resources from Capella University in March of 2007. She has maintained the designation of certified professional in human resources (SPHR) for more than six years.

A Delta
delta.com

Melanee Haywood is vice president of engineering and common services at Delta Technology, LLC, a wholly-owned subsidiary of Delta Air Lines. Her responsibilities include providing leadership and strategic direction for 200 engineers and developers who design technology solutions for Delta Air Lines.

Melanee began her career with Delta Air Lines in 1980. She has held various positions of increased responsibility within Delta and its information technology subsidiaries. An experienced leader, Melanee consistently seeks to influence direction throughout the company. One of her primary objectives is to build strong leadership competencies at all levels of the organization. She is committed to leadership development through formal mentoring to facilitate positive individual career growth.

Melanee received a bachelor of arts degree in psychology from Spelman College in Atlanta. She is a member of the infrastructure executive council of the Corporate Executive Board. She also serves as the executive sponsor of Delta Technology's Medallion Toastmasters chapter, completed the Women in Technology Executive Coaching Program, and was recognized as a Technology All-Star by Women of Color in Technology.

Melanee Haywood
Vice President
Engineering and Common Services
Delta Technology, LLC

A native of Jacksonville, Florida, Alonzo Howell received a bachelor's degree in business management from Florida State University in Tallahassee, Florida and a master's degree in information systems from American University in Washington, D.C.

With 20 years of experience in the information technology industry, Alonzo led the development of numerous large-scale technology solutions for companies including Electronic Data Systems, Advanced Technology Inc., CSX Transportation and BNSF Railway Company. Alonzo and his family moved to Atlanta in June of 2000 after he joined Delta Technology as a director responsible for many enterprise technology components.

Alonzo is a member of the Information Technology Senior Management Forum and Alpha Phi Alpha Fraternity, Inc. He has held leadership positions in the Black Data Processing Associates and served on the board of directors for Big Brothers Big Sisters.

Alonzo was recognized as a Minority Achiever by the YMCA, where he also served as a mentor to several inner-city youth. Alonzo and his family are members of Elizabeth Baptist Church.

Alonzo and his wife, Jeanette, have a son, Alonzo Jr., 22, and a daughter, Brittany, 18.

Alonzo Howell
Director of Revenue Pipeline
Revenue Accounting &
Flight Profitability
Delta Technology, LLC

▲Delta
delta.com

Corporation of the Year

Keyra Lynn Johnson
Director, Internal Communications
Delta Air Lines, Inc.

Keyra Lynn Johnson is director of internal communications for Delta Air Lines. She sets the course for the company's employee communications strategies and oversees Delta's internal news vehicles, leadership communications and the corporate intranet. She is an advocate for Delta's goal of direct, honest, collaborative communications with its more than 45,000 employees worldwide.

Keyra began her career with Delta in 1994 as a customer service agent. In 2000 Keyra joined Delta's corporate communications team as manager of strategic communications. She served as general manager and program director of internal communications before being promoted to her current position in 2005.

Prior to joining Delta, Keyra was a consultant for the Parents Resource Institute for Drug Education (PRIDE), representing the organization in 17 states, Canada and Japan. She also co-authored a grant to establish and manage PRIDE youth teams throughout the Atlanta Public Schools.

Keyra graduated from Georgia State University with a bachelor of arts degree in speech communication. A believer in giving back to the community, she is the co-founder of Girls In Transition, a youth mentoring program.

Thonnia Lee
Senior Manager & Editor
Corporate Communications
Delta Air Lines, Inc.

Thonnia Lee is the senior manager and editor in corporate communications at Delta Air Lines. She is responsible for the monthly employee magazine, *NewsDigest*, as well as the editorial direction, look and feel for company news on the intranet. Her team provides employee news in real time on a site that is updated with breaking news several times a day.

Prior to joining Delta, Lee was editor of the Morehouse College alumnus magazine and acted as lead on the media team as interim director of public relations. An award-winning journalist, Lee has written for *Atlanta Magazine*, *Essence*, *Black Enterprise* and a number of other local and regional magazines. She spent six years with the *Atlanta Journal-Constitution*.

A graduate of Hampton University, Lee has served as an adjunct professor of journalism at Clark Atlanta University, and taught magazine freelance writing at the Callanwolde Fine Arts Center. Under her leadership, Delta's *NewsDigest* has received several awards from the International Association of Business Communicators and is acknowledged by communications professionals as an industry leader in internal communications.

WHO'S *who*

Valerie S. Nesbitt is general manager of supplier diversity for Delta Air Lines. She is responsible for developing and implementing the corporation's strategy for building and maintaining partnerships with small, minority-owned and women-owned businesses. Prior to joining Delta, Valerie held the position of purchasing manager at Scientific-Atlanta, Inc., where she was responsible for the purchase of general office and computer supplies, and capital equipment.

Valerie spent 12 years with Martin Marietta Specialty Components Inc., (formerly General Electric) where she gained an extensive background in supply chain management through a variety of assignments.

Valerie's memberships and board affiliations include the Georgia Minority Supplier Development Council, the Florida Minority Supplier Development Council, and the U.S. Pan Asian American Chamber of Commerce-Southeast. She has received numerous awards and recognition for her business and community contributions.

A native of Aiken, South Carolina, Valerie is a certified purchasing manager. She holds a bachelor of arts degree in psychology from the University of South Carolina, and a master's degree in public administration from Golden Gate University.

Valerie and her husband, Donas, reside in Smyrna, Georgia.

Valerie S. Nesbitt
General Manager, Supplier Diversity
Delta Air Lines, Inc.

Jill Pemberton, 36, is director of finance for Delta Air Lines. She leads all financial activities for the airport customer service and air logistics business units.

Since joining Delta in 1998, Pemberton has held various positions of increasing responsibility. She began her career as manager of financial planning. She then joined the strategy and business development group as general manager of corporate planning before returning to finance as general manager of investor relations. Pemberton was also executive assistant to the chief marketing officer. Prior to her current role, she was general manager of finance for Delta's Atlanta airport operations. Prior to joining Delta, Pemberton held various finance positions within TRW, Inc.

A native of Reston, Virginia, Pemberton graduated from Yale University with a bachelor's degree in economics. She received her master of business administration degree from Harvard Business School.

Pemberton serves on the board of Create Your Dreams, a nonprofit enrichment program for underserved kids in northwest Atlanta.

Jill Pemberton
Director of Finance
Delta Air Lines, Inc.

Delta
delta.com

Corporation of the Year

William E. Settle is the program manager for global diversity, talent acquisition and retention for Delta Air Lines at the world headquarters in Atlanta, Georgia.

Settle is responsible for the management of Delta's global diversity community outreach initiatives. For 12 years, he served as dean of students and vice president for student affairs at Morris Brown College in Atlanta. He entered the corporate world with Delta Air Lines on June 1, 1998.

A native of Charleston, South Carolina, Settle received his bachelor's degree from Fisk University in Nashville, Tennessee and his master's degree in education from Western Carolina University in Cullowhee, North Carolina.

Settle serves on the minority advisory council of the Metropolitan Atlanta Chapter of the American Red Cross. He is a board member of the Salley Foundation and a vice chair of the Southern Region of the General Alumni Association of Fisk University.

He and his wife, Michelle, have two sons, Matthew, a junior at Clark Atlanta University and Christopher, a freshman at Starr's Mill High School. They currently reside in Fayetteville, Georgia.

William E. Settle
Program Manager, Global Diversity
Talent Acquisition & Retention
Delta Air Lines, Inc.

As a finance director for Delta Air Lines, Charles White is responsible for the financial planning, business case analysis, and controller activities for the company's network and revenue management, marketing and SkyMiles loyalty program divisions.

Charles joined Delta in April of 2000 and served as manager of financial and strategic analysis, supporting the reservation sales division. In October of 2002, he was named general manager of finance, supporting reservation sales and consumer marketing. He assumed his current position in July of 2006.

Prior to joining Delta, Charles served as a financial services manager for the Coca-Cola Company in Atlanta. He had several financial and controller roles within the Coca-Cola Company from 1990 to 2000, supporting global procurement and trading, corporate services and the Coca-Cola fountain divisions.

An Atlanta native, Charles received his bachelor of science degree from the Georgia Institute of Technology.

Charles and his wife, Shelley, reside in Stockbridge with their two children, Kyle and Tai-Alysia.

Charles White
Finance Director
Delta Air Lines, Inc.

WHO'S *who*

The only thing we like better than being part of this community is helping ensure its future.

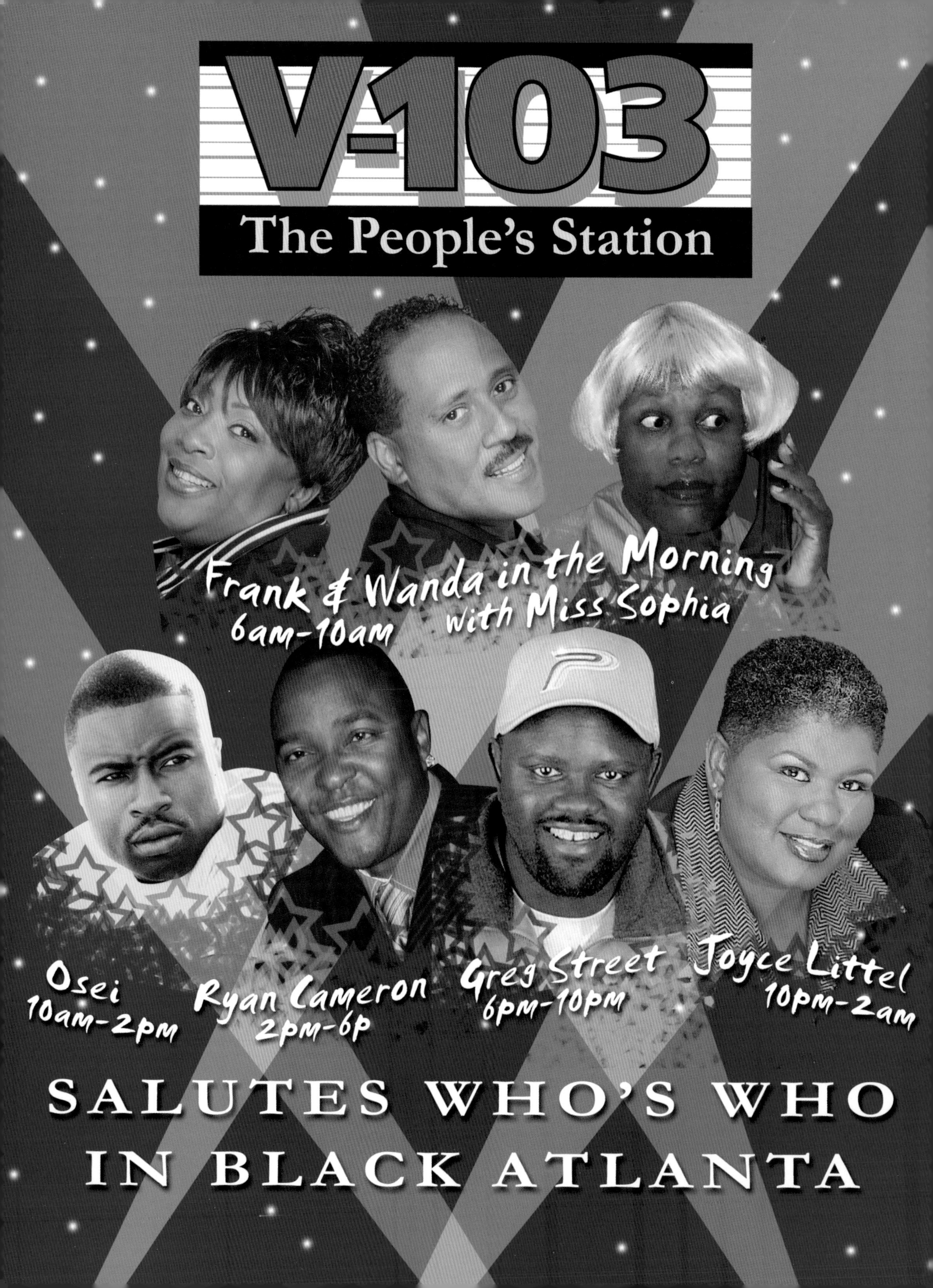

V-103

The People's Station

Frank & Wanda in the Morning
6am-10am
with Miss Sophia

Osei
10am-2pm

Ryan Cameron
2pm-6p

Greg Street
6pm-10pm

Joyce Littel
10pm-2am

SALUTES WHO'S WHO
IN BLACK ATLANTA

V-103
The People's Station

In 1976, there were 1.2 million total residents in the Atlanta Metro Area, and now in 2006 there are 1.2 million African Americans that reside in the Metro Area. Launched in October of 1976, V-103 has literally grown up with Atlanta. The station soared to the top of the ratings from the start and continues to be the dominant station in the market and the most listened to station among multiple generations of African Americans, age 12-54, in Atlanta.

For three decades the station has been the voice of the community and has influenced everything from economic growth and empowerment to politics and of course entertainment and the music industry. V-103 has been instrumental via partnerships with every major organization within our community including the UNCF, NAACP, 100 Black Men of Atlanta, Hosea Feed the Hungry, the APEX Museum, The King Center and the church community. We value these partnerships and are proud to have been with many of them from our beginning, working together to impact social and economic change.

V-103's programming and on air talent have always maintained the highest standards with the purpose to entertain, inform and inspire. Although a music intensive station, V-103 will stop the music when an issue needs to be discussed and our airwaves are the tool to spread the message. A major influence in the music industry, breaking new artists or showcasing a new genre…from disco to rap to hip hop or neo-soul…you hear it first on V-103. The station has been the winner of the National Association of Broadcasters prestigious Marconi Award for an impressive five times for "Station of the Year"

Former V-103 personality Mike Roberts sums it up best, "V-103 is THE model for what an FM Heritage stations impact should be in the community, its longevity and clout is unsurpassed in the entire country."

Mike & Carol

Frank & Wanda

October 23, 1976 WVEE V-103 launched with an all disco format at the beginning of the "Disco Fever" era. The station's team consisted of General Manager/VP; C.B. Rik Rogers, Program Director and morning show host, Scotty Andrews. Soon other personalities were on the air including Wanda Ramos in middays, Billy D in afternoon drive and Joanne Haynes.

However, Disco was soon fizzled and in 1980, after a few years of development and fine tuning, V-103 evolved into the Urban Contemporary format it's known for today.

1986 Mike Robert's debut as the new morning show host, soaring to the top of the ratings. Mike was an influential figure on the air and in the community and he established the standard of excellence to "Entertain, Inform and Educate". He worked in the community with many organizations including the Carrie Steel Pitts home, NAACP, the Apex Museum, the King Center and more.

Over the years, co-host Carol Blackmon, Sports Director; Robin Roberts and comedian Wanda Smith joined the show maintaining the #1 spot in mornings for an amazing 10 years. In 1998, Mike Roberts passed the baton to Frank Ski to carry on the tradition. Mike went on to become one of the country's select few African American radio stations owners, with properties in Macon, Ga.

JULY, 1990 Joyce Littel launches the Quiet Storm. Joyce's sensual voice and relaxing love songs provide the "soundtrack" for Atlanta's adults winding down after a long day at work. The show is the perfect blend of music, spoken word and celebrity interviews. Joyce also focuses on various issues pertaining to "Love & Relationships", providing an outlet for our listeners to discuss the challenges that face them with the relationships in their lives.

FEBRUARY, 1995 Larry Tinsley, the "Triple Threat from Tennessee" becomes the host on Sunday mornings with "Sunday Morning Praise". Each week, over 157,000 listeners tune in to Larry, making him the #1 Sunday morning program.

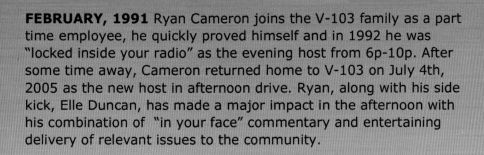

FEBRUARY, 1991 Ryan Cameron joins the V-103 family as a part time employee, he quickly proved himself and in 1992 he was "locked inside your radio" as the evening host from 6p-10p. After some time away, Cameron returned home to V-103 on July 4th, 2005 as the new host in afternoon drive. Ryan, along with his side kick, Elle Duncan, has made a major impact in the afternoon with his combination of "in your face" commentary and entertaining delivery of relevant issues to the community.

MAY, 1995 It's 6 O'Clock, Time for Greg Street to Rock. Greg Street takes over evenings, 6pm-10pm and brings hip hop credibility to the ATL. Nationally respected in both the radio and music industry, Greg attracts listeners of all ages, 12-54.

1998 Frank Ski takes over the reigns in the am drive. The Frank Ski Morning Show continued to uplift, inform and entertain our listeners while taking the show to the next level. He challenged our listeners to educate themselves on a variety of topics such as home ownership, financial investments, spiritual enlightenment, family values and more.

Wanda Smith continued to play a major role with Frank, giving the comic relief for the show but also being the "voice" for the women and many community organizations. The latest team member, Miss Sophia, gives a new "twist" to the show as the entertainment reporter. The Frank & Wanda Morning Show consistently ranks #1 in all of the key demographics.

JANUARY, 2006 Osei takes over the mid day sp from 10am-2pm. Known a "The Dark Secret", Osei entertains Atlanta "at wor with his unique style and special features. His at work audience anticipates The "O Spot", a segment love songs and the "Free Lunch Old Skool Mix" to provide a musical break during their day.

V-103

The People's Station

News & Talk
1380 WAOK
The Voice of the Community

Atlanta's Best News
Jean Ross & Rick Blalock
M-F 5:30am-8am

Power Talk
Lorraine Jacques-White
M-F 8am-12n

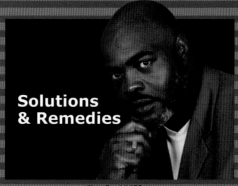

Solutions & Remedies
Rob Wilson
M-F 12n-2pm

The Right Side
Shelley Wynter
M-F 2pm-6pm

Auto Scoop
Adam Goldfein & Joyce Littel
Sat 8am-1pm

Real Estate
Ronnie DeVoe
Sat 1pm-3pm

Sunday Morning Praise
Larry Tinsley
Sun 6am-12noon

SALUTES
WHO'S WHO
IN BLACK ATLANTA

*The true worth of a race must be measured
by the character of its womanhood . . .*

Mary McLeod Bethune

Pink Pages designed by Zakkee and Associates

Photo by Denise Gray Photography

Fulfilling a Prophecy

Scarlet Pressley-Brown

by Jacquee Minor

As a little girl in Anderson, South Carolina, Scarlet Pressley-Brown's dreams of flying off to exotic, faraway destinations were held aloft on the planes soaring by overhead. How poetic that she landed in the airline industry. General manager in global diversity and community affairs at Delta Air Lines, Pressley-Brown says her job is a dream come true.

She is responsible for managing Delta Air Line's philanthropic giving, both cash and in-kind donations, which include sometimes life-saving transportation. In establishing her company as a good corporate citizen, she also fulfills a personal goal.

"I enjoy the fact that the work I do has a positive impact on so many lives," says Pressley-Brown. Because of the commodity that we give, transportation, we're able to do some incredible things… sometimes as incredible as saving lives."

Pressley-Brown points to the organizations they support, such as Children's Miracle Network, transporting children with rare illnesses to critical health care wherever it is available in the world. They also transport Red Cross and UNICEF caretakers to disaster sites of human tragedy. "I'm glad to be instrumental in making sure those things happen," she says proudly.

It's a long way from her adolescent dreams of "owning the biggest modeling agency in the world." As a teenager and young adult, Pressley-Brown pursued her modeling passion, despite the fact that, at 5'5", she didn't fit the bill of a top model, and the opportunities in her market were slim and none. With little income, she realized she would need an education to move forward.

Pressley-Brown went back to earn a bachelor's degree in her '30s, and a master's in her '40s. She says it was the best thing she could have done, discovering that education makes winning easier.

While at Oglethorpe University, Pressley-Brown encountered a professor who had a profound influence in her life. Dr. Virginia Kemp Leslie was a professor of women's studies who "constantly sent messages that reassured me who I was and what I could be," she recalls. "One day she looked me in my eyes and said 'You will make wonderful things happen for a lot of people. You're going to change lives."

In fulfilling the prophecy, Pressley-Brown has changed many lives. Previously, she worked with the East Lake Community Foundation, where she helped transform the East Lake Meadows public housing community, once known as "little Vietnam," into a vibrant, thriving neighborhood. As part of the restoration, she helped establish Drew Charter School, Atlanta's first charter school, and proudly reports that of the 12 students she worked with, over half have gone on to secondary education.

Pressley-Brown always involved her own children in her civic activities, partly as a way to spend time with them when her jobs kept her away for long hours. Inspired by the East Lake experience, her youngest daughter has gone on to become an award-winning fifth grade teacher in Atlanta Public Schools. Pressley-Brown says, "She goes to work with the idea of doing something good in a child's life today."

Life is good for Pressley-Brown. She and husband, Wendell, headed off to Rome to celebrate their seventh wedding anniversary. Working in the airline industry has its privileges.

Photo by Denise Gray Photography

Paying it Forward

Billye S. Aaron

by Jacquee Minor

It is a long way from hard times in a rural Texas farming community to the grand lifestyle of a celebrated benefactor. Billye S. Aaron has made the journey fabulously, with a good measure of class and style.

The memories of childhood ever-present, Aaron conjures up images of poverty and deprivation. Her father died when she was only 12 years old, leaving her mother to raise eight children on her own. She tells of a time when they made clothes from the printed fabric of sacks that were used in those days to package cooking flour, passed on from a neighbor lady. And Aaron recalls dreaming of one day being able to buy "as many clothes as I can hang up."

The former teacher, television talk show host, United Negro College Fund executive and fund-raiser extraordinaire, Aaron, who is married to baseball great Hank Aaron, can afford just about anything she wants these days. And while she does love a good sale, giving is more her style.

"To whom much is given, much is required," Aaron says earnestly. "That is imbedded in me. I feel that God has blessed me tremendously, and it is required."

Aaron, who remains grateful to the people who helped her family when they needed it, takes satisfaction in paying it forward. She co-founded, with her husband, the Hank Aaron Chasing the Dream Foundation, to provide grants for children with special talents. Her years as a development executive with UNCF brought in significant dollars, and despite retiring more than ten years ago, she continues to chair its annual fund-raising campaign. In fact, her fund-raising prowess is often called on to attract donors as generous as the Aarons.

This year, she was asked to co-chair the Schomburg Center for Research in Black Culture Museum's 80th anniversary celebration gala at Lincoln Center in New York, honoring the likes of Maya Angelou, Harry Belafonte, John Hope Franklin and Ruby Dee. Marveling at the opportunity, Aaron says, "If you're a southern girl from Palestine, Texas, and somebody asks you serve in this capacity, you're gonna say yes."

Just don't call her a philanthropist. Aaron, famously generous, is offended by the term that she thinks should be reserved for folks like the Rockefellers, (Warren) Buffets and (Bill) Gates of the world.

"I don't call it philanthropy," she insists. "I just want to do God's will. It is incumbent upon me to do what I can."

Education at a black college got her out of her small town life, and Aaron believes it can deliver today's youth from their own Palestine. That is why she gives so generously in support of black colleges. "I feel it is my responsibility to do what I can to help other African-American young people coming behind me to have opportunities as well."

In a milestone year for Aaron, turning 70 years old, she is celebrating the joys of a life well lived. There have been no further signs of breast cancer, diagnosed six years ago. The experiences of a charmed adult life are enough to soften those of the early days. "I've had an unbelievable life," she says in awe. "People I've met, places I've been. Sometimes, I think this is too good to be true."

Still Going Strong

Evangelist Dorothy Norwood

by Alonia Jernigan

When turning the pages of the history of gospel music, it is inevitable that the story of Evangelist Dorothy Norwood will appear. In fact, there is no way to talk about the history of gospel without including the countless contributions of Norwood. A native Atlantan, she began singing and touring with her family at the tender age of 8. Today, at age 71, she boasts a 50-year career as a professional gospel singer. But what most people do not know is that she is still physically fit, and there is no retirement in sight or mind for her any time soon. "I have a trainer, and I do everything from riding the bike to walking on the treadmill. I even work on the Ab Lounge!" So when asked about retirement, she joyfully shares, "As long as I've got my health and strength, I'll be here. In the words of my mother, 'if it works for you, stick with it.'"

Without a doubt, Norwood's career has certainly worked for her. In addition to being a part of the legendary Caravans (an ensemble that gained notoriety from the late 1950s to the mid 1960s as the nation's most popular touring gospel group), Norwood has recorded 47 albums, received five gold records, eight Grammy nominations, one Stellar award and three Stellar nominations. And, she won the 2005 Soul Train Lady of Soul award for best gospel album, *Stand on the Word.* Her uncanny ability to tell stories that relate to people's lives, and then climax the story with a soul-stirring song earned her the title, "The World's Greatest Gospel Story Teller." Norwood's renown eventually introduced her to European audiences including Germany, France and England.

Norwood's storytelling not only became a delight of the gospel community, but in 1972 she had the opportunity to tour with famed rocker Mick Jagger, who attributes his selection to her storytelling. "He said that he was really moved by the stories *Johnny and Jesus* and *Denied Mother*," she recalls. This experience brought her before an audience of 62,000 people in 30 states and 42 cities.

Reflecting on her career, Norwood states, "My latter is greater than my past. Now, I find myself handling not just one career but two," which references a vision God gave her that the Caravans would reunite. "We recorded a new CD entitled, *Paving the Way*, which was recorded in September of 2006." And to her excitement, the group started traveling before the project was released.

As with any career, Norwood was not immune from options to explore other aspects of her professional industry of music. "I've worked with many secular artists—Stevie Wonder, Johnny Taylor, Natalie Cole," she says. "But I've always stayed true to gospel. I didn't give in to the option to cross over to secular music, although one of my recordings did actually cross over," she adds.

The facts that Evangelist Norwood didn't give in and that she is still making an impact around the world are testaments that people are glad she stayed in the game. Still going strong, she is an excellent example that with God, professional longevity and success are indeed possible.

A Life Overflowing

Evern Cooper Epps

by Jacquee Minor

In a life overflowing with accomplishment, Evern Cooper Epps is at the height of her career. President of the UPS Foundation and vice president of corporate relations, she is the first woman and the only minority to ever head the foundation in its 55-year history. She develops strategic programs that, with the help of her board of directors, have grown the company's philanthropic presence from domestic to worldwide.

And yet, every now and again, Epps admits to still having a "pinch me moment."

There are those moments when this self-described "country girl from Arkansas" recognizes the grand scale of her life, like a recent trip to China, in which she traveled across the country, being one of only a handful of dark people in sight. As she stood up as a woman and a minority addressing company employees through a translator, it struck her like a wave. The sense of accomplishment about making a difference in the quality of life for people in a foreign land brought on an overwhelming surge of emotion.

"Being part of something greater than yourself is really a blessing," Epps explains. "You can never take life for granted." At the end of the day, I think I can lay my head down and hear the Lord say, 'job well done.'"

The special moments have not come without struggle. Epps started her career with UPS more than 30 years ago as a part-time clerical worker. She worked her way through the organization, at one point driving the brown delivery truck, before joining the executive management circle.

A former high school teacher, Epps did not picture herself in the philanthropic world. A strategic thinker who loves taking charge, she now knows she is where she is supposed to be.

"It's who I am," she confesses. "I have to be in a position to know I'm being used in a way God intended for my life to be used."

Epps credits the religious values she grew up with for helping her to stay focused on her real purpose. This drives her commitment to community and her work with organizations such as the Northwest Georgia Girl Scouts Council, Atlanta Partners for Education, Metro Atlanta YWCA, and Andrew Young School of Public Policy, among many others.

The greatest challenge for high-powered women, Epps acknowledges, is giving yourself permission for personal time. Living her personal motto of "make it happen, make it fun," Epps makes sure there is time for the things that love her back, like golfing, reading, cooking and spending time with her family.

With culinary skills that range from roast duck to neck bones, Epps takes great pride in the fact that her husband of two years enjoys her cooking. "He told me before we married that I was more than just a pretty face," she laughs. Epps, who refused to settle, counts him among the many blessings in her life; the best friend who she says "helped complete my circle."

Epps also places a premium on creating a personal space. She uses this metaphor: "It's like going into the closet with the Lord; you have to surround yourself with people and things that keep you focused, keep you balanced, and keep you true."

Building Communities ... One Dream at a Time

Autaco
DEVELOPMENT
A BROWN GROUP COMPANY

Audra Brown Cooper
Developer

AUTACO DEVELOPMENT, LLC

3099 Washington Road
Atlanta, Georgia 30344
P 404.559.1805
F 404.761.0020
www.autaco.com

LAND DEVELOPMENT • INFRASTRUCTURE • DESIGN/BUILD • RENOVATIONS
COMMERCIAL/RESIDENTIAL • PROJECT MANAGEMENT • NEW CONSTRUCTION

Project
words that inspire
we can show you how...

Jacquee Minor
President

A good speech has the power to reach out and touch someone. It weaves a tale that captures the imagination. At the heart of a good speech is a story that grabs hold and won't let go. Minorlogues can help you make the connection. We craft messages that inform, entertain, and delight.

Messages that create a lasting bond.

What's your story? It's all in the telling.

Let Minorlogues create your

monologue masterpiece.

Project...Engage...Connect.

J.MINORLOGUES
speeches scripts profiles

Photo by Denise Gray Photography

Keeping it Real

Jackie Parker

by Jacquee Minor

When major consumer and commercial product marketer Newell Rubbermaid decided to add a diversity program to its business model this year, the company considered only one person for the job. As it turns out, Jackie Parker is exactly what was needed to open the doors to a more inclusive environment.

"I honestly feel my unique quality is keeping it real with them," Parker tells. "That's what you hire me for, to bring a different perspective. I need to stay true to who I am so that the message is heard."

The message she must reinforce is that a company has to reflect its marketplace in order to be competitive. With a new, forward-thinking CEO and new headquarters located in Atlanta, Newell, a more-than-a-century-old company whose brands touch millions of people every day, is ready to change its traditional ways.

Parker, whose early career in customer marketing and consumer products sales ended when her job was transferred to another city, feels that her life experiences have prepared her for this ministry in the workplace. She makes it clear, "I believe my steps have been ordered by God."

After a position with Pepsi-Cola Company ended, Parker was introduced to the practice of diversity and inclusion. With marketing degrees, the Baltimore, Maryland native had worked for companies like General Foods and Nabisco. A prayer minister in her church, she often led intercessory prayer group meetings. On one such occasion, after hearing her powerful delivery, a member of the group approached Parker about becoming a facilitator for Roosevelt Thomas Consulting.

Parker became a certified trainer with Thomas, considered the pioneer of the diversity practice, and, while doing classroom facilitation, got what she called "the bug." Oftentimes reluctant participants would approach her after a class to say they got the message. "That was the divine transition for me into this business."

She was working for Russell Corporation as diversity director when word of the Newell position reached Parker. Eager to build a world-class diversity initiative from the ground level, she is inspired to give a voice to people in the workplace who feel powerless to make changes. Her own encounters with exclusion and discrimination add purpose and passion to her mission.

"I've lived it, I know what other employees are going through," Parker says. "I'm in this role for a reason...to make a difference, to educate and bring a level of awareness about treating women and minorities with respect and dignity. Just give us the fair opportunity you give everybody else."

Parker's diminutive frame packs a powerhouse of energy, fueled in large part by frequent exercise. She plays mixed tennis with her husband in several leagues and plays on a singles' team. The mother of two daughters, ages 14 and 9, she loves shopping and eating out with the girls.

Her story is unfolding as if from the pages of an engrossing novel and the one about how Parker met her husband is another thriller. In the short version, after praying for someone who would appreciate all of her, their lives intersected in the sky on a flight from Los Angeles. Parker's husband of two years is her dream come true.

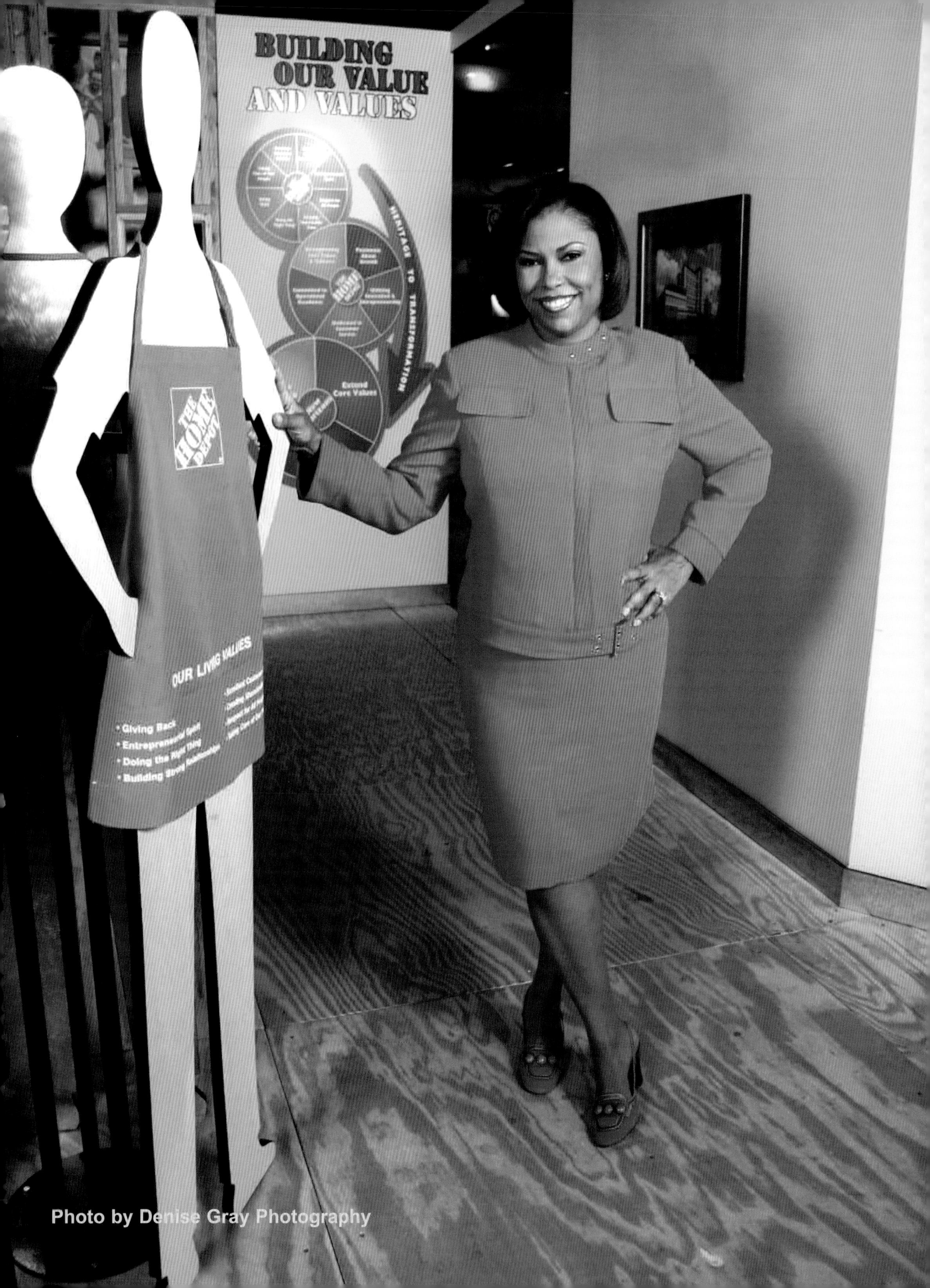
BUILDING
OUR VALUE
AND VALUES
HERITAGE TO TRANSFORMATION
Extend Core Values
THE HOME DEPOT
OUR LIVING VALUES
• Giving Back
• Entrepreneurial Spirit
• Doing the Right Thing
• Building Strong Relationships

Photo by Denise Gray Photography

A Life of Advocacy

Gloria Johnson Goins

by Jacquee Minor

When she was just 6 years old, Gloria Johnson Goins told her dad she wanted to be a lawyer when she grew up so that she could "use the law to help people." True to her personal vision and philosophy, Goins became a successful trial attorney although, these days, her advocacy takes on a different form.

Vice president of diversity and inclusion for the world's third-largest retailer, The Home Depot, Goins says it is important to her that she is doing something to change people's lives. "I became a lawyer to be an advocate," she says. "Every day, I advocate for making sure we have a culture and a company which welcomes all people."

As chief architect of The Home Depot's strategy to truly be a global company that mirrors its marketplace, Goins influences everything the company does. She was recruited from her role as vice president of diversity at Cingular Wireless, where she created a diversity practice that became nationally recognized for its progressive leadership in the industry. Goins notes that companies must be nimble in order to stay competitive.

"This is the first time in American history that four generations are at work, all with different opinions and different philosophies about work. A company has to respond to all the generational needs within the workplace."

A member of the bar in both her birth state of Florida and in Georgia, Goins says the lion's share of her career was spent in the courtroom as a trial lawyer. Whether representing individuals or companies, the theme of her life has been to have a positive impact in people's lives.

"My spiritual connection is at the core of who I am," Goins says. One way she exercises it is through teaching others the principles of good finance. Having had access to information that helped her to make good financial decisions, Goins feels obligated to share it with as many people as she can. She counsels others about the economic principles of wealth building, how to get out of debt, and sound investment. She is especially concerned about news reports indicating young women are leaving college saddled with debt. She laments that "Young people are mortgaging away their futures before they can start it."

The daughter of a Bahamian immigrant living in Miami, Goins says she grew up in a stable, loving environment. She didn't know they were poor until much later in life because her parents always provided them with what they wanted. Goins says her dad would often work six jobs at a time to provide for the family. "My father only had a sixth grade education, but insisted that his children get the best education available. He was going to do whatever it took to afford it."

That work ethic and the family's strong Christian values are certainly reflected in Goins' life. She devotes time to her church, New Birth Missionary Baptist Church. Married now for four years, Goins, who got pregnant on her honeymoon, is the mother of a sassy, smart 3-year-old daughter. "I'm blessed to have an incredible spouse and partner who does what it takes to make sure the home is taken care of. It allows me to be the woman I am."

All Things Are Possible

Stephanie Odom

by Alonia Jernigan

A foundational principle of leadership, according to renowned football coach and motivator Vince Lombardi, is the power to inspire others to follow. With that being said, Stephanie Odom is quite a leader. Barely 40 years old, Odom has achieved a measure of professional success that many merely dream of achieving within their entire lifetime. As CEO of Christian Ministries Hospice, she is responsible for the operation and stewardship of four subsidiary businesses: Southern Crescent Personal Care Home, Victorian Manor Personal Care Home, Special Occasions Events Center and Christian Ministries Residential Palliative Care Suites, with locations in Riverdale and Griffin, Georgia and approximately 100 employees.

Odom's journey to success was not tread upon a crystal stair. The Zebulon, Georgia native not only experienced growing up in a small, rural community, but she also faced a situation that could have shattered her dreams, as it has many other teen mothers. "I am a living testimony that anyone who desires to rise above their circumstances certainly can do so," reflects Odom. "I was determined that I was not going to take second best in life, and it's a blessing to now be an inspiration to other young women," she adds.

And so her journey began when she completed high school and further completed the nursing program at Gordon College. Prior to matriculating through Gordon, she worked private duty and she also worked as an oncology nurse for approximately ten years. "After spending so much time in this field, I began to see that there was a tremendous need for support for the families of those with terminal illnesses,"

Odom says. "As I began to research, I discovered that there was a terrible void within our community. Knowing my heart's desire to assure that families have a place of dignity where their loved ones could make their last days their best days, and seeing that there was a poignant need, I began Christian Ministries Hospice in 1998."

Because of Odom's leadership, Christian Ministries Hospice is an icon in the community. Her organization founded and organized Griffin's annual community health fair in 2005. Drawing over 3,000 citizens, public safety personnel and medical professionals, the event was Griffin's first and spawned an incredible additional 2,000 people in 2006. She nurtures her commitment to the community through her membership with the National Hospice Palliative Care Organization, Spalding County Rotary Club and the Georgia Hospice Organization.

Odom's dynamic leadership and sincere concern for humanity has gained the attention of her alma mater, and she recently received the Gordon College Alumnae Achievement Award. Also, former Secretary of State Cathy Cox bestowed upon Odom the Outstanding Citizen Award and said, "There is no one with more vision for the people of Georgia than Stephanie Collier Odom." Described by her colleagues as one who is innovative, hardworking, kind and loving, the healthcare industry is a much better place, thanks to Ms. Odom. And while business and community are important, she also understands the importance of balance. As such, Odom enjoys shopping, traveling, swimming and cooking. She is the proud mother of four children: Anthony (22), Jeremy (15) and twins, Calyn and Collin (5).

A
DAY
IN
THE
LIFE OF
AFRICA

Crusader for Good Health

Melissa Bishop-Murphy

by Jacquee Minor

When it comes to your health, what you don't know can hurt you. Melissa Bishop-Murphy, southeastern director of government relations for Pfizer, Inc., is committed to making health and wellness information readily available, especially to minorities. She considers it critical to our survival.

"The biggest challenge in the African-American community is access to health care and medications," says Bishop-Murphy. "African Americans are disproportionately impacted by disease. My passion is to get the message of preventative health care to the minority community."

Lobbying public officials and lawmakers, Bishop-Murphy advocates for easy access to medications that treat, and better yet, prevent illness. Working with advocacy organizations like the American Diabetes Association, she has been instrumental in helping to make medications more readily available to more people by removing some of the barriers to access.

Pfizer manufactures many of the maintenance drugs that treat chronic conditions prevalent in the African-American community. Bishop-Murphy wants more people to know they do not have to choose between buying food and medications. The pharmaceutical company offers a number of reduced cost and no-cost programs for those who qualify, yet Bishop-Murphy laments, "we're the last to know about them." Working with more than 100 faith-based organizations throughout the southeast region conducting informational workshops, she is spreading the word that drugs are available to those who need them most.

Watching her parents struggle with illness has been a catalyst for the mission. Her mother has hyperten-

sion; her father's uncontrolled blood pressure led to kidney failure at the age of 48 and a kidney transplant. Bishop-Murphy says there are simple messages that we all can pass along. "Just losing 10 to 20 pounds makes a difference," she suggests. "It is a message we can carry to our children, our parents, our friends. It takes a community effort."

Community is paramount in Bishop-Murphy's life. But for a community of friends, family and educators who encouraged and supported her dreams, she wonders where she would be today. As the second of six children growing up poor in Alabama, she became the first in her family to graduate from college. Books opened the door to a whole new world. "Reading took me to places I couldn't afford to go. It gave me something to emulate."

A graduate of Georgetown University Law School, Bishop-Murphy began her career in the practice of law. She was recruited by Pfizer while serving as general counsel for the Georgia Department of Medical Assistance.

While she deals with a lot of serious issues, Bishop-Murphy knows how to have fun. And while she is health-conscious, she admits to a weakness. "I have to tell you, I love chocolate," she says with a giggle. "That is my weakness. I've never seen a piece of chocolate cake I can resist."

Married 14 years, Bishop-Murphy wants to someday travel the world, leisurely. And she always encourages her nieces and nephews to read, telling them, "Reading will take you everywhere you want to go. You can find all the answers in a book."

rolonda wright
lifestyle management

- Run Errands

- Personal/ Grocery Shopping

- Prescription Delivery

- Waiting Service

- Event Planning

- Event Tickets

- Travel Arrangements

- Reminder Service

- Motor Vehicle Issues

OOdlez
personal concierge service

3150 norman berry drive

suite b

atlanta, georgia 30344

o: 404.234.5886 | f: 404.607.1406

www.oodlezllc.com

Plus OOdlez More . . .

Living and Giving Large

Wanda Smith

by Jacquee Minor

You would expect the co-host of a popular morning radio show to have a big personality. Wanda Smith is no exception. The comedic half of Atlanta's V-103 *Frank and Wanda in the Morning* show is bold, brash and irreverently funny. More surprising is the enormous size of her heart. Smith's generous nature flows from a wellspring of compassion that appears bottomless.

A humanitarian at heart, Smith would find a way to help people no matter what she was doing. It just happens that this position makes her accessible to throngs of people who have come to know and love her like a big sister. The better half of the Frank and Wanda show on WVEE, V-103 FM, Smith co-hosts the region's No. 1 radio show and, after ten years on air, boasts the highest ratings of any of the station's personalities. The show has become the pulpit of her ministry.

"V-103 helped me to become the woman I am," says Smith. "I'm using the talent God gave me to make people laugh. And I can speak up and help people who need me."

Making people laugh is how she got the radio gig. Smith came to Atlanta in the early '90s in search of a better place to raise her young son. She was making the rounds on what is known as "the chitlin' circuit," performing wherever she could book a gig. The word on her raunchy comedy act got around, drawing hundreds of people to a local club.

A V-103 manager who had been watching her performance for a while invited her to sit in on the morning show one day a week. Research indicated how much she connected with the audience, and they asked her to stay for a year. Now ten years into her morning routine, Smith has a new contract with a new title… show co-host.

"If you put God first, He will put you where you need to be," she reflects.

Smith's listeners know she will go the extra mile. Within days of Katrina's rampage through the Gulf coastal region, Smith spearheaded a call to action, collecting three planeloads of food and supplies that were shipped in to those who needed it most. She helped raise more than $250,000 for MARDS, Metro Atlanta Respite & Developmental Services, a favorite charity that provides respite care services to disabled children in Atlanta.

A simple phone call can launch her into action, pulling in all the resources at her disposal. When a single mom called to say she was about to lose her home, Smith rallied the troops to get her a new apartment with a two-year lease, new furniture, a trip to Disney World for the kids, health services and a host of other freebies.

Still, no one would imagine the breadth of her kindness. A listener with seven children told Smith how she was struggling to get on her feet. After arranging for help, Smith went a step further, taking in one of the children. With her oldest son now off to college, Smith's 5-year-old adopted daughter, Kennedy, lives with Smith, along with her son, 9-year-old Giovanni. A recipient of the 2006 Humanitarian Award from Omega Psi Phi Fraternity, Wanda Smith is living and giving large.

Be Prepared, Be Available, Be Involved

Harriette Watkins

by Jacquee Minor

Everything she needed to know, Harriette Watkins learned working in a high school classroom. What she learned there about patience, motivating people, being creative, organizing and being an administrator was useful in every subsequent career move. Recently retired as president of AGL Resources Foundation, Watkins has had ample opportunity to put those principles to good use.

A descendant of three generations of educators, teaching came naturally to Watkins. Her mother retired after 30 years in the Columbus, Georgia school system. Her grandfather, a teacher most of his life, taught Watkins a valuable lesson: always learn and then teach. "I found out the more you learn, the better you are…the more you teach, the better you get because you teach what you most need to learn," says Watkins. "That message helps prepare you for whatever life has to offer."

Watkins' career was an ever-evolving entity. Her first job after earning a master's degree in special education was teaching special ed students at Therrell High School. Later, she was introduced to adult learning at Atlanta Area Technical College and then Atlanta University.

Watkins left the classroom for a corporate position managing special development training at Georgia Power. It was there that she gained entry into the community affairs arena. "It gave me the exposure, skills and training to do community service well," she reflects. "AGL Resources was an opportunity to do it at its highest level."

Before her retirement in the summer of 2006, Watkins headed up the company's philanthropic efforts, connecting the company to the community, putting foundation dollars where they were needed. "I was able to put a face on AGL Resources and bridge the gap between the community and the company."

At no time during her rising career did Watkins ever have to look for a job. "Every job I had came from a phone call and someone asking me if I was interested in doing it," she says with amusement. "God cut through the weeds and bushes and allowed this course to happen. It certainly was not my doing." Watkins says the best way to move ahead is to be prepared, be available and be involved.

She considered her job at AGL Resources "the best job in the world. Can you imagine getting paid to make a difference in the community? It doesn't get any better than that."

Maybe a little better. With retirement comes the freedom to set your own agenda. She and her husband, who retired from IBM last year, are spending a lot of time traveling. She was also able to spend time planning her mother's surprise 90th birthday party in Columbus.

Perhaps her greatest pleasure is that she is now free to get involved in helping to manifest her sons' dreams. She has agreed to work with son Derrick Watkins (aka Fonsworth Bentley) on writing a book on manners, dress and etiquette for young people. She marvels at the ingenuity and creativity of his fictitious character, which started as a personal assistant to Sean "P. Diddy" Combs, and has morphed into a celebrity hip-hop figure. And now her youngest son is applying his creative skills, attending film school at USC in Southern California.

The Woman Changing Her World

Xernona Clayton

by Jacquee Minor

Xernona Clayton has enjoyed an exciting career. She has always worked in positions of great influence, with high profile people, under exceptional circumstances. In 1967 she was the first black person in the South to have her own television show. She spent 31 years as a high ranking corporate executive with Turner Broadcasting Systems. As creator and executive producer of the famed Trumpet Awards, Clayton has crafted a signature event. With such a rich pedigree, no one could ever challenge her place in history. She is, in the simplest terms, an icon.

So when Time Warner acquired Turner Broadcasting System's fleet of companies, it seemed like a good time for the media maven to retire. The new company, after all, did not always share her vision of how the Trumpet Awards should be presented. She was weighing the option until the most amazing turn of events.

Turner Broadcasting offered her a five-year, $5 million deal, giving her complete creative control of her program. It is not the kind of thing that happens every day, unless you're Xernona Clayton, founder, president and CEO of the Trumpet Awards Foundation.

Clayton tells young people to prepare for rare moments. "It's important to go to school to become well trained, so that when opportunity presents itself, you can be ready to respond."

"I didn't go to school to meet Martin King (or wife Coretta) and become his confidant. I didn't go to school to meet Ted Turner. Now, I'm tied to him in spirit forever," she says.

Throughout her career she has been the only woman, and usually the woman changing the men around her. Yet Clayton credits Turner with revealing her full potential. "When people believe in you," she explains, "it's amazing how far you will expand your talents beyond the boundaries even you thought you had. Now I'm so rich, so expansive because of the opportunities that have come my way through that relationship."

Clayton created the Trumpet Awards to herald the tremendous accomplishments and contributions African Americans have made to the world. Now in its 13th year, it is a showcase of talent, hard work and ingenuity, and a who's who of Hollywood celebrities, athletes, politicians, entrepreneurs and titans of industry.

A spectacle of remarkable good health and high energy, Clayton, at "31" years of age, has no aches, no pains, and takes no medication. Averaging only about four hours of sleep a night, she is up and in her office by four o'clock every morning, staying until at least six o'clock every evening. With no exercise or diet, she weighs exactly 4 pounds more than she did in college.

Clayton's petite frame possesses a bigger-than-life personality, and her irreverent humor can bring the house down.

Even as a child growing up in Muskogee, Oklahoma, Clayton remembers always being different from the other kids. "I never wanted to go where everyone else was going," she remembers. "I didn't want to follow the crowd." And while she never had children of her own, she has nurtured many. "I feel like I've given life without giving birth," she says.

A Career of Longevity and Consistency

Carolyn Jones Cartwright

by Jacquee Minor

As director of corporate diversity for SunTrust Banks, Carolyn Jones Cartwright thinks of herself as the thought leader on strategic planning for diversity. Her biggest challenge, as she sees it, is reaching out to all the partners, both inside and outside the organization, and keeping them all engaged.

"I've been with SunTrust longer than my husband," she jokes. With SunTrust more than 35 years working primarily in human resources functions, the diversity role is the first position she has held that had no predecessor. Cartwright was given the task of creating and coordinating the company's diversity initiatives. Her efforts over the past six years in building a centralized diversity focus, spanning across all the company's geographies and regions, has gained SunTrust recognition as a leader in the diversity arena.

"Having the opportunity to shape it, influence what it was going to be, and influence the company's activities in this space is one of the things I'm most proud of," she says. In addition to institutionalizing diversity throughout the organization, Cartwright believes "our greatest accomplishment has been making sure there is consistent, ongoing conversation about diversity."

Longevity and consistency are hallmarks of Cartwright's character. A fan of road races, she has run the six-mile Peachtree Road Race for 20 years, missing only a couple of races over the years. Her longest run, the Atlanta Marathon, was 26 miles. As an avid runner, she would enter races in cities she was visiting as a way to learn the lay of the land, and to see the local sights. She recalls a run through San Francisco as one of her most fun races. "It was about a 12-mile run through lots of eclectic neighborhoods through San Francisco to the Bay. People dressed up in that race. It was like one big party," she recalls. Cartwright says bad knees have taken her off-road for the longer races. Although she still gets in her walks on the treadmill and around the neighborhood.

Much of Cartwright's work in the community has been in support of children's issues. She has worked as a board member with Inner Harbour, a treatment facility for young people, and has served on the board of the Georgia Center for Children and worked with United Way. Her work with Atlanta Public Schools programs stems from a desire to help people become independent. "Freedom comes from education," she says. "You gain economic empowerment through education."

The Spelman College alum says she has always been drawn to the idea of teaching at the college level, and it still holds her interest.

Being someone who often does the right thing has earned Cartwright a nickname from her husband, "Ms. Do Right." Married 35 years, she and husband, Kenneth, share a commitment to volunteerism and to church activities at Ben Hill United Methodist Church. They spend much of their free time together working around the house and gardening, and they both love spending time with the family dog. "She is our heart." The key to a long marriage, according to Cartwright, is compromise.

DENISE GRAY

dg

PHOTOGRAPHY

DENISE GRAY
PHOTOGRAPHY

Specializing in:
- **Promotional Portraits**
- **Corporate Events**
- **Public Relations**
- **Seniors**
- **Special Events**
- **Weddings**

**Denise
Gray**
*On-Site
Photographer*

770.969.5639

770.969.7740 fax

email: dgrayphoto@yahoo.com

www.denisegrayphoto.com

Post Office Box 474

Union City, Georgia 30291

We bring the studio to you . . .

Photo by Denise Gray Photography

The Thrill of the Hunt

Sonia "Sunny" Franklin

by Jacquee Minor

In the fierce competition for top business talent, Sonia "Sunny" Franklin, head of talent management for Avon North America, knows exactly what to look for. She is interested in people who can move through the ranks of the organization to fill high level positions, and to do it within a specific window of time. Whether she is looking within the company ranks or locating outside talent, Franklin just loves the thrill of the hunt.

"There's a war on talent these days," she says. "Everybody's going after good talent, especially looking for diverse candidates."

In this newly created position at Avon, Franklin has been given responsibility for leading the search for the company's next generation of leaders. She is charged with identifying top talent that can step in to fill key positions, like that of president in the North American business. As one of just five people given the role in the organization across Avon's vast territory of 120 countries, she helps to design the talent management process for the entire company. With her human resources background, Avon has placed a lot of confidence in Franklin's ability to help shape the company's future.

"I always wanted to be in a position to make a significant impact to the business, and put leaders in place who will move the stock price and take care of employees," she says.

Franklin understands what it takes to drive operations and how to market a business. Before going to work for Avon 13 years ago, she held marketing positions at Sara Lee. An interest in developing human potential led her to pursue human resources, knowing the old adage, "If you do what you like, the money will follow," would be true. She lives by her philosophy, "Everything that happens in your life is intended to prepare you for something bigger and better in the future."

Franklin maintains a grueling travel schedule, working in New York during the week and returning to her Atlanta home and husband on weekends. She recognizes how important it is that her husband of 30 years, a military man, understands and respects what she does. "My career," Franklin concedes, "would not be where it is without him."

She also credits her parents, both now deceased, for setting the standards high and demanding that their children live up to them. As Seventh Day Adventists, they grew up in the confines of a deeply religious family. "My only role model is my mom," says Franklin. "She was humble, compassionate, giving and hardworking."

Perhaps that is why Franklin emphasizes humility as an important character trait. "I treat the janitor the same as I would the president of the company. For me, it's not about the title, it's about people."

When time permits, Franklin indulges her creative passion for decorating, both in her own home and the homes of family and friends. Few people know she has a yellow belt in karate. Franklin has studied tae kwon do over the years as a means of learning discipline, focus and for keeping her mind razor sharp.

Photo by Denise Gray Photography

A Strong Sense of Ethics

Rhonda Mims Simpson

by Jacquee Minor

At just 39 years old, Rhonda Mims Simpson has made a lot of big steps in her career. As a lawyer, she headed up a district attorney's office in South Carolina, managing 35 people when she was 28 years old. She has worked as a civil litigation attorney with the United States Justice Department, and as a senior attorney with the National District Attorney Association's American Prosecutor's Research Institute. Now, as president of ING Foundation, she leads the philanthropic efforts of the world's 13th largest financial services company.

"God placed me in the right places at the right time," is Simpson's explanation for the meteoric rise. "I've always had a very strong ethical way of doing things, and I've always been noticed a lot."

A love of politics and government, sparked by a fourth grade trip to the South Carolina State House, was ignited with a position in the Justice Department. Working at the very seat of power, Simpson felt at ease among the power brokers, even though she can't see herself as an elected official. "I like politics, but I don't like the politic," she explains. "I'm more of the chief of staff type, running the show, while someone else does the politicking."

Simpson says her career has been defined by a strong sense of ethics, something ingrained in her as a child. She describes her mother as someone who always did right by people. Recalling a childhood incident in which her mother diplomatically told a friend that her outfit looked good when, in fact, it did not, Simpson says she was blown away to know that her mother even knew how to lie. Dad also has a sound moral compass. And grandmother reinforced the need to always tell the truth. "Lying was like stealing in my house," she remembers.

Carrying that code of conduct throughout her life, Simpson has found it useful in every phase of her career. "Being a prosecutor wasn't just about winning the case, but about seeking justice. I just wanted to make sure the right thing was done." Only recently has Simpson relinquished a role as ethics officer with ING, giving her more time to focus on running the foundation.

With such a serious façade, Simpson says her wicked sense of humor often goes unnoticed. She looks for opportunities to let more people in on her lighter side.

Up until recently, Simpson would have said her amazing career ascent was her proudest achievement. Then came Ansley Gabriel, her 8-month-old daughter, and suddenly the focus of her world has shifted.

"I'm surprised at how much I'm enjoying it, based on who I thought I was," muses Simpson. "I never saw myself as a mother." Married two years to husband James Simpson, a sales and marketing manager, the driving career woman is adapting seamlessly to her new role as parent.

A strong fashion sense could influence her destiny. Simpson, who describes her style as "traditional, with flair," says she would love to someday own a clothing specialty boutique, offering upscale clothing and accessories. She says it is the only thing she has not done that she would still like to do someday.

Empowered to Excel

Justine Boyd

by Alonia Jernigan

Sitting at the helm of a branch of the nation's oldest organization for women is a vibrant young woman. Emerging from a professional background wherein each position has served as a stepping stone to future and better opportunities, Justine Boyd, CEO of the YWCA of Greater Atlanta, is a force to be reckoned with in the non-profit community.

As the YWCA's leader since January of 2005, Boyd has impressively exceeded expectations in the organization's primary area of concern. "The biggest challenge for most nonprofits is that of fund-raising," states Boyd. "It's important that a strategic, comprehensive plan be developed, which will play a key role in helping gain support for the organization." Understanding this concept and focusing on growth, Boyd is pleased that the organization's signature event, the Annual Salute to Women of Achievement Luncheon, raised a half-million dollars in 2006. "We are really excited about this accomplishment because the constant figure for a while was in the $400,000 range," she shares. Boyd served on the organization's board of directors for two years before being asked to be the CEO.

Was it in the cards for this Lincolnton, Georgia native to find herself in such a prominent position? She answers, "I wish I could say that I had big dreams of growing up and becoming this or that, and then have a plan to get there. But it didn't happen for me that way." Boyd made Atlanta her home after transferring to Georgia State University from the University of Georgia. She served as county clerk for the Fulton County Board of Commissioners, a position which she says was tough, yet beneficial. "Being in the middle of politics really taught me how to build relationships. It laid the foundation for helping me to build the rest of my career," she says. "The experience gave me an opportunity to manage the staff and helped bring out the best in the people I worked with," she shares. Prior to joining the YWCA, Boyd served as assistant general manager for external affairs for MARTA.

Raised by a mother who was a school teacher and a father who was chairman of the church's deacon board for several years, Boyd has always had a heart for serving others. "From my upbringing, it was expected that you work in the community. In fact, I never thought about not being a part of the community. So, when I came here, the first thing I tried to do was find a church family and community activities in which to get involved," she says. A daddy's girl at heart, Boyd credits her 79-year old father with playing an integral role in helping to shape her leadership abilities. "He has a lot of wisdom on how to handle life. He has a great personality, and he believes in community and family."

An avid traveler, Boyd enjoys visiting as many places as possible. "I try to get away at least twice a year, and I'll stay gone for a week, including weekends," she says. She also enjoys interior design, reading and calligraphy. Married for 15 years, Boyd's husband is a banker and one whom she refers to as a wonderful man.

Nothing Short of Excellence

Rebecca Franklin

by Jacquee Minor

An invitation from Rebecca Franklin always signals something special. The founder and CEO of Women Works Publishing, Inc., Franklin has a reputation for putting on the Ritz. Whether she's inviting you into her home, or to one of her signature events, you know it's going to be a memorable occasion.

Listed in the portfolio of the Roswell, Georgia-based firm is its premiere publication, *Women Looking Ahead News Magazine*; the newly created *Men Looking Ahead* magazine which debuted in 2003; and *Doctors Orders*, a special market publication for medical professionals introduced in 2006. The company also sponsors a series of annual events, including Georgia Entrepreneurs Night, the WLA 100s List of Georgia's Most Powerful and Influential Women, the Woman of the Year Luncheon honoring "Ordinary Women with Extraordinary Talents and Men Who Soar," and the ever-popular WPP Power Networking Breakfast at Tiffany's.

Conceived out of a desire to spotlight the achievements of women of color, Franklin took inspiration from *Essence* magazine, and her cues from George Frazier's *Success Guide*, to create her first publication in 1993. *Women Looking Ahead News Magazine* has gone on to earn awards and accolades primarily because, according to Franklin, she expects nothing short of excellence.

"I am successful," Franklin says matter-of-factly, "because I expect it to happen. I don't expect to fail."

Her business prowess, coupled with a disarming Southern charm, has opened many doors. On display throughout her showplace home visitors see Franklin cozying up with the rich and famous. Among the publicity shots are Franklin's White House meeting with Hillary Clinton, and another

mentor, Johnny Cochran. Still, it's her daughter, Shanika Joshua, who she most wants to impress. The mother who shields and protects her daughter from harm, even though Shanika is now a married woman, takes great pride in what she calls "my biggest production."

A natural people broker, Franklin has won an A-list of admirers who surround her with support, both professionally and personally. With so many experiences to share, she sees it as her responsibility to help others succeed. "I've had so many women to teach me the ropes," says Franklin. I want to teach other women to believe in themselves."

Had she pursued her childhood dreams, Franklin would be a district attorney, prosecuting criminals. Instead, she reads design books and peruses furniture stores, always on the look out for something to satisfy her admitted sofa fetish.

Above all, Franklin is the consummate hostess. Even the printed announcement itself is a work of art. Once there, guests receive the royal treatment. A beautifully appointed setting that's pleasing to the senses, a tasteful spread of delicious food, a cheerful smile and a good word to lift your spirit await those who enter her domain. A self-described Southern belle from Houston, Texas, Franklin always makes her visitors feel at home.

If only she could learn to relax. So much of her time and energy is dedicated to the business that Franklin rarely takes vacation. And when she does take time off, it's usually only a few days before she's answering calls and e-mails again. It is the kind of dedication that is often the curse and the catalyst of a successful entrepreneur. Franklin wouldn't have it any other way.

RITA TUCKER WILLIAMS
Attorney at Law

The Law Firm of
Williams & Associates, P.C.

220 CHURCH STREET | DECATUR, GEORGIA 30030 | 404.370.3783 | 404.370.0884 FAX

WWW.AtlantaInjuryLawFirm.com

PERSONAL INJURY • TRANSPORTATION WRECKS • DEFECTIVE PRODUCTS • WORKPLACE INJURIES

A Sonja Strayhand Design… It's You, Only Better

Residential Interior

Commercial Interior

Sonja Strayhand, President
Allied ASID, Associate II IIDA

Award Winning Interior Designs
- Atlanta Woman Magazine *"25 Power Women to Watch of 2006"*
- Atlanta Business League *"Outstanding Achievement in Creative Style Award"* 2005
- *"Best Interior Design Award"* 2004 Street of Dreams Luxury Home Tour

Commercial & Residential Interiors
- Selected one of premier showcase designers for the exclusive Bryan Jordan Le Jardin community of South Fulton
- Skyloft Business Center in West End for the Russell Corporation
- Renaissance Walk on Auburn Avenue for the Integral Group
- Celebrities, athletes, dignitaries, bishops, and top corporate executives in Atlanta, New York, Philadelphia and Houston live with a Sonja Strayhand design.

Sonja Strayhand designs interiors for you, always exceeding your expectations.

SONJA STRAYHAND
INTERIOR DESIGN

5601 Fulton Industrial Blvd.

Suite 120

Atlanta, GA   30336

404-629-0044 office

404-629-0047 fax

678-596-3044 cell

Sonstra@aol.com

AWARD WINNING INTERIOR DESIGN FIRM | COMMERCIAL AND RESIDENTIAL INTERIORS

"I was raised around strong, powerful women."

Myrna White

by Jacquee Minor

Myrna White's job as director of public affairs at Hartsfield Jackson International Airport is a lot like the city's famous slogan. "Everyday is a brand new day," she chuckles, describing the dynamic environment of managing multiple issues simultaneously at the breakneck pace of the world's busiest airport. At any moment of any given day, the unexpected crisis can arise to upset the perilously balanced apple cart. Believe it or not, it is that sense of daring she loves most about her high-flying career.

White credits her dexterity to the women who shaped her. "I was raised around strong, powerful women," she says. Most influential is her mother, a retired school teacher. Although very prim and proper, her mother, much to White's amusement, has returned to her roots in the Dublin, Georgia farm country to become a prize-winning Black Angus cow farmer.

Mother's advice to "do it right the first time," has been the clarion call of White's career. "I always wanted to do my best," she says, reflecting on her ascent to the heights of the aviation industry. She excelled in her first job out of the School of Journalism at University of Georgia, and was made bureau chief of the *Columbus Ledger-Enquirer* newspaper.

When the constant deadline pressures of journalism lost its allure, White transitioned into public affairs/public relations by way of the Atlanta Public Safety.

In the early '90s, White was hired by the Atlanta Airport to promote the controversial fifth commuter runway. The $1.2 billion runway, considered the most important runway in America, opened in 2006,

dramatically increasing Hartsfield Jackson's capacity to move people around the world. Since then, White has created the office of intergovernmental affairs, and is now building the office of public affairs for the Department of Aviation.

The Georgia General Assembly gave her a huge vote of confidence this year with resolutions from the Senate and the House, commending her outstanding achievements. Having her family join in for the ceremony made it all the more special.

With all of her success, White says the role of mom gives her the most joy. "I longed to be a mother," she recalls, recounting an incident that crystallized her desire. "I was standing on the mezzanine at the airport, and I remember distinctly seeing a mother playing with her (infant) and I got teary eyed because I wanted to be a mommy so bad." When Floyd, III was born eight years ago, she nicknamed him "Tad," the Greek word for "gift of God."

In homage to an influential fraternal grandmother with a college degree who taught English and home economics, and a maternal grandmother who raised eight children on a farm, White reaches out to other young people. "I attempt to repay my gifts by motivating young women and pushing them to recognize the talent they have and helping them to build on them."

Her relationship with a young adolescent girl earned White the "Big Sister of the Year" title from Big Brothers Big Sisters, Inc. in 1987. The two have remained good friends and her little sister, now a police officer who is married with children of her own, reminds White what it means to nurture a young person's life.

The Sweet Sound of Music

Tanya Coleman

by Jacquee Minor

You may not have heard her name, but you've certainly seen her work. Tanya Coleman is the creative force behind all the advertising materials for Publix Super Markets, Inc. As marketing advertising manager, Coleman produces all the printed materials, such as weekly newspaper circulars, and has a hand in developing television and radio spots. Managing the chain's image in the Atlanta division, which includes Georgia, South Carolina, Alabama and Tennessee, falls solely within her province.

Oddly enough, Coleman's consumer product sales expertise was acquired on-the-job. She came to Publix with experience in fund development for non-profit organizations such as the United Negro College Fund and Families First. Her fund-raising skills were finely honed working during the Johnnetta Cole administration at Spelman College. An engaging personality caught the attention of one of her board members, who ultimately became her calling card to get in the Publix door.

Publix hired Coleman to work in its Cascade store shortly after it opened, where she captivated the neighborhood, building strong community ties for the store. The company sent her back to school to learn marketing and made her field marketing manager before promoting her to the current position.

It is a role for which Coleman seems uniquely suited. Intellectually, she thinks analytically, with a vision for what the end product should look like. Intuitively, she closely identifies with customers and she is a good listener who genuinely cares about people. "I strive to educate, stimulate and motivate others," Coleman says. "Doing these things brings me a sense of satisfaction, fulfillment and joy."

Above all, Coleman is a woman who makes music, literally and figuratively. "I don't want my life to be ordinary," she says. To that end, Coleman fully inhabits every moment. A classically trained lyric alto and Spelman College music major, she sings in three choirs at St. Paul's Episcopal Church. At the time of the interview, she was preparing for a concert at Cathedral of St. John in New York. Her love affair with music includes playing piano and listening to jazz and blues.

Spending time with her daughter and three granddaughters is cause for celebration. "We cook together, laugh a great deal, sing silly songs, travel together and enjoy music, books, storytelling and movies together," Coleman says.

In seeking balance between work, family and community, Coleman finds harmony in her life. Her social life fits seamlessly into the professional. She loves entertaining friends at home, shopping for the right ingredients to make the perfect dish for each guest, and then pairing it to the perfect wines. Given the right circumstances, Coleman admits, "I would love to write and illustrate a book about fine dining: the food, the linens, the flowers, the joy."

Blending work and community service gives both extra mileage. Her Links chapter, in partnership with Atlanta Public Schools, is developing the first all-girls' school in public housing. The school, in the Capitol Homes community, is being built in the next couple of years and is intended to nurture the girls into proud, productive women. Demonstrating her passion for children, Coleman says "this is how we create a lasting legacy in the African-American community."

Photo by Denise Gray Photography

Connecting With Your Health

Dr. Debra Carlton

by Earnestine Perry

Since she can remember, Debra Carlton has always been intrigued by science and technology. Imagine having the opportunity to guide Kaiser Permanente's electronic medical records implementation at 12 local medical centers, subsequently providing nearly 300,000 Georgians with online access to their health records. Dr. Debra Carlton did just that and more.

After obtaining an undergraduate degree in biology at the prestigious Massachusetts Institute of Technology (MIT), Carlton earned a medical degree from Vanderbilt University in Nashville and completed her internal medicine residency at the UCLA Sepulveda VA Hospital. These educational choices were contributing factors that placed Carlton in a distinct league of African-American physicians. Carlton says MIT taught her to embrace and love technology; to be curious about it; and not to be afraid of it. This helped her prepare Kaiser Permanente physicians and other staff for the massive transition from paper medical charts to electronic medical records.

As associate medical director of clinical affairs for The Southeast Permanente Medical Group, Inc., Carlton oversees 250 physicians who provide care exclusively to Kaiser Permanente patients in Georgia. For more than 15 years, she has kept Kaiser Permanente in the forefront of medicine and innovation.

Carlton is on the board of directors of the Care Management Institute, a Kaiser Permanente organization that works to assure the delivery of high quality, evidence-based care. She was integrally involved in helping the medical group earn the prestigious 2002

Preeminence Award from the American Medical Group Association.

Carlton is married to William Craven, M.D., an orthopedic surgeon in Decatur. After moving around most of her life — she has lived in Boston, Los Angeles, Baltimore and Nashville—she has called Atlanta home for 16 years. "We love Atlanta," she says. "The climate is wonderful, and it still has some of that friendliness that you find in a small town while also being very cosmopolitan."

Carlton is a proud mother of three accomplished daughters: Mariah, a television news producer for WHAS in Louisville, Kentucky; Morgan, a graduate from Stanford University currently applying to law school; and Meredith, a freshman at Williams College in Williamstown, Massachusetts.

Now an avid gardener, Carlton shares, "My favorite thing to do is spend time in my yard. When we moved into our current home, it was brand new and had no shrubbery on the side. That was what started me planting, and I haven't stopped since." On Mother's Day that's how I celebrate. Neighbors used to think it was strange, but now they know that's what makes me happy. My mother and I have spent a couple of Mother's Days together in our yards, first in hers, then in mine."

Her other hobbies and interests include exercising, skiing and reading books, with her favorites being *The Kite Runner* by Khaled Hosseini and *Secret Life of Bees* by Sue Monk Kidd.

Footprints of a Change Agent

Equilla Wainwright

by Jacquee Minor

The way she sees it, you must be willing to leave your comfort zone in order to move forward. Equilla Wainwright, diversity director for Johnson Controls, has often gone into less than desirable territory as a means to an end. This pioneer in opening doors to other minorities has a clear mission. "My contribution," Wainwright says, "has been to drive change."

Now responsible for developing and implementing the diversity platform for Johnson Controls' business unit, Wainwright's core training in human resources led her to positions at Ford Motor Company and MCI Worldcom. Upon arrival at Johnson Controls ten years ago, just as in her previous jobs, Wainwright found herself in the role of "first." She became one of the first African-American women in Johnson Controls to run an entire organization throughout the country.

Johnson Controls, a major supplier of automotive seating, interior systems and batteries, as well as electric room thermostats, is a $31 billion global enterprise headquartered in Wisconsin. Wainwright recalls being totally unprepared for the environment, but says she stuck it out because she saw it as a bigger place to make a difference.

Reflecting on the sacrifices of change, Wainwright says you have to find courage. "As African Americans, we have to think about our legacy. You can make a footprint for those who come behind. Just think, if Martin (King), Xernona Clayton, Andy Young, or Maynard Jackson didn't take the hard stand, many of us wouldn't have a place today."

Wainwright is currently heading up the company's diversity initiative they call Metro Market Strategy, partnering with minority businesses and community organizations in five pilot cities, including Atlanta. This socioeconomic strategy, what Wainwright considers a holistic approach to diversity, means investing in existing minority businesses and in local communities, in order to grow the local workforce and give the company entry into new lines of business.

Juggling two home fronts in Atlanta and Wisconsin, Wainwright travels most of the week but is always eager to return to Atlanta on weekends. "I would always find my way back to Pastor Dale Bronner on Sunday mornings," she confesses. "His teachings are fundamental to the way I handle things in my day-to-day life."

With such a demanding job, it is easy for Wainwright to daydream about wearing braids and sandals. Perhaps in homage to her mother, who has run a small boutique in Muncie, Indiana for more than 50 years, Wainwright sees herself naturally as being more creative than her job requires. Her daughter, a Spelman College graduate, on the other hand, shows a predilection for her grandmother's entrepreneurial spirit.

Although her job makes it difficult to give much time to the community issues important to her, Wainwright still feels it is important to give as much as she can. "We all have to find our way of making change and driving our passion in whatever way God presents it to us," she says.

Wainwright hopes an opportunity will present itself for a possible assignment that will extend her reach internationally. "I would love to be able to take what I've learned here and apply it to make a difference in Africa," she says. Considering her driving passion, don't be surprised when it happens.

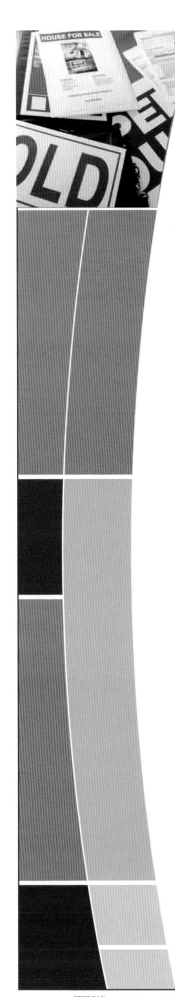

SHANNON J. HARRIS

REALTOR
KELLER WILLIAMS REALTY
ATLANTA PARTNERS

Shannon Harris is "Turning Dreams-2-Reality" by living and working by Keller Williams' Culture of "Win-Win" - or no deal, "Integrity" - do the right thing, "Communication" - seek first to understand, "Creativity" - ideas before results, "Customers" - always come first, "Teamwork" - together everyone achieves more, "Trust" - starts with honesty and "Success" - results through people. She has built a successful real estate business from referrals specializing and concentrating in working with clientele who are buying first or second homes, relocation, investment, multi-family and commercial properties. She is dedicated to educating her clientele on current market trends of the real estate industry. Shannon facilitates home ownership seminars and her clientele state that her devotion and dedication goes beyond the inception and completion of a transaction.

Shannon is a member of NAMAR - Northeast Atlanta Metro Association of Realtors in Gwinnett and a member of the Million Dollar Club. She has also served on Keller Williams Realty Sugarloaf Office ALC (Agent Leadership Council) ranking among the top agents in her office. She has been selected twice in her career as the year's "Top Recruiting Agent" at the Sugarloaf office. Shannon contributes her real estate success to her many career experiences as well as 23 years of military affiliation and traveling.

Shannon holds a Masters degree in Executive Development for Public Services from Ball State University in Muncie, IN and a Bachelor of Science degree in Business Education from Virginia State University. A native of Smithfield, Virginia, Shannon, her husband Anthony, their son Taj, and daughter Stanicia resides in Stone Mountain.

KELLER WILLIAMS ®
REALTY

Office: (678) 775-2710　|　Fax: (678) 775-2637　|　Res. (770) 413-4591
email: shannonjharris@aol.com

"Dreams-2-Reality"

"Women can do everything."

Miranda Mack McKenzie

by Jacquee Minor

Miranda Mack McKenzie has been part of an industry for a dozen years that has not always been accepting of women. One of the pioneering women in the beverage business, specifically in distribution, she is happy to have other female colleagues and proud that her company is leading the sea of change that is bringing in more women.

McKenzie, with her recent promotion to community affairs director of Anheuser-Busch, stepped into a traditionally male-dominated arena with her eyes wide open. She was bolstered by her faith, believing "I can do all things through Christ who strengthens me." She also called on friends and mentors who offered valuable guidance.

McKenzie is excited to report, "More and more women are coming into the industry every day. Finally, the world has accepted that women can do everything. I'm seeing opportunities for women… from all aspects (of the business), from technology to manufacturing."

From the very start, she found the challenge exhilarating; each day different, each new situation unique. "Being a female and being able to thrive and survive in this gender-based industry has been challenging, and it has propelled me to try and be the best in all that I do."

Traveling the country representing the company's community affairs programming in support of African-American markets, McKenzie is on the road at least 50 percent of the time. A typical junket might include attending the National Council of Negro Women's annual event in D.C., a taping of the UNCF telethon in Los Angeles, Russell Simmon's Hip-Hop Summit in Philadelphia, or following the Tom Joyner Sky Shows around the country.

McKenzie was recruited into the industry while working as a journalist at WAOK radio, which at the time was Atlanta's top R&B station for African Americans. She was offered a position with City Beverage Company, a black-owned beer distributorship owned by Herman Russell, and has been working in the industry every since.

An Atlanta native, a "Grady baby," and the youngest of 14 siblings, McKenzie says she has only lived outside Atlanta once, when she went to work briefly for Coors Brewing Company. Four months later, she negotiated her way back to Atlanta. A divorcee, she loves the closeness of her large, extended family and friends and the village of support she relies on to help raise her 11-year-old son, Terrence McKenzie. Having a son is among her proudest achievements, especially thinking for much of her life that she would not have children.

Insisting that she was not spoiled, this baby of the family marvels at her mother's endurance. Having lost count of the number of people now in the family, she knows she is a great-great aunt. Having a child of her own has led her to focus her efforts on the needs of young people, especially their education. "I'm more interested now in trying to help young people find direction in life. I support the things they need to do to be successful in life," she says.

McKenzie is responsible for coordinating the scholarship program at Greater Piney Grove Baptist Church, raising funds to help support church members who are going to college. If she were to leave the beverage industry, it would be to run an organization that supports youth development.

Photo by Denise Gray Photography

Influence Through Collaboration

Sandra Simpson Mitchell

by Jacquee Minor

When in college trying to determine her career path, Sandra Mitchell was given advice that she still passes on to today's young students. Now senior vice president and general manager for Home Box Office, Mitchell says she was told to look for a career that she could be passionate about and to consider a field that provides opportunities for entry and advancement.

Derailed from her original career track, Mitchell learned she was not naturally suited to accounting. "I don't get great pleasure in discovering mistakes," she teases. The detour into consumer package goods provided good training in the principles of marketing and led her to pursue an MBA from the University of Wisconsin. On her way, she landed a position with General Mills in product management, and in her five-year tenure she became assistant brand manager on the Trix and Lucky Charms accounts.

Had it not been for the brutal winters in Minneapolis, Mitchell may not have found her way to a rising career in the burgeoning cable industry. After 24 years with HBO, rising through the ranks, she manages a 35-person sales team with responsibility for affiliate sales customer accounts in Atlanta and St. Louis, Missouri.

Mitchell finds it important to support young people coming into the organization who are trying to gain a foothold in the industry. "I always wanted to have a positive influence. I would rather influence through collaboration than through fear or intimidation." She earned the Tony Cox Award in 2002 from the National Association of Minorities in Cable as a key mentor of African Americans in the cable industry.

Dramatic changes in the industry over the years, reflecting the rapid pace of technological advances, have meant inevitable consolidations. Mitchell has gone through three reorganizations and says people would be surprised to know how much she agonizes over the decisions each time. "For months I couldn't sleep. I would wake up at 4 o'clock in the morning wide awake," she recounts.

Although she finds it sometimes hard to believe that a southern girl from Laurel, Mississippi could wind up in her position, Mitchell is proud of the way she has stood up against adversity and for making the tough decisions. "I feel I made the best decision I could make at that time," she concedes.

With two teenage sons to raise, Mitchell shares, "My greatest accomplishment will be getting my sons established as independent, productive young men." She has found balancing the demands of work and home, especially after a divorce, to be her greatest challenge. "Having children took on a significance I never imagined."

She has found a better sense of the things she has a passion for since turning 50. A woman who seeks adventure and the thrill of competition, Mitchell would choose a hiking vacation over a cruise. Knowing what she does now, Mitchell says that she probably would have preferred a career in landscape architecture. "I would enjoy being outside every day." While she still loves business, Mitchell says you often don't get to appreciate what you have done because you have to move on to the next challenge. "Being able to beautify the environment and to create something from nothing would give me joy."

Photo by Denise Gray Photography

When God Has Other Plans

Brenda Wood

by Jacquee Minor

With an illustrious career spanning nearly three decades, she is an award-winning journalist, which includes winning 15 Emmy Awards. Her work is respected among peers and viewers trust her to tell them the truth. It is hard to imagine that if things had been left up to her, Brenda Wood would not be a television news anchor. Left to her own devices, Wood would have been in Hollywood, with an Oscar on her mantle.

"It was never my dream to be in front of the television camera. I always wanted to produce and direct and write feature films," she reveals.

By way of explanation, Wood, WXIA 11 Alive news anchor, conjures up an old Beatle's tune. "Life is what happens when you make other plans," and that's exactly what happened to her.

Armed with a degree in speech communications from Loma Linda University in California, Wood went home to Huntsville, Alabama for the summer before heading off to The Ohio State University to take advantage of a master's fellowship program and pursue her dream of being a groundbreaking filmmaker. Wanting to earn a little money while waiting, she sent out her resume and received an interview from the local television station.

In a calamity of errors, Wood, with no previous reporting experience whatsoever, said all the wrong things. "I told the news director I was only gonna be there for six months, that I was leaving in January for my master's, that I wasn't interested in television news, that I wanted to be a filmmaker, not a reporter." Wood laughs, "He hired me. Go figure."

It was the summer of 1977. Wood has been a television journalist ever since.

Initially, she did general assignment reporting. The news director told her to forget about her master's fellowship, telling her she wouldn't need it, that she had a great future in this business. She agreed to stay, aided by the fact that the young Wood was falling in love with a local cutie-pie and wasn't eager to leave him.

Later, she went to work for a station in Nashville, but admittedly unhappy being away from "the cutie-pie boyfriend," she returned to Huntsville and her old station. It was not long before she became an anchor.

"I've done with life what it's handed me," Wood says with no regret. "I really feel like God was orchestrating the whole thing for a purpose. This was not anything I planned." While not sure of the purpose, Wood says she tries to use her success to make a difference wherever she can.

Wood's news career propelled her to unimagined heights. Along the way, Wood tried resisting, asking God to give her something else. "He kept giving me newer, bigger markets, bigger salaries, greater prestige, higher profile positions. After a while, I just gave up wanting something else."

Yes, she married the cutie-pie boyfriend. Together, she and Keith Wood have raised two lovely daughters, one attending graduate school at Emory, the other an undergraduate at Duke University. Wood encourages her daughters to pursue their passions, and at least one of them is showing signs of Mom's creative gene. And somewhere just beneath the surface, Wood clings to her lifelong desire to make a documentary someday.

Photo by Denise Gray Photography

Family Matters

Julia H. Jones

by Alonia Jernigan

Every child is born to fulfill his or her unique destiny. For Julia H. Jones, she was born to make a difference in the lives of others. In the dual capacities of vice president and administrator for DeKalb Regional Healthcare System (DRHS) and administrator for DeKalb Medical Center at Hillandale (DRHS' third hospital), she is entrusted to do just that. Armed with a bachelor's degree from Georgia Tech in health systems, an MBA from Georgia State University and more than a decade of experience, Hunter is making an indelible mark in the health care industry, and she is impacting families at the same time.

While growing up in Augusta, Georgia, Julia was challenged to explore leadership as well as health care. "I had a military father, so for a brief period I thought I'd be an officer in the military or that I'd go into management somewhere," she remembers. "Health care came from exposure from an older sister who worked in a hospital. She's a nurse, and she'd come home and tell us what her day was like. By listening to her, I was actually piquing my interest in the health care industry, although I didn't know that's what I was doing at the time." She further adds, "My dad also worked as a contractor for a few of the hospitals in Augusta."

From where she stands today, one could say that the youthful Julia had a keen insight into her future. Beginning with DeKalb in 1990 as a planning analyst, she experienced a colorful journey to her current destination. "I've developed projects such as the Urgent Care Center and the SurgiCenter," she states.

Along the way, I also worked in marketing, public relations, community relations, lab and environmental services." Little did Jones know that her assignment would evolve into an entire hospital.

With such a huge responsibility, Jones says it is still important for her to achieve balance in her personal life. Married to Bernard Jones and the mother of 2-year-old Julian and 3-year-old Adrianna, she credits a strong support system with helping her maintain balance. "I remember panicking because Bernard and I had miscommunicated about who was to pick up the kids. When I got to the babysitter's house, Elder Canty (the babysitter's husband) told me, 'Why are you worrying? If you *never* get back here, the kids will be fine.'"

This reassurance makes it easy for Julia to enjoy downtime. "Bernard and I are really old school," she says. "Put on a little Prince or Earth, Wind and Fire and it will be on!" If she wasn't running a hospital Julia firmly believes, "I'd be a jazz singer with my own little intimate nightclub. It would be very upscale, nice romantic experience. People would want to just drop in." She also likes to travel, and the islands are her favorite. From a spiritual standpoint, Jones has spent a considerable amount of time working with youth through the YoungLife program. She is also a trained lay counselor and once pursued a master's degree in Christian education. "You never forget the teachings, but right now my ministry is to my husband and children." Yes, family really does matter.

ALL n 1
S E C U R I T Y

Integrating People and Technology to Provide a Total Security Solution

SECURITY PERSONNEL

SPECIAL EVENTS

CONSTRUCTION SITES

ELECTRONIC SECURITY

ALL n 1 SECURITY SERVICES, INC.

is a Full Service Security Company providing highly trained and professional security personnel 24 hours a day, 7 days a week for construction sites, warehouse facilities, office buildings, residential communities and schools. We also handle special events such as concerts and sporting events. In addition, we provide detailed background checks, electronic security technology and security consulting services. Certified with organizations such as The Women's Business Enterprise National Council (WBENC), The Georgia Minority Supplier Diversity Council (GMSDC) and The Georgia Women's Business Council (GWBC).

ALL n 1 SECURITY SERVICES, INC.

is the nation's only certified African-American Woman-Owned Security Firm offering a full line of services to businesses and individuals.

MARY PARKER
President/CEO

FOR MORE INFORMATION, PLEASE VISIT US AT
WWW.ALLN1SECURITY.COM

ALL n 1

3915 Cascade Road | Suite 360
Atlanta, Georgia 30331
T 404.691.4915 | F 404.691.3279

Woman of the Movement

Evelyn Gibson Lowery

by Jacquee Minor

Keeping history alive for another generation and making certain all the stories of the people of the civil rights movement are told motivates Evelyn Gibson Lowery these days. A key figure of the movement, Lowery's activism started long before the movement itself and continues to shine long after its conclusion.

For Lowery, activism is a way of life. Only the times have changed. The daughter of a Methodist minister who was also president of the NAACP, she learned early on to fight for what you believe in and not give in to fear. There were times as a child when church members guarded their home. "You get stronger and more determined that something has to be done. You keep up the fight," she says, looking back.

Growing up surrounded by ministers—her father, brothers and grandfather were all ministers—Lowery recalls with a chuckle that she swore she'd never marry one. When she and Joseph Echols Lowery met and married 58 years ago, he was not. Dr. Lowery went on to become ordained and one of Rev. Martin Luther King Jr.'s closest associates.

A fearless freedom fighter, Lowery grew accustomed to the constant threat of bombings and attacks. She participated in every significant march of the movement, once marching for three entire months from Alabama to Washington, D.C. to extend the Voting Rights Act. She recalled an incident in Decatur, Alabama in which bullets were fired into her vehicle, barely missing their mark when she dove down on the seat for cover. "I was too shocked to be afraid," she recalls, even now unperturbed.

Women in the movement, many of them already working for change, were a steady presence—marching, cooking, raising money—supporting the male leaders from the background. In an effort to empower her female colleagues, Lowery organized a meeting in her home to organize their participation. "Finally, the men recognized the fact that women could add something to the cause," she says.

Forming SCLC/Women's Organizational Movement for Equality Now, a movement within a movement, Lowery created a platform to champion the rights of women, children and families. The programs, designed to help the poor and disenfranchised, include a mentoring program for girls age 8 through 18, and a learning center that trains women for the workplace.

Most important, Lowery says, is to keep the legacy alive in the hearts and minds of young people. "They need to know about the sacrifices. If we don't tell them, who will?" she asks. Every year since 1987, Lowery has organized a two-day motor coach tour to Alabama for youth, tracing the steps of the movement. She also created the Drum Major for Justice Awards Dinner to recognize all of those whose contributions have gone unheralded. "I'm concerned about the unsung she-roes of the movement," she says. "Women are still struggling for equality."

Remarkably, Lowery has never drawn a salary from SCLC/W.O.M.E.N. And while she would love to retire, Lowery says she can't because no one is willing to take the job without pay. Even if she could, her passion and energy wouldn't let her walk away, she admits. "I would miss it if I could not be involved. I think I'll always be involved as long as I'm able."

A Voice and an Advocate

Connie Stokes

by Jacquee Minor

In politics more than ten years, first as a Georgia state senator and now a DeKalb County commissioner, it is not politics that keeps Connie Stokes engaged. Rather, it is the opportunity to change lives that drives her ambitions.

"It doesn't matter what I do... I want to be able to make a difference in the lives of people and be able to change the world. I'll work on that work, and believe in that the rest of my life," she says adamantly.

Stokes' introduction into the political arena came while trying to help customers of her real estate business purchase homes. Many of them having blemished credit records, or no credit history at all, Stokes began advocating with mortgage companies, lobbying on behalf of those who wanted to realize the American dream. It was while lobbying HUD officials in Washington, D.C. that she got to taste the real power of policy making. That was the start of her advocacy career.

"I'm in public service," she explains, "but I'm an advocate at heart for people who need an advocate." She has found that while the issues change, the skills for getting things done are the same.

Stokes was elected this year in a landslide victory to represent Super District 7 on the DeKalb County Board of Commissioners. As super commissioner, she speaks for more than half the county, consisting of nearly 400,000 constituents. What people want most from elected officials, according to Stokes, is not necessarily a vote but leadership on critical issues. "It's to understand issues, be a voice on issues, advocate for issues, and put forth change on issues that are relevant today," says Stokes, "and the impact it will have 20 years from now."

Stokes may have had her greatest impact while serving in the state senate. As the first woman to chair the health committee, Stokes set the health agenda for the entire state. As Governor Roy Barnes' floor leader, she points to the many Democratic victories in the legislature, including the creation of the Georgia Regional Transportation Authority. She is especially proud of domestic violence legislation that has helped reduce violence against women and children.

Her childhood is a tragic tale that could have ended much differently. Growing up in Atlanta's Old Fourth Ward, deserted by her mother when she was 6 years old, and never knowing her father, Stokes was raised by a great-great grandmother. Only recently has she begun to reveal her childhood, having difficulty still in discussing the details. She refers to traumatic experiences she has had to overcome, like becoming a mother at age 16.

With a strong faith to carry her, Stokes' vulnerability holds a message for other young people. "On those experiences, my character was developed so that I can be a mentor for young women to encourage them to know they can do whatever they want to do." She is heartened that two of the young ladies she mentors are interested in public service.

Married for 25 years, Stokes' husband is her greatest advocate, and her two grandchildren, her greatest joy. "That's a part of your legacy. You see the future through their eyes."

Living up to Expectations

Renee Glover

by Jacquee Minor

Growing up in the Jim Crow South during the era of civil rights, Renee Glover was instilled with a sense of purpose that she was here to make an impact on her world. Despite the limitations of segregation, there was never any suggestion that she couldn't achieve anything she set her mind to. "We were raised," she recalls, "to be the future leaders of our nation."

The adult Renee Glover has risen to those expectations. Chief executive officer of the Atlanta Housing Authority, Glover has been the catalyst behind a complete overhaul of Atlanta's public housing communities and a massive transformation of Atlanta's urban core.

She credits former Mayor Maynard Jackson for helping her make the best professional decision of her career. "He saw something in me I hadn't contemplated myself," she says. "It all lined up with my personal beliefs and my strong sense of commitment."

A lawyer by training and former partner in a Wall Street firm, Glover came to Atlanta in 1986 as a partner with the Mike Trotter law firm. After working on Maynard Jackson's second successful run for mayor, he asked her to serve on the Atlanta Housing Authority board. It took some convincing, but she came around to the idea of making a difference.

In the years leading up to the Olympics, the housing authority's reputation was in jeopardy, with the resignation of its director and a scathing HUD audit. By now chairman of the board, Glover was convinced to take charge of the agency. "It was a big change in what I had done professionally," she recalls, "but it aligned with my desire at the time to give something back to the community."

Glover was persuaded by a "throw out the rulebook" direction from HUD, in an effort to rewrite the sullied history of public housing. It became a personal mission to break up the warehouses of hopelessness and despair.

"It was personal in the sense that problems facing a racial group, it's up to members of that group to find solutions. If we don't bring our skills, our backgrounds, and our exposure to solving problems that help our people, what in the world are we doing?"

With low expectations and standards, public housing, intended to be a temporary measure for people down on their luck, had become a multi-generational trap. Through the use of Hope VI funds, the housing authority is partnering with the private sector to create market rate communities that include a place for families who need assistance. Glover says it's important to note, "We're not creating a newer version of public housing; this is a community building strategy."

Since taking the position, AHA has been involved in developing 13 mixed-use, mixed-income communities in Atlanta, the first of which, Centennial Place, was the first of its kind in the nation. It has become the prototype for all other similar properties being developed.

High expectations are part of her DNA and Glover points to her great-great grandfather who, in 1901, founded Florida's first life insurance company. She believes today's youth will also respond when expectations are set high. "It will pay dividends for future generations that we can't even imagine. It's from that perspective I have been engaged in this work."

RALPH D. ABERNATHY TOWER
1055

Photo by Denise Gray Photography

A History of Service

Juanita Abernathy

by Jacquee Minor

If there is one thing Juanita Abernathy wants young people to know about the civil rights movement, it is that Martin Luther King and other leaders in the movement were ordinary people who did extraordinary things. The widow of Rev. Ralph David Abernathy and a lifetime activist, she challenges the notion that leaders of the past were a singular phenomenon. To suggest they were anything more than mortal men and women is to her, akin to heresy.

"The greatest leader has never been born," she insists, voice rising with passion. "We can't limit young people. Tell them they can be better than anybody else. God hasn't stopped creating."

Abernathy believes young people need the hope of knowing that with hard work and strong conviction, they can be anything and can do anything they choose. "That's the legacy we've got to leave our children," she says.

History records her legacy as being a central figure of the movement, working alongside her husband, a close associate and confident of Dr. King. Abernathy insists that her role started much earlier in Uniontown, Alabama, where she grew up in a deeply religious household under parents who stood up for what they believed.

Her father was a wealthy farmer and dairyman. With an eighth grade education, he built an empire and financial independence. "My father," she recalls fondly, "believed whoever controlled your purse, controlled you. He felt you had to be independent of the white man in order to achieve any rights."

When the phone company refused to bring phone lines into their homes, her dad and his brothers connected all of their properties to the central operator in Selma. Abernathy found her own voice of protest when, forced to attend a school she did not choose, she refused to pledge allegiance to the flag in the fifth grade. She has not uttered the words "liberty and justice for all" since.

"That's how I came to be," says Abernathy. "My fight for justice and civil rights did not start with Montgomery or when I married Ralph Abernathy. I had my philosophy set long before that."

Her beliefs carried her through the movement's turbulence when her Montgomery home was bombed with her baby inside and people called daily to harass her family. It did not waver when they moved to Atlanta and organized campaigns to open retail stores and businesses to black patrons and employees. Her fervor and passion did not die with Dr. King, her husband, or any of the era's lost warriors. She reminds us that many lives were lost. "We forget the thousands of people whose names are not in our forefront, but their lives were given."

While she has worked as a teacher and a super director in the Mary Kay organization, Abernathy says she is and will always be a civil rights activist. "I've always worked for peace; I am still going to work for peace and for women," she says. "I've always been passionate about what women can and need to do, because we carry the balance of power." Abernathy uses her voice to speak to groups throughout the world. And one of these days, she intends to write the story that has never been told.

Angelia
Gay-Northern
President

Angel's Paradise Higher Learning Academy has been serving the community for over 30 years. The original preschool was founded in 1968 on a foundation of love and caring. Our school is a year round pre-school that offer programs for children six weeks through twelve years old.

Angel's Paradise's mission is dedication to the total development of your child by providing a quality, nurturing, safe, and fun-filled environment.

Angel's Paradise takes special care to identify and reinforce the needs of each and every child to ensure that they are prepared for the future. Our excellence can be measured by Angel's well stocked and equipped classrooms, degreed and credential teachers, low child to staff ratios and NAEYC accreditation.

- Serving Children 6 weeks - 12 year olds
- GA Lottery - Funded PreKindergarten (all 4 year olds FREE)
- School-Age Program
- After School Program
- Summer Camp
- Holiday Care
- Family Resource Advocacy

595 Joseph Lowery Boulevard
Atlanta, GA 30310
(404) 755-8493

2038 Stanton Road
East Point, GA 30344
(404) 762-1133
FAX (404) 758-1506
www.angelsparadisehla.com

Angel's Paradise
HIGHER LEARNING ACADEMY
Specializing in Developing Future Leaders

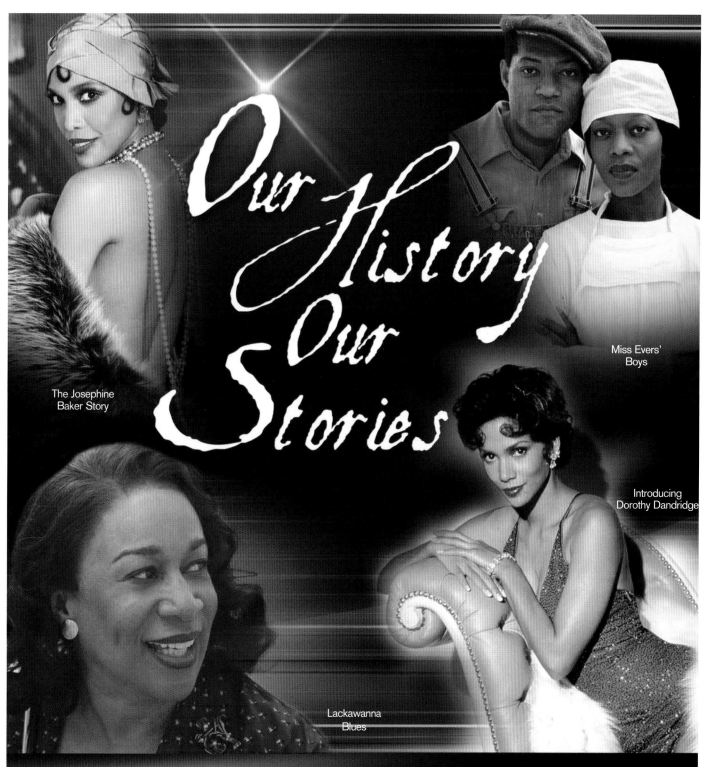

Miss Evers'
Boys

The Josephine
Baker Story

*Our History
Our
Stories*

Introducing
Dorothy Dandridge

Lackawanna
Blues

IN THE SPIRIT OF THESE EXTRAORDINARY WOMEN WHOSE LIVES HAVE INSPIRED US,
HBO® PROUDLY SALUTES ATLANTA'S FEMALE POWERHOUSES.

Photo by Denise Gray Photography

Opportunities to Serve the Cause of Justice

Thelma Wyatt Cummings Moore

by Jacquee Minor

After 29 years on the bench, Judge Thelma Wyatt Cummings Moore has seen just about everything. Her courtroom in the Fulton County Superior Court, where she hears both civil and criminal cases, is a microcosm of social ills. Rather than throwing up her hands in dismay, Judge Moore seizes every opportunity to make a difference.

"It's my duty and burden to do something about what I see," declares Moore. "I have worked consistently to make the family stronger, to make the young people stronger."

Moore's leadership is anchored in the pursuit of justice and equality. Always concerned about the general welfare of her community, she looks at each case as an opportunity to serve the cause of justice, one individual at a time.

In one of her most heralded acts, Moore designed and crafted the Fulton County Family Court and the Family Law Information Center, coordinating all available resources into a state-of-the-art justice information system. The entire system is designed to streamline the legal court process, making it more accessible and available to those who need it most.

Moore's innovations have impacted the entire justice system. In addition to creating a family court system, she worked to expand alternative resolution in civil cases and brought together the various divisions of the criminal court in unprecedented collaboration.

These systemic changes, serving very basic needs and helping citizens, have become a part of Moore's legacy. "I feel I have brought home to the people the court system which is theirs," she says.

Growing up in Amarillo, Texas, Moore says there were no black lawyers. She has vivid memories of her family's home being burned by the Ku Klux Klan and crosses being burned in her yard. After the *Brown v. Board of Education* decision, her father ran for a seat on the Amarillo School Board, sparking another flame, this time in the heart of a young woman motivated to change her world.

"The notion of justice and equality resonated with me," says Moore. After earning her law degree from Emory Law School, she worked for the Equal Employment Opportunity Commission under the tutelage of civil rights legend Donald E. Hollowell.

First appointed to the bench by Atlanta Mayor Maynard Jackson in 1977, Moore continues to set the standard. She is the first woman on the Atlanta Municipal Court and Atlanta City Court, the first African-American woman on the State Court of Georgia, and the first woman chief judge of the Superior Court of Fulton County. The first African-American woman to serve as chief of any judicial circuit in Georgia, she has been reelected to the bench six times.

As compassionate as she is in the courtroom, Moore is equally passionate about her life. You might see her out stepping, Chicago style. "Life is short," she declares. "I'm going to have as much fun as I can. I'm just waiting on the gift to play the piano, so that I can become a cocktail singer," she laughs.

Never one to hold her tongue, Moore points out injustice with moral authority. "It's troublesome to see the justice system mete out injustice," she says. Anticipating that the next movement will be for economic justice for African Americans, Judge Moore will no doubt be a part of it.

Dr. Beverly L. Hall
SUPERINTENDENT

Photo by Denise Gray Photography

A Track Record of Success

Dr. Beverly L. Hall

by Jacquee Minor

A reputation for transforming troubled public schools preceded Dr. Beverly Hall before answering the call to lead Atlanta Public Schools. She had built an impressive track record as a turnaround specialist, going into the most dysfunctional schools, reforming them and moving on to the next challenge.

"I seem to have a history of picking the big challenge," Hall chuckles. "Each time, I've gotten tremendous satisfaction from working hard and seeing progress. That motivates me to take on bigger challenges."

As superintendent of the Newark Public Schools System in New Jersey, deputy chancellor for New York City Public Schools, and superintendent of the Queens District of New York, Hall had major victories. While proud of the successes over the last seven years in Atlanta, she is not satisfied. "I won't be satisfied until the gains made on the elementary level are matched at the middle and high school levels. I believe it can be done," she insists. "I will be relentless until it's done."

Most likely, her temerity emanates from a history of success. Admittedly a good student with a competitive nature, Hall says, "I gained self-confidence in the ability to achieve. I had faith in my competence. That had a lot to do with my willingness to take on tough roles."

Any doubts about her decision are fleeting. She is often reminded of what is at stake, such as the letter she received from a young man doing his Ph.D. work. He wrote to thank her for the difference she made in his life as a sixth grader when she came to his school as principal.

Still, challenges remain. The greatest, according to Hall is "widespread disbelief in the educability of *all* children." If more people were willing to invest in educating all the children, she believes it would happen.

Engaging the entire community is part of her strategy for success. Since coming to Atlanta, Hall has reached out to every segment of the community, building alliances and partnerships to benefit children.

Ironically, she stumbled upon her calling. With the original intent of becoming a journalist, she took a summer job teaching in New York City schools between undergraduate and graduate studies. "From the minute I got into that classroom, I knew I had found my calling. I just loved teaching," she recalls.

Because she was so good at it, she was encouraged to pursue administrative positions. One assignment as an assistant principal led to another as a principal, still another as superintendent and the rest, as they say, is history. Each successful position solidified her reputation as a problem solver. "I didn't have all the answers, but I wasn't afraid to look for them."

A native of the West Indies, with still a slight hint of an accent, Hall has a delicious sense of humor, contrary to a rather reserved demeanor. Her husband, whom she married shortly after starting her teaching career, is a sounding board. They have an adult son. Relocating from New York to Atlanta, the hardest adjustment according to this news junkie is its size. "I go nowhere without being recognized in Atlanta," she laughs. "I can't go out looking tacky."

Charting a New Course

B.J. Walker

by Jacquee Minor

Commissioner B.J. Walker, having spent the last two years redirecting the course of Georgia's human services division, seems to have turned the massive ship around. Since her appointment in May of 2004 as commissioner of the Georgia Department of Human Resources, the child welfare system case load, overrun with crisis, is now below 2001 levels. She gained control by setting clear direction and values.

At the time she came onboard, the ship was sinking in a sea of awful cases and bad press. Too few case workers were struggling to manage a spiking case load that had increased 40 percent in about six months. The highly publicized tragic death of Terrell Peterson at the hands of his family became the rallying cry of child welfare advocates. Fear and trepidation ruled the department. The commissioner charted a new course around a core belief.

"Families are the foundation of most societies," says Walker, who believes the best use of government funds is to invest in families so they can take care of themselves. "Strengthening families makes a difference."

Walker says strong families must work. "Welfare may be good enough for trifling adults, but it's not good enough for children. It means we have to do everything we can to help adults get up and go to work and be responsible for raising their children."

The actions of adults, according to Walker, are the biggest threat to her business. "I'm amazed at what adults do to children," she muses. She admits some of the stories have sent her home to curl up in a ball, only to return the next day with a new sense of purpose. Admittedly a hands-on manager, Walker says the idea of getting up every day with a mission in her face is what makes her day. "I like making decisions."

Previously, Walker worked in Chicago Mayor Richard Daley's administration, overseeing the human service needs of that city's residents. Now managing 19,000 people and a budget of $2.4 billion, she oversees every health and human services program in Georgia, including mental health, aging, developmental diseases, addictive diseases, child welfare and public health. A no-nonsense, demanding, yet even-handed administrator, she often relies on prayer to cope. "A lot of my own balance, sense of urgency and justice comes through prayer."

Walker feels balance is important and says she plays as hard as she works. "I love to shop," she laughs, while describing her elaborate shopping system for getting the best deals. "I love the sport of it all."

Walker learned a thing or two about sports and teamwork playing pitcher on a women's softball team. She took up softball as an adult, playing for ten years with women from every walk of life. Walker thinks every girl should be on a team because of the lessons learned. "You learn the value of contribution of everybody on the team and that the team is greater than the sum of its parts." Some of the lessons are important in her career, such as learning to trust your team, the value of contribution, and how to put team goals ahead of your own. Perhaps most important, she says, "You learn you have to play. You just gotta play."

Photo by Monica Morgan

What Being Great Really Means

Vanessa Williams

by Jacquee Minor

You might say Vanessa Williams has activism is her blood. Her parents were longtime stakeholders in the Las Vegas community; her mother a warrior in the civil rights struggle. Her godfather was the first black assemblyman elected in Vegas. Being involved wasn't an option, it was simply expected. It is no wonder that Williams, executive director for the National Conference of Black Mayors, Inc. (NCBM), is putting her stamp on the family tradition, and at just 32 years old, she is breaking new ground for another generation of leaders.

With empowerment as her mantra and information the tool, Williams is a force to be reckoned with. Years of attending community meetings with her parents, campaigning for candidates, organizing, and canvassing neighborhoods led the teenage Willams to a role organizing West Las Vegas in establishing community development corporations. She discovered a power she never knew existed.

"Doing my first development deal, and watching an area in West Las Vegas that was dilapidated and drug infested… to take that block and watch that block transform. I discovered a new way to fight," she marvels.

Williams found this was more than the political empowerment she had become accustomed to; it was socioeconomic justice. "I was sold on CDCs and understanding the power of real estate and our people's participation in it."

Through a position with one of the CDCs, Williams developed about 200 units of affordable housing in Las Vegas. She was then offered the opportunity to learn the financing side of the industry, packaging development deals and putting together funding. Realizing that many small town mayors have few resources, Williams began assisting some of them in developing and financing local community projects. The relationships formed with black mayors across the country ultimately led to an offer from NCBM to take the helm. But at age 29, Williams was uncertain about her readiness for the role. "That was the lie I told myself," she says. "In fact, God was preparing me all my life for this position." Recently, she coordinated with New Orleans Mayor Ray Nagin and other U.S. mayors to bring desperately needed relief to Hurricane Katrina victims.

While attending the University of California at Berkeley, Williams' father died in her sophomore year, prompting her to organize Positive Choices for Academic Success, a program designed to encourage young African-American students to complete higher education. The economic reality of her father's passing meant that she had to transfer to UNLV. In offering support to other young people, Williams received the support she needed to complete her own education. President Bill Clinton recognized her with a Presidential Exemplary Award. Today, Positive Choices is the largest, funded after-school tutorial program in Nevada, helping nearly 600 African-American students attain higher education.

The next time NCBM called, she answered. Williams, who has built relationships with people from heads of state to hip-hop artists, has set in motion plans to make NCBM an international organization. Since she became executive director in early 2006, the organization has established chapters in Columbia, Haiti and Uganda.

Williams and her husband involve their two young children in their community activities, passing on the family legacy. She tells young people, "Help somebody. For those of us who want to be great, you have to serve."

Partial Client Listing:

- Agape Communications Technology Systems (ACTS)
- Atlanta Business League
- Denise Gray Photography
- Greater Bethany Baptist Church
- National African American & Culinary Arts Association
- National Bar Association
- National Black McDonald's Owners Association
- National Conference of Black Mayors, Inc.
- Reynolds ADsociates
- Sasha's Day Spa & Wellness Center
- The Coca-Cola Company
- Vases With Faces
- Who's Who in Black Atlanta
- Zakkee and Associates

Partial Listing of Services Provided:

Writing

Corporate and Individual Profiles
Ghost Writing
Newsletters
Press Releases
Program/Souvenir Journals
Proposals
Scripts
Speeches
Verbiage for Website Development

Speaking

Keynote Addresses
Panel Moderating
Event Host/Mistress of Ceremonies
Motivational Messages

Training

Workshop series based on The Effective Communicator's series, "The Essentials"

- Writing Winning Grant Proposals, Part I: Effectively Positioning Your Nonprofit for Financial Success
- Writing Winning Grant Proposals, Part II: Show Me the Money
- Talking Loud and Saying Something: Delivering Unforgettable Messages

THE Effective COMMUNICATOR

Professional Communication. Transformative Results™.

www.TheEssentialsOnline.com
(770) 256-4337

The Effective Communicator provides professional writing, speaking and training services, and we empower others to do the same through our dynamic workshop series, The Essentials.

Alonia Jernigan
President
The Effective Communicator

The next time you need a message conveyed effectively, remember me.

Ever since I can remember, I've been able to effectively express myself. God has blessed me with the awesome ability to communicate ideas, and I am delighted to share my gifts with others as they seek to reach their next level of success.

As a speaker, I've touched the lives of the young and old, sacred and secular. As a writer, I've written features on everyone from Attorney Willie Gary to Bishop Eddie Long. I've even done ghost writing for various individuals, businesses and religious organizations. And, I'm very proud of the fact that I earned my scholarship for excellence in essay writing under Mayor Andrew Young's administration. The essay was entitled, "If I Were Mayor." That was 21 years ago, and I'm still creating ideas of substance and impact; and I'm still inspiring audiences to excellence.

Let us show you how easy moving can be!

Leave the hard work to us.

We know how quickly moving can become a stressful and exhausting experience. That's why B&B Movers is dedicated to making your move practically relaxing. Our unique approach to excellent service reflects our mission to be a friendlier kind of moving company.

B&B Movers has come a long way since being founded ten years ago by Barbara Billingsley. Thanks to her award-winning leadership and the dedication of our associates, we've grown significantly while staying true to our founding values. Although our success can be attributed to hard work and superior customer service, we go beyond simply moving belongings. As our motto states, "We really treat you like family."

Call us at **404-212-0819** or visit **www.bbmovers.com** today!

A Solid Structure of Support

Sharon S. Hall

by Jacquee Minor

Sharon Hall knows the source of her power. Partner, managing director and board member of Spencer Stuart, a leading global executive search firm, Hall credits her success to one simple thing.

"Structure. I couldn't be a powerhouse woman if I didn't have a solid structure of support," Hall acknowledges.

A single mother of two teenage sons, Hall can wear multiple hats on the job, maintain a global travel schedule, and keep her clients satisfied because, in her estimation, she can rely on her family for support. Hall says her mom and dad are there to back her up.

It is the same structure she grew up with. Reflecting back to the childhood experiences that helped to shape her, Hall recounts Sunday family meetings in which all important decisions were made. Those times, as she recalls, taught her the art of debate, and how to present her case and reach consensus.

Keeping the family tradition alive, Hall moved her parents in when she relocated to Atlanta in 1997 to take a position with Stuart Spencer. With all the years of experience as a marketer, strategist and developer/general manager of significant business units, Hall knew what she needed to succeed was that same structure she grew up with.

"I made my Dad VP of procurement, and put him in charge of the people at the middle school my son attended at the time. Mom was VP of administration, and she was responsible for staying in touch with my oldest son's high school," Hall explains.

While the roles and titles have changed over the years, with both parents getting promotions and corresponding raises, everyone knows their contribution keeps the wheels turning smoothly. It is a serious framework, one in which everyone plays a role and everyone has fun.

Taking pleasure in the work you do and making the most of life are prevailing themes running throughout Hall's life. She laughs readily and heartily, and loves to make others laugh with her. A woman unafraid of pursuing her interests, Hall once played second flute in a symphonic orchestra and competed as a synchronized swimmer.

In a high-powered career that includes a role as general manager with Avon Products, Inc., and founder of Spencer Stuart's diversity practice, Hall says she would just as happily be a chef, running her own restaurant. "Cooking is my passion," she admits.

Hall says her life is really about improving the planet and the lives on it. It is a mission and a faith that takes on greater urgency from the desire to turn her teenage sons, ages 17 and 13, into men who take responsibility for themselves and for others. "My faith is living productively among mankind… it's about giving and loving and helping each other. That's what I want them to learn."

This baby boomer has no qualms about aging. She is taking her cue from her mother who, at 73 years of age, Hall considers a model for living the fullness of life. As she approaches her 50th birthday this year, Hall says she is excited to discover what lies ahead. "I can't wait to see what the 50s hold," she says. "Bring it on."

Continuing a Legacy of Excellence: Keeping Spelman ALIVE

Dr. Beverly Daniel Tatum

by Alonia Jernigan

Being an institution of excellence in higher education is a legacy that Spelman College is proud to call its own. For 125 years, the institution has nurtured and produced leaders all over the world, including actress Keisha Knight-Pulliam, author Pearl Cleage, child advocate Marian Wright Edelman, minister Bernice King, State Representative Alisha Thomas Morgan and Dr. Deborah Prothrow-Stith, among countless others. Under the visionary leadership of Dr. Beverly Daniel Tatum, the college's ninth president, Spelman intends to continue its legacy and become known as not just a historically black college and not simply a college for women. "My goal is to assure that Spelman is seen as one of the best colleges period, without the classification," she says.

Tatum's method for achieving this goal is through a strategic, five-part initiative called Spelman ALIVE: **A**cademic Excellence; **L**eadership Development; **I**mproving our Environment; **V**isibility of our Achievements; and **E**xemplary Customer Service. "Spelman ALIVE presents an awesome opportunity for people to take a closer look at our institution and realize that we really are an institution worthy to be classified outside of the box in which people generally perceive us," adds Tatum. "We present our students with a wealth of experiences that are uniquely Spelman, including the fact that we sent six young women to compete in a robotics competition in Japan."

Tatum's task may not appear to be the simplest that one could be given. Yet, she is performing so phenomenally that her original five-year contract has been renewed by Spelman's board of directors. The proficiency that Dr. Tatum exemplifies can be attributed to her love for what she does, even though she did not leave college with her eyes set on becoming a college president. After spending years as a fourth generation professor, she began a career in educational administration. "I knew since high school that I wanted to be a psychologist," Tatum imparts. "But once I had the opportunity to teach, I found that I enjoyed that as well. What led me to the administrative roles was the desire to have a wider impact on the students."

Prior to coming to Spelman, Tatum spent 13 years at Mount Holyoke College where she worked as acting president and dean of the college. She is well known as a scholar, teacher, author and race relations expert. Her critically acclaimed book, *Why Are All the Black Kids Sitting Together in the Cafeteria? And Other Conversations About Race* (published in 1999) is still receiving positive feedback. This is particularly exciting for Tatum because it reinforces her innate desire to write more books, including one on the subject of leadership.

Appropriately, Tatum is a recent graduate of Leadership Atlanta, involved with the Metro Atlanta Chamber of Commerce, and a board member for Woodruff Arts Center. In her spare time, she enjoys reading, listening to music, taking walks and spending time with her husband. She is the mother of two adult sons.

When asked what kind of community issues concern her, she answered, "Education, broadly. Education in our society is so critical." From all indications, Dr. Tatum is truly making a difference. In keeping Spelman ALIVE, others may live to continue the legacy.

Lisa M. Borders

Finding the Sweet Spot of Compromise

Lisa Borders

by Jacquee Minor

Since being elected president of the Atlanta City Council two years ago, Lisa Borders has made a few discoveries, not just about the job, but also herself.

"I've learned I am proud, yet practical about serving the people of Atlanta," Borders offers, adding, "I never imagined it could be so fulfilling, or how wonderful it would feel to be entrusted with this tremendous responsibility."

Looking back to the many times she would visit City Hall during Mayor Maynard Jackson's administration, Borders recalls being fascinated by what she observed about the operation of city government. Now a part of the process, she applies much of what she learned from Jackson in executing her duties.

"It's important to acknowledge his value of service to the city," she says, giving him "props" as an elected official, as a citizen, a husband and father.

That she chose the path of public service was almost inevitable, considering the family tree. Borders is a descendant of Atlanta's prominent first family of community and social activism, of which Jackson is also a member. Her grandfather, the late Reverend William Holmes Borders, as pastor of Wheat Street Baptist Church, was a major figure in Atlanta's involvement in the civil rights movement. Both her parents have been lifelong community activists. Learning to revere public service as one's duty, Borders is carrying on a family tradition.

The old saying about ministers can be said for public servants as well: few are called, while others call themselves. For Borders, public service is a higher calling that rarely comes without personal sacrifice. "It is giving of the total self, without regard for personal gain."

Thoughtfully articulate, Borders has earned a reputation among her colleagues as a bridge builder. "I think my greatest gift is bringing people together," she says. "I am able to help people listen to one another and to broker the best solution for everyone," what Borders refers to as the "sweet spot of compromise."

With no prior legislative experience, Borders was elected to lead the City Council, her first public office, in a special election. In a sometimes contentious battle, she ran a respectful race, unafraid to put up her dukes when challenged, but always with a sense of fair play. Borders credits her mother with instilling the moral compass that clearly delineates right and wrong.

Juggling the demands of two responsibilities, she maintains her job of six years as senior vice president of marketing communications and public affairs for Cousins Properties. "I've certainly had to learn to delegate more," Borders acknowledges, while giving praise to her staff in both jobs. Getting the most out of a 12- to 15-hour workday, she must stay on task. "I can never procrastinate; it's imperative that I use every moment efficiently."

Should she lose sight of the need for balance, Borders says her son reminds her to take care of herself. At 24 years old, he has become the protector, the one looking out for her well-being. "I'm most proud of raising a male child alone," she says "helping him to become self-sufficient, considerate, kind, and compassionate. That is most rewarding. I recognized the need to replace myself with an even better contributor."

Photo by Denise Gray Photography

A Common Touch

Rogsbert F. Phillips, M.D., F.A.C.S.

by Jacquee Minor

Breast cancer is a frightening disease, representing the second leading cause of cancer-related death in women. Still, Dr. Rogsbert F. Phillips, leading expert in the field of breast cancer surgery, offers encouraging words.

"I think there will be a cure in my lifetime," Phillips says confidently. While she expects it to come on many levels, Phillips believes, based on current research, the breakthrough will come in learning to manipulate cells on the DNA level. "We will be able to stop the growth of abnormal cells, and/or to prevent growth of abnormal cells. It's going to be huge."

With more than 23 years in practice, Phillips has gained prominence as a surgeon specializing in laparoscopic and breast surgery. Her community-based practice, Metro Surgical Associates, has earned a reputation as a pioneering practice in the forefront of breast cancer research, diagnostics and treatment. She is also chief of surgery at DeKalb Medical Center at Hillandale. For Phillips, it is a rewarding way of life.

"I love what I do. It's awesome to be in a position to impact someone's life, day in and out. It gives me satisfaction that what I do is important to mankind."

As a native Georgian, she grew up with a strong emphasis on helping your neighbor. That upbringing has given her a common touch, which along with spirituality, is made all the more refreshing in a physician. "You are here for a purpose, not to just do everything that makes you happy. We have to live outside ourselves. That's what defines us as a person."

Surprisingly, her entry into medicine almost didn't happen. An excellent academic record earned her a spot at the University of Georgia in Athens during the height of the civil rights era. Recalling the racial tensions of the time, she was constantly faced with proving her right to be there. The sleights, insults and mistreatment could have made her bitter but instead, made her stronger. She credits the UGA experience with helping to shape who she is today.

She reconnected with the idea of medicine while pursuing her master's degree and tutoring med students in English. Her application to Columbia University School of Medicine was accepted without ever having to take a medical admissions exam. Discovering during internship that she enjoyed the definitive nature of surgery, she chose it as a practice, despite the paucity of women role models in the field. A Trojan-like focus during her residency earned the recognition of her peers and respect for her intellectual ability, her skills as a surgeon, and her approach with patients.

While the same work ethic drives her practice, Phillips says she takes time to nourish herself. "I realize I'm a better doctor when I take care of myself," she offers. She would have liked to have had kids, but says she didn't find her soul mate during her childbearing years. With someone special sharing her life today, she is content with her many godchildren, nieces and nephews to spoil.

Dealing with life and death issues can take its toll, but Phillips says she has put into practice something a dying patient once told her. "She taught me how to live in the moment, plan for tomorrow, and make the best of today."

Photo by Denise Gray Photography

Virtuously Diligent, Dynamic and Devoted

Carolyn Young

by Alonia Jernigan

A popular scripture raises the question, "Who can find a virtuous woman?" From the perspective of those who know her well, the city of Atlanta is highly esteemed to identify one of its citizens, Carolyn Young, as one of such caliber. Donning a heart of gold, a spirit of compassion and a mind to do good, Young is a virtuous woman in every sense of the word. In all that she does, she is diligent, dynamic and devoted.

Though most people know Young as the wife of former mayor Andrew Young, Carolyn Young has quite an identity of her own. She is a former educator within the Atlanta Public Schools system and an executive with GoodWorks International, a specialty consulting group that provides strategic services to corporations and governments operating in the global economy. In the latter role, she diligently hosts the various dignitaries that grace our fair city. "This experience is a sheer delight because it provides me with an opportunity to offer hospitality, as well as exchange cultural awarenesses," says Young. "It's like a classroom away from a classroom."

A self-defined people person, Young delights in making an impact on the lives of others, particularly youth. When visiting Bethesda House, an orphanage in Soweto for children living with AIDS (adopted by her husband), she takes pride in encouraging them. "I'm a firm believer that you cannot achieve unless you feel good about yourself," she says, "So, I don't mind telling them that they are beautiful, that they can make it in the world. And as a former Sunday school superintendent, it's just in me to instill within them the power of a higher being that made them a wonderful creation."

Young's dynamism is further evidenced in the outcomes of the number of students she has educated. And, she considers teaching as one of her life's greatest accomplishments. "I had a mother to come to me and tell me that her son was suicidal. But after being in my class, he went on with his life, graduated from Oberlin College, and now has a Ph.D. in music," she informs. "I've also taught students who are now attorneys, doctors, TV commentators and businessmen."

Reared by a loving mother and grandmother, Young knows no other way to live life than being devoted to service. "I've always served; it's only right to do so," she says. "And in serving others, I don't see it as 'giving back,' because in and of myself, I have nothing. It all comes from God and I just pass it on." The Carolyn McClain Young Scholarship empowers students to obtain master's and Ph.D. degrees through the Georgia State University Foundation.

Young is also an elite socialite, being present at essentially every major activity in the city. As such, one may find it interesting to know that she doesn't drive. Not one to enjoy being alone, she shares, "Some of my friends tease me and tell me the real reason why I don't drive is so I can have some company!"

In her spare time, the Delta loves to shop, read, go to the movies and enjoy her two South African-born dogs.

REYNOLDS
ADSOCIATES

Applauds the Accomplishments

of

Mayor Shirley Franklin

Atlanta's Female Powerhouses

and

The Pink Pages Sponsors

"WOMEN IN THE ATL - Making it Happen!"

Yolanda Reynolds

Atlanta Publisher

PINK POWER!!!

At the Georgia International Convention Center, we celebrate our diversity and are proud of the professional, exceptional women on our team.

Congratulations to all of our staff members who have been selected for *Who's Who in Black Atlanta* and the *Pink Pages*!

GEORGIA INTERNATIONAL CONVENTION CENTER

2000 Convention Center Concourse
College Park, Georgia 30337
P 770.997.3566
F 770.994.8559

VISIT OUR WEBSITE AT WWW.GICC.COM

Pictured from left to right: Iris Owens, Darcel Ivey, Tamara McLaurin, Denise Cole, Mercedes Miller, Sonia Williams, Andrea Smalls and Cindy Sumter

Photo by Tony Duffy

SALUTING ATLANTA'S
Female Powerhouses

Every business needs to JUMP OUT OF THE BOX with creative ideas that POP!

Go the distance with a marketing campaign beyond measure. For example, make a statement with a 'walking billboard' that brings your brand image to life. Let your business take flight with: A corporate spokesperson, Olympic-bound athlete and marketing guru - ALL IN ONE.

Monica Cabbler, empowering audiences across America.

"...one of metro Atlanta's intriguing business personalities" - Atlanta Journal & Constitution

Cabbler & Associates
P.O. Box 3424 - Atlanta, GA 30302
For Bookings: mcabbler@monicacabbler.com

www.MONICACABBLER.com

CONTINUE TO LET GOD SHINE THROUGH YOU TO MAKE A DIFFERENCE IN THE COMMUNITY"

You can do it.
We can help.^{SM}

At The Home Depot, we firmly believe that talent comes in many forms and we celebrate each and every one of them. Diversity is the catalyst for innovative thinking, entrepreneurial spirit and new ways of building our communities. The greater the diversity of our people, the greater our ability to serve our customers. It is talent above all else that is cultivated, nourished and considered to be the foundation of our culture. At The Home Depot, we are committed to creating a diverse work environment where all associates are included, respected and supported to do their best work.

Just look at how we've created one of America's strongest teams, combining the strength of more than 365,000 associates.

One Team.
Many Talents.
CELEBRATING DIVERSITY & PRACTICING INCLUSION

The Luxury Real Estate Specialist

FOR ALL YOUR REAL ESTATE
NEEDS PLEASE CALL

Rhonda A. Crockett
**LUXURY REAL ESTATE
SPECIALIST**

(770) 849-8537
www.galuxuryrealestate.com

We Put Our Energy Here!

For nearly 150 years, Atlanta Gas Light has been connected to the people of Georgia, serving 1.6 million natural gas consumers in 237 communities across the state.

Natural gas is used to heat 85 percent of homes in Georgia. Homes that use electricity for heat also depend indirectly on natural gas, which fuels electricity-generating plants in Georgia.

The employees of Atlanta Gas Light remain committed and dedicated - to their jobs, and you. We are the people behind the pipes, flowing clean, natural gas across Georgia.

It's a promise we've kept since 1856.

Atlanta Gas Light
An AGL Resources Company

A COMMITMENT
To Excellence
since **1990**

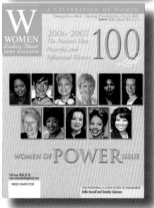

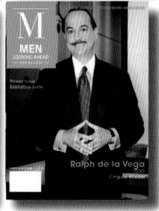

Women Looking Ahead was the first company (1990) and publication (1993) that caters exclusively to the wants, needs and lifestyles of today's business woman. These women range from your average college student to the retired woman.

Men Looking Ahead has an allure that appeals to men readers of all backgrounds, ethnic groups, races and diversities. It is a celebration of the printed word designed to highlight the accomplishments of men, provide viable information and serve as an echoing voice for every man of the 21st century.

Rebecca Franklin is the spirit behind Women Looking Ahead, Inc. Women Looking Ahead, Inc. is a company that recognizes the progress and achievements of people across the globe and works endlessly to further the prosperity and growth of all individuals

WOMEN WORKS PUBLISHING, INC.

Mailing Address: P.O. Box 767277
Roswell, Georgia 30076
Phone: 770.993.1173
Fax: 770.993.1179
Email: wlanews@bellsouth.net
Website: www.womenlookingahead.com

WE'D ALSO LIKE TO BE THOUGHT OF AS
YOUR EM**POWER**ING COMPANY.

Georgia Power's commitment to our customers goes beyond providing reliable and affordable power. We believe in giving back to the communities we serve. That's why we have partnered with programs like the 100 Black Men of Atlanta's Project Success and the Atlanta University Center Dual Degree Engineering Program to help our young people succeed in the workplace and strengthen our communities. While supplying electricity is our business, showing our support of higher education is equally powerful. To learn more about your power company, visit **georgiapower.com.**

GEORGIA
POWER
A **SOUTHERN COMPANY**

BRUCE H. DOBBS

PRESIDENT & CEO

Be In It 2 Win It!

Bruce Dobbs is a specialist at helping people free themselves from the bonds that inhibit their success, allowing them to be more innovative and resourceful at getting what they want out of life. He is a highly successful entrepreneur, investment banker, certified financial manager, speaker, author, business consultant, personal development coach/motivator and educator.

Whether it's coaching "one-on-one" with senior level executives, presidents and CEOs to help them improve personal performance or motivating your entire staff towards competitive excellence, Bruce brings a solid background of proven achievement, learned wisdom through experience and a "never give up – never give in" spirit that will infect your business and your personal life and drive you towards the success you deserve.

Are you looking for the yet to be discovered "breakout" stars on your staff?

Through interactive and customized programs, Bruce provides the tools necessary to change attitudes and behaviors, increase productivity, and enhance and improve leadership skills.

If you want to increase sales, identify or create leaders, build cohesive teams and retain clients and staff then **"Be In It To Win It!"** is the motivational and training program for any member of your company from the back office to the front desk. Offering more than a keynote speech or a simple "pep talk", Bruce provides a roadmap that you or your staff members can follow to achieve your business goals.

"Be In It To Win It!" programs are designed to be customizable for the startup entrepreneur, the seasoned manager or supervisor, senior level executives and CEOs.

"Be In It To Win It!" programs will improve your staff attitudes and perceptions, inspire them to put more of themselves into your business and help them to understand and learn to achieve your company or corporate mission.

"Be In It To Win It!" programs will help your frontline supervisors and managers learn the underlying causes of staff burnout and dissatisfaction and teach them proven techniques of motivating which will result in dynamic staff performance. "Be In It and Win It!" programs will provide your leadership with the necessary skills to bring out the best in almost anyone on your staff.

For more information call (404) 246-7899 or email bruce.dobbs@comcast.net.

From diversity comes strength...
and success

At Comcast, we are committed to connecting people to what's important in their lives. A key to our success is our commitment to embrace and celebrate what is unique about our employees, our customers and our communities.

This celebration of diversity is evident in our workforce, our programming, the suppliers with whom we do business and our community investment efforts.

We salute the extraordinary Comcast Employees highlighted in this 2007 edition of Who's Who In Black Atlanta.

Michael Hewitt   Stacy Cole

Lillian Harding   Jason Biske

Tina Capers-Hall   Angela Gray

They represent what we stand for — the strength and success that come from embracing diversity.

comcast

KISS 104.1

ATLANTA'S OLD SCHOOL R&B STATION

Art Terrell:
3PM - 7PM
Art.Terrell@kiss1041fm.com

Stacy D:
7PM - 12M
StacyD@kiss1041fm.com

Sasha the Diva:
10AM - 3PM
SashatheDiva@kiss1041fm.com

Tom Joyner:
The Tom Joyner
Morning Show
6AM -10AM

WWW. KISS1041FM.COM

Washington Mutual

DIVERSITY CORPORATION
OF THE YEAR

Reginald Bynum
Small Business Relationship Manager
Washington Mutual, Inc.

Ruth Charles
Assistant Vice President
Small Business Relationships
Washington Mutual, Inc.

Reginald Bynum is the small business relationship manager for Washington Mutual's Region Two in Tucker, Georgia. In this position, he manages the acquisition, retention and expansion of assigned small business customer portfolios. Reginald joined Washington Mutual in August of 2002 as a financial center manager in Norcross, Georgia, and accepted his current position in July of 2006.

Prior to joining Washington Mutual, Reginald held management positions in the consumer finance industry with American General, NationsCredit and Avco.

Reginald was born in Greenville, Mississippi, and graduated from Mississippi State University where he majored in business administration with an emphasis in finance.

Reginald and his wife, Toni, have been married for 15 years. They have two children, Ambrea and Reginald Jr.

Ruth Charles is assistant vice president of small business relationships for Washington Mutual Bank. In this position, she manages the small business sales and service initiatives for her region, which includes 23 financial centers around Atlanta.

With 19 years of banking experience, Ruth has held various positions including sales and service manager, branch manager and small business development officer at key banks throughout Georgia and Florida.

Ruth is an avid soccer player, having enjoyed the sport all her life, both as a dedicated player and fan. Currently, she plays the middle field position on a local women's soccer team in Stone Mountain.

The quote that means the most to Ruth in both her professional and personal life is: "It's better to try and fail than to fail to try." She also lives by these sayings: "Just do it!" and "Failure is not an option."

A native of Trinidad and Tobago, Ruth migrated to New York at the age of seven and has lived in Georgia for 14 years. She and her family live in Conyers.

Washington Mutual

Dana D. Chestnut
First Vice President
Southeast Regional Manager
Washington Mutual, Inc.

Beverly H. Dabney
First Vice President
Washington Mutual, Inc.

Dana D. Chestnut is first vice president and southeast regional manager with the Washington Mutual Community Lending and Investment Group. Dana has worked in the banking industry for more than ten years. His current responsibilities include the management of the Florida and Georgia markets and assisting for-profit and not-for-profit entities with the development of affordable multi-family communities.

Prior to joining Washington Mutual, Dana held the position of vice president with Bank of America.

A native of Tallahassee, Florida, Dana earned a bachelor of science degree in business economics from Florida A&M University, where he was a member of the varsity baseball team.

Beverly Dabney is first vice president and community affairs relationship manager with Washington Mutual's community and external affairs division, covering the Georgia, Orlando and Tampa markets. She is responsible for identifying and building strong community partnerships that promote affordable housing and financial empowerment. A 31-year banking veteran, Beverly began her career as a bank examiner with the Federal Reserve Bank of Atlanta.

Throughout her career, Beverly has been actively involved with community development organizations. She has served on the board of the Initiative for Affordable Housing, the Latin American Association, the Metropolitan Atlanta Youth Opportunities Initiative, the Hughes Spalding Children's Hospital, and Eastlake YMCA. She is a member of Leadership Atlanta and a life member of the NAACP.

Beverly has been recognized throughout her career with many awards for leadership and work performance. Most recently, she was recognized as the Eastlake 2006 YMCA Volunteer of the Year.

A native of Mount Airy, North Carolina, Beverly received her bachelor of science degree in business administration from Winston-Salem State University.

She is married to Dexter Dabney and they have one son, Duane.

Debra T. Griffin
Small Business Relationship Manager
Washington Mutual, Inc.

Reneé Knorr
Assistant Vice President
Small Business Relationships
Washington Mutual, Inc.

Debra T. Griffin is a small business relationship manager with Washington Mutual. She began her career in retail sales with a major department store. During her ten years in retail sales, Debra held many positions including supervisor and trainer. In 1993 she made the transition to banking. During the last 13 years, she has also worked as a loan manager and branch manager.

Debra has been recognized with many honors throughout her career. She has received a variety of awards including employee of the month, outstanding community leader and top performing branch.

Debra serves on numerous boards and committees including the Gwinnett County apprenticeship board, the Covenant House Georgia financial committee and ACCION USA. She is very active in the community and is an advocate for promoting financial education. She can also be found teaching budgeting classes, volunteering at schools and hosting financial seminars for business owners.

An Ohio native, Debra has lived in Atlanta for six years. She attended Columbus State University and Youngstown State University where she studied business. She resides in Suwanee with her daughter.

Reneé Knorr is an assistant vice president of small business relationships at Washington Mutual where she is responsible for developing and managing sales and service initiatives for small business owners.

For the past ten years, Reneé has enjoyed creating expert solutions in the financial services industry. Prior to joining Washington Mutual in 2005, she worked for SunTrust Bank where she was inducted into the Hall of Fame for exemplary sales achievement.

A New Orleans native, Reneé has lived in Atlanta for 13 years. Her community involvement includes volunteering for Sisters Network Breast Cancer Organization, the March of Dimes, the United Way, the Open Hands Project and the Sickle Cell Anemia Foundation. She is also involved with the Melanoma Skin Cancer Foundation, Junior Achievement, the American Cancer Society and V-103's For Sisters Only.

Reneé is the proud mother of a 6-year-old daughter.

Regina Murray
Vice President & Senior Sales Manager
Washington Mutual, Inc.

Silah Williams
Assistant Vice President
Business Banking Division
Washington Mutual, Inc.

Regina Murray is very passionate about "the power of yes." A California native, she began her career in mortgage more than 20 years ago in Oakland, California. Since then, she has held leadership and management positions with Century 21, Bank of America, Nations Bank and Washington Mutual.

While embracing her vision of sharing financial literacy with the masses, Regina earned a bachelor's degree in biblical studies, a master's degree in Christian education and a doctorate in the ministry of Christian education.

Currently, Regina is the only African-American female in the Southeast region of Washington Mutual Home Loans to hold the position of vice president and senior sales manager in the emerging markets division. She heads three offices in the metropolitan Atlanta area.

Understanding the cultural nuances that many minorities face, Regina is committed to building a team that will commit to meeting the needs of Atlanta's underserved urban communities. Under her leadership, the focus is to promote financial empowerment by providing access to the funds needed, while guiding one family at a time through the process of buying a home.

Silah Williams is an assistant vice president in the business banking division of Washington Mutual Bank. There, he works closely with business owners to help them obtain business accounts and lending products. He is also an instructor at Clayton State University where he teaches "Banking for Your Small Business," a course he developed for business owners.

Prior to joining Washington Mutual in 2005, Silah was an assistant vice president in the wealth management division of Bank of America. He served in a variety of roles including banking center manager, business development representative, insurance representative and investment representative with Fifth Third Bank in Lansing, Michigan. He began his banking career as a sales and service specialist with Central Carolina Bank in Durham, North Carolina in 1998.

Silah holds a bachelor of science degree in business management from North Carolina A&T State University. He also holds licenses to sell investment and insurance products.

A native of North Carolina, Silah and his wife, Yolanda, call Georgia home.

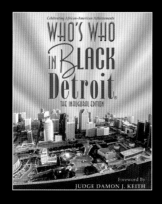
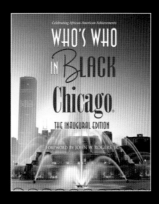
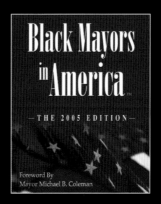
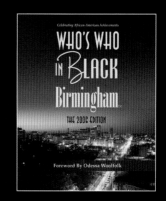
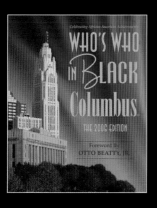

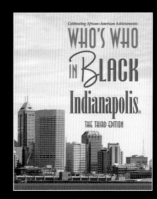
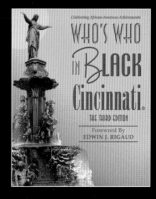
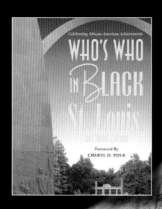
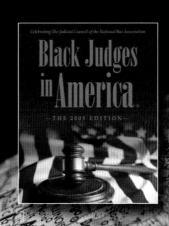
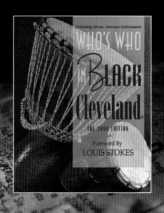

THOMAS, KENNEDY, SAMPSON, & PATTERSON
ATTORNEYS AT LAW

For over thirty-five years, perseverance has been the axiom of **Thomas, Kennedy, Sampson & Patterson**. Founded in 1971, the firm serves the legal needs of major corporations, governmental authorities, small businesses and individuals. The oldest minority-owned law firm in Georgia and among the largest minority-owned law firms in the southeastern United States, Thomas, Kennedy, Sampson & Patterson is rated *a v* by Martindale-Hubbell and is listed in the *Bar Register of Preeminent Lawyers*, published by Martindale-Hubbell.

In May of 2006, **Thomas, Kennedy Sampson & Patterson**, was awarded The Coca-Cola Company's "Partner in the Promise" Award, as the minority business enterprise supplier of the year.

The firm was recognized as one of the top "go to" companies in the country, as listed in the May 2006 Fortune magazine, placing **Thomas, Kennedy, Sampson & Patterson** among the top 5 percent of law firms in the country.

"These recognitions are a tremendous honor and is an affirmation of the hard work we've invested over the years," says Managing Partner and co-founder Thomas G. Sampson. It is quite an honor, and a testament to the skills of everyone at the firm."

Thomas, Kennedy, Sampson & Patterson is committed to excellence and is dedicated to meeting the needs of a broad-based practice.

Thomas, Kennedy, Sampson, & Patterson

3355 MAIN STREET

ATLANTA, GEORGIA 30337

404.688.4503 TEL

404.681.2950 CORPORATE FAX

404.684.9515 LITIGATION FAX

WWW.TKSP.COM

To experience Anthony Davis Designs
is to indulge your imagination.

404.368.2416
www.adavisdesigns.com
Fashion Designer, Stylist, Interior Consultant

remember

... a world safe from risk?

The world today is a risky place to live, work and do business.

People need reliable and timely information to help make the decisions that will lead to a safer, more secure world. ChoicePoint delivers this promise to thousands of people every day in business and government. To nonprofit organizations and consumers.

One event can change lives. One solution can impact the future. One company can help make our world a safer place.

Smarter Decisions. Safer World.™

1000 Alderman Drive Alpharetta, GA 30005 800.342.5339 www.choicepoint.com

Jazz
never goes
out of style!

www.wclk.com

There's something important we'd like you to know about Publix: showing our appreciation to our customers is the cornerstone of our culture. It's not just something we do when we think about it. It's who we are. We want you to always feel good about shopping at Publix, and that everything you buy will meet your expectations. In fact, we feel so strongly about it that we've put it in writing. Come by and let us prove it. Publix Super Markets. Where shopping is a pleasure.

Historic College Park's Newest Fine Dining Restaurant

Located minutes from airport area hotels, Hartsfield-Jackson International Airport, Georgia International Convention Center and Fort McPherson. The Pecan fuses Classic Southern Cuisine with modern eclectic influences. Visit us in Historic College Park and experience contemporary style and southern elegance.

<u>Lunch</u>	<u>Dinner</u>	<u>Brunch</u>
Tuesday-Friday	**Tuesday-Saturday**	**Sunday**
11:30 am - 2:30 pm	**5:30 pm - 10:30 pm**	**11:00 am - 3:00 pm**

3 7 2 5   M a i n   S t r e e t ,   C o l l e g e   P a r k ,   G A   3 0 3 3 7
(4 0 4)   7 6 2 - 8 4 4 4   •   w w w . t h e p e c a n o n l i n e . c o m

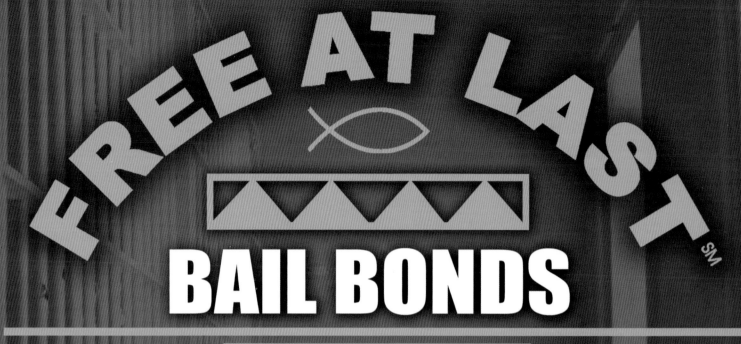

SPECIAL OCCASIONS EVENT CENTER

- Your Complete Wedding, Party & Event Facility -

The Pleasure of Your Company Is Requested

The Chapel & The Gardens, in addition to the Special Occasions Reception Room, provide the best settings for simple, but warm and elegant year-round entertaining. The reception room is spacious, tastefully decorated and has an adjoining catering kitchen.

Reunions

Weddings

Events

Meetings

Parties

The Chapel is quaint and elegant... perfect for a memorable, intimate wedding. Stained glass windows, a candle lit altar, bridal parlor, chandeliers and seating capacity for 150 guests are a few of the features which are a part of this historic and architecturally unique setting. Plan your wedding your way and choose or bring in the services that you want. Special Occasions offers many additional services to assist you.

The Gardens adjoining the Chapel is a pleasant and tranquil space with a tiered fountain as its centerpiece. Arbors, flowers and trees make this an ideal setting to entertain guests.

For an elegant and special wedding or event, reserve your day with Special Occasions. Please contact us for more information.

Mobile Concession Unit
Available for
Craft Shows • Festivals • Events

Concession Equipment
Snow Cone • Corn Dog • Cotton Candy
Pop Corn • Funnel Cakes

Assorted Catering Equipment
Tents of All Sizes
China • Candelabras
Tables & Chairs • Linen
Brass & Silver Accessories
PA Systems • Staging
Dance Floor • Karaoke Machine
Hot & Cold Beverage Containers
Moon Walks & Slides for Kids
Cash Vault Blow Up for Adults
Commercial Grills & Smokers
Generators

• • •

232 S 10TH STREET
GRIFFIN, GA 30224
PH 770-229-8588
FAX 770-229-8558

MORE THAN 200 PLACES TO CONNECT...

1050 Lenox Park, AmeriSuites Downtown, AmeriSuites-Airport, METROPOLIS, AmeriSuites- Stonecrest, BUCKHEAD LIBRARY, Arbor Gates at Buckhead, AT&T TLC COMMITTEE, METRO ATLANTA CHAMBER OF COMMERCE, Aveda Institute, Berkeley Run, Berkeley Trace, Best Western, BORDERS AT STONECREST, Bryson Square at City PK, Camden Brookwood, Camelot at Buckhead, Canten Walk, Centennial Tower, CENTENNIAL HOUSE, Charleston Courts, Churchill Grounds, Comfort Inn Stone Mtn, Country Inn & Suites, Crown Plaza-Ravinia, Crowne Plaza – Buckhead, Curves Fitness, DE'AMAR SALON & SPA, Doubletree Club Atlanta, EMBASSY SUITES, ENTERPRISE RENTAL CAR, Five Oaks, Georgia International Convention Center, HERTZ RENTAL CAR, Hilton Garden Inn, 330 Ponce, Historical Hair & Barber, Hilton Atlanta Downtown, Hotel Indigo, Hyatt Regency Atlanta, Intercontinental Hotel, J. W. Marriott Hotel Lenox, JAVAOLOGY, Lexington Glen, Longwood Apartment Homes, The MANUEL J. MALOOF CENTER, Marriott Hotel, MARRIOTT MARQUIS HOTEL, Marriott-Perimeter, Morningside Courts, NAIL 1ST, NAIL TALK & TAN, Nancy's Pizza, Omni Hotel @ CNN Center, On The Move Lending, OUTWRITE BOOKS, Paces Park, PLANET SMOOTHIE, Ponko Chicken, Post Briarcliff, Post Gardens, Post Glen, Post Lenox Park, Post Lindbergh, Post Oak Apartment, POST Peachtree Apts., Poster Hut, Red Roof Inn, Renaissance Hotel, RESIDENCE INN, Ritz Carlton, Savannah Midtown Apts, HARTSFIELD-JACKSON INTERNATIONAL AIRPORT TRAVEL CENTER, Sheraton Atlanta Hotel, Sleep Inn, Smash Inc., Smoothie King, Summit Properties, SUN CITY TAN, Thai Palate, The Columns at River Pkwy, SHOEMAKERS WAREHOUSE, The Conservatory at Druid, The Georgian Terrace, The Reserve at Lenox Park, The Standard@ Lenox Park, Tiburon of Buckhead, Town Place Suites, Vinings Gallery, W HOTEL ATLANTA, Waldenbooks, Waterford On Piedmont, WESLEY TOWNSEND APTS, Westin Peachtree Plaza At Windsor at Briarhill, Woodland Hills Apartment, WVEE, Coldwell Banker, The Westin Buckhead, Fairfield Inn & Suites, The Lofts at 5300, ReMax of Buckhead, Holiday Inn Express, Sheraton Buckhead Hotel, ReMAX GREATER ATLANTA, Staybridge Suites, Coldwell Banker, Harry Norman Realtors, Jenny Pruitt & Assoc., Harry Norman Realtors, ReMax Greater Atlanta, Keller Williams Realty, ReMax Around Atlanta, Hampton Inn, AmeriSuites, Homewood Suites, Wingate Inn, Keller Williams, PEACHTREE-DEKALB AIRPORT SIGNATURE FLIGHT SUPPORT, Jenny Pruitt, Courtyard by Marriott, Doubletree Guest Suites, Comfort Inn, Keller Williams, Grand Hyatt Atlanta, Keller Williams, Metro Brokers GMAC, Fairfield Inn & Suites, Staybridge Suites, Hyatt Place AmeriSuites, THE WESTIN HOTEL-DOWNTOWN, Microtel Inn & Suites, FAT BURGER, Courtyard by Marriott, La Quinta Inn, Doubletree Inn, Comfort Suites, Holiday Inn Hotel, Holiday Inn Express, Marriott Atlanta N Central, Karafotias Realty Co., POST WOODS, Crown Plaza Marietta, Especially for You, AMA EXECUTIVE CONFERENCE CENTER

CONNECT ATLANTA

www.connectextra.com
678.476.0274

CONNECT is a complimentary, quarterly magazine distributed in more than 200 high traffic outlets in and around metro Atlanta. Call today to get CONNECTed.

NATIONAL COALITION of 100 BLACK WOMEN

NCBW 100

BY ALONIA JERNIGAN

NATIONAL COALITION *of* 100 BLACK WOMEN

Metropolitan Atlanta Chapter
STRENGTH IN NUMBERS

Deloitte & Touche LLP Corporate Partnership -left to right- President Virgina Harris, Partner Avery Munning, Deloitte & Touche LLP and Partner Joanne Kelly, CPA.

Standing strong with 104 members, the Metropolitan Atlanta Chapter of the National Coalition of 100 Black Women, Inc. is the organization's third largest chapter. Founded in 1998, the Metropolitan Atlanta Chapter represents its share of 14 million African-American women in the United States. In keeping with the national office's mission, the Metropolitan Atlanta Chapter focuses on four core initiatives: teen mentoring, education, health and economic empowerment. The chapter boasts of strong ties to the corporate community, which reinforces the fact that they are a community advocacy organization.

Of the four initiatives, the Metropolitan Atlanta Chapter's flagship program is their teen mentoring program, Teens on the Move. The program, which has received national acknowledgement, invites ninth grade students to participate in activities that will better prepare them for their future. The previous class, comprised of students from Crim and Washington High Schools, included 33 young ladies who completed the program after an original enrollment of 72. The Metropolitan Atlanta Chapter has awarded over $350,000 to 250 students since its inception in 1995. The current class of 2010 began in September of 2006 and has enrolled 120 students.

Another exciting feature of the Metropolitan Atlanta Chapter is Gourmet Gents, an extravaganza where Atlanta's finest amateur, professional and celebrity gents dish out samplings of their favorite recipes. The annual event generally draws over 4,000 attendees and serves as a major fundraiser for Teens on the Move.

For ten years the chapter has held its Unsung Heroine Gala, recognizing women in the community whose work often goes unnoticed without the chapter's salute. Over 100 women have been honored for their unselfish acts of kindness. "During the past three years, we added a new twist and honored notable community leaders including the late Coretta Scott King, Judge Leah Sears, Monica (Kaufman) Pearson and Tommy Dortch," said President Virginia Harris. Proceeds from this event go to the chapter's economic empowerment initiative, Adopt-A-Shelter program, in partnership with the Achor Center. The goal of this program is to provide transitional shelter for women and children.

For more information on the Metropolitan Atlanta Chapter, visit them online at www.ncbw-metroatlchapter.org

NATIONAL COALITION of 100 BLACK WOMEN

MECCA Chapter

INTERNATIONAL IMPACT WITH LOCAL APPEAL

Members of MECCA and the Little Ladies of MECCA with Ambassador Andrew Young at a Voters' Reauthorization March.

In April of 1990, Winifred E. Saulter called together a group of friends on Emory University's campus who were concerned about the growing issues of teen pregnancy and other issues affecting youth in Atlanta. This group has now evolved into a prominent chapter of the National Coalition of 100 Black Women Inc., MECCA (Metro Ebone Civic Club Association).

Over the course of three years, MECCA made a name for itself, with its Teen Mothers program becoming the group's most visible and momentous. This program assisted young mothers with workshops on parenting skills, self-esteem and the importance of prenatal doctor visits. Elizabeth Wilson, director of the Oakhurst Community Center, played an instrumental role in implementing the Teen Mothers program. As an enhancement to the program, MECCA enlisted help from volunteer Emory students to tutor girls in setting the groundwork for returning to school so they could earn their high school diplomas.

MECCA officially became a chapter of the National Coalition of 100 Black Women, Inc. in 1993. Immediately gaining the recognition of a local principal, Dr. Charles Hawks, MECCA began a mentoring program for girls at English Avenue Elementary School. The program followed Dr. Hawks to Perkerson Elementary. The program is still active today and is known as Little Ladies of MECCA, starting at fifth grade and following the girls to high school. The Little Ladies of MECCA graduated its first group in May of 2006. All of the Little Ladies received a $1,500 scholarship from the chapter and are college bound.

MECCA's exemplary commitment to the community has gained many accolades. Among them is the Martin Luther King, Jr. Community Service Award for exemplary community service. This award was bestowed in 1999 by the Emory University School of Public Health and the Goizueta Business School. MECCA's close involvement with Emory gives the chapter an international appeal because of the Little Ladies of MECCA's exposure to students from various countries. The chapter provides an excellent vehicle that enlightens the young ladies in the areas of education and cultural enrichment.

For more information on the MECCA Chapter, visit them online at www.nc100bwmecca.org

Decatur/DeKalb Chapter

CREATING LEGACIES, CHANGING A GENERATION

Chef Marvin Woods from Home Plate (Turner South Network) did a cooking demonstration during the chapter's Wellness Day. He is pictured here with members of the chapter.

The Decatur/DeKalb Chapter of the National Coalition of 100 Black Women, Inc. is most widely known for its signature program, Legacy, which, since 1997, has been the foundation for leadership and mentoring of African-American girls in grades nine through 12 who attend school in DeKalb County. For eight months, participants are exposed to life's lessons through seminars and other empowering activities in the areas of health awareness, self-esteem, civic responsibility, cultural awareness, economic development, entrepreneurship and financial literacy. A community service project is also a part of the program, and juniors are given the opportunity to go on a college tour. The end result is that seniors receive a scholarship upon successful completion of the program. "Legacy, by far, is our most celebrated program," says Chapter President Kimberly Cameron. "Since its inception ten years ago, 200 girls have matriculated through our program and subsequently achieved significant levels of accomplishment. We have watched our young ladies become attorneys and enter various other disciplines. This gives us a sense of pride in knowing that we've helped play an integral role in these young ladies' lives."

Additionally, the Decatur/DeKalb chapter hosts an annual Wellness Day, a community service event that focuses on health education and disease prevention. "While we realized that health is important, we also wanted to present a program that would not be the typical health fair," Cameron adds. The chapter's most recent Wellness Day featured in-depth seminars on cardiovascular health, nutrition and psychological health. The chapter also hosts a Pink and Black ball, which is a fund-raiser for breast cancer research. Proceeds from this event benefit the Legacy program.

Although the chapter's membership base is relatively small, the group enthusiastically anticipates its 20th anniversary, and increasing its membership will be a key component of its focus for the year. "I also hope to concentrate on empowering the younger women to come in and be leaders of the future," says Cameron. Commendably, some of the chapter's charter members are still active. For more information on the Decatur/DeKalb Chapter, call (770) 322-8049.

Northwest Georgia Chapter, Inc.

POSITIVE MENTORING TO THE DISADVANTAGED WITH A SPIRIT OF UNITY AND SISTERHOOD

Induction of new members during an installation ceremony.

What began as a vision to combine the vast and varied expertise of professional women from Cobb, Cherokee and Douglas counties and surrounding areas to build a bridge for the future has blossomed into the Northwest Georgia Chapter, Inc. of the National Coalition of 100 Black Women, Inc. Under the leadership of its visionary and president, Alice Archey, the Northwest Georgia Chapter was officially chartered in March of 2004 with 60 women.

Understanding that the National Coalition of 100 Black Women, Inc. presented the best platform where women could unite and affect changes in their communities, Archey began the Northwest Georgia Chapter with hopes of not only impacting young women in the community, but she also saw it as an opportunity for professional women to become better protectors and supporters of each other. "So much is thrown at the sisterhood of African-American women. I would love to see us unify and be a bridge for each other."

The Northwest Georgia Chapter takes pride in being advocates for change. "Our first advocacy platform took place in Cherokee County when an image that depicted an African-American girl with no shoes was posted on one of the school's Web sites," states Archey. "We wrote a letter to the superintendent, explaining our disdain. The picture was immediately pulled from the Web site, and officials promised not to use the photo in the upcoming brochure," she adds. The chapter also took a lead role in partnering with the Cobb County Health Department and the Cobb County Sheriff's Department for the purpose of showing students in Cobb's alternative schools (middle and high schools) the legal ramifications of sexual misbehavior.

Among the chapter's major activities are two fundraisers: the charity golf tournament and the Sadie Hawkins charity dance. Funds from both events go toward the chapter's scholarship program, which is a mentoring program called Teen 100. This particular program targets middle and high school girls and helps prepare them for a successful future.

For more information on the Northwest Georgia Chapter, visit them online at www.nc100bwnwga.org

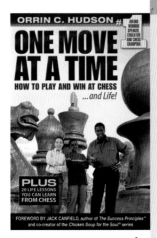

HYATT REGENCY ATLANTA
ON PEACHTREE STREET ®

CORPORATE SPOTLIGHT

Angie Howard
Director of Human Resources
Hyatt Regency Atlanta

A ngie Howard started her career with Hyatt in 1982 in Florida as an administrative assistant to the human resources director. She quickly moved into management after being in her position for five months. She held positions as the benefits manager, employment manager and assistant human resources director.

During her 23-year tenure with Hyatt, Angie has been director of human resources at Hyatt Regency West Houston, Hyatt Regency Orlando International Airport, Hyatt Regency New Orleans and Hyatt Orlando. In 2004 she transferred to her current position as director of human resources at Hyatt Regency Atlanta, a city in which she has always wanted to live.

Before joining Hyatt, Angie worked as an employment specialist for the Hillsborough County Employment and Training Department in Florida. She attended Hillsborough Community College and the University of Phoenix.

During her time away from work, Angie is a volunteer director of human resources for Antioch-Lithonia Missionary Baptist Church and a board member of EduPAC of Atlanta.

Angie is married to Michael Weir and is the proud parent of three wonderful children.

La Tonya Hunter
Assistant Director, Human Resources
Hyatt Regency Atlanta

L a Tonya Hunter is the assistant director of human resources at Hyatt Regency Atlanta. Now in her 12th year with the Hyatt Corporation, she began her Hyatt career as a PBX operator in her hometown of San Antonio, Texas. An avid learner, she quickly fast-tracked into management, having served in various positions including reservations, front office, sales and human resources.

Hunter received her bachelor of science degree in business management from the University of Phoenix. She is currently working on certifications in human resources management.

In addition to a flourishing career, Hunter enjoys helping others and is very active in community building. As one who believes that education is key to success, she actively participates in her local PTA. She serves on the business advisory council board at Warren Technical School and is a Make-A-Wish Foundation volunteer. She enjoys spending time with her family and is an active member of her church. Hunter's ultimate goal is to find the path in life she was created to follow.

Kayla began her career in the hospitality industry in 1998 with Hyatt Regency Orlando International Airport as a corporate management trainee. There, she was promoted to several management positions and gained experience in all areas of the human resources function.

Kayla transferred to the Hyatt Regency Atlanta in September of 2005 as the assistant human resources director. In this position, her work-related responsibilities include benefit administration, compensation, recruitment and retention, employee and labor relations, counseling, safety, and training and development.

As a hospitality management major at Bethune-Cookman College, Kayla was affiliated with and received scholarships from many hospitality organizations including the National Society of Minorities in Hospitality and the Coalition of Black Meeting Planners. She graduated with honors in 1998. She is presently an active member of the Society of Human Resource Management.

A native of the Bahamas, Kayla is happily married with two children. Her hobbies include cooking native Bahamian foods, watching HGTV and shopping. She is known for her ability to see the good in any situation and her favorite quote is: "Look on the bright side."

Kayla Dionne Jones
Assistant Human Resources Director
Hyatt Regency Atlanta

Tracey E. Martin is convention services manager for Hyatt Regency Atlanta. She began her career with Hyatt Hotels and Resorts in 1990 at the airport property as a part-time front desk agent. Following a fulfilling and rewarding management career in the retail industry, she joined the Hyatt Regency Atlanta family full-time as an administrative assistant in January of 1997.

In 1999 Tracey was promoted to her current position of catering/convention services manager, where she services all market types from family reunions to major corporations. Her responsibilities include managing sleeping rooms, planning food and beverage functions and coordinating all other convention activities with the meeting planner. Over the years, she has received several leadership awards for dedication and outstanding performance.

Outside of work, Tracey enjoys reading, traveling and spending time at the park with her husband Greg, and her daughters, Jill and Clarke. An advocate for helping others, Tracey and her family volunteer regularly with the Atlanta Community Food Bank and the Atlanta Fire Department.

A native of Atlanta, Tracey holds a bachelor of business administration degree from Georgia State University.

Tracey E. Martin
Convention Services Manager
Hyatt Regency Atlanta

ON PEACHTREE STREET

Maxine Matheson
Catering Sales Manager
Hyatt Regency Atlanta

Maxine Matheson is catering sales manager with Hyatt Regency Atlanta. Following her collegiate achievements from the College of Arts, Science and Technology in Jamaica, she accepted a position as catering sales trainee. Maxine joined the Hyatt family in 1997 on the island of Grand Cayman as food and beverage manager. There, Maxine worked predominantly with incentive groups, local banks and investment companies to develop and coordinate social and business meetings, galas, tours and events.

In 2002 Maxine was awarded the Manager of the Year Award for outstanding performance, service and dedication.

In December of 2002, Maxine was given the opportunity to move to Hyatt Regency Atlanta as catering sales manager. In her new position, her responsibility is to support event planning through sales and service. She works closely with the community in areas including education, and with marketing and advertising companies, media and meeting/event planners to coordinate successful functions.

Maxine is a member of the International Business Association and enjoys its monthly activities. Outside of work, Maxine enjoys spending time with her daughter, Tamara, and her husband, Trevor.

Jessie Moore
Credit Manager
Hyatt Regency Atlanta

Jessie Lee Moore is the credit manager in accounting at Hyatt Regency Atlanta. As accounting credit manager, he oversees accounts receivable staff regarding credit approvals and billing.

Jessie began his career with Hyatt Hotels and Resorts in 1991 at the Hyatt Regency in the great city of Chicago, where he worked for 14 years in various departments and divisions. On February 15, 2005, he relocated to the Hyatt Regency Atlanta with a plethora of opportunities to excel in his career. His ultimate career goal with Hyatt Hotels and Resorts is to become a controller.

A native of Blytheville, Arkansas, Jessie studied at Truman College in Chicago and the Metropolitan College of Business Training. Jessie is one of 15 children in his family and spent most of his youth in Chicago.

I yanna Newborn, sales manager for Hyatt Regency Atlanta, began her career with Hyatt as an intern upon graduation from Spelman College. With a degree in political science, she came to Hyatt with very little knowledge of the hotel industry, but it did not take her long to adjust to the fast-paced climate. With a tenacious spirit, she has quickly moved up the ranks.

After six months, Iyanna entered into the Winter 2006 Corporate Management Trainee (CMT) class. She became a sales manager in July of 2006, handling the meeting connections market, multicultural and association business.

A native of Southern California, Iyanna came to Atlanta to attend Spelman College, and has since adopted the city as her second home. She is active in the National Alumnae Association of Spelman College and Delta Sigma Theta Sorority, Inc.

Iyanna Newborn
Sales Manager
Hyatt Regency Atlanta

J ustin L. Page has been with Hyatt for more than four years. He began his career with Hyatt as a sales/marketing intern while attending Morehouse College. As a sales manager, Justin now manages all multicultural and diversity accounts for Hyatt in the group sales market segment.

Additionally, Justin serves on the board for Go Help Others, Inc., a nonprofit organization designed to better educate children. He also serves on the diversity committee for the City of Atlanta.

While in college, Justin was a member of the Morehouse Business Association and participated in the national INROADS program which places talented, qualified minorities in business positions to develop their corporate leadership skills. Consistently on the dean's list, he made time to tutor and mentor children at St. Anthony's Elementary School and Thomasville Heights Elementary School.

Justin's commitment to community involvement has not diminished. He currently supports the Habitat for Humanity home building project, and in the past he served as a positive role model and sounding board for many children at the Atlanta Children's Shelter.

Justin L. Page
Sales Manager
Hyatt Regency Atlanta

Rudy Parsons
Chief Engineer
Hyatt Regency Atlanta

Rudy Parsons is chief engineer at the Hyatt Regency Atlanta. He is primarily responsible for maintaining the physical plant and day-to-day management of the engineering department. Rudy leads a team of three assistant directors with a staff of approximately 30 technicians. He provides leadership, direction, coordination, scheduling, training and review to ensure safety, comfort and security for guests and staff.

Rudy began his Hyatt career in 1990 as a plant supervisor at Hyatt Regency St. John, and later became assistant director of engineering. Shortly thereafter, he transferred and held positions as assistant director of engineering for Hyatt Orlando and director of engineering for Hyatt Regency Suites in Georgia.

Rudy received his undergraduate degree in diesel and automotive technology from Lincoln Tech. A St. John, Virgin Islands native, he was an affiliate of Hyatt Corporation's Diversity Council in 2004. He serves as a board member of the Southwest Youth Baseball Association and is a member of the Mustang Powerhouse of Atlanta.

Rudy is an avid professional sports enthusiast, and enjoys spending time with his wife, Jannis, and three children, Rasheed, Rahmoi and Jayda.

Lawrence Williams
Senior Food and Beverage Director
Hyatt Regency Atlanta

Lawrence Williams is the senior food and beverage director for the Hyatt Regency Atlanta. Born in August of 1961 in Evansville, Indiana, he is a graduate of Indiana State University's two-year business program.

Lawrence started his career with Hyatt Hotels and Resorts in August of 1982 and has worked in seven cities. He has held positions including catering and convention service manager, director of outlets, director of catering, assistant food and beverage director, and food and beverage director.

Following his time as a corporate operational review leader, Lawrence was appointed senior executive director of food and beverage in 2005.

Lawrence and his wife, Deanna, have been married for 14 years and have two sons, Lawrence and Sidney. Lawrence enjoys fishing, golf, wine tastings, traveling and cooking. His favorite quote is: "You can't separate peace from freedom because no one can be at peace unless he has his freedom."

CORPORATE SPOTLIGHT

Ronald E. Frieson
President of Georgia Operations
BellSouth Corporation

Ronald E. Frieson is president of Georgia operations for BellSouth Corporation. He is responsible for the regulatory, legislative, public policy and external affairs for BellSouth's operation in Georgia. From 2002 until his appointment to his current post in 2005, Frieson was vice president of transition and strategy for BellSouth's consumer services. Previously, he was vice president and chief of diversity for BellSouth Corporation.

Frieson began his BellSouth career at TechSouth Publishing Services, holding positions of increasing responsibility in the company, both nationally and internationally. Before joining BellSouth, he worked in the banking industry.

Frieson is currently a board member of the Georgia Chamber of Commerce, Hands on Atlanta, the Atlanta Police Foundation, the American Kidney Fund and 100 Black Men of DeKalb. He was also a member of the Leadership Atlanta Class of 2002.

Frieson holds a bachelor of science degree in finance from the University of Tennessee and a master of business administration degree in information systems from Georgia State University. He is married to Belinda Stubblefield and they have two adult children.

Belinda Grant-Anderson
Vice President, People Development
BellSouth Corporation

Belinda Grant-Anderson is vice president of people development for BellSouth Corporation. In this role, she is responsible for staffing and training, the overall corporate governance process, and creating a three-year workforce transformation plan. Her previous roles at BellSouth include vice president of policy resolution for regulatory and external affairs, division president of BellSouth's operator services, and executive director of the strategic management unit.

Prior to joining BellSouth, Grant-Anderson spent seven years as a consultant with the Atlanta office of McKinsey & Company, a global management consulting firm. She began her career with Procter & Gamble's research and development division in Cincinnati, Ohio.

A native of Jacksonville, Florida, Grant-Anderson received her bachelor of engineering degree and master of business administration degree from Vanderbilt University in Nashville, Tennessee. She served on the board of the Vanderbilt University Alumni Association. Currently, she serves as board secretary for St. Jude's Recovery Center and Imagine IT!: The Children's Museum of Atlanta.

She is married to Brad Anderson and they have two children.

As president of BellSouth's advertising and publishing group, Ike Harris is responsible for the marketing and publishing of *The Real White* and *Yellow Pages* from BellSouth. Harris also serves on the board of yellowpages.com, a joint venture with AT&T that serves the online yellow pages market. He co-chairs BellSouth's diversity council.

Before joining BellSouth in 1997, Harris served as vice president and corporate controller of Supervalu, Inc. He also spent 13 years with KPMG Peat Marwick. Prior to this, he spent eight years in the NFL with the St. Louis Cardinals and the New Orleans Saints.

Harris' current professional affiliations include board membership at Deluxe Corporation, CIGNA Corporation, the Henry W. Grady Foundation and the Iowa State University Foundation board of governors. He also serves on the finance committee for the United Way of Metropolitan Atlanta. He is a member of the American Institute of Certified Public Accountants and the Minnesota Society of CPAs.

Harris holds a bachelor of science degree from Iowa State University and a master of business administration degree from the University of Minnesota.

Isaiah "Ike" Harris Jr.
President
Advertising & Publishing Group
BellSouth Corporation

George E. Hill III is vice president for product management at BellSouth Corporation. He is responsible for the operational planning, program management, and office and portfolio management of BellSouth's product portfolio.

Previously, Hill led a team of product managers and developers who were responsible for the strategy and portfolio management of BellSouth's wireless assets. The portfolio includes the Cingular Wireless agency agreement, fixed mobile convergence, and wireless broadband initiatives including Wi-Fi and Wi-Max. He led the technology organization responsible for next generation operations planning, portal/applications strategy and development, wireless/wireline integration, and home networking development to enable new products and services.

Prior to returning to BellSouth domestic operations, Hill was executive vice president and chief technology officer for BellSouth International.

A Washington, D.C. native, Hill has more than 20 years of experience in the telecommunications industry. He has a master of business administration degree from Emory University and a diploma in industrial electronics. He also attended the University of Phoenix where he studied business management. Hill speaks four languages and was an expatriate for five years in Sao Paulo, Brazil.

George E. Hill III
Vice President, Product Management
BellSouth Corporation

BELLSOUTH
Listening. Answering.®

Dallas LeDuff
Senior Director
Customer Care Operations
BellSouth Corporation

Dallas LeDuff is senior director of customer care operations for the retail market division of BellSouth Corporation. In this role, he is responsible for a myriad of support functions for the various sales channels in retail markets.

Dallas began his career with BellSouth in 1977 in New Orleans. He moved to Atlanta in the summer of 1995 with the assignment of centralizing all staffing operations for BellSouth. This goal was accomplished by the end of 1996, and it remains centralized as of today.

Prior to his current assignment, Dallas was senior director of field interface and planning for the largest retail channel, consumer services.

A native of New Orleans, Dallas earned a bachelor of science degree in accounting from Xavier University. He earned his master of business administration degree from Loyola University in New Orleans.

Necole J. Merritt
Senior Director
Corporate Communications
BellSouth Corporation

Necole Merritt is the senior director of corporate communications for BellSouth Corporation. She is responsible for the development and execution of the employee communications strategy for the company's approximately 60,000 employees.

An 18-year corporate communications executive, Merritt has held a variety of leadership positions across multiple industries. She has served as senior director of corporate communications since 1999, and recently served as senior director of public policy communications.

Before joining BellSouth, Merritt worked in communications for General Motors and Saturn Corporation, where she was an integral member of the Saturn project launch team and General Motors' electric vehicle launch team.

Additionally, Merritt is an adjunct professor at Georgia Perimeter College. She was featured in *PRWeek* and *USA Today* as a panel member commenting on *The Apprentice*. Merritt is involved in the community as a member of various committees for nonprofit organizations, serving as a mentor and an active member of her church.

A native of Detroit, Merritt earned her bachelor of science degree in journalism from Northwestern University and her master of arts degree from California State University at Northridge.

Corporate Spotlight

⚉ BELLSOUTH
Listening. Answering.®

Clarence O'Banner is assistant vice president of strategic relations and diversity initiatives for BellSouth Corporation. He is responsible for managing many of BellSouth's external stakeholder relationships, developing and implementing diversity communications strategies, and serving as a spokesperson on diversity matters.

O'Banner began his professional career with BellSouth in Jackson, Mississippi. Progressing to increasing levels of responsibility, he was appointed director of education affairs at BellSouth's headquarters in Atlanta in 1990. In this assignment, he was responsible for directing the corporation's efforts to promote educational excellence in the Southeast.

In 1999 O'Banner was appointed director of strategic relations, where he was responsible for company efforts aimed at enhancing customer and brand loyalty with minority and special interest organizations at the national level.

A native of Jackson, Mississippi, O'Banner received a bachelor's degree from Ithaca College, a master's degree from Southern Illinois University, and a master of business administration degree from Mercer University.

O'Banner is active in several community organizations, serving on the board of directors of 21st Century Leaders and on the NAACP's national board of trustees.

Clarence O'Banner
Assistant Vice President
Strategic Relations &
Diversity Initiatives
BellSouth Corporation

Gloria R. Reese, president of operator services for BellSouth Telecommunications, is responsible for operator services, business strategy and operations. The operator services organization is responsible for providing 0, 411 and database services to retail and wholesale markets. Gloria's responsibility includes every aspect of the business, from marketing and product management to overseeing management of call centers.

Gloria has more than 25 years of experience in the telecommunications business, including positions in consumer operations, business sales, technology planning and design, and diversity and training.

In addition to her support of the United Negro College Fund, Gloria is a member of the board of trustees for Winston-Salem State University, the Center for the Visually Impaired and the Charlotte Housing Authority scholarship board. She is an advisor to the BellSouth Network of African American Telecom Professionals and a member of the BellSouth Women's Networking Association.

Gloria is a proud graduate of Winston-Salem State University. She completed executive education programs at Penn State University and the Harvard Business School.

Gloria and her husband, Michael, reside in Snellville where they enjoy Cajun cooking and entertaining.

Gloria R. Reese
President, Operator Services
BellSouth Telecommunications

BELLSOUTH
Listening. Answering.®

Scott Spivey
Vice President &
Chief Financial Officer
Advertising & Publishing Group
BellSouth Corporation

As vice president and chief financial officer for the BellSouth advertising and publishing group, Scott Spivey is responsible for financial and business planning, revenue assurance, and controller activities for BellSouth's print and electronic directory advertising businesses.

Spivey joined BellSouth in February of 1999 and served as assistant vice president and controller for BellSouth Telecommunications. In April of 2000, he was named assistant vice president of finance and business planning for BellSouth Corporation, and he assumed his current position in February of 2002.

Prior to joining BellSouth, Spivey served as vice president of finance and operations for the Stride Rite Shoe Corporation in Lexington, Massachusetts.

A native of Minneapolis, Minnesota, Spivey received his bachelor of arts degree in accounting from Clark Atlanta University, and his master of business administration degree from the University of St. Thomas in St. Paul, Minnesota.

In his spare time, Spivey studies acting through the Alliance Theater education program. He and his wife, Wanda, have three wonderful daughters, Jayci, Rori and Hayley.

Atlanta's
BLACK DOCTORS

Sponsored By

KAISER PERMANENTE®

Ade Aderibigbe, M.D.
Chairman of Pediatrics
Southern Regional Medical Center

Ade Aderibigbe, M.D., works in the Southern Regional Medical Center's neonatal intensive care unit. He has been a member of the Southern Regional family for eight years and is chairman of pediatrics at Southern Regional Medical Center.

Ade received a bachelor of science degree and a doctor of medicine degree in health services from the University of Ife in Nigeria. He completed his pediatric residency at the State University of New York at Stony Brook, Nassau County Medical Center. He completed his fellowship in neonatal and perinatal medicine at Duke University.

Ade has been married to Joko for 17 years, and is the proud father of two children, Mayowa, 16, and Sadé, 11.

In his spare time, Ade enjoys golfing, traveling and reading. He and his family attend Mt. Zion Redeemed Christian Church in Riverdale.

Dr. Marco Antonio Belizaire
Sports & Family Chiropractor
AGAPE Chiropractic and
Wellness Center, LLC

Dr. Marco Belizaire has been a practicing chiropractor for more than 13 years. He practices both in Atlanta and Panama, Central America, where he initially founded and established the AGAPE Chiropractic Center. His practice is focused on family practice with an emphasis on sports biomechanics to enhance peak performance and optimum well-being.

Marco is a former member of Panama's Olympic track team. His extensive and continual postgraduate training in sports chiropractic, in conjunction with being bilingual, has allowed him to work with many national Olympic teams. He is presently working with an elite group of Olympians in the City of Atlanta.

He received his bachelor of science degree from Fairleigh Dickinson University in New Jersey, and his doctorate of chiropractic degree from Life University.

A New Yorker raised in Panama City, Panama, he is married to his lovely wife, Virginia, and has two sons, Stephen and Sterling. He is very strong in his Christian faith and active in his church, Faith Christian Center. Marco enjoys salsa dancing, reading and watching sports.

Dr. Robin T. Bingham is a St. Louis, Missouri native. After serving five years as a commissioned naval dental officer, she moved to the metropolitan Atlanta area in the spring of 2002. She practiced in several Atlanta suburbs before deciding to settle in her own private practice.

Bingham is the owner of Bingham Dental Group in Conyers, Georgia. Her practice is a state-of-the-art dental office that offers general and cosmetic dentistry for the family. The facility boasts the latest dental technology including intra-oral cameras, digital X-ray technology and the latest in teeth whitening techniques. Her ongoing commitment to continued education allows her to remain on top of cutting-edge procedures and techniques. She strives to provide quality healthcare to all of her patients.

Bingham attended Tennessee State University and is a Meharry Medical College graduate. Her professional affiliations include the American Dental Association, the Georgia Dental Association, the Georgia Dental Society, the American Association of Women Dentists and the American Academy of Cosmetic Dentistry. She is a life member of the Meharry Medical College Alumni Association.

Dr. Robin T. Bingham
General Dentist
Bingham Dental Group, LLC

William Boddie, M.D. is associate medical director for professional development and human resources for the The Southeast Permanente Medical Group, Inc., which exclusively treats Kaiser Permanente patients in Georgia. In addition to his administrative responsibilities, Boddie continues to practice gastroenterology.

Boddie is a member and fellow of the American College of Physician Executives. He also belongs to the American Gastroenterological Association. Previously, he worked at Stanislaus Medical Center in Modesto, California, where he served as medical director of the center and chief executive officer of the faculty practice.

Boddie is actively involved in the community. He has served on the board of directors for the United Way of Metropolitan Atlanta, Project Open Hand, the Modesto Community Hospice and the Modesto Visiting Nurse Association.

Boddie earned a bachelor's degree from Howard University and his medical degree from the University of Maryland School of Medicine. He interned at Maryland General Hospital and completed his residency in internal medicine at the University of Maryland Hospital.

William Leon Boddie, M.D.
Associate Medical Director
The Southeast Permanente
Medical Group, Inc.

Sandra Ford Bouchelion, M.D.
District Health Director
DeKalb County Board of Health

Dr. Sandra Ford Bouchelion has been the district health director for the DeKalb County Board of Health since February of 2005. Bouchelion, a board-certified pediatrician, is the first African-American health director in DeKalb County's history. She oversees clinical and population-based services for an area with 685,000 residents, focusing on emergency preparedness, health disparities, infant mortality, asthma and obesity.

During her short tenure, Bouchelion orchestrated the reorganization of the agency in order to deliver quality services, despite the current healthcare financing crisis. She has partnered with the DeKalb board of county commissioners, local community agencies and legislators to educate the public and promote healthcare advocacy.

Bouchelion received an American Academy of Pediatrics Scholarship, a Commonwealth Fund Fellowship, the Robinson/Dickens Award and a National Medical Fellowship.

She holds a bachelor's degree from Stanford University, a medical degree from Howard University College of Medicine and a master's degree in business administration from Howard University Graduate School of Business.

Bouchelion's experiences as a primary care provider and her extensive business training give her a unique insight into the challenges facing the healthcare system today.

Otis W. Brawley, M.D.
Medical Director
Georgia Cancer Center of Excellence
Grady Memorial Hospital

Otis W. Brawley, M.D. is chief medical director of the Georgia Cancer Coalition Center of Excellence at Grady Memorial Hospital. He is a professor of hematology, oncology and medicine at the Emory University School of Medicine, and professor of epidemiology at the Emory Rollins School of Public Health. He also serves as deputy director of the Winship Cancer Institute at Emory University.

From 1995 to April of 2001, Brawley served as assistant director of the Office of Special Populations Research at the National Cancer Institute. Previously, he was a senior in the Division of Cancer Prevention and Control at the National Cancer Institute.

Brawley graduated from the University of Chicago and was an internal medicine resident at University Hospitals of Cleveland at Case Western Reserve University. IIe trained in medical oncology at the National Cancer Institute. Recently, he was named a Georgia Cancer Coalition Eminent Scholar.

Dr. Howard M. Bryant presently serves on the podiatric surgical staffs of Northlake Regional Medical Center and Decatur Hospital. Additionally, he is the director of the Absolute Foot & Ankle Center, serving the community since 1985.

In 1981 Bryant graduated with a bachelor's degree in chemistry from Lincoln University in Pennsylvania. He received his doctor of podiatric medicine degree from Ohio College of Podiatric Medicine, and performed his postgraduate residency at the Veterans Administration Medical Center in Tuskegee, Alabama and The Ohio College of Podiatric Medicine in Cleveland, Ohio.

Board certified by the American Board of Podiatric Surgery, Bryant is a fellow of the American College of Foot & Ankle Surgeons and the American College of Foot & Ankle Orthopedics & Medicine. He served on the surgical staff and the credentials committee of the former Atlanta Hospital and the Podiatry Hospital of Pittsburgh teaching and research facilities.

Bryant has written numerous public educational articles and is a member of the National Podiatric Medical Association. He is also the former HMO committee chairman of the Georgia State Insurance Task Force.

Dr. Howard M. Bryant
Podiatric Surgical Staff
Northlake Regional Medical Center
Decatur Hospital

A native of Atlanta, Georgia, Dr. Winston Kyle Carhee Jr. is the founder and owner of Pain 2 Wellness Center. He received a bachelor of science degree from Morehouse College and a doctor of chiropractic degree from Life University. During his education, Winston conducted research and studies at Yale University, Emory University and Morehouse School of Medicine.

Winston enjoys taking time to empower the community about the importance of staying healthy and living a life free from nerve system interference (subluxation). He regularly volunteers at community events and health fairs sponsored by community, church and fraternal organizations.

An active participant of several business and civic organizations, Winston currently serves as vice president of Georgia Chiropractic Association, District 1; board member of Cascade Business and Merchants Association and Fulton County Work Force Development, and ambassador of the South Fulton Chamber of Commerce.

Winston is married to Dr. Chantaye Evans-Carhee, who is also a chiropractor. When he is not engaged in professional or civic duties he enjoys spending quality time with his wife, listening to music, and practicing his golf swing.

Dr. Winston Kyle Carhee Jr.
Owner & Chiropractor
Pain 2 Wellness Center

Darrell J. Carmen, M.D., FACS
Partner
Georgia Urology, PA

Darrell J. Carmen, M.D., FACS, is a partner with Georgia Urology, one the nation's largest private practice groups, and provides comprehensive urological care in metropolitan Atlanta. He has a very active adult urology practice with expertise in erectile dysfunction, stone disease and urinary incontinence. Actively involved with clinical research, Carmen serves as a principal investigator of several research projects with Georgia Urology Research Institute.

Carmen is also a consultant to several pharmaceutical and device manufacturers, and has been able to offer his patients access to new drugs and treatments unavailable elsewhere. He remains active in the community by educating the public through hospital and local seminars as well as several media programs.

He holds memberships in the American Urological Association, the American College of Surgeons, the American Association of Clinical Urologists, the National Medical Association, the Atlanta Medical Association, and Alpha Phi Alpha Fraternity, Inc.

Carmen earned a bachelor of science degree from Southern University and a medical degree from Louisiana State University. He received internship training at Loyola University and urology training at Northeastern Ohio University.

Juanita Cone, M.D.
Chief, Population Care
Prevention & Health Promotion
Kaiser Permanente

Internist Juanita Cone, M.D., is dedicated to promoting good health through public education. As chief of population care, prevention and health promotion for Kaiser Permanente, she helps support health activities that enhance the quality of life for members. In addition to seeing patients, she provides clinical expertise for special events, including Diabetes Alert Day and the Great American Smokeout.

Cone received her bachelor of science and medical degrees from Howard University in Washington, D.C. After completing an internship and residency at Bridgeport Hospital in Bridgeport, Connecticut, she became a solo practitioner in Jacksonville, Florida. Since moving to Atlanta, she completed a residency in preventive medicine and earned a master of public health degree from the Morehouse School of Medicine. She is currently completing a master of divinity degree from the Interdenominational Theological Center in Atlanta.

Cone currently serves as co-chairperson for Services to Youth for the Azalea City chapter of The Links, Inc., and is actively involved in St. Phillips African Methodist Episcopal Church as an ordained elder. She has been married for 24 years to Cecil Wayne Cone, Ph.D.

LIFE IS BETTER WHEN YOU'RE
WELL CONNECTED.

Wouldn't it be nice if you could send your doctor's office a secure e-mail* with questions or concerns any time you wanted? With Kaiser Permanente, you can. No phone tag. And no waiting for an appointment. You can even access parts of your health record online — including certain lab results and past office visit summaries.* The convenience of online access to your health record and email access to your personal doctor with Kaiser Permanente. Just one more way we make it easier to live well, be well, and thrive.

To find out more, log on to *experiencekp.org*.

*Available to members receiving care at Kaiser Permanente Medical Centers.

**Opening February 2007 in Austell -
New Kaiser Permanente West Cobb Medical Center**

KAISER PERMANENTE® **thrive**

influence
You have the power to beat the flu.®

Over the past

Unfortunately, some people think you can get influenza (flu) from the injectable vaccine. **NOT SO.**

Injectable influenza vaccine is made from killed virus, so you cannot get the flu from the vaccine. Some people may experience a sore arm or a fever that usually goes away within 24 hours, but these side effects are not symptoms of the flu. You can easily catch influenza from an infected person—so vaccination is your best defense against the flu.

While most people get immunized in October or November, vaccination is beneficial throughout influenza season because most people get infected from December through March.

years,
hundreds
of millions
of influenza (flu) shots
have been administered

Immunization offers **SAFE** and **SIMPLE** protection against influenza. So join the crowd and get IMMUNIZED.

William Kevin Dancy practices general, restorative cosmetic dentistry in southwest Atlanta. He believes that aesthetic dentistry gives him the opportunity to provide patients with the beautiful smiles they have always desired. He enjoys seeing patients of all ages, and building professional, confident and long-lasting relationships with them and their families.

In August of 2006, Dancy was awarded a fellowship into the Academy of General Dentistry. He has been featured in several publications and honored by many organizations as one of Atlanta's leading dentists.

Dancy received his bachelor of science degree from Morehouse College, his doctor of dental surgery degree from Meharry Medical College, and his master's degree in restorative dentistry from the University of Michigan.

Dancy is a member of Friendship Baptist Church. His affiliations include Omega Psi Phi Fraternity, Inc., 100 Black Men of South Metro, the National Dental Association and the American Dental Association.

A native of Atlanta, Dancy is blessed to be able to serve the community in his hometown. He is married to Dr. Measha Pcterson Dancy, an internist, and they have one daughter, Ryli McKinna.

William Kevin Dancy, D.D.S.
Family & Cosmetic Dentist

Dr. Camille Davis-Williams is a trailblazer in women's health as founder and managing provider of care for Greater Atlanta Women's HealthCare. Her staff is committed to the reproductive and gynecologic health of females in the greater Atlanta area. Davis-Williams developed an interest in women's health because a community's reproductive health has a direct impact on its future generations.

Davis-Williams completed her internship and residency training in obstetrics and gynecology at Emory University, and started her career at Oakhurst Health Center. Appointed by Emory University, she now serves as chief of obstetrical services at Crawford Long Hospital, where she previously served as president of the medical staff.

Davis-Williams holds several national and local medical society memberships. She has served on advisory boards for the Medical Association of Atlanta and the Georgia State OB/GYN Society. She has received numerous honors, awards, and citations.

Davis-Williams earned her bachelor's degree at Emory University, and her medical doctorate from the Emory University School of Medicine.

She is married to Dr. Melvin Williams and has two children, Vincent and Melanie.

Dr. Camille Davis-Williams
Founder
Greater Atlanta Women's Healthcare

Dr. Brian S. Deas
Dentist & Chief Executive Officer
Creekside Dental, Inc.

Creekside Dental is proud to have as its chief executive officer Dr. Brian S. Deas, a native of West Georgia. After graduating from Bowdon High, Deas attended the University of Georgia, where he majored in biology. He obtained a doctorate of dental surgery from the University of Tennessee.

A graduate of the prestigious Las Vegas Institute for Advanced Dental Studies, Deas is a member of the American Dental Association, American Academy of Cosmetic Dentistry, Georgia Dental Association and the North Georgia Dental Society. He is also a member of the Douglasville Chamber of Commerce.

Deas is a talented and trusted dentist known for his comforting chairside manner and upbeat, infectious attitude. He works hard to put patients at ease and answer any questions because he knows that the more informed patients are about their procedures, the less anxious they will be.

Creekside Dental is a warm, friendly office nestled in Douglasville where patients come first. When people visit the office, they see the difference that outstanding customer service, a commitment to patient education and top-notch clinical skills make.

Paul L. Douglass, M.D., F.A.C.C.
Cardiologist
Metropolitan Atlanta
Cardiology Consultants, P.C.

Paul L. Douglass, M.D., is a native of Nashville, Tennessee. He joined Metropolitan Atlanta Cardiology Consultants in 1982 and practices clinical and interventional cardiology. He is chief of the division of cardiology, director of cardiovascular services and chairman of the hospital board at Atlanta Medical Center. Douglass received his undergraduate degree in biology from Northwestern University and his doctor of medicine degree from Meharry Medical College. He completed his postgraduate training in medicine and cardiovascular diseases at Emory University School of Medicine.

Douglass is the recipient of numerous professional awards from the Atlanta Medical Association, the Georgia State Medical Association and the Association of Black Cardiologists. He has served as president of the Atlanta Medical Association, the Georgia State Medical Association and the Association of Black Cardiologists. Currently, he sits on the board of trustees of the American College of Cardiology.

Dr. Douglass has three children, Toi, Paul III, and Travis. He is married to Sheila Robinson, M.D., F.A.C.C., also a cardiologist and partner in Metropolitan Atlanta Cardiology Consulatants.

Tonya Echols, M.D.
Radiation Oncologist
GA Radiation

A specialist in cancer radiation therapy, Tonya Echols, M.D. is founder of Greater Atlanta Radiation Oncology Consultants, LLC (GA Radiation). GA Radiation is the only radiation oncology practice in Atlanta that is owned by an African-American female.

Echols was recognized as an Alpha Kappa Alpha, Educational Advancement Scholar and received the Roentgen Resident Research Award. She was also honored as a valedictorian of the Nx Level Entrepreneur training program at New Birth Missionary Baptist Church.

A member of Alpha Kappa Alpha Sorority, Inc., Echols she serves on the board of Youth Vibe, Inc. and minority recruitment for the American Red Cross. Her professional memberships include the American Society for Therapeutic Radiology and Oncology and the Atlanta Medical Association.

Echols received her bachelor of arts degree from The Johns Hopkins University in Baltimore, Maryland, and her doctor of medicine degree from the University of Cincinnati College of Medicine. She trained in radiation oncology at the University of Cincinnati's Barrett Cancer Center.

Ericka M. Edmonds, D.D.S.
Owner & Dentist
Camp Creek Smiles

A native of Augusta, Georgia, Dr. Ericka Edmonds attended a health science and engineering magnet school where her interest in dentistry was initially sparked. Upon graduation, she attended Mercer University and earned a bachelor of science degree in biology. During her undergraduate years, she worked as a dental assistant to gain experience in the field.

Edmonds moved to Nashville, Tennessee to earn a doctor of dental surgery degree from the historic Meharry Medical College School of Dentistry in 2002. She completed her postgraduate general dental residency training at the University of Alabama in Birmingham.

Edmonds worked with a large group dental practice in the metro Atlanta area for two-and-a-half years before opening Camp Creek Smiles. The goal of Camp Creek Smiles is to provide comprehensive cosmetic and general dental services with a personal, faith-based touch in a luxurious environment.

Kevin Edmonds, M.D.
Medical Director
Camp Creek Women's Health
Specialist, LLC

A native of Birmingham, Alabama, Kevin Edmonds graduated salutatorian from A.H. Parker High School in 1993. He earned his bachelor's degree in biology from Morehouse College in 1997 and his medical degree from Meharry Medical College in 2001. He continued his postgraduate medical training at Grady Memorial Hospital in the Morehouse ob-gyn residency program, during which time he developed his interest in female sexual dysfunction and satisfaction.

After completing residency training in 2001, Edmonds spent the past year studying and training in laser cosmetics, aesthetics and skincare. He recently established the Camp Creek Laser Vaginal Rejuvenation Institute after completing cosmetic surgery training in Los Angeles with Dr. David Matlock, one of the world's foremost authorities and pioneers in the field.

Edmonds is the proud husband of Dr. Ericka Edmonds, owner of Camp Creek Smiles. He is the father of a 5-year-old son. Camp Creek Women's Health Specialist embodies Edmonds' passion to care for women completely in a faith-based environment.

Charles Fowler Jr., M.D.
Managing Physician
Kaiser Permanente
Cascade Medical Center

D r. Charles Fowler Jr. is the managing physician for the Kaiser Permanente Cascade Medical Center. His professional interests include hypertension control, diabetes and health education for the African-American community.

Prior to joining The Southeast Permanente Medical Group, Inc., which exclusively treats Kaiser Permanente patients in Georgia, Fowler served in the U.S. Air Force. He was stationed at Langley Air Force Base where he served as chairman for the department of internal medicine. From 1994 to 1996, Fowler was stationed at the Air Force Regional Hospital in Riverside, California. He served as chairman for the department of internal medicine and deputy director of hospital services.

Fowler earned his undergraduate degree at Huntington College of Health Sciences in Knoxville, Tennessee. He received his medical degree from the Uniformed Services University F. Edward Hébert School of Medicine in Bethesda, Maryland. He is board-certified in internal medicine.

When he is not seeing patients, Fowler enjoys photography, home improvement, vacationing, physical fitness, church and spending time with family. He has one daughter who resides in Lexington Park, Maryland.

Clayton Gibson III is co-founder and chief executive officer of Vitality Health Care, Inc., a rehabilitation and human performance center. Gibson believes that through advanced health care and innovative rehabilitation everyone can maximize their genetic potential. He developed a comprehensive system to prevent injury and improve neuromuscular efficiency, allowing individuals to reach optimal performance. He is the personal sports physician and performance consultant to numerous professional and Olympic athletes.

Gibson received a bachelor's degree from Furman University, a master's degree from Central Michigan and a doctoral degree from Life University. He became the first certified myoneural medicine physician in the U.S. by the Trigenics Institute and Canadian Board of Natural Medicine. He is certified by the National Academy of Sports Medicine, National Strength & Conditioning Association and as a Golf Bio-mechanist (CHEK Institute).

He is team doctor and performance consultant for Westlake High School. As service to the community, he provides off-site rehabilitation and technique sessions to student-athletes in six schools.

Gibson resides in Powder Springs, Georgia. Married with one child, he is an active member of Cascade United Methodist.

Clayton Gibson III
Co-Founder & Chief Executive Officer
Vitality Health Care, Inc.

Valda Gibson is a physician in internal medicine at Northside Hospital in Atlanta. She has served as a hospitalist with the internal medicine service at Northside for 11 years. She delivers care to patients as an attending and consulting physician, and has served on multiple committees within the hospital.

Valda is involved in the Atlanta Medical Society, the Alliance of Women Physicians and the Rebecca Lee Medical Society. She participates in many organizations including the Metro Atlanta Chapter of 100 Black Women, Alpha Kappa Alpha Sorority, Inc., and the Atlanta Chapter of Jack and Jill of America. She is an active member of Zion Hill Baptist Church in Atlanta.

In 1981 Valda graduated cum laude from Howard University with a bachelor of science degree in zoology. She received her doctor of medicine degree from the University of North Carolina at Chapel Hill in 1985. She completed her internship and residency at the Emory/Grady residency program.

Valda is the proud mother of Bethany Gibson. A native of Fayetteville, North Carolina, she has lived in Atlanta since 1995.

Valda O. Gibson, M.D.
Hospitalist & Physician
Northside Hospital

Sandea Greene-Harris, M.D.
Neurosurgeon
Metro Atlanta Neurosurgery, PC

Dr. Sandea Greene-Harris is originally from Huntsville, Alabama. She joined Metro Atlanta Neurosurgery on September 1, 2003.

Greene-Harris received her undergraduate degree from Tulane University. She earned her medical degree from Tulane University Medical School, and completed an internship in neurology, critical care and surgery, and a neurosurgical residency program at Tulane University Hospital. During her residency, she completed a spine fellowship at the Barrow Neurological Institute in Phoenix, Arizona.

Greene-Harris is the recipient of numerous awards recognizing her humanism and excellence in teaching and patient care. She has co-authored articles that were published in the *Neurosurgery Journal* and has presented at national meetings.

Greene-Harris is a member of numerous professional organizations including the Atlanta Medical Association, the Georgia Neurosurgical Association, the American Medical Association, the Congress of Neurosurgeons and the American Association of Neurological Surgeons. She is a member of Delta Sigma Theta Sorority, Inc.

She and her husband, Willie, are the proud parents of William. They attend Our Lady of Lords Catholic Church and Antioch North in Atlanta.

Leon L. Haley Jr., M.D.
Deputy Senior Vice President
Medical Affairs &
Chief of Emergency Medicine
Grady Health System

Leon L. Haley Jr. is deputy senior vice president of medical affairs and chief of emergency medicine for the Grady Health System. Additionally, he is vice chairman for Grady clinical affairs and associate professor of emergency medicine at Emory University.

A Pittsburgh native, Haley holds degrees from Brown University and the Universities of Pittsburgh and Michigan. Board certified in emergency medicine, he is a fellow and member of the American College of Emergency Physicians. He is also a member of the American Colleges of Healthcare Executives and Physician Executives.

Named one of *Georgia Trend's* 40 Under 40, Haley has received several honors and awards. These include *Atlanta Business Chronicle's* Healthcare Heroes and Up and Comers Awards and Georgia Association of Physician Assistants' Physician of the Year Award.

Haley volunteers with Leadership Georgia, Leadership Atlanta, the Society for Academic Emergency Medicine, Atlanta Children's Shelter, and The Junior League of Atlanta community advisory board.

A member of Omega Psi Phi and Sigma Pi Phi Fraternities, Haley is married to Dr. Carla Y. Neal-Haley and they have three children, Grant, Wesley and Nichelle.

No prescription coverage? Need Pfizer medicines?

One call fits all™

If you don't have prescription coverage, it can be hard to get the medicines you need. We understand that. That's why we're here to help.

At Pfizer Helpful Answers, we have many programs to help you save on Pfizer medicines, no matter your age or income. You may even get them for free, depending on your income.

Contact Pfizer Helpful Answers to get help today.

Some restrictions apply.

Call 1-866-706-2400
or visit **www.PfizerHelpfulAnswers.com**
for help getting your Pfizer medicines.

If you take medicines that are not made by Pfizer, you may still get help paying for your medicines. Contact the Partnership for Prescription Assistance (PPA) at **1-888-4PPA-NOW (1-888-477-2669)** or visit **www.PPARx.org**. Pfizer participates in the PPA.

Partnership for Prescription Assistance

Look beneath

all the layers of advanced technology, rigorous medical training, high-tech protective wear and real-world experience and what will you find?

A doctor who really cares about helping you feel better.

Simple things like a smile don't come in a medical textbook. Or from the latest equipment. But, at Southern Regional, we know they're just as important to healing. That's why the doctors, nurses and staff of Southern Regional are determined to provide our patients with the best balance of technology and personal attention. To assure our patients of true state-of-the-art treatment, we've added advances like our new all-digital cardiovascular imaging system and positron emission tomography system (PET) that tracks cancer cells. More importantly, all 2,500 of our employees have signed a personal commitment to outstanding customer service.

At Southern Regional, we're striving to make every person who comes to us feel they've come to the right place. Because, with all our advanced technology and treatments, it's the human connection that people respond to – and remember.

Southern Regional
HEALTH SYSTEM
Committed to You.

---

11 Upper Riverdale Road, S.W., Riverdale, Georgia 30274 • 770-991-8000 • www.southernregional.org
For a free physician referral call HealthCall at 770-541-1111.

A native of Atlanta, Karen Harris-Moore, M.D., earned her medical degree from Howard University College of Medicine and completed her internship and residency at Howard University Hospital in Washington, D.C.

Harris-Moore was an assistant professor at the Morehouse College of Medicine and medical director with the W.T. Brooks Medical Center. She is board-certified in family practice, and is a diplomat of the American Board of Family Practice. In addition, she is board eligible in geriatric medicine.

Harris-Moore was recognized as one of America's Top Family Doctors in 2002-2003 by the Consumers' Research Council of America. Criteria for this award includes experience, training, professional associations and quality care to patients. She joined Piedmont Physicians at Peachtree City in 1995.

Karen Harris-Moore, M.D.
Family Practitioner
Piedmont Physicians at Peachtree City

J effrey Freeman Hines, M.D., is a native of New York. He received his bachelor of science degree in biology from Brown University, magna cum laude, in May of 1983. He received his medical degree from Brown University School of Medicine in May of 1986.

Hines completed a four-year residency program in obstetrics and gynecology at Fitzsimons Army Medical Center in Aurora, Colorado. He completed a three-year fellowship in gynecologic oncology at Georgetown University Medical Center in Washington, D.C., and then served as attending staff gynecologic oncologist at Brooke Army Medical Center from 1995 to 2000.

Hines joined Southeastern Gynecologic Oncology in Atlanta as an attending gynecologic oncologist. He primarily sees patients in southern Atlanta at Southern Regional Medical Center, and in western Atlanta at Cobb Hospital.

In addition, Hines is a clinical instructor of obstetrics and gynecology at the Morehouse School of Medicine. He is a diplomat of the American Board of Obstetrics and Gynecology, with special competence in gynecologic oncology. He was named one of Atlanta's Top Doctors in the July 2005 edition of *Atlanta* magazine.

Jeffrey Freeman Hines, M.D.
Gynecologic Oncologist
Southeastern Gynecologic Oncology

Paul King, M.D.
Neurosurgeon
President & Chief Executive Officer
Metro Atlanta Neurosurgery, PC

Dr. Paul King founded Metro Atlanta Neurosurgery in 1999. He is a board-certified neurosurgeon, specializing in complex spinal surgery, cerebrovascular disease and neurotrauma. Before coming to Atlanta, King was in academic practice in Detroit, Michigan, where he was the chief of neurosurgery and the co-director of a spinal cord injury unit.

In 2001 King founded Metro Atlanta Neurosurgery Foundation to advance health care resources for people in third world communities. To date, he has organized three medical missions to Ghana, Africa, and is helping to furnish, equip and train personnel for the health center under construction in Prampram, Ghana.

King graduated from Fisk University, received his doctor of medicine degree from Michigan State University, and completed a spine fellowship at Emory University's department of neurosurgery.

King is a member of numerous organizations including the Atlanta Medical Association, the American Association of Neurosurgeons, the Georgia State Medical Association, the National Medical Association and the American Medical Association.

He and his wife of 33 years, Monica, are the proud parents of three sons, Paul II, Kimani and Aaron.

Dr. Christopher Leggett
Cardiologist
St. Joseph's Hospital

Dr. Christopher Leggett is a clinical academic interventional cardiologist at St. Joseph's Hospital of Atlanta. He attended the preparatory school of Phillips Academy in Andover, Massachusetts. After graduating from Princeton University, he went on to receive his medical degree from Case Western Reserve University in Cleveland, Ohio and completed both his internship and residency at the world-renowned Johns Hopkins Hospital in Baltimore, Maryland. His cardiology fellowship training was performed at the Emory University School of Medicine in Atlanta.

A member of the Center for Disease Control board of visitors and the national board of directors of the American Heart Association, Leggett is the recipient of numerous citations and awards for clinical excellence. He was recently recognized as one of America's Leading Physicians by *Black Enterprise*.

Leggett has been privileged to enjoy more than 20 years of marriage to his wonderful wife Denise Cleveland-Leggett, a successful attorney. They are the proud parents of Alexandria Nichol and Christopher James II. He is a member of Berean Seventh Day Adventist Church and enjoys basketball, golf, traveling and exercising.

Dr. Kaneta R. Lott
Pediatric Dentist & Owner
Lake Oconee Smile Center

Dr. Kaneta R. Lott has helped to shape the smiles of children for more than 20 years. A renowned national speaker and motivator, Lott is one of the most respected pediatric dentists in the United States. Lott is the owner of Lake Oconee Smile Center, and she has appeared as an expert on CNN and its affiliates.

The owner of metropolitan Atlanta's most successful pediatric dental practices, Lott provides strategic advice to her patients and to organizations concerned about quality healthcare. A board-certified pediatric dentist, she earned her doctor of dental surgery degree from Emory University, and completed her residency at Emory University and Scottish Rite Hospitals. She is a consultant to the Georgia Board of Dentistry and served as an assistant clinical professor in the department of pediatric dentistry at the Medical College of Georgia.

Lott is a founding member of the board of directors of Capitol City Bank & Trust Company, the Atlanta Technical College Foundation board, and numerous civic and social organizations in Atlanta. She is married to Attorney Thomas F. Cuffie.

Dr. Reggie Mason
Chief of Medical Subspecialties
The Southeast Permanente
Medical Group

From his stethoscope to running sneakers, Reggie Mason, M.D., is devoted to medicine, family and community. As chief of medical subspecialties for The Southeast Permanente Medical Group, Inc., which exclusively treats Kaiser Permanente patients in Georgia, Reggie is an expert in pulmonary and critical care medicine.

Reggie attended Stanford University and earned a bachelor's degree in biology. He attended the University of California, San Francisco School of Medicine and performed his internal medicine internship and residency at George Washington University Hospital in Washington, D.C. He completed a pulmonary fellowship at the University of California—San Francisco.

When he is not seeing patients, Reggie is an avid runner. In 2000 he earned the country's No. 3 ranking in the 400-meter dash in his age group. He trains at the Atlanta site used during the 1996 Olympics and participates in about ten races a year.

Reggie and his wife, Karen Goodlett, M.D., also a doctor with The Southeast Permanente Medical Group, Inc., have a 19-year-old son and a 15-year-old daughter, who is also a budding track star.

Dr. Calvin Wayne McLarin
Co-Founder
Metropolitan Atlanta
Cardiology Consultants, P.C.

D r. Calvin Wayne McLarin is co-founder of Metropolitan Atlanta Cardiology Consultants, P.C., in downtown Atlanta. He is board certified in internal medicine and cardiology.

McLarin has received many awards in medicine. Most recently, the Atlanta Medical Association gave him the Nash-Carter Award. The Heritage Fund of the Atlanta Medical Association named their highest award the Calvin Wayne McLarin Award, naming him the inaugural recipient. He received the O.T. Hammonds Award from the Hammonds House Galleries in 2003 and the Distinguished Perseverance Award from the Eta Omega chapter of Omega Psi Phi Fraternity, Inc. in 2002.

He is a member of the Sigma Pi Phi Fraternity, Inc., Omega Psi Phi Fraternity, Inc. and the Guardsmen. Additionally, he is past chairman of the board for the Association of Black Cardiologists.

In 1968 McLarin received his bachelor of science degree from Morehouse College. He earned his doctor of medicine degree from Emory University's School of Medicine in 1972.

A native of Atlanta, McLarin is married to Deborah Sarita Cathcart and has four children and one grandchild, Rayne Haile.

Adrienne Mims, M.D.
Medical Doctor
The Southeast Permanente
Medical Group, Inc.

A drienne Mims, M.D., MPH, is highly regarded in the metro Atlanta community for her medical expertise and community advocacy. She practices with The Southeast Permanente Medical Group, Inc., which exclusively treats Kaiser Permanente patients. Mims served as the chief of health promotion and disease prevention and has now returned to full-time clinical practice.

A former spokesperson for the Georgia Quit Line, Mims currently serves as the national clinical lead for Kaiser Permanente's Garfield Weight Management Initiative. She oversees grants to evaluate reducing obesity in adults and children. She is featured in a national video produced by Kaiser Permanente, the American Academy of Family Physicians and the Institute of Church Administration and Management that encourages African Americans to maintain healthy lifestyles.

Mims serves as vice chair of the public education committee of the American Geriatric Society and is a member of the American Academy of Family Physicians and the National Medical Association. She earned her bachelor's degree from George Washington University, her doctor of medicine degree from Stanford University, and her master's degree in public health from UCLA.

Kelly DeGraffenreid Organ, M.D.
Lead Physician & Family Practitioner
Kaiser Permanente of Georgia
Southwood Medical Office

D r. Kelly DeGraffenreid Organ wears many hats. In addition to her role as lead physician and family practitioner for Kaiser Permanente of Georgia's Southwood Medical Office, she is also chief of coding and data quality.

In 2003 Organ joined The Southeast Permanente Medical Group, Inc. (TSPMG), which provides exclusive care for Kaiser Permanente patients in Georgia. She quickly became a respected physician and leader. In 2005 she was named Team Player of the Year for TSPMG. She was also honored as the Glaxo-Wellcome Resident Scholar for leadership at Emory University.

Organ completed her undergraduate degree in pharmacy at Purdue University, earned her doctor of medicine degree at Case Western Reserve University, and completed her family practice residency at Emory University. She is licensed with the American Board of Family Practitioners and is certified as an American Cancer Society breast test educator.

She lives in Atlanta with her husband, David Organ, M.D., and two children, Nicholas and Sherry. When she is not seeing patients, she enjoys listening to music, playing the piano, singing, playing tennis and dancing.

Dr. Nelson M. Oyesiku
Neurosurgery Residency
Program Director
Emory University School of Medicine

D r. Nelson Oyesiku is professor of neurosurgery and director of the neurosurgery residency training program at Emory University. Particularly renowned for the surgical treatment and molecular biology of pituitary tumors, he has received research awards from the National Institute of Health and the Robert Wood Johnson Foundation. He has authored several manuscripts, book chapters and a book. He has also served on various institutional, state and regional committees, such as president of the Georgia Neurological Society.

Nelson is past president of the Congress of Neurological Surgeons, on the editorial board of *Neurosurgery* and a reviewer for several journals.

His peers have selected him as one of The Best Doctors in America and the Consumer Research Council of America named him one of America's Top Surgeons. He is a fellow of the American College of Surgeons, and named in *Marquis Who's Who in America*.

Nelson obtained his neurosurgical training and a doctorate of medicine degree in neuroscience at Emory University.

He is married to Lola and they have three children, Angela, Linda and Nelson III.

Karyl C. Patten, D.D.S.
Vice President
Perimeter Medical Associates

Karyl C. Patten, D.D.S. serves as the director of dental services for the Whitefoord Elementary School and Coan Middle School school-based clinics. This clinic is a part of the Whitefoord Community nonprofit program in east Atlanta.

Karyl's work as a general dentist in the east Atlanta community addresses oral health disparities. She has established herself in the public health community by providing services to the Fulton County Jail and maintaining community outreach as a volunteer dentist for the Good Samaritan Health Clinic. Karyl continues to lecture for the National Association of School-Based Clinics and is a passionate advocate for equal access to oral health care for the underserved.

Karyl received her bachelor of arts degree from Fisk University, her doctorate degree from Meharry Medical College, and is completing the master of public health program at Emory University's prestigious Rollins School of Public Health. A native of Jefferson City, Missouri, she is the wife of Steven A. Patten, M.D., and proud mother of Katherine, Celeste, Thomas and Steven.

Steven A. Patten, M.D.
President & Chief Executive Officer
Perimeter Medical Associates, PC

A native of Atlanta, Dr. Steven Patten attended Northside High School. He received his undergraduate degree in biomedical engineering in 1980 from Vanderbilt University. He earned his medical degree from the Emory University School of Medicine in 1984. Patten completed his internship at Georgetown University/D.C. General Hospital. He served as chief resident at the Alvin C. York VA Medical Center in Tennessee. He received his board certification in internal medicine in 1989 and in geriatrics in 1998.

Patten holds an honorary doctorate of science. He belongs to the Alpha Omega Alpha Honor Medical Society.

Patten belongs to numerous professional and community organizations including the Poetry Society of America, Alpha Omega Alpha National Honor Medical Society, the American College of Physicians, the National Medical Association, the American Medical Association and 100 Black Men of Atlanta.

He is married to Karyl C. Patten, D.D.S., and has four children, Katherine, Celeste, Thomas and Steven.

Dr. Marcus Polk
Anesthesiologist
Southern Regional Medical Center

Dr. Marcus Polk is a board certified anesthesiologist currently practicing anesthesia at Southern Regional Medical Center. He is also a full partner with Riverdale Anesthesia Associates and has been with the group since 1999.

Polk received his undergraduate degree while on a golf scholarship from Jackson State University. He received his medical degree from Oregon Health and Science University, then completed his residency training at Emory University. Following residency he completed a one-year fellowship in pediatric anesthesiology at Egleston Children's Hospital.

Aside from medicine, Polk is an entrepreneur. A Subway franchisee, he owns and operates three Subway restaurants, with another currently in development.

In his spare time, Polk enjoys being with family and playing lots of golf. He is the husband of Debra Polk, and the father of three children.

Willie Rainey, M.D.
Chief of Internal Medicine
The Southeast Permanente
Medical Group

Diabetes expert Willie Rainey, M.D. is chief of internal medicine for The Southeast Permanente Medical Group, Inc., which exclusively treats Kaiser Permanente patients in Georgia. He combines a deep understanding of diabetes, hypertension and preventive medicine to take excellent care of his patients.

Rainey is board-certified in internal medicine and holds memberships with the American Diabetes Association and the American College of Physician Executives. He serves on the board of directors of the Diabetes Association of Atlanta. He is also an active supporter of the annual Diabetes University in metro Atlanta, an educational community forum for people living with diabetes.

A native of Macon, Georgia, Rainey completed his undergraduate degree at Tuskegee University and attended medical school at the Medical College of Georgia. He completed his residency at Emory University, where he also earned an internal medicine certification. Rainey also holds a certificate in executive management from the University of North Carolina Kenan-Flagler Business School.

D r. Stephen Tates has served Atlanta, the nation and the international community for more than 30 years by providing natural approaches to good health. A world-renowned herbalist and nutritionist, Tates is director of the Carter-Tates Wellness Center of Atlanta and chief financial officer of Carter-Tates Enterprises, Inc. He is also the creator of the all-natural product line, Dr. Tates Herbal Tinctures & Tonics. These all-natural tonics are found in health food stores, wellness centers, fitness centers and doctors' offices nationwide.

Tates is host of *Dr. Tates: Adventures In Good Health*, a weekly television series about holistic healthcare. His goal is to help educate others on natural approaches to good health. His lectures and speaking engagements have taken him around the world.

Tates has trained with other world-renowned herbalists. He was personally honored by the American Integrative Medical Association and was awarded the status of diplomat in integrative medicine.

Tates' greatest gift is his partnership with his business partner and wife, Velva Carter.

Dr. Stephen Tates
Director
Carter-Tates Wellness Center

T homas K. Taylor III, M.D., is a respected gynecologist and one of the original founders of Northwest Women's Care in Marietta, Georgia. As such, he helps provide quality perinatal health care to women of all races by shedding light on important health issues. Patients, doctors and midwives make up the multicultural diversity at Northwest Women's Care. Because of Taylor's commitments and contributions to the medical field, the mortality rate of high-risk pregnancies has decreased significantly.

A native of Durham, North Carolina, Taylor attended Morehouse College in Atlanta, where he received his bachelor's degree in biology. He then attended North Carolina A&T University, where he earned a master's degree in biology. Taylor received a medical degree from East Carolina University and then trained in Baltimore, Maryland. He later received his master of business administration degree from the Michael Coles School of Business in Kennesaw, Georgia.

Taylor is a member of the Atlanta Medical Association, the Georgia Medical Association and the National Medical Association.

Taylor plans to pen a book on his experiences as a doctor and his extensive travels.

Thomas K. Taylor III, M.D.
Obstetrician/Gynecologist
Wellstar Northwest Women's Care

Earl Thurmond, M.D.
Director of Network
Development & Affiliated Care
The Southeast Permanente
Medical Group

Earl Thurmond, M.D. lives by the Winston Churchill proverb, "We make a living by what we get. We make a life by what we give." He practices with The Southeast Permanente Medical Group, Inc., which exclusively treats Kaiser Permanente patients in Georgia. He is the director of network development and affiliated care.

A native of Augusta, Georgia, Thurmond pours his time and energy back into the community when he is not at the medical center. Since 2001, he has made a great impact at Peachtree Pine Men's Homeless Shelter, where he counsels and treats patients and performs routine screenings. Thurmond also volunteers with the March of Dimes, the Cascade United Methodist Church Health Fair and Bouie Elementary School.

Thurmond graduated from the Georgia Institute of Technology. He attended medical school at the Howard University College of Medicine and obtained his master of business administration degree from Kennesaw University. He was named Primary Care Practitioner of the Year in 2004 by Kaiser Permanente and is a fellow with the American College of Physicians.

He and his wife, Phyllis Kitchens, live in Lithonia.

Sandra White, M.D.
Medical Director,
Medical Management
Blue Cross Blue Shield of Georgia

As medical director of medical management at Blue Cross Blue Shield of Georgia, Sandra White is responsible for case management and utilization management. She leads quality initiatives related to health disparities, breast cancer and specialty pharmacy. She also participates with network management and provider relations for assigned hospitals and geographic areas.

White's areas of interest include health and disease management and improving consumer understanding of health-related information to improve health literacy and facilitate self management.

White received her bachelor's degree from the City College of New York. She earned her doctor of medicine degree from Mount Sinai School of Medicine and her master of business administration degree from Kennesaw State University.

White is a diplomate of the American Board of Internal Medicine and Rheumatology and the American Board of Quality Assurance and Utilization Review Physicians. She holds certifications in managed care.

Dr. Carolyn Williams
Lead Pediatrician
Cumberland Medical Center

Carolyn Williams, M.D., is a committed and caring pediatrician who always puts her patients first. She practices with The Southeast Permanente Medical Group, Inc., which exclusively treats Kaiser Permanente patients in Georgia. Williams is the lead pediatrician at Kaiser Permanente's Cumberland Medical Center and is dedicated to advancing the medical, educational and social needs of children of all ages.

Williams played a significant role in Kaiser Permanente's implementation of a computerized medical record system, which puts the health plan at the forefront of health care. Professionally, Williams is a diplomat for the American Board of Pediatrics, a fellow for the American Academy of Pediatrics and a member of the National Medical Association. She obtained her medicine degree from Howard University in Washington, D.C. and has a master of business administration degree in management from St. Thomas University in Minneapolis.

When she is not treating patients, Williams is actively involved in the community. She does volunteer work with the March of Dimes, local influenza vaccine clinics and the Awana Club, a local nondenominational youth ministry in Atlanta.

Having experienced congenital cardiac problems in infancy through adulthood, Barbara Lynne Ivey Yarn, M.D., MPH, yearned to help treat these conditions in others. While her interests in cardiology morphed into anesthesiology, she found great reward in teaching residents the art of administering anesthesia to infants and children for cardiac surgery. She served as a faculty member at the University of Louisville School of Medicine. Yarn trained at Emory University Hospitals in anesthesia and received a master of public health degree from the University of Minnesota. She currently practices solo, specializing in anesthesiology for pediatric dental restorations, orthopedics and pain management.

Previously, Barbara was chair of the department of anesthesiology and director of respiratory therapy at Humana Hospital Newnan. She also practiced in private partnership at Atlanta Outpatient Peachtree Dunwoody Medical Center.

A board member of SCLC/W.O.M.E.N., Barbara has served as president of the Buckhead Cascade Chapter of The Links, Inc., The Sophisticates, Inc., and is the current national executive board treasurer.

Barbara is married to Tyrone Yarn, retired special agent for the Department of Justice, Drug Enforcement Administration.

Barbara Lynne Ivey Yarn,
M.D., MPH
Anesthesiologist

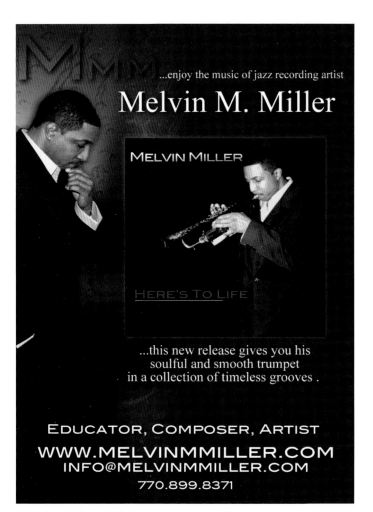

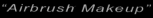

AmeriPlan USA Can Make Your American Dream A Reality

Jerome & Debera Scott - National Vice Presidents - $300,000. Founders' Ring Club - AmeriPlan USA®

⌐rmer School Teacher Jerome Scott and his wife, Debera, are living the American Dream

⌐ey've achieved financial success beyond most people's ⌐dest dreams, They're working within a career they love, ⌐d more than that, they're helping people in the process.

⌐w are they doing this? **Simple** - ⌐ey're involved with one of the most dynamic and ⌐-coming companies in the country - AmeriPlan USA®. ⌐eriPlan® is the nation's leading provider for discounted ⌐pplemental health benefits.

⌐is program allows members to save up to 80% on ⌐ntal, Vision, Prescription and Chiropractic services. ⌐eriPlan USA® is now offering ⌐meriPlan Health® ⌐edical discount benefits) ⌐ most states.

⌐eriPlan® brings healthcare to ⌐llions of uninsured and under- ⌐sured Americans. AmeriPlan® is ⌐t insurance. It is the nation's leading ⌐ovider of discount health benefits.

⌐e Scott's saw the brilliance in AmeriPlan® a few years ⌐o, and have turned this opportunity into the American ⌐eam. Now, they want to share this opportunity with **You**. ⌐coming an AmeriPlan® Independent Business Owner ⌐O) is as easy as a phone call to Jerome or Debera Scott, ⌐d an investment of as little as $50. Training classes are ⌐mplimentery and conducted on a weekly basis. No prior ⌐perience or licenensing is required.

⌐e've got IBO's from all walks of life," Jerome Scott said. ⌐e Scotts' team includes former school bus drivers, fast-food ⌐nployees, teachers, pastors, attorneys, FBI agents, ⌐surance agents, single parents, doctors, nurses, hair ⌐signers, accountants and politicians. "This really is a great ⌐portunity for everyone."

By making a simple phone call to 1-877-212-8100, you'll be taking the first step to becoming an AmeriPlan® IBO and the Scotts newest business partner. "I've seen so many people achieve so much by seizing this opportunity," Scott explained. "It's so nice to know that you've helped someone reach their goals and achieve their dreams."

With the addition of **Medical discount** benifits to the program, consumers are now interested more than ever in AmeriPlan®USA. There's no better time to act than now.

It's easy to become an IBO for AmeriPlan®, Scott emphasizes. "There's a great **window of opportunity** for people right now." With corporations slashing employee medical benefits on a daily basis, and the cost of medical care rising, it's certain that AmeriPlan USA's cutting-edge benefits and programs will grow increasingly popular with citizens all over the country.

This is why becoming an AmeriPlan® IBO, and making that call to 1-877-212-8100, is so important to those who may be looking to improve the quality of life for themselfs and their families. Whether it's a new car, a new home, a comfortable retirement, or a college education for your children, becoming an AmeriPlan® IBO can help make these things happen - just look what it did for a former school teacher and his wife (former Blue Cross representative).

The Scotts' Team Includes

a former school bus driver, fast-food employees, teachers, pastors, attorneys, FBI agents, insurance agents, single parents, doctors, nurses, hair designers, accountants and politicians.

For more information, we invite you to visit our website - **www.myteamprosperity.com/jerome**
or call us @ 1- 877-212-8100

Atlanta's

LITERARY

"I speak to the black experience, but I am always talking about the human condition -- about what we can endure, dream, fail at, and still survive."

MAYA ANGELOU

NOVELIST AND POET

Tanya Finney
Poet & Author

D. Lee Hatchett
Founder
The Urban Speculative Fiction
Literary Foundation

Tanya Finney began writing poetry after inspiring her students to write based on a conversation she had with a nationally known poet. She has been selected for her poetic skills to participate in numerous forums. Her first collection of poetry, *Love Letters: Connecting the heart of man to God*, was released in February of 2006 to rave reviews.

Tanya is a first-year graduate and former leader of Women on the Path, a women's ministry group at New Birth Missionary Baptist Church. She is often sought after for counsel and prayer among church members and friends.

Tanya received a bachelor of arts degree in secondary English from Wesleyan College and an educational specialist degree in educational leadership from Georgia College and State University. She serves as a gifted education teacher and English department chairperson in a metro Atlanta high school.

A native of Milledgeville, Georgia, Tanya currently resides in the Atlanta area and is working on her first novel and a second book of poetry.

D. Lee Hatchett is an African American Literary Award nominee and self-published speculative fiction author. Inspired by a fascination with religion, science and African-American history, Lee is a contributing writer for *Black College Today*, *Urban Influence* and *Booking Matters Magazine*. His interests collide in an explosive three-part science fiction series, The Black Angel Trilogy.

Lee is the founder of the Urban Speculative Fiction Literary Foundation (USFLF). The USFLF is a Georgia nonprofit organization with a single mission: to stimulate and cultivate the imaginations, hopes, dreams, literary talents and life skills of underserved youth through speculative fiction.

Lee holds a bachelor of science degree in engineering from North Carolina State University and a master of business administration degree from Georgia State University.

Lee is devoted to exploring the world, having worked in various corporate positions in Italy, Spain, China, Japan, Germany and several cities within the U.S. He currently serves as the executive vice president of the Atlanta division of U.S. Foodservice.

A resident of Atlanta, Lee is the husband of Lillie Hatchett and the proud father of three children, Olivia, Zachary and Channing.

LITERARY

Patricia Heggs
Author

Shunda Leigh
Editor in Chief & Publisher
Booking Matters Magazine

*R*oad to Two Hearts is Patricia Heggs' first fiction novel. It is a wonderful story of love recognized too late.

Patricia is a graduate of Clark Atlanta University. She received a degree in fine arts and education. Previously, she served as a director for the City of Atlanta, a school teacher and a youth development coordinator.

Patricia currently lives in Locust Grove, Georgia.

*S*hunda Leigh is the editor in chief and publisher of *Booking Matters Magazine*, established with her husband Jamill in November of 2002. The magazine chronicles and promotes African-American authors, bookstores, book clubs and businesses. The Memphis Black Writers and Southern Film Festival named *Booking Matters Magazine* the Best New Literary Magazine for 2004. Shunda is no stranger to the literary arena as she is also the founder of Circle of Friends II Book Club in Atlanta, one of the largest book clubs in the country. Shunda led the efforts of her book club's appearance on *The Oprah Winfrey Show*.

Shunda has been featured in numerous national magazines and newspapers. Her fully sponsored wedding was featured on ABC News *Primetime* in June of 2004, and she also appeared in *Modern Bride* magazine's April/June 2005 issue. She is currently working on her first published book which will be released in 2007.

A native of Valdosta, Shunda currently resides in Ellenwood, Georgia. She is happily and permanently married to her business partner, Jamill. They are the proud parents of two young adults, Courtney and LaMonté.

Angela D. Lewis
President
Speaking Concepts & Publications, LLC

Tia McCollors
Author

Angela D. Lewis, known to family and childhood friends as "CheeChee," is a full-time account manager for a Fortune 500 company, president of Speaking Concepts & Publications, LLC, and a contributing columnist for the *Wyngate Gazette*'s monthly newsletter.

In September of 2006, Angela published her first book, *Ssss Single, Sensational, Significant, Sisters... We Sizzle!!! A Single Woman's Guide To Attracting and Meeting Men. Ssss* is creating a buzz as Angela shares practical techniques and guidance on how any woman can enjoy a more exciting single life while attracting and meeting lots of good men in the process.

In Angela's second book, *The Midnight Clear*, she is part of an anthology. The book consists of 21 short stories about love, hope and inspiration written by various authors.

Angela holds a bachelor of science degree in business administration from the University of South Carolina and is currently pursuing her executive master of business administration degree from the University of Phoenix.

Angela makes her home in south Atlanta. She is single and has one son, Brandon.

A national bestselling author, Tia McCollors secured her spot in the publishing industry with the release of her debut novel and *Essence* bestseller, *A Heart of Devotion*, followed by her second release, *Zora's Cry*. After ten years as a public relations professional in the corporate arena, she is now emerging as a steadfast author of faith-based novels.

In addition to being a novelist, Tia is a motivational speaker and instructor for writing workshops. A member of the American Christian Fiction Writers (ACFW) organization, she serves as vice president of Visions In Print, the Atlanta Southeast Chapter of the ACFW. Tia also facilitates a writer's critique group that she co-founded in 2003. In 2006 she was voted the Breakout Author of the Year by the Open Book Awards of the African American Literary Awards Show.

Tia received a bachelor of arts degree in journalism and mass communication from the University of North Carolina in 1996.

A native of Greensboro, North Carolina, she is the wife of Wayne McCollors and the proud mother of one son.

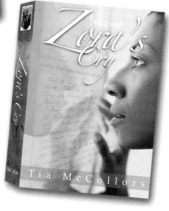

Kendra Norman-Bellamy
Author & Publisher
KNB Publications, LLC

Theron J. Parker
Poet & Author

Kendra Norman-Bellamy is a national bestselling author and president of an independent self-publishing house that produces the works of rising authors. Since 2003, Kendra has been sole proprietor of KNB Publications, LLC, a company that assists aspiring writers of Christian-based literature to realize their publishing dreams.

Kendra's own literary works are currently produced through Harlequin Books, Moody Publishers and Urban Books. Additionally, she is the editorial consultant for *Booking Matters Magazine* and a columnist for *Hope for Women Magazine* and *Global Woman Magazine*. Kendra is also the Georgia area coordinator for the American Christian Fiction Writers. She is founder of Cruisin' For Christ, a cruise that celebrates Christian artistries.

Among her most recent recognitions, Kendra's titles have repeatedly graced *Essence* magazine's Best Seller List. She received the 2006 Open Book Award for Best Christian Fiction from the New York-based African American Literary Awards Show.

A native of West Palm Beach, Florida, Kendra is a graduate of Valdosta Technical College. She resides in Stone Mountain, Georgia with her husband, Jonathan, and her daughters, Brittney and Crystal.

Theron J. Parker is an award-winning poet. He has received numerous accolades from the International Library of Poetry, Poetry.com and the American Poets Society. Theron has written two poetry books, *Poems From The Heart* and *Visions of True Love*.

Inspired by the movement of Atlanta's fiction authors, Theron collaborated with co-author Patricia A. Heggs in writing his first fiction novel, *Road to Two Hearts*.

Theron attended Georgia Military College in Milledgeville, Georgia and Alabama State University in Montgomery, Alabama. After graduating from college, he entered the U.S. Army, eventually retiring as an Army major.

Theron is currently a resident of DeKalb County, Georgia.

Help us make a difference by exposing our children to positive role models!

At Who's Who Publishing Co. LLC, we are dedicated to making an impact in our communities across the nation and in the lives of the next generation. Our coffee table-quality publications highlight the outstanding and significant achievements made by legendary and contemporary African Americans.

They are essential guides in acquainting our youth with people in their community who sacrificed, overcame and excelled.

While the ancient African proverb wisely notes that "It takes a whole village to raise a child," we also realize that what our children see is what they become. Our books broaden the landscape of career opportunities for the next generation while inspiring them to reach for the top.

Who's Who publications are designed to encourage and inspire, to uplift and unite, and to forever memorialize the culture, contributions, and history that represents our rich heritage.

ORDER ONLINE OR CALL 614-481-7300
www.whoswhopublishing.com

Atlanta's
MOST INFLUENTIAL

*"Women, if the soul of the nation is to be saved,
I believe that you must become its soul."*

CORETTA SCOTT KING, 1927-2006

HUMAN RIGHTS ACTIVIST AND LEADER

Hank Aaron
President & Owner
Hank Aaron BMW

Born in Mobile, Alabama, Henry L. "Hank" Aaron has been an active and influential leader in the business and civic communities for more than 20 years. Prior to joining Turner Broadcasting System, Inc., Aaron enjoyed a 23-year major league career during which he rewrote baseball's hitting record book. Nicknamed "The Hammer," Aaron holds more major league batting records than any other player in the game's history, including most home runs and most runs batted in. Along with Frank Robinson, Aaron was inducted in the Baseball Hall of Fame on August 1, 1982.

Aaron is senior vice president of the Atlanta National League Baseball Club, Inc., vice president of business development for the CNN Airport Network, and president of Henry Aaron, Inc. and Henry Aaron Uniform Company. He is also a long-time Church's and Arby's restaurant franchisee. Aaron has now put together an all-star team as president and owner of Hank Aaron BMW.

In 1995 he and his wife, Billye, established the Hank Aaron Chasing the Dream Foundation to give children with limited opportunities a chance to pursue their dreams.

Valencia Adams
Vice President & Chief Diversity Officer
BellSouth Corporation

Valencia Adams is vice president and chief diversity officer for BellSouth Corporation. She has oversight for diversity and inclusion strategy development and implementation across BellSouth Corporation. She has been with BellSouth for 36 years.

Valencia received the 2006 Compass Award from the Women's Leadership Exchange®. She was named one of the 25 Influential Black Women in Business for 2006 by *The Network Journal*. In 2005 she received the Millennium Pacesetter award from the Atlanta Business League and was named among the Top 100 Blacks in Corporate America by *Black Professionals*.

A lifetime member of the Atlanta Chamber of Commerce, Valencia has a long history of community involvement and fund-raising. She was appointed by Governor Sonny Purdue to the state's Workforce Investment Board Coordinating Council in 2006. She also serves on the boards of the Possible Woman Foundation, Women's Resource Center to End Domestic Violence, St. Joseph's Hospital, *Atlanta Woman* and the BellSouth Foundation.

Valencia is a graduate of Georgia State University with a bachelor of business administration degree. She has also completed management courses at Columbia University and Emory University.

Cynthia Robinson Alexander has more than two decades of experience in commercial real estate development and investment. She has direct, hands-on experience in asset managing and positioning of large, multi-tenant office buildings throughout the country. She was directly responsible for the development of more than 1.2 million square feet of Class A office space in Atlanta. The largest of these projects, Promenade, was completed in 1990 while she served as development officer for The Landmarks Group.

Cynthia is extremely involved in various civic, charitable and professional organizations. She currently serves as one of the founding board members of the Midtown Community Improvement District. Cynthia is the immediate past president of Commercial Real Estate Women, having also served on the board for several years. She also serves on the board of Big Brothers Big Sisters of Metro Atlanta.

Cynthia has a passion for reading and cooking, and finds comfort in entertaining at her home in Decatur. She has two sons and attends Mount Zion AME Church, where she is involved in various church activities.

Cynthia Robinson Alexander
Senior Vice President
Southeast Regional Office
Sumitomo Life Realty

The Reverend Al Anderson has spent the last 40 years as a pioneer in marketing, with an emphasis on the African-American consumer. He is chairman and founder of Anderson Communications Inc. (ACI), the second-oldest African-American-owned firm in the country.

Now in its 35th year, ACI is known as one of the best sources for companies that wish to market their products and services to African Americans. ACI has developed a variety of marketing services for a host of Fortune 500 companies.

Al has served as an adjunct professor of marketing and is a collector of African and African-American art. Though he has many achievements, he takes the greatest pride in his family. He is the husband of Jeanette; father to Albert III, 27, and April, 36; and grandfather to Mejona, Kaleb, Kade and Kash.

A native of Winston-Salem, North Carolina, Al is a graduate of Morehouse College. He also completed studies at Rutgers University and Georgia State University. He is the recipient of an honorary doctorate of medicine from the University of Dar es Salaam in Tanzania.

Rev. Al Anderson
Chairman & Founder
Anderson Communications

Bernard Anderson, AIF®
President
Anderson Financial Solutions, Inc.

Bernard Anderson is an independent financial advisor whose practice focuses on the wealth management needs of medical professionals, senior executives and directors, and successful small business owners. His clients benefit from holistic planning and proactive strategies that help reduce taxes, enhance wealth, protect assets and fulfill philanthropic objectives. He has an extensive background in retirement income and distribution planning, estate planning, executive benefits and charitable planning.

Recognized by *Who's Who in American High Schools and Colleges*, Anderson earned a bachelor's degree in business from North Carolina A&T State University and a master's degree from Florida Institute of Technology. He is a retired military officer and serves on the advisory boards of several local nonprofit organizations.

Anderson completed the Ed Slott, CPA Advanced IRA Rollover and Distribution Expert Training Course. He holds memberships with the Georgia Planned Giving Council, the Financial Planning Association, the National Association of Securities Professionals and the National Association of Health Services Executives. Additionally, he is a registered representative of member firm NFP Securities, Inc. A frequent speaker, Anderson has been featured in local publications and media.

**The Honorable
Thurbert E. Baker**
Attorney General
State of Georgia

Since June of 1997, Thurbert E. Baker has served as Georgia's 52nd attorney general.

In 1988 Baker was elected to the Georgia House of Representatives, representing the 70th House District. After one term in the General Assembly, former Governor Zell Miller selected him to serve as his assistant administration floor leader, and later appointed him to the position of administration floor leader.

Baker is a trustee on the Ebenezer Baptist Church board and the National Medical Society, Emory University. He also serves on the board of governors of the State Bar of Georgia and as a member of the Judicial Nominating Commission. He has served as vice chairman of the National Association of Attorneys Generals' Conference on Violence Against Women in Washington, D.C.

Born in Rocky Mount, North Carolina, Baker received his bachelor's degree in political science from the University of North Carolina at Chapel Hill. He received his law degree from the Emory University School of Law in Atlanta.

He lives in Stone Mountain with his wife, Catherine, and their two daughters, Jocelyn and Chelsea.

Gregory Baranco is president of Baranco Automotive Group, consisting of Baranco Acura, Baranco Lincoln, and Baranco Pontiac GMC. A native of Baton Rouge, Louisiana, he graduated from Southern University with a bachelor of science degree in business administration.

In 1978 Baranco founded Baranco Pontiac, Inc., and he has since received numerous awards sponsored by General Motors, Ford and American Honda. Since 1990, his automotive group has remained one of *Black Enterprise*'s top 100 businesses, and he has received the coveted *Time* magazine Quality Dealer Award. He presently serves on the board of the Georgia Automobile Dealers Association.

As chairman of the board of the First Southern Bank of Lithonia, Baranco negotiated a merger with Citizens Trust Bank of Atlanta, making the new Citizens Trust Bank the third-largest minority bank in the U.S. He serves on several other boards and is an active member of 100 Black Men of DeKalb County, the Maynard Jackson Youth Foundation, Arrive Alive and the United Way, to name a few.

Baranco is married to Juanita Powell Baranco, and together they have four children.

Gregory T. Baranco
President
Baranco Automotive Group

Juanita Baranco, along with her husband, Gregory, co-owns Baranco Automotive Group.

Born in Washington, D.C., Baranco was raised in Shreveport, Louisiana, where she earned bachelor of science and juris doctorate degrees from Louisiana State University. She holds memberships with the American Bar Association and the State Bar Associations of Georgia and Louisiana.

A community servant, Baranco actively supports the Scottsdale Child Development Center and is a board director for Georgia Power Company, the Federal Reserve Bank of Atlanta, the John H. Hartland Company and the Woodruff Arts Center. A member of Delta Sigma Theta Sorority, Inc., she is also a board member of the Sickle Cell Foundation of Georgia and a Clark Atlanta University trustee. Since 1991, she has served on the board of regents of the University System of Georgia, serving as board chair and vice chair. Additionally, she is a member of Saints Peter and Paul Church, where she sings in the choir.

A sought-after speaker, Baranco has received numerous awards, including election into the YWCA Academy of Women Achievers. She and husband Gregory have four children.

Juanita Powell Baranco
Co-Owner & Executive Vice President
Baranco Automotive Group

The Honorable Joann Bayneum
Chief Judge
Magistrate Court of Fulton County

Appointed to the bench in 1984, Joann Bayneum is chief judge of the Magistrate Court of Fulton County in Atlanta. She also serves by special appointment as a superior court judge. As chief judge, she oversees the management of cases of the court's more than 40 part-time and full-time judges. She serves as the official spokesperson for the court, whose jurisdiction is civil claims up to $15,000, criminal arrest warrants and criminal commitment hearings. The Superior Court is the highest trial level court and involves felony trials, family matters and civil claims exceeding $15,000.

Bayneum is the recipient of a number of awards, but she is most proud of her role in the establishment of court-annexed alternative dispute resolution programs in metropolitan Atlanta courts in the 1980s.

Bayneum received a bachelor of arts degree from Morgan State University in Baltimore, Maryland, a master of arts degree from Clark Atlanta University, and her juris doctorate from the Woodrow Wilson College of Law.

She is a native of Maryland's eastern shore, Cambridge.

The Honorable Eldrin A. Bell
Chairman
Clayton County Board of Commissioners

The Honorable Eldrin A. Bell was elected in 2004 as chairman of the Clayton County Board of Commissioners. His election was historic in that he is the first African American in this position. Bell also served as the first African-American chief of police for the City of Atlanta to hold every rank from patrolman to chief.

Bell is a member of many civic and professional organizations including the Gate City Bar Association, the National Organization of Black Law Enforcement Officers, the Georgia International Law Enforcement Exchange, the Governor's Martin Luther King Holiday Commission and the National Academy of Recording Arts and Sciences (Grammy Awards).

Bell received his education in Atlanta Public Schools. He completed undergraduate studies at Morris Brown College and Georgia State University. Bell completed graduate studies at Harvard University Law School, Northwestern University Traffic Institute and Atlanta University. He also received training at the FBI Academy, the National Executive Institute, and is a Secret Service Academy graduate.

A member and minister at Salem Bible Church in Atlanta, Bell is the proud father of 12 children (eight adopted).

Justice Robert Benham is a cum laude graduate of Tuskegee University. He received his juris doctor degree from the University of Georgia, and his master of law degree from the University of Virginia. Additionally, he has received honorary doctorate of law degrees from John Marshall Law School and Tuskegee University.

Benham served as a judge on the Georgia Court of Appeals for six years until his appointment to the Georgia Supreme Court, where previously he served as chief justice. To his credit, his court was listed as one of the most progressive supreme courts in the nation by the American Bar Association. He is a master in the Bleckley Inn of Court and served as the late Chief Justice Rehnquist's appointee to the Federal-State Jurisdiction Committee.

Benham holds membership in numerous local, state and national professional organizations, and he serves on the boards of many civic, fraternal, business and religious organizations.

A recipient of many distinguished awards, Benham is married to the former Nell Dodson, and they have two sons, Corey Brevard Benham and Austin Tyler Benham.

The Honorable Robert Benham
Justice
Supreme Court of Georgia

Ernestine Bennett owns and operates six Wendy's Old Fashioned Hamburgers restaurants in the Atlanta metropolitan area. She majored in business education at North Carolina A&T State University, where she developed the passion to become an entrepreneur. She matriculated graduate school at George Washington University with a major in public administration.

E B Enterprise Unlimited, Inc. serves as a vehicle to mentor future entrepreneurs, enhance economic growth through employment opportunities and revenue, promote productive and ethical work standards, and to give back to the communities it serves.

Ernestine received the 2005 Atlanta Business League's Outstanding Achievement Woman of the Year Award. She also recieved Infinity Broadcasting's 4th Annual For Sisters Only Community Service Achievement Award in 2004.

Ernestine is an advisory board member of minority recruitment for the American Red Cross, Southern Region. She is a trustee of Cascade United Methodist Church and a board member of the Metropolitan Atlanta Coalition of 100 Black Women and Bridgebuilders, Inc. She is also a member of the Atlanta Suburban Chapter of Delta Sigma Theta Sorority, Inc.

Ernestine Bennett
President & Chief Executive Officer
E B Enterprise Unlimited, Inc.
dba Wendy's

Kathleen Jackson Bertrand
Vice President of Community
& Government Affairs
Atlanta Convention & Visitors Bureau

Kathleen Jackson Bertrand is a native Atlantan and graduate of Spelman College. In 1983 she joined the staff of the Atlanta Convention & Visitors Bureau (ACVB). She has worked as membership account executive, advertising and membership manager, and vice president of membership and community affairs.

In January of 2003, Bertrand assumed the title of vice president of community and government affairs. She has been instrumental in the ACVB's development of its diversity marketing programs. Through her concept and direction, the ACVB published its first visitors guide aimed at the African-American visitor in 1992.

Bertrand is also a well-known jazz recording artist and writer. She has performed in a variety of settings, including at two Olympic Games, before two presidents and at jazz festivals worldwide. She was honored by the United Negro College Fund as one of Atlanta's Legends and by Spelman College with its 1998 Alumnae Achievement Award for the Arts and Entertainment. Additionally, Bertrand was an invited performer for both the 1999 and 2000 Montreux Jazz Festivals in Switzerland, as well as the Atlanta Jazz Festival.

J. Veronica Biggins
Managing Partner
Heidrick & Struggles

J. Veronica Biggins is managing partner of Heidrick & Struggles in Atlanta, managing partner of the firm's diversity services practice, and an active member of the board of director functional practice.

Previously, Veronica served as assistant to the President of the United States and director of presidential personnel. She also served as vice chairman of the United States delegation to the United Nations' Fourth World Conference on Women in Beijing, China, and she continues to serve her country as chairman of the Czech Slovak American Enterprise Fund.

Veronica's background includes 20 years of experience with NationsBank (now Bank of America) and its predecessor, The Citizen and Southern Bank. When she left NationsBank to join the White House, she was one of the highest-ranking female bankers in the country.

Veronica serves on the boards of AirTran Airways, Avnet and NDC Health. She also serves on the trustee boards for the Georgia Research Alliance, Woodruff Arts Center, the Downtown Atlanta Rotary and the International AIDS Fund.

Veronica holds a master's degree from Georgia State University and a bachelor's degree from Spelman College.

Johnnie B. Booker was named director of supplier diversity for The Coca-Cola Company in 2001. As such, she is responsible for assuring that minority- and women-owned businesses have equal access to contracting opportunities. Under her direction, the company's profile as a strong supporter of supplier diversity has grown substantially in actual dollars expended and in national recognition.

Previously, Booker was vice president of Resolution Trust Corporation and deputy assistant secretary for Fair Housing, U.S. Department of Housing and Urban Development. Additionally, she served in senior management positions with the Federal Home Loan Bank Board and the National Urban League.

Booker serves on several boards including D.C. Chartered Health Plan and the Women's Business Enterprise National Council. She is the recipient of numerous honors and awards for outstanding accomplishments and contributions.

A native of Fort Valley, Georgia, Booker received a bachelor of science degree from Hampton University and a master of social work degree from the Atlanta University School of Social Work.

She is the proud mother of an adult son, S. Courtney Booker III, and has a wonderful granddaughter, Dalyn.

Johnnie B. Booker
Director, Supplier Diversity
The Coca-Cola Company

A New York City native, Commissioner Nancy A. Boxill has been a resident of Atlanta since 1971. She began her political career in 1987 when the governor appointed her interim commissioner on the Fulton County Board of Commissioners. Boxill subsequently ran for the office and was elected in June of 1988 and was reelected in 1990, 1994, 1998, and 2002. She is the first female commissioner and vice chair of the Board of Commissioners. In addition, Boxill is a full-time graduate faculty member of The Union Institute in Cincinnati, Ohio.

She holds a bachelor's degree in psychology from Duquesne University in Pittsburgh; a master's degree in psychology from the New School for Social Research in New York; and a doctor of philosophy degree in child psychology from Union Graduate School in Cincinnati.

Boxill's community service history is extensive and varied. She currently serves as chair of the National Black Arts Festival board of directors, chair of the Fulton-Atlanta Land Bank Authority, vice chair of the Atlanta-Fulton County Recreation Authority, and a member of The Atlanta Opera board of directors.

The Honorable Nancy A. Boxill
Commissioner, District Six
Fulton County Board of Commissioners

Rickford D. Bradley
Executive Vice President
Human Resources
Cingular

Rick Bradley is executive vice president of human resources for Cingular. He is responsible for the development and direction of human resource strategies, plans, programs and policies corporate-wide.

Before joining Cingular, Bradley was president of interconnection services for SBC Telecommunications, Inc. Prior to SBC's merger with Pacific Telesis in 1997, Bradley was vice president and general manager of operator services for Pacific Bell, and he led an organization of more than 7,000 employees. He was named managing director of corporate development for SBC Communications, where he was responsible for identifying, cultivating and evaluating merger, joint venture and new international business opportunities for SBC.

In 1998 Bradley was appointed president of SBC's Center for Learning. He became president and general manager of public communications in 1999, where he oversaw all coin phone operations for Southwestern Bell, Pacific Bell, SNET and Nevada Bell.

Bradley is a graduate of Santa Clara University and completed the Program for Management Development at the Harvard University Graduate School of Business. He serves on the advisory board of Coles College of Business at Kennesaw State University.

Shirley Bradley-Carmack,
CRN, Ph.D.
Founder
GNLD Wellness Center

Dr. Shirley Bradley-Carmack's lifelong desire to help others led her to pursue a career in anesthesia and studies in psychology. She left the field of anesthesia and has been active in the direct selling industry for more than 25 years. She is the founder of the GNLD Wellness Center, which provides numerous health services.

The Carmacks' multimillion-dollar worldwide team has more than 38,000 members. Her accomplishments have brought her many awards and acknowledgements. Her special calling is to help people rise above the limitations of race, gender and economics.

Recently, Carmack was named co-author for the book *More Build It Big: 101 Insider Secrets from Top Direct Selling Experts*, created by the Direct Selling Women's Alliance (DSWA).

"The individuals who contributed to this book were selected not just because they have attained considerable success in direct selling, but because they have done so with a spirit and sense of integrity that exemplifies the best of our profession," said Jane Deuber, co-founder and president of the DSWA.

Dr. Carmack's future plan is to mentor young people in the industry.

Rosalind Brewer is president and corporate officer of Kimberly-Clark Corporation. She currently leads the global nonwovens sector that includes research and development, engineering and manufacturing. This particular sector operates nonwoven base machines in North America, Mexico, Europe and Asia, with sales value of just over $1 billion and 2,000 employees internationally.

In addition to her responsibilities at Kimberly-Clark, Rosalind serves on the Board of Directors Network, Inc. and on the Molson Coors Brewing Company board of directors. She is a member of the Executive Leadership Council, America's most prestigious association of African-American corporate executives from Fortune 500 companies. She also serves on the board of councilors for the Carter Presidential Center.

Rosalind received the 2005 Legacy of Leadership award from Spelman College; was voted one of 25 Power Women to Watch by *Atlanta Woman*; and was granted the DIVA award by *Business-To-Business*.

Rosalind completed the advanced management program at the Wharton School of Business in 2001. She earned her bachelor of science degree in chemistry from Spelman College in Atlanta. She is married with two young children.

Rosalind Brewer
President & Corporate Officer
Kimberly-Clark Corporation

Walter D. Broadnax has served as president of Clark Atlanta University since August of 2002.

A nationally and internationally known scholar, practitioner and accomplished speaker in the field of public policy, Broadnax served as deputy secretary and chief operating officer of the U.S. Department of Health and Human Services from 1993 to 1996. From 1980 to 1981, he was principal deputy assistant secretary for planning and evaluation of the U.S. Department of Health, Education and Welfare.

Broadnax served as director of Children, Youth and Adult Services for the State of Kansas, and president of the New York State Civil Service Commission. He was director and lecturer of the Innovations in State and Local Government programs at the John F. Kennedy School of Government at Harvard University, senior staff member at the Brookings Institution, and dean of the School of Public Affairs at American University.

Broadnax earned a doctorate from the Maxwell School at Syracuse University, a master of public administration degree from the University of Kansas and a bachelor of arts degree from Washburn University.

Dr. Walter D. Broadnax
President
Clark Atlanta University

The Honorable Tyrone Brooks
Representative, District 63
Georgia House of Representatives

The Honorable Tyrone Brooks is a 26-year member of the Georgia House of Representatives, representing District 63. He serves on the economic development and tourism, governmental affairs and retirement committees.

His career in public service began as a 15-year-old civil rights activist and volunteer with the Southern Christian Leadership Conference. In 1967 Brooks became a full-time staffer and has been jailed 65 times for civil rights work.

Brooks led the movement to reactivate the town of Keysville, Georgia and helped to pass the anti-terrorism law, the Max Black Reapportionment Plan, and repeal of Jim Crow laws. He also helped pass a law to bring African-American law enforcement officers into the Peace Officers Benefit Annuity Retirement Fund, denied because of race prior to 1976. His House Bill 16 resulted in winning an almost 20-year battle to change the Georgia state flag. He is known as "the man who changed the Georgia flag."

Brooks is a member of the Georgia Legislative Black Caucus, president of the Georgia Association of Black Elected Officials and co-founder of the Coalition for the Peoples' Agenda.

Marjorie M. Brown
Postmaster, Atlanta
United States Postal Service

A Jacksonville, Florida native, Marjorie Brown began her postal career as a distribution clerk. Appointed the first female postmaster of Atlanta in 1996, she is responsible for an annual revenue exceeding $614 million, and she directs delivery to more than 421,000 addresses in Atlanta.

Previously, Marjorie served as district manager for the Westchester District in White Plains, New York. She held executive positions as director of marketing and communications, manager of retail sales and service and manager of station/branch operations in Miami, Orlando, and Jacksonville.

In 2003 Marjorie received the Vice President's Award for Leadership at the National Executives Conference and the Vice President's Team Award. She has been selected as one of Atlanta's Top 100 Black Women of Influence for five consecutive years. She is also an active member of Atlanta's Chamber of Commerce.

Marjorie attended Edward Waters College and completed studies at Duke University, Emory University and the University of Virginia. Additionally, she is a 2001 graduate of Leadership Atlanta. She is the very proud mother of five adult children and a grandmother of seven.

T arlee W. Brown is chairman and chief executive officer of the Brown Design Group, Inc., which he founded in 1975. For more than 30 years, he has led the company which provides professional services in architecture, urban planning, engineering and project management.

Licensed and registered as an architect, Brown holds national certification from the National Council of Architectural Registration Boards and the American Institute of Certified Planners. He has practiced professionally in a number of states including Alabama, Georgia, Colorado, Florida, Ohio, Massachusetts, North Carolina, South Carolina, Texas, Washington and others.

Mr. Brown is married to Grace Brown. He enjoys spending time with their three children, Audra, Gayle and Robert Jr.

Tarlee W. Brown
Chairman & Chief Executive Officer
Brown Design Group, Inc.

G overnor Roy E. Barnes appointed David Burgess to fill a commission seat on April 8, 1999. His appointment is one of several firsts. Burgess is the first African American to serve on the vital utility board; the first former Public Service Commission staff member to hold a commission seat; and the first Georgia Institute of Technology graduate on the commission. He was elected to a six-year term in November of 2000, and served as chairman of the commission in 2002. He is the only African-American statewide elected public service commissioner in the nation.

Burgess graduated from Georgia Tech in 1981 with a degree in electrical engineering. He served as a member of the PSC staff for 17 years and is recognized nationally as an expert in telecommunications policy.

Burgess serves as chairman of the commission's telecommunications committee and a member of the advisory board of the Georgia Center for Advanced Telecommunications Technology. He was inducted into the 2006 class of the Georgia Tech Engineering Hall of Fame, and received the 2006 Catalyst Award from the Atlanta Business League.

The Honorable
David L. Burgess
Commissioner
Public Service Commission

The Honorable Gloria Butler
Senator, 55th District
Georgia Senate

Senator Gloria Butler, a Democrat, began her first term as a state senator during the 1999-2000 legislative session, representing the 55th District in DeKalb County. She serves on several committees, including the Senate public safety and homeland security; regulated industries and utilities; health and human services; and the powerful committee of rules. Butler was appointed by Lieutenant Governor Mark Taylor to serve on the Georgia Workforce Investment Board.

The highest-ranking female in the Georgia Senate, Butler is the minority whip and chair of the DeKalb Senate Delegation. Likewise, she is tri-chair of the Women's Caucus, a nonpartisan body providing women legislators opportunities to develop relationships across party lines and enhance the quality of life for women and Georgia families. She also formed the Dynamic 55th Senate District Advisory Council.

Butler has sponsored or co-sponsored more than 90 pieces of legislation. During her first term, she received the Freshman Legislator of the Year Award from the Georgia Legislative Black Caucus.

A Daytona Beach, Florida native, she is the mother of Felicia and Leslie and grandmother of Corey and Courtney.

Rick Caffey
Senior Vice President &
Market Manager
CBS Radio East, Inc.

Rick Caffey began his career at WAOK/WVEE radio as vice president and general manager on October 1, 1995. On January 27, 2003, he was named senior vice president and market manager of CBS Radio East, Inc. He currently oversees a four-station cluster, which includes urban giant WVEE, WAOK and the new adult rock format, dave fm and Falcons Radio.

Prior to joining WAOK/WVEE, Caffey was station manager of WALR and general manager of the Atlanta Urban Radio Alliance (AURA). Prior to coming to Atlanta, he ran the number one and two stations in Memphis, WHRK-FM and WDIA-AM, for US Radio. He was previously the general sales manager for Bonneville's WTMX-FM, Chicago. Caffey, the recipient of numerous community service awards, has been named to *Radio Ink*'s 25 Most Successful African-Americans in Radio for the past six consecutive years.

He is a graduate of Northern Illinois University with a bachelor of science degree in advertising and marketing. Rick is married to Jacqui Caffey, and he is the proud father of a son, Parris, and a daughter, Ciara.

Kimberly A. Cameron is owner and chief executive officer of Chase Real Estate/Project Resources & Solutions, LLC, a real estate development consulting company. As chief executive officer, Kimberly has established a business focus to work with clients that lack the personnel or experience in the real estate development process so they can have a profitable real estate development project. She plans, directs and coordinates activities related to specific projects including obtaining and managing third-party consultants; arranging for financing; acting as liaison with governmental agencies and neighborhood groups; and creating project timelines and parameters. Kimberly advises clients on alternate methods of solving needs or problems and she recommends specific solutions.

Kimberly is president of the National Coalition of 100 Black Women-Decatur/DeKalb Chapter and board chair of the Women in Construction Scholarship Foundation. She is an adjunct professor in the school of business at DeVry University.

In 1990 Kimberly was the first African-American woman to receive a construction management degree from the University of Wisconsin-Madison. In 1996 she earned a master of business administration degree in finance from Concordia University Wisconsin.

Kimberly Cameron
President, Decatur/DeKalb Chapter
National Coalition of 100 Black Women

Ryan Cameron is radio host for V-103's (WVEE-FM) afternoon drive. In 1991 he was trailblazing his way through radio in the nation's capital at WKYS-FM when Radio One mogul Kathy Hughes and son, Alfred Liggens, decided to bring a true hip-hop station to Atlanta; Ryan Cameron was their first choice as the morning man. After nine years, Ryan decided to make a power move to secure his place in the city as a radio icon at Atlanta's heritage station, WVEE-FM, an Infinity Broadcasting station. The move was well received by V-103 listeners.

Always ready to give "good television," Ryan has appeared on *The Jamie Foxx Show*, *MONTEL*, *Rolanda* and BET's *Comic View*. Recognized by many for his crazy antics, which won him first place as a contestant on BET's *Comic View*, Ryan won an Emmy in 1994 for Best On-Air Personality for hosting former Atlanta television news magazine *Noon Day* (WXIA-TV 11 NBC).

Born in Atlanta on November 29, 1966, Ryan reflects on his grandmother Lonnie Cameron's positive attitude, strong spirituality and ironclad belief that "anything is possible."

Ryan Cameron
Host, Afternoon Drive
WVEE V-103 FM

**The Honorable
Elaine L. Carlisle**
Judge
Atlanta Municipal Court

Judge Elaine L. Carlisle is a graduate of Howard University with a bachelor's degree in communications. She graduated from the John Marshall Law School with a doctor of jurisprudence, magna cum laude, in 1982.

In October of 1989, Mayor Andrew Young appointed Carlisle to the Atlanta Municipal Court. She was reelected in 1994, 1998, 2002 and 2005. Carlisle is a member of the State Bar of Georgia, the Atlanta Bar Association, the Gate City Bar Association, and the Atlanta alumnae chapter of Delta Sigma Theta Sorority, Inc.

In 1990 Carlisle was honored by the Southern Bell Corporation as an outstanding Woman Achiever in the Judiciary. In 1996 she was appointed a lieutenant colonel, aide de camp, to the governor's staff by Governor Zell Miller for public service work.

Carlisle is a member of the Ormewood Park Presbyterian Church where she serves as elder. She is director of Christian education and vacation Bible school and also teaches Sunday school to first graders.

A graduate of Gary Roosevelt High School, Carlisle is an avid professional basketball fan and enjoys playing golf.

The Honorable Joe Carn
Councilmember
City of College Park

Joe Carn is the City of College Park's youngest councilman. The son of R&B vocalist Jean Carn, Joe set his sights on the music industry early. After graduating from Benjamin Mays High School, he attended DeVry Institute of Technology to pursue a music career. Composing songs for major labels including MCA, Arista, Sony and Disney, Carn wrote and produced national Top 10 singles and albums, selling more than two million copies worldwide.

A devoted husband and father, Carn has been instrumental in the transformation of College Park. He is committee chairman for Concerned Black Clergy, an elected state committee member of the Democratic Party of Georgia, and a Fulton County deputy registrar. He has worked on campaigns for Vice President Al Gore, Mayor Shirley Franklin, State Senator Donzella James, Councilman Tracey Wyatt, Senator Greg Hecht and Congresswoman Cynthia McKinney.

Vice president of the local PTA, Carn is a member of the ACLU, the Young Entrepreneurs Association and the RainbowPUSH Coalition. He is the national treasurer and youngest board member to serve for the National Organization to Insure a Sound-Controlled Environment.

William "Bill" Clement Jr. is chairman and chief executive officer of DOBBS, RAM & Company. DOBBS, RAM & Company is the primary contractor engaged by the Internal Revenue Service (IRS) to maintain the IRS E-Filing system, the national system used to electronically receive federal income tax returns.

Appointed by President Carter, Bill served as associate administrator of the U.S. Small Business Administration in Washington, D.C. during the Carter Administration. He also served as vice president and senior loan officer of Citizens Trust Bank.

Bill is chairman of the boards of directors of Atlanta Life Financial Group, Inc. and the Atlanta Life Insurance Company. He is also a board member of Radiant Systems, Inc. and The Commerce Club. He is co-chairman of the Atlanta Action Forum, a trustee of the Maynard Jackson Youth Foundation and a charter member of the 100 Black Men of Atlanta.

Born in Atlanta, Bill received his bachelor of arts degree from Morehouse College and his master of business administration degree from the Wharton Business School at the University of Pennsylvania.

William A. Clement Jr.
Chairman & Chief Executive Officer
DOBBS, RAM & Company

Rosemary Roberts Cloud is fire chief for the City of East Point and is the first African-American female fire chief in the U.S. In her position, she is responsible for managing five fire stations and 120 employees in a city with 40,000 residents. She began her career in the fire service 27 years ago with the City of Atlanta Fire Department and worked her way up the ranks, from firefighter to chief officer.

Cloud holds a bachelor of science degree in applied behavioral science from National-Louis University. She received additional training at Harvard University's John F. Kennedy School of Government, Dillard University and the National Fire Academy.

Cloud's professional affiliations include the International Association of Fire Chiefs, Women in Fire Service, Women Chief Officers, the International Association of Black Professional Fire Fighters, the National Association of Black Public Administrators, and the National Fire Protection Association.

Cloud has received many awards for her outstanding work in the community.

The youngest of 14 children, Cloud was born and raised in Atlanta and has one daughter and one granddaughter.

Rosemary Roberts Cloud
Fire Chief
City of East Point

The Honorable Brenda H. Cole
Judge
State Court of Fulton County

Judge Brenda Hill Cole was appointed to the State Court of Fulton County in 1998. She previously served as a deputy attorney general in Georgia and West Virginia.

Cole holds a bachelor's degree from Spelman College, a master's degree from Clark Atlanta University and a juris doctorate from Emory University.

Cole was honored in 2004 as a YWCA Woman of Achievement and was recognized as a distinguished alumna by both Spelman College and Emory University. A member of several boards, she serves as board secretary of the Council of State Court Judges and on the Chief Justice's Commission on Professionalism.

The founder of the Clark Atlanta University Guild, Cole is a member of the Atlanta and Gate City Bar Associations and the Georgia Association of Black Women Attorneys. Likewise, she is a member of Cascade United Methodist Church, The Links, Inc. and Alpha Kappa Alpha Sorority, Inc.

She is married to Dr. Thomas W. Cole Jr., president emeritus of Clark Atlanta University and chief executive officer of Great Schools Atlanta. They are the parents of Kelley Susann and Thomas III.

Dr. Thomas W. Cole Jr.
President Emeritus
Clark Atlanta University

Thomas Winston Cole Jr. was appointed the first president of Clark Atlanta University in 1989. He retired in 2002. He is currently president and chief executive officer of Great Schools Atlanta.

Cole joined Atlanta University as an assistant professor of chemistry in 1966. While there, he served as chairman of the department of chemistry, provost and vice president for academic affairs. Cole held visiting professorships at Massachusetts Institute of Technology and the University of Illinois at Champaign-Urbana. He was president of West Virginia State College and chancellor of the West Virginia Board of Regents.

Cole's professional activities and honors are numerous. He is nationally recognized for his scholarly contributions to science and his leadership in higher education administration.

A Texas native, he graduated summa cum laude from Wiley College in 1961. He earned a doctorate of philosophy in organic chemistry from the University of Chicago in 1966.

A second-generation college president, his father, the late Thomas Winston Cole Sr., was president of Wiley College. He is married to Brenda Hill Cole. They have two children, Kelley Susann and Thomas III.

An active participant in the civil rights movement of the 1960s and a staunch advocate for social, economic and political change, Carolin Martin Collins brings more than 40 years of experience to the MECCA Chapter of the National Coalition of 100 Black Women. Championing against racism, sexism and classism through letter-writing campaigns, lobbying and demonstrations, Carolin hopes to keep major issues affecting women's lives in the forefront.

A native of Houston, Carolin began her career in 1968 at one of the largest newspapers in the Southwest, the *Houston Chronicle*. Ten years later, she joined IBM, and through a partnership with inner-city schools, she began tutoring students in math and reading. Today she takes great pride in the chapter's signature mentoring program, the Little Ladies of MECCA.

Now retired, Carolin is a missionary and a Sunday school teacher in the African Methodist Episcopal Church. She is the wife of Jackie Collins, vice president and director of internal auditing for Southern Company.

Carolin Martin Collins
President, MECCA Chapter
National Coalition of 100 Black Women

As a two-term commissioner for the City of Decatur, Kecia A. Cunningham sets policy and enacts legislation for the city's 18,000 residents. Additionally, she is active with the Georgia Municipal Association and sits on its legislative policy committee and congressional action team. In these roles, she helps craft the legislative agenda and priorities for the GMA's 500 member cities.

Cunningham is active with numerous community groups and chairs the DeKalb Rape Crisis Center. She graduated from Leadership Georgia in 2005, and previously from Leadership Atlanta and the Regional Leadership Institute. She has been recognized by the Georgia Municipal Association, the *Atlanta Journal-Constitution* and *Women Looking Ahead* magazine. Her awards include the GA Equality Political Animal Award, the Human Rights Campaign Community Leadership Award, and being named an Agnes Scott College Outstanding Young Alumna.

Cunningham received her bachelor of arts degree from Agnes Scott College. She resides in Decatur and is employed by A.G. Edwards & Sons in capital markets.

Kecia A. Cunningham
Commissioner
City of Decatur, District 2

Benjamin R. DeCosta
Aviation General Manager
Hartsfield-Jackson Atlanta
International Airport

Benjamin R. DeCosta assumed leadership of Hartsfield-Jackson Atlanta International Airport in June of 1998. During his tenure, his priorities have been customer service, security and the airport's $6.2 billion capital expansion program.

In May of 2006, DeCosta commissioned the airport's long-awaited fifth runway, considered the most important runway in America. He and his team are committed to passenger delight and have developed a fitting mission statement: To be the world's best airport by exceeding customer expectations.

Under DeCosta's guidance, Hartsfield-Jackson continues to be the world's busiest airport, accommodating nearly 86 million passengers in 2005. Additionally, the Air Transport Research Society designated it the most efficient airport in the world for five consecutive years.

Formerly, DeCosta worked for the Port Authority of New York and New Jersey and served as the general manager of Newark International Airport.

A native New Yorker, DeCosta received a bachelor of arts degree in physics at Queens College and a juris doctorate from New York Law School. He also completed a program for senior executives at Harvard University.

Terri L. Denison
District Director
U.S. Small Business Administration

Terri Denison has served as the district director of the U.S. Small Business Administration, Georgia District Office since May of 2002. In this position, she manages the SBA's operations and delivery of financial assistance, entrepreneurial development, and 8(a) business development programs in Georgia.

During her tenure, the SBA's lending activity has increased over 142 percent with loans to African-American businesses increasing 398 percent. In 2004 she and the Georgia office received a Builder Award from the Georgia Microenterprise Network. In 2006 Terri was recognized as one of "Atlanta's Top 100 Black Women of Influence" by the Atlanta Business League and included in the *Atlanta Business Chronicle*'s "Who's Who in Banking and Finance" issue.

Terri holds a bachelor's degree in American government from Cornell University and a master's degree in urban studies from Trinity University in San Antonio, Texas. She is a member of the Georgia Economic Developers Association and the Georgia Department of Economic Development's Entrepreneurs and Small Business Coordinating Network.

A native of Corpus Christi, Texas, Terri enjoys international travel and ballroom and Latin dancing.

Roslyn Neal Dickerson is senior vice president and chief diversity officer for InterContinental Hotels Group (IHG), the world's largest hotel group by number of rooms. She is responsible for leading, developing and implementing diversity and inclusion strategies. This includes assessing IHG's organizational needs and identifying solutions that will contribute to a more diverse and inclusive organization. She also furthers the development of IHG's external relationships and partnerships with diverse suppliers, vendors and franchise prospects.

Dickerson most recently served as corporate vice president, chief diversity officer for Honeywell. Joining in 2002, she initiated a complete redesign of strategy, operating structure and governance model for Honeywell's diversity management and provided leadership for business unit leaders. Before her tenure at Honeywell, Dickerson held various senior-level positions with several financial services organizations in New York.

Dickerson earned her bachelor of science degree in education and health sciences from Boston University and holds an MBA from Cornell University. She is a board member for the American Hotel & Lodging Association Multicultural and Diversity Advisory Council as well as the W.E.B. DuBois Society.

Roslyn Neal Dickerson
Senior Vice President &
Chief Diversity Officer
InterContinental Hotels Group

The Honorable Myra H. Dixon was appointed by Governor Roy Barnes to the State Court of Fulton County in 1998. Dixon presides over civil cases involving product liability, personal injury, medical malpractice, contracts and criminal misdemeanors.

Dixon's legal career has been one of much distinction and diversity. Previously, she was a partner at Thomas, Kennedy, Sampson & Patterson, assistant U.S. attorney for the Northern District of Georgia, assistant public defender in Fulton County, and associate to general counsel of the U.S. Navy.

Dixon was honored in the 2005 edition of *Who's Who in Black Atlanta®* and *Black Judges in America®*. She was awarded the Pinnacle Leadership Award in 2002 by Delta Sigma Theta Sorority, Inc., East Point Chapter, and was honored as an Outstanding Former Memphian by the City of Memphis.

A graduate of Tennessee State University, Dixon received her bachelor of science degree in 1975. She graduated cum laude from the Howard University School of Law in 1978.

She is married to attorney Pat D. Dixon Jr., and they have two children, Kyra and Pat.

The Honorable Myra H. Dixon
Judge
State Court of Fulton County

Thomas W. Dortch Jr.
President & Chief Executive Officer
TWD, Inc.

Thomas W. Dortch Jr. is president and chief executive officer of TWD, Inc., a consulting firm with emphasis on business development, public relations and fund-raising. He is also chairman emeritus of 100 Black Men of America's national board of directors. Under his guidance, the 100 expanded to include 102 chapters throughout the United States, Africa, England and the West Indies.

The author of *The Miracles of Mentoring: The Joy of Investing in Our Future*, Dortch is also the voice of the 100's *Four for the Future*.

Dortch is the recipient of numerous awards and honors including a U.S. Presidential Citation for Volunteerism and the Martin Luther King Jr. Distinguished Service Award. He was among *Ebony* and *Atlanta Business Chronicle*'s 100 Most Influential Black Leaders in 2004.

Dortch earned a bachelor's degree in sociology and pre-professional social work from Fort Valley State University, and a master of arts degree in criminal justice administration from Clark Atlanta University. He also attended Georgia State University as a Ford fellow in the urban administration program, and he holds two honorary doctor's degrees.

Curley M. Dossman Jr.
President
Georgia-Pacific Foundation

Curley Dossman is responsible for community relations program development for plant communities and administration of the Georgia-Pacific Foundation and its community programs department. Dossman works closely with executive leadership on Atlanta- and Georgia-focused programs important to the company. In directing the activities of the Georgia-Pacific Foundation, he is responsible for developing and implementing the company's overall philanthropic strategies.

A member of numerous boards of directors, Dossman's board memberships include the Metro Atlanta YMCA, the National Black Arts Festival, the Professional Association of Georgia Educators, the High Museum of Art, Leadership Atlanta, Camp Best Friends (chairman), and the Atlanta Downtown Improvement District (chairman). Likewise, he is executive committee chairman for Great Schools Atlanta, vice chairman of operations for 100 Black Men of America, and chairman of the Metro Atlanta Chamber of Commerce education committee.

Curley received his bachelor's degree from Morehouse College in 1973, and his law degree from Washington University School of Law in 1976.

A native of Louisiana, Curley's wife, Jennifer, is an honors graduate of Spelman College, and their son, Jonathan, is attending Morehouse College.

A native Atlantan, Dr. Clinton E. Dye Jr. attended the Atlanta Public Schools and graduated from Morehouse College, Atlanta University and Clark Atlanta University. He has more than 40 years of professional experience in the field of human services.

Dye is a veteran of the Urban League movement, having previously served as director of community services and vice president of the Atlanta Urban League. From 1990 to 2000, he held senior management positions in the Georgia Department of Human Resources before returning to the Urban League as president and chief executive officer.

Dye has served on several committees including the Governor's Advisory Council on Mental Health for the State of Georgia; the Regional Development Advisory Council for the Atlanta Regional Commission; and the board of visitors at Grady Memorial Hospital.

Dye serves in adjunct faculty positions at Spelman College, and the Whitney M. Young Jr. School of Social Work at Clark Atlanta University.

He and his wife of 41 years, Dr. Myrtice Willis Dye, are the proud parents of two sons, Clinton E. Dye III and Trevin Gerard Dye.

Clinton E. Dye Jr., Ph.D.
President & Chief Executive Officer
Atlanta Urban League, Inc.

DeKalb County Commissioner Burrell Ellis is a partner with the national law firm of Epstein Becker & Green. He is a renowned public speaker, a dedicated community volunteer, a husband and a father.

Ellis holds a degree in economics and finance from the Wharton School of the University of Pennsylvania, and a doctor of jurisprudence degree from the University of Texas School of Law. At the University of Texas, he was elected student body president of one of the nation's largest and most prestigious law schools.

As presiding officer of the DeKalb County Board of Commissioners, Ellis has been deeply involved with the National Association of Counties (NACo), a bipartisan organization that works to protect the interests of counties across the country. He currently serves as vice chair of NACo's Large Urban County Caucus (LUCC). LUCC plays a vital role in influencing national policy because it represents the 100 largest urban counties in the U.S.

Burrell's community involvement is extensive and his volunteer activities have included leadership roles in his church, 100 Black Men, Big Brothers and the Georgia Democratic Party.

The Honorable Burrell Ellis
Commissioner, District 4
DeKalb County

Atlanta's
MOST INFLUENTIAL

Celebrating African-American Achievements

Marvin R. Ellison
President, Northern Division
The Home Depot

Marvin R. Ellison is president of the northern division for The Home Depot. He joined the company in 2002. During this time, he has held several officer positions including senior vice president of global logistics, vice president of logistics and vice president of loss prevention. In his current role, Ellison is responsible for the sales, profit and operations of more than 650 stores in the Midwest and the Northeast. He has more than 110,000 employees in his division and is responsible for more than one third of the total sales volume of The Home Depot U.S. stores.

Ellison has 23 years of retail experience with an extensive background in operations. Prior to joining The Home Depot, he spent 15 years with Target stores in a variety of operational roles.

Ellison earned a business administration degree in marketing from the University of Memphis and a master of business administration degree from Emory University.

He and his wife, Sharyn, and their two children reside in Marietta, Georgia.

Sidmel Estes-Sumpter
President
Breakthrough, Inc.

Sidmel Estes-Sumpter, president of Breakthrough, Inc., a dynamic executive media management-consulting firm, has worked in the industry for more than a quarter of a century.

She received her bachelor's and master's degrees as an honors graduate of Northwestern University's Medill School of Journalism, and later returned to be honored with one of Northwestern's most prestigious recognitions, an Alumni Service award, after she was elected president of the Northwestern University Black Alumni Association.

Estes-Sumpter made history in 1991 when she was elected as the first woman president of the National Association of Black Journalists. She has won several local Emmy awards and in 2003 received the highest honor of the television academy, the Silver Circle award, which celebrates 25 years of service in the television industry. She was also honored in 1988 with the National Association of Media Women's Media Woman of the Year award.

She has been married for more than 23 years and has two beautiful boys, Joshua and Sidney, who are growing into wonderful young men each and every day.

272 WHO'S WHO

S teven R. Ewing is president of Wade Ford, a dealership that offers new, pre-owned, and fleet vehicles from three properties located on South Cobb Drive in Smyrna, Georgia. Consistently a top-performing franchise, Wade Ford is the recipient of the President's Award for outstanding customer service.

A native of New Jersey, Steve began his career at Apple Chevrolet in Fairlawn, New Jersey. After he opened his first car dealership, Crossroads Ford, in 1989, Ford Motor Company purchased the franchise in 1992 and offered Steve a position with Ford overseeing the company's franchises.

Steve left Ford Motor Company to open Champion Fordland in 1993 under the auspices of Ford's Dealer Development Program. Within four years, he paid off Ford's stock in his dealership. He then opened Champion Nissan in Scranton, Pennsylvania, followed by Champion Lincoln Mercury in Hazelton, Pennsylvania. Steve sold the dealerships in 2002 and purchased Wade Ford in Georgia.

A graduate of Delaware State University, Steve resides in Atlanta with his wife, Terri, and his two children, Halle and Stephen.

Steven R. Ewing
President
Wade Ford

I saac Newton Farris Jr., nephew of Dr. Martin Luther King, Jr., is president and chief executive officer of the Martin Luther King, Jr. Center for Nonviolent Social Change. The organization is dedicated to educating the public about Dr. King's life, work and teachings. Isaac oversees the King Center's programs, serves as the primary spokesman, and meets with heads of state and business, religious, academic and grassroots leaders.

Isaac has also served as Georgia field coordinator of Walter Mondale's presidential campaign, deputy manager for the reelection of Andrew Young as mayor of Atlanta, and campaign manager for Martin Luther King III in his successful bid to become a Fulton County commissioner. In addition, he held executive posts in government and served as president of Clean Air Industries, Inc., a company that has provided innovative leadership in environmental reclamation and development of clean-burning combustion engines.

Isaac attended his uncle's alma mater, Morehouse College, where he majored in political science. His background and experience have given him a unique perspective on many of the pressing issues of our times.

Isaac Newton Farris Jr.
President & Chief Executive Officer
The King Center

Gwendolyn Keyes Fleming
District Attorney
DeKalb County

Gwen Keyes Fleming is the first African American and first female elected as DeKalb County district attorney. Previously solicitor-general for DeKalb County, she was the first African American, first female, and youngest person elected to that position.

Gwen was one of *Georgia Trend*'s Top 40 Under 40 and an Outstanding Atlanta Awardee. *Ebony* recognized her as a Woman to Watch in the 21st Century. The Georgia Supreme Court's Commission on Professionalism recognized Gwen for community service in 2001. The DeKalb Rotary Council honored her in 2003 for distinguished service and leadership.

Gwen is the immediate past president of the Emory Law School Alumni Association. She is an active member of the DeKalb Lawyers Association, the DeKalb Bar Association, the Georgia Association of Black Women Attorneys, the National Council of Negro Women, and the NAACP. Likewise, she is a member of the 1999 Leadership DeKalb class and the 2000 Leadership Georgia class.

Gwen received a bachelor of science degree in finance from Douglass College and graduated from Emory University School of Law.

A New Jersey native, Gwen is married to Randal Fleming.

The Honorable Virgil Fludd
Representative, 66th District
Georgia House of Representatives

The Honorable Virgil Fludd is a state representative for the State of Georgia's 66th District. He serves on the administrative services, natural resources and education committees, and he is the secretary of the banking committee.

Fludd is also president and chief executive officer of the Carvir Group, Inc., an executive recruiting firm with clients nationwide. He has more than 20 years of sales, marketing, management and consulting experience. Previously, he worked for Bank of America and Xerox Corporation.

Fludd serves on several boards including the board of trustees for the Clayton State University Foundation; the board of directors of the Jordan Foundation; and the board of advisors for Christian City and the Community Foundation of Fayette County. He is a founding member of the NBCSI Financial Literary Task Force, a graduate of Leadership Fayette, and a mentor with the Georgia 100 Mentor Exchange Program.

Virgil holds a bachelor of arts degree in economics from Davidson College.

He has been married to Carolyn for more than 20 years, and they are the proud parents of Christine and Brendan.

Mr. Darryl Ford is a highly-motivated professional with a successful background in marketing, management, employee development, customer handling and automotive operations.

Ford began his automotive career with the Chrysler Corporation in 1987 and held a variety of marketing positions before moving his family to Atlanta. There, he opened Stone Mountain Chrysler Jeep Dodge, which is currently DaimlerChrysler's newest minority dealer in the metro Atlanta area. Stone Mountain is a family-owned-and-operated dealership determined to build lifelong relationships within the community.

As owner and general manager, Ford manages daily operations, provides vision, leadership and the inspiration to create an environment that motivates employees to effectively implement business plan objectives. He brings passion and a wealth of work and life experiences to support this role. His automotive retail experience provides the development needed to successfully implement daily operations. By combining quality products with the professional customer care, his organization is committed to providing the very best to the community served, the people employed and the brand represented.

Darryl Ford
General Manager
Stone Mountain Chrysler Jeep Dodge

Judge Crystal A. Gaines presently serves on the Municipal Court of Atlanta. Prior to becoming a judge in 2001, she was chief public defender in the City Court of Atlanta for four years. She has also worked with the Fulton County Conflict Defender, Inc., the Georgia Indigent Defense Counsel, the Georgia State Employees Union and the Georgia House of Representatives.

Gaines is a graduate of Albany State University, North Carolina Central University and Atlanta Law School.

Active in the legal community, Gaines currently serves with the Georgia Association of Black Women Attorneys, the Georgia Association of Women Attorneys and the indigent defense committee of the State Bar of Georgia. She is also involved in the National Bar Association, the Atlanta Bar Association, the Council of Municipal Court Judges, the judicial section of the Gate City Bar Association and the DeKalb Technical School paralegal program board.

Gaines is the wife of Eric Bond. She is a member of Friendship Baptist Church and Zeta Phi Beta Sorority, Inc.

The Honorable
Crystal A. Gaines
Judge
Municipal Court of Atlanta

N. Russell Goldston IV
Senior Vice President
Business Development
The Gourmet Companies

N.Russell Goldston IV is senior vice president of business development for The Gourmet Companies. Russell's current areas of concentration are in the development and expansion of The Gourmet Companies' services in the international food service arena, as well as the development of creative, alternative lifestyle, health-conscious food products and concepts. Recently, in coordination with Soul Vegetarian Restaurants, he created Taste Buds Health Foods, specializing in vegan alternative food products. The first product to come forth is a line of premium quality, non-dairy, frozen soy "kreme."

In addition to his tenure at The Gourmet Companies, Russell has had the opportunity to live in northeast Africa; the city of Dimona in southern Israel; and the East African country of Uganda. While in Uganda, Russell had the opportunity to establish the country's first pan-African radio station. He was also able to travel to Tanzania, Kenya, Rwanda, the Democratic Republic of Congo, Ethiopia and Egypt.

Russell is a graduate of the Cornell University School of Hotel Administration. He enjoys music, golf, world travel, hermeneutical scholarship and pan-African pursuits.

The Honorable
Phaedra Graham
Mayor
The City of Riverdale

When the Honorable Phaedra Graham became mayor of Riverdale, Georgia, she set a new standard. She became Clayton County and Riverdale's first African-American mayor. With hard work and a strong team of supporters, Graham's vision for a new Riverdale was set in motion in 2003.

Graham loves being the "People's Mayor" because she enjoys direct involvement in government and the opportunity to enhance the lives of others. She lives by her own words, "As in life, and in any race, enter to win."

Graham participates in the Clayton County National Council of Negro Women, Toastmasters, the East Point/College Park Chapter of Delta Sigma Theta Sorority, Inc. and many other community groups.

A graduate of the University of North Florida and Clark Atlanta University, Graham knows the importance of getting a good education and using that knowledge to improve the lives of people in the community. Currently, she is a high school English instructor in Clayton County, Georgia. Graham loves to read, listen to classical music, and she aspires to become an author of children's books.

John Thomas Grant Jr. is chief executive officer of 100 Black Men of Atlanta, Inc. (100) and has been a member of the organization for almost 20 years. As chief executive officer, Grant is responsible for managing the organization's day-to-day growth and direction. Under his leadership, 100 has attained a level of visibility and prominence that underscores the importance of the philanthropic mission established by its founders.

Grant serves on several boards including the Alliance Theatre, the American Red Cross Southern Region, True Colors Theatre Company and the Atlanta Convention & Visitors Bureau. He also serves on the Emory University board of advisors.

Grant's achievements have been recognized throughout Atlanta. He has participated in such programs as Leadership Atlanta, Leadership Georgia and the Diversity Leadership Academy. He was selected by the *Atlanta Business Chronicle* as one of the 96 Most Influential Atlantans and was voted an Outstanding Young Atlantan. Grant was selected as the WTBS Super Citizen of the Week. He has also received the President's Service Award and the Atlanta Technical College Foundation Bridge Builder Award.

John Thomas Grant Jr.
Chief Executive Officer
100 Black Men of Atlanta, Inc.

Garfield Hammonds Jr. is an executive member of the Georgia State Board of Pardons and Paroles. He served as parole board chairman in 1996. He also served as vice chair on Georgia's Peace Officers Standards and Training Council from 1996 to 2002.

Prior to joining the parole board in 1995, Hammonds served as commissioner of Georgia's Department of Children and Youth Services. He retired from the Drug Enforcement Administration (DEA) after serving 25 years as a special agent. During his tenure with the DEA, he served as country attaché in Kingston, Jamaica, and as special agent in charge of the DEA's southeast region. Hammonds was responsible for 19 offices throughout North Carolina, South Carolina, Tennessee and Georgia. Before his retirement in 1994, he received six Senior Executive Performance Awards, and President Clinton's Meritorious Senior Executive Performance Award.

Hammonds is an active member of 100 Black Men of Atlanta, Inc., Kappa Alpha Psi Fraternity, Inc., and the National Organization of Black Law Enforcement Executives. He also belongs to numerous professional law enforcement and civic organizations.

Garfield Hammonds Jr.
Executive Member
Georgia State Board of
Pardons and Paroles

Judge Glenda A. Hatchett
Syndicated TV Host
Sony Pictures Television

Judge Glenda A. Hatchett is the jurist of the award-winning television series, *Judge Hatchett*. The author of *Say What You Mean and Mean What You Say*, she serves as national spokesperson for CASA (Court Appointed Special Advocates).

After graduating from law school, Hatchett took a position at Delta Air Lines, where she was the highest-ranking African-American woman. She later accepted an appointment as chief presiding judge of the Fulton County Juvenile Court.

The local chapter of the National Bar Association selected Hatchett as Outstanding Jurist of the Year, and she won a Prism Award in 2003 for *Judge Hatchett*. The 100 Black Men of America named her Woman of the Year, and the Girl Scouts of America named her one of the 10 Women of Distinction.

Hatchett serves on the board of directors for the NFL's Atlanta Falcons and the Hospital Corporation of America.

She graduated from Mount Holyoke College and Emory University Law School. Emory named her Outstanding Alumni of the Year and presented her the Emory Medal.

An Atlanta native, Hatchett resides in Atlanta with her two sons.

The Honorable
Joseph B. Heckstall
Representative, 62nd District
Georgia House of Representatives

"Mr. Energizer," the Honorable Joseph B. Heckstall, is a successful lecturer, television talk show host, trainer and radio commentator. He has spent many years sharing his message of power-filled thinking, which reminds his audiences that there are no limited opportunities, only limited thoughts.

A New York City native, Joe earned his undergraduate degree from Saint Augustine College in Raleigh, North Carolina.

He is currently the state representative of Georgia's 62nd House District. Joe is also certified in Neuro-Linguistic Programming (NLP) and hypnotherapy language, which are innovative approaches to understanding and directing human experiences, communication and behavior. In addition, Joe is a real estate broker.

His most recent venture, however, is that of being an author. He released his first book, *Grandparents Aren't Goofy: Yes They Are, Too*, which captures his humorous side and offers his own experiences of the joys of grandparenting.

Joe and his wife, Andrea, have four children, an adopted niece, and two grandchildren. They reside in Atlanta.

Glenn Henderson is chairman and co-founder of AFC Worldwide Express, a global transportation company headquartered in Kennesaw, Georgia. Under his leadership, the company was established with one office in 1987. There are currently 15 offices in key cites nationwide. The company is tracking to exceed $100 million in sales by 2007.

AFC Worldwide Express was recognized as Small Business of the Year by Hallmark Cards and as Carrier of the Year for three consecutive years. AFC was relied upon to assist in delivering business and critical shipments to the White House, the FBI and other government agencies during the aftermath of 9/11.

Henderson has been featured on the *Minority Business Report,* a television broadcast of WGN and similar leadership broadcasts in Atlanta. Under his direction, AFC continues to remain consistent with its core values in developing and investing in people, as well as being involved in the community.

Henderson was born in Louisiana, grew up in Chicago and now lives in Georgia with his wife, Regina. He is the proud father of Valerie, Cameron and Allegra.

Glenn Henderson
Chairman & Co-Founder
AFC Worldwide Express, Inc.

Robert M. Henderson was named Atlanta regional director of the U.S. Department of Commerce's Minority Business Development Agency (MBDA) in October of 1994. Prior to joining MBDA, Henderson was deputy director for the U.S. Small Business Administration in Madison, Wisconsin. Additionally, he served in positions including deputy district director in U.S. Small Business Administration offices nationwide.

Henderson's civic and professional affiliations include Beta Epsilon Sigma, Phi Beta Sigma Fraternity, Inc., the Shriners, the Association of Government Accountants, and the Society of Government Meeting Planners. Likewise, he is a member of the Morris Brown College International Trade Institute advisory committee, the Atlanta Metro Kiwanis Club and the DeKalb Rotary Club. He also serves on the boards of directors for the Georgia Minority Supplier Development Council and the Wisconsin Minority Supplier Development Council.

Henderson is a retired military veteran who holds, among other medals, the Bronze Star for service in Vietnam.

Henderson attended the University of Alabama and the University of Nebraska, majoring in business. He is married to Ethel M. Dexter and has two children, six grandchildren, and four great-grandchildren.

Robert M. Henderson
Atlanta Regional Director
U.S. Department of Commerce
Minority Business Development Agency

Paul Hewitt
Head Basketball Coach
Georgia Institute of Technology

Named Georgia Institute of Technology's 12th head basketball coach in 2000, Paul Hewitt has led the Yellow Jackets to the NCAA tournament three times, including a berth in the national title game in 2004.

Hewitt has a record of 107-83 at Georgia Tech, and his overall record as a head coach is 173-110, with six post-season appearances in nine years. Ranked 17th among the nation's top 40 coaches by *Hoop Scoop*, Hewitt was given a new six-year contract in the spring of 2004. He earned his 100th victory on December 10, 2006.

Prior to arriving in Atlanta, Hewitt posted a 66-27 mark as head coach at Siena College. He spent five seasons as an assistant at Villanova University, and served for two years as assistant coach at Fordham University. Previously, he was a graduate assistant at Southern California and an assistant coach at Long Island University's C.W. Post.

Hewitt spent three years as junior varsity head coach at his alma mater, Westbury High School on Long Island, following graduation from St. John Fisher College.

The Honorable Juanita Hicks
Clerk
Superior Court of Fulton County

The Honorable Juanita Hicks is a dynamic, highly-effective elected official recognized for conceptualizing and implementing total automation and renovation of the Superior Court Clerk's Office. She coordinates the management of 205 professional, technical and clerical employees. She is directly responsible for overseeing the administration of an annual budget in excess of $12 million. Hicks has been elected to five terms as clerk of the Superior Court of Fulton County.

Some of her noteworthy achievements include creating a quality control panel to oversee document processing; installing public access computers for viewing real estate, civil, criminal and domestic records; and implementing an automated intangible tax system.

She is a former president and board member of both the National Association of Clerks, Recorders and Election Officials and the National Association for Court Management.

Hicks holds a bachelor of arts degree in history from Bennett College, and a master of science degree in urban administration from Georgia State University. She also completed doctoral studies in public administration at the University of Georgia.

Archibald B. Hill III is the director of Fannie Mae's Atlanta Partnership Office. The Atlanta Partnership Office is one of 55 offices in the nation that helps increase affordable rental and homeownership opportunities for low-, moderate- and middle-income families and first-time homebuyers. Hill is responsible for implementing HouseAtlanta, a ten-year, $26 billion program that finances affordable housing for 220,000 families in Atlanta and five surrounding counties, Clayton, Cobb, DeKalb, Fulton and Gwinnett.

Prior to joining Fannie Mae, Hill served as vice president and state director for community reinvestment at First Union National Bank of Georgia.

Hill is active in several organizations including the Atlanta Community Food Bank, 100 Black Men of Atlanta, Atlanta College of Art, Rotary Club of Atlanta and Leadership Atlanta.

Hill was appointed by Mayor Franklin to serve on the Mayor's Housing Task Force. He is also a member of the Mayor's Commission on Homelessness and chairman of the permanent supportive housing committee.

Hill graduated from Morehouse College with a degree in business management and marketing.

Archibald B. Hill III
Director
Atlanta Partnership Office
Fannie Mae

In 2004 Victor Hill was elected the first African-American sheriff of Clayton County. Since his election, Hill has created an anti-drug, anti-gang "Cobra" Unit to strike the county's rising crime rate; a proactive Stalking Unit to protect victims of domestic violence; the S.O.R.T. (Sexual Offender Registry & Tracking) Unit to protect children from sexual predators; and the SCCIP (Sheriff's Clean Community Initiative Program) to assist in cleaning roads and parks of graffiti and trash.

He is a Charleston, South Carolina native and attended Trident Technical College. A member of Phi Beta Sigma Fraternity, Inc. and a Prince Hall Mason, Hill began his law enforcement career at age 18 with the Charleston City Police Force. He became a certified police officer at age 21. He began studying martial arts at age 14 and at age 20 attained a first-degree black belt. Hill joined the Clayton County Police Force in 1992 and later became Clayton County's first African-American hostage negotiator.

In 2002 Hill was elected to the Georgia House of Representatives, District 81. He sponsored four bills that were passed into law.

Victor Hill
Sheriff
Clayton County

Richard L. Holmes
Senior Vice President
Metro Atlanta Region
Georgia Power

Richard Holmes is senior vice president of the metro Atlanta region for Georgia Power. He joined Georgia Power in 1974. In this role, he has operational responsibilities for Georgia Power's 1.2 million customers in the metropolitan Atlanta area.

Richard earned his bachelor's degree from Columbus State University and his master of business administration degree from Clark Atlanta University. He also completed the Harvard University Business School Program for Management Development.

Richard is chairman of the board of the Georgia State Department of Community Health. He serves on the boards of Literacy Action, the Kennesaw State University Foundation, the American Association of Blacks in Energy, the NAACP-Atlanta Branch, the Atlanta Beltline Partnership, the McPherson Local Planning Redevelopment Authority and the Atlanta Police Foundation. In 1999 he served as chairman of the Cobb Chamber of Commerce, becoming the first African American to lead the second-largest chamber of commerce in Georgia. He is a member of 100 Black Men of Atlanta.

A native of Columbus, Georgia, Richard and his wife, Linda, reside in Peachtree City. They have two sons, Stephen and Mark.

The Honorable
Robert A. Holmes
Representative, District 61
Georgia House of Representative

Bob Holmes has served 32 years in the Georgia legislature. A former chair of the Black Caucus, he has served on committees for education, governmental affairs and appropriations. He has successfully sponsored and passed more than 200 bills.

Bob received his bachelor's degree in political science from Shepherd College, and his master's degree and doctorate from Columbia University. He was a founding faculty member of the Ph.D. program in political science at Clark Atlanta University. Bob is an editorial board member of the *Journal of Social and Behavioral Sciences*, the *Journal of Black Political Economy* and *Phylon*, and is editor of *Status of Black Atlanta*. He retired as a distinguished professor in 2005.

Bob served as president of the National Conference of Black Political Scientists and the Association of Social and Behavioral Scientists. He has received numerous awards and a portion of I 285 in Atlanta is named the Bob Holmes Freeway.

A native of Shepherdstown, West Virginia, Bob is married to Gloria Carey Holmes. He is the father of Robert Jr., Donna and Darlene, and is grandfather of eight children.

Outside of the ring, Evander Holyfield continues to complete impossible dreams while helping others. A participant with the United States Olympic boxing team and the Boys and Girls Clubs of America, he is an advocate of youth. He founded the Evander Holyfield Foundation, which provides college scholarships to Atlanta high school students.

Born in Atmore, Alabama, Holyfield moved to Atlanta when he was 3. He began his boxing career at the age of 8 when he entered a peewee tournament. He went on to compile an amateur record of 160-14, with 75 knockouts. As an amateur boxer, Holyfield supported himself by pumping airplane fuel for Epps Air Service and as a swim instructor, working summers as a lifeguard. He would later become one of the most talked about Olympians of 1984.

In his historic heavyweight career, Evander the "Real Deal" Holyfield has 50 fights with 40 wins, eight losses, two draws and 26 knockouts. The first four-time heavyweight champion of the world, his most notable victories include wins over James "Buster" Douglas, George Foreman and Mike Tyson.

Evander Holyfield
Co-Vice Chair
Black Family Channel

Currently serving his third term, Paul Howard was first elected as district attorney of Fulton County in 1996, becoming the first African-American district attorney in Georgia history. He previously served as Fulton County solicitor general.

Howard's career began in 1976 as a City of Atlanta assistant solicitor. He left to join Fulton County as an assistant district attorney. Upon leaving the county, he joined the firm of Thomas, Kennedy, Sampson, Edward & Patterson.

Howard serves on the board of directors for the Partnership Against Domestic Violence, the Fulton County Child Advocacy Center, and Georgians for Children. He is a member of the Georgia Association of Black Elected Officials, the National Black Prosecutors Association and 100 Black Men of Atlanta. He has received numerous awards including the Georgia Women's Political Caucus Good Guy Award and Gammon Theological Seminary's Outstanding Community Service Award.

Howard graduated cum laude from Morehouse College, and earned a scholarship to Emory University's School of Law. While there, he served as president of the Black American Law Students Association and vice president of the Student Bar Association.

The Honorable
Paul L. Howard Jr.
District Attorney
Fulton County

Stephanie S. Hughley
Executive Producer
National Black Arts Festival

As executive producer of the National Black Arts Festival (NBAF), Stephanie S. Hughley has been responsible for creating the unique artistic vision of the festival since 1999. She is responsible for artistic and programmatic policy, external and community relations, fund development and strategic planning, and management.

As the founding artistic director of NBAF, Hughley conceptualized and implemented the artistic content for each festival. She was the theatre and dance producer for the Atlanta Committee for the Olympic Games Cultural Olympiad. She also played an integral role in creating the Olympic Arts Festival.

Currently, Hughley serves on the board of the Metro Atlanta Arts and Culture Coalition and the Atlanta Convention & Visitors Bureau. She is a member of the Association of Theatrical Press Agents and Managers.

Hughley was recognized as one of Atlanta's Top 100 Black Women of Influence in 2006 by the Atlanta Business League. She was also recognized by *Atlanta Woman* magazine as Woman of the Year in July of 2005.

Hughley is a graduate of Kent State University, Antioch College and Harvard University.

John W. Jackson
President & Chief Executive Officer
Bank of Atlanta

John W. Jackson has been in banking in Atlanta for more than 28 years. He has advanced through the leadership ranks of Atlanta's most prominent middle market banks. He spent 15 years with Bank South focused on retail banking, consumer lending, mortgage lending and commercial lending.

In 1991 Jackson moved to SouthTrust where he remained until December of 2004. His leadership responsibility at SouthTrust included serving as regional manager of East Metro in 1991 and managing an $800 million loan portfolio. In August of 2004, following the Wachovia acquisition announcement, Jackson became the Jacksonville, Florida regional chief executive officer to help prepare the bank for the merger. In December of 2004, he joined Atlanta Bancorporation and currently serves as president and chief executive officer of Bank of Atlanta, a community bank located in the Midtown area.

Mr. Jackson is a graduate of the University of Georgia with a bachelor of business administration degree.

Maurice E. Jenkins, southeast region vice president of the United Negro College Fund, directs the fund-raising activities of six southeast area offices, with an annual goal of $15.7 million. He is a graduate of the University of Maryland and attended Atlanta University.

Maurice serves on the boards of MEA, Atlanta Centennial YMCA and the Dr. Martin L. King Jr. National Memorial Project in Washington, D.C. He is a member of Alpha Phi Alpha Fraternity, Inc., Leadership Atlanta's Class of 2003, the Association of Fundraising Professionals, and the Diversity Leadership Academy, 2003 spring class. A charter member of 100 Black Men of DeKalb, he is chairperson of stewardship at Allgood Road United Methodist Church.

Maurice has earned numerous awards and commendations including the Anheuser-Busch/WVEE Citizen of the Week Award, the NAACP Charles L. Harper Leadership Award and the 2004 United Methodist Man of the Year Award of Allgood Road United Methodist Church. Likewise, for three years, he has received the UNCF President's Award for outstanding achievement.

Maurice and his wife, Gina, have a son, Maurice III, and a daughter, Mia.

Maurice E. Jenkins Jr.
Vice President, Southeast Region
United Negro College Fund, Inc.

Celeste Johnson is the first African American to be elected as state representative in Georgia District 75 in Clayton County. She will be serving as a freshman legislator in the 2007 legislative session. With a passion for the arts and education, Celeste sets a new precedent for the community.

Celeste enjoys involvement in organizations that directly impact the community and she is humble in accepting the opportunity to enhance and educate people on relevant issues.

An accomplished musician, Celeste is the fine arts lead teacher for Clayton County Public Schools. She has more than ten years of teaching experience and has performed in many different venues across the nation. She is a member of Delta Sigma Theta Sorority, Inc., the Georgia Music Educators Association and the National Arts and Recording Academy. Additionally, she serves with several community groups.

Celeste is a graduate of Florida State University and is very aware that education is the key to success. She is married to the Reverend Rod Johnson and has one daughter, Genesis.

The Honorable
Celeste Johnson
Representative, District 75
Georgia House of Representatives

The Honorable Hank Johnson
Representative
Georgia's 4th Congressional District
U.S. House of Representatives

The Honorable Hank Johnson (D-Ga.) represents Georgia's 4th Congressional District in the 110th Congress. Prior to his election to Congress, he served 12 years as a DeKalb County magistrate judge, five years as a county commissioner and three years as chair of the DeKalb budget committee.

Johnson has practiced law in DeKalb County for 27 years, handling civil and criminal cases. A staunch supporter of public education, he graduated from the District of Columbia Public Schools, Clark College and the Thurgood Marshall School of Law at Texas Southern University. His mother is a retired public school teacher and his father served as a high-ranking civil servant in the Kennedy and Johnson administrations.

Johnson's wife of 27 years and law partner is Mereda Davis Johnson. They have two children attending DeKalb Public Schools.

Khalil Johnson, CFE
General Manager
Georgia Dome

Khalil Johnson, CFE, became general manager of the Georgia Dome in 1989. He was project manager for the design and construction phase of the facility, which opened on schedule and under budget. He currently has responsibility for overall facility management, including special event marketing, operations, budget and staffing.

Previously, Johnson was director of event services for the Georgia World Congress Center, and sales manager and director of sales and services for the Washington Convention Center. Prior to his positions in Washington, D.C., he worked at the Georgia World Congress Center in the operations department.

Johnson has served on the boards of directors of the International Association for Exposition Management and the International Association of Auditorium Managers, which recognized him as a certified facility executive. He has also served on Super Bowl, NCAA Final Four, Olympic and Peach Bowl host committees. As a result, *The Atlanta Journal-Constitution* named Johnson one of the 25 Most Influential People in Georgia Sports.

Active in numerous local community organizations, Johnson is a frequent guest lecturer for the Georgia State University sports management master's degree program.

Lonnie Johnson is founder and president of Johnson Research & Development Co. Inc., and its spin-off companies, Excellatron Solid State and Johnson Electro-Mechanical Systems. These Atlanta-based companies are developing revolutionary energy technologies to harness, store and manage energy for a wide variety of applications.

With bachelor's, master's and doctorate degrees from Tuskegee University, Lonnie Johnson is a rocket scientist who has worked on space programs for the Air Force, NASA's jet propulsion laboratory and as an inventor with over 90 patents. While much of Johnson's early work flew on satellites to Jupiter, Saturn and Mars, perhaps his most famous invention is a toy, the SuperSoaker® water gun. Becoming the #1 selling toy in America just two years after its launch in 1989, it has since generated almost $1 billion in retail sales worldwide.

Johnson has been featured in numerous publications and science-related television productions. He serves on the boards of the Georgia Alliance for Children and the Hank Aaron "Chasing the Dream" Foundation, and he is a member of the 100 Black Men of Atlanta.

Lonnie Johnson
Founder & President
Johnson Research &
Development Co. Inc.

The Honorable Michael Johnson serves as a judge on the Superior Court of Fulton County. In this role, Johnson is responsible for presiding over all aspects of general civil cases including domestic and real estate matters and disputes emanating from the state legislature. Likewise, he presides over all aspects of felony criminal cases. Johnson actively participates in public speaking engagements designed to educate the public on the role of the judge and the judicial system.

Prior to ascending to the bench in 2005, Johnson argued before the Georgia Supreme Court and clerked for the Georgia Court of Appeals. He also practiced as a litigator in the areas of labor and employment law and insurance defense. Johnson practiced in the public sector as an assistant prosecutor both in DeKalb and Fulton Counties, in the Office of the Attorney General and as a special assistant U.S. attorney. He has served as chairman of the City of Atlanta board of ethics and is a member of numerous bar organizations.

Johnson graduated from Morehouse College and Syracuse University College of Law.

The Honorable
Michael Johnson
Judge
Superior Court of Fulton County

William E. Johnson III
City Manager
City of College Park

William E. Johnson III serves as city manager of the City of College Park, a municipality with more than 20,000 citizens, 400 employees and corporate citizens that include the world's busiest airport, Hartsfield-Jackson International Airport. The first African-American city manager in the city's 110-year history, he is responsible for all city departments including fire, police, power, finance, personnel and the Georgia International Convention Center, amongst others.

Joining College Park in 2005, Johnson has a distinguished career in public administration that includes serving as deputy county administrator of King George County, Virginia and deputy city manager of Richmond, Virginia. His other career highlights include director of finance and county administrator positions for Prince George County, Virginia.

Johnson holds an MBA degree from Averett College and an undergraduate degree in accounting from Hampton University. He is a member of the Georgia Municipal Association, the Georgia City-County Management Association, the National Forum for Black Public Administrators (NFBPA), and Kappa Alpha Psi Fraternity, Inc. Recently named vice chairman of NFBPA's membership committee, Johnson is a member of their fund development committee.

Brenda Watts Jones, Ph.D.
President
Atlanta Technical College

Dr. Brenda Watts Jones is president of Atlanta Technical College, the largest single-site technical college in Georgia. She oversees a budget of more than $22 million and a staff of 500. As the first and only African-American woman to lead a technical college in the state, she is recognized as a visionary trailblazer.

Jones advances education through a multitude of board appointments, memberships and honors. She heads the President's Council of the Georgia Department of Technical and Adult Education. She is active in the Georgia Economic Development Association, the National Coalition of 100 Black Women, the Atlanta Workforce Development Agency, the Metro Regional Educational Service Agency, the Fulton County Workforce Development Agency and Project GRAD. She is a founding member of the Atlanta Health Services CEO Forum, and the Atlanta Business League named her one of Atlanta's most influential women.

Jones is an active member of Cascade United Methodist Church. She and her husband, Morris, have a 12-year-old son, Brandon.

In November of 2004, the Honorable Emanuel D. Jones was elected to the Georgia Senate, Tenth District. Jones also owns the Atlanta area's third-largest African-American-owned business. He is president and owner of Legacy Ford of McDonough; Legacy Toyota of Union City; Legendary Ford-Mercury of Marion, North Carolina and ANSA Automotive in Macon and Los Angeles, California.

Valedictorian of West Fulton High School in 1977, Jones was commissioned as a second lieutenant in the U.S. Army Corps of Engineers in 1980, eventually becoming a captain. He holds a master of business administration degree from Columbia University and a bachelor's degree from the University of Pennsylvania.

Jones is chairman of the Henry County YMCA and Henry County's United Way campaign. His honors include Businessman of the Year in 2005 from the Concerned Black Clergy of Atlanta, the Ford Motor Minority Dealer Executive Director's Award in 2003, and *Black Enterprise*'s Top 100 Minority-Owned Companies (2000-2004).

Jones resides in Ellenwood with his wife, Gloria, sons, Emanuel II and Elam and daughter, Emani. He is a member of the Shiloh Baptist Church in McDonough.

The Honorable
Emanuel D. Jones
Senator, Tenth District
Georgia Senate

A teacher by training, Ingrid Saunders Jones now works for The Coca-Cola Company. A Detroit native, Jones earned a bachelor's degree at Michigan State University and a master's degree in education at Eastern Michigan University. She has held leadership positions in the educational, nonprofit, city, government and corporate sectors.

As senior vice president of corporate external affairs, Jones directs The Coca-Cola Company in community, humanitarian and civic affairs. As chair of The Coca-Cola Foundation, she leads the company's philanthropic commitment to education. Under her leadership, the foundation has contributed more than $150 million to education initiatives that increase access to higher education. Jones also serves on the board of The Coca-Cola Scholars Foundation, providing scholarships to high school students, and Camp Coca-Cola, a leadership development program.

Jones chairs the United Way of Metropolitan Atlanta board of directors. She is a member of the Andrew Young School of Policy Studies at Georgia State University, the Rotary Club of Atlanta, the Desmond Tutu Peace Foundation, Clark Atlanta University and the Woodruff Arts Center.

Jones received the National Urban League's 2004 Leadership Award.

Ingrid Saunders Jones
Senior Vice President
The Coca-Cola Company

Atlanta's
MOST INFLUENTIAL

T he Honorable Vernon Jones is the chief executive officer of DeKalb County, Georgia, overseeing a $2.6 billion budget in the state's second most populous county. He is the youngest person ever elected to this position, one that is unlike any other political leadership post in Georgia. Jones presides over the twice-monthly meetings of the board and manages the day-to-day county operations involving 7,000 employees.

Jones' strategic public policy blueprint will leave a lasting legacy upon DeKalb County and the state of Georgia. His demonstrated leadership has enabled him to enact many key measures, and is a testament to the bipartisan support that he has enjoyed.

A graduate of Harvard's John F. Kennedy School of Government's Executive Program, Jones serves on many boards that impact lives in Georgia and the nation.

Jones community and civic affiliations include New Birth Missionary Baptist Church. He is a founding member of Kappa Alpha Psi Fraternity, Inc., Stone Mountain Alumni Chapter, Advocates for Seniors and Youth Prevention Services, Inc.

The Honorable Vernon Jones
Chief Executive Officer
DeKalb County

D r. B. Waine Kong is a member of the Georgia Bar and an educational psychologist. He held several positions before assuming his present responsibilities with the Association of Black Cardiologists, Inc. (ABC) in 1996. He was director of the Urban Cardiology Research Center in Baltimore and director of research and grants at Provident Hospital.

The *Georgia Informer* designated Kong one of the 15 Most Intriguing Citizens of Georgia in 2002. He is a deacon at Providence Missionary Baptist Church, and a member of Alpha Phi Alpha Fraternity, Inc. He has published widely and made presentations in Egypt, Israel, the Virgin Islands, Zimbabwe, Cameroon, Nigeria, South Africa and Kenya.

Professionally, Kong has worked with ABC's leaders for 15 years to develop it into a bona fide institution that is making a difference in peoples' lives. ABC's slogan is "Children should know their grandparents and become GREAT grandparents themselves."

Kong suggests that his greatest accomplishments are marrying a good wife, Dr. Stephanie Kong, having four successful children, Jillian, Fredie, Melanie and Aleron, and having three happy grandchildren, MacKenzie, Brooks and Audrey.

Dr. B. Waine Kong
Chief Executive Officer
Association of Black Cardiologists, Inc.

Atlanta's
MOST INFLUENTIAL

J ohn Lewis is serving his tenth term representing Georgia's 5th Congressional District, which encompasses the city of Atlanta, parts of Fulton, DeKalb and Clayton counties.

Lewis, the son of sharecroppers, was born on February 21, 1940 outside of Troy, Alabama. He grew up on his family's farm and attended segregated public schools in Pike County, Alabama. By 1963 Lewis was recognized as one of the "Big Six" leaders of the civil rights movement.

Having braved more than 40 arrests, physical attacks and serious injuries, Lewis remains a devoted advocate of the philosophy of nonviolence.

In 1977 President Jimmy Carter appointed Lewis to direct ACTION and its more than 250,000 volunteers. Lewis' first electoral success was his election to Atlanta City Council in 1981.

Lewis holds a bachelor's degree from Fisk University. He is a graduate of the American Baptist Theological Seminary and holds numerous honorary degrees.

John and his wife, Lillian, live in Atlanta. Lillian is the director of external affairs for the office of research and sponsored programs at Clark Atlanta University. They have one son, John Miles.

The Honorable John Lewis
Representative
Georgia's 5th Congressional District
U.S. House of Representatives

E bony magazine named Joseph Lowery one of the nation's 15 greatest black preachers: "The consummate voice of biblical-social relevancy, a focused prophetic voice, speaking truth to power." Additionally, the NAACP labeled him "Dean of the civil rights movement."

Co-founder with Martin Luther King, Jr. of SCLC, Lowery served as president and CEO from 1977-1998. King named him chair of the delegation, delivering the demands of the 1965 Selma-Montgomery March to Governor Wallace. Lowery is a founder of the National Black Leadership Forum and serves as chairman emeritus.

Lowery was one of the first five arrested at the South African embassy in Washington D.C. in the Free South Africa movement. Former pastor at Atlanta's oldest predominantly black United Methodist congregation for 18 years, Lowery added thousands of members and a 240-unit housing development. Likewise, he was pastor at Cascade United Methodist Church from 1986-1992. Upon retirement, he left ten acres of land, $1 million and plans for a new edifice.

Lowery is also credited with helping black farmers win a $2 billion federal court settlement (reparations) against the U.S. Department of Agriculture.

Rev. Dr. Joseph Echols Lowery
Co-Founder, President Emeritus
Southern Christian Leadership Conference

Sheila Maddox
President
Sheila Maddox, Inc.

As president of Sheila Maddox, Inc. and associate broker with Coldwell Banker Residential Brokerage, Sheila Maddox has been the voice of experience in Atlanta real estate for more than two decades. She is recognized and respected for her integrity, competence, business acumen, customer service and civic involvement.

Sheila is consistently ranked among Coldwell Banker's top one percent. She received the International President's Elite Award, recognizing the top Coldwell Banker agents internationally. She also received the Atlanta Board of Realtors Phoenix Award in 2006 and is a member of the Empire Board of Realtists Million Dollar Club. Sheila is the founding president of the Southwest Atlanta Real Estate Focus Group.

An Atlanta native, Sheila graduated magna cum laude from Howard University. She served on the Howard University board of trustees and is a past president of the Howard University Alumni Association-Atlanta Club.

An actress and voice-over talent, Sheila serves on the executive board of the Screen Actors Guild of Georgia.

Sheila is the daughter of Atlanta City Councilman Jim Maddox and retired Atlanta Public Schools teacher Alice Wise Maddox.

The Honorable
Clarence Terrell Martin
Councilmember, District Ten
Atlanta City Council

An Atlanta native, the Honorable Clarence Terrell "C. T." Martin received a presidential appointment to the White House Office of Domestic Affairs in 1972, and was elected to the Atlanta City Council in a 1990 special election. His career includes tireless activism and advocacy for civil rights, higher education, civic citizenship development for African-American youth, equal opportunity for economic development in the disenfranchised small business entrepreneurial community, adequate family recreation opportunities, and public safety as key budget, policy and program priorities.

Martin holds a master's degree from Atlanta University, a bachelor's degree from Shaw University, and is a graduate of Leadership Atlanta.

Some of Martin's career highlights include founding Youthfest, an annual civic leadership development event for 3,000-plus youth, securing design and construction funding for the $20 million Adamsville Natatorium, and impacting college minority recruitment policy nationwide for 20 years by serving in leadership capacities for NSSFNS.

A recipient of some 150 community service awards, Martin is a board member of the Southwest Hospital Medical Center Foundation, the West End Medical Center and Another Way Out, Inc.

D r. Walter E. Massey is president of Morehouse College, the nation's largest liberal arts institution for men. Massey is a former provost and senior vice president of the University of California system, former director of the National Science Foundation and founding director of the Argonne National Laboratory at the University of Chicago. He received a bachelor's degree from Morehouse, and master's and doctorate degrees from Washington University, St. Louis.

Massey is a member of the Atlanta University Center Council of Presidents, the Atlanta Committee for Progress, the Atlanta Regional Commission for Higher Education, the Rotary Club of Atlanta and the President's Council of Advisors on Science and Technology. Also, he is a board member of the Atlanta Symphony Orchestra, the Marine Biological Laboratory and Great Schools Atlanta.

Massey serves on the boards of the Gates Millennium Scholars Advisory Council, the Mellon Foundation, the Commonwealth Fund and the board of regents of the Smithsonian Institution.

Born in Hattiesburg, Mississippi, he and his wife, Shirley Anne, have two sons, Keith and Eric.

Dr. Walter E. Massey
President
Morehouse College

R andall March is a consumer bank first vice president regional manager for Washington Mutual's metropolitan Atlanta market. He is responsible for service management to banking customers in the metropolitan Atlanta market in 24 stores with more than 200 employees.

A 19-year banking veteran, Randall began his career as a teller with Great Western Bank in California. Over the years, he has held positions as a personal financial representative, loan officer, operations manager, sales manager and financial center manager. His promotion to regional manager relocated him to the Atlanta area in 2003. Before joining Washington Mutual, Randall spent ten years as a manager at Edison Brothers, a clothing retailer.

Randall has received numerous awards at Washington Mutual, including the prestigious Premier Group Award in 2000, 2001 and 2003. He also received the 2000 Angels Among Us Award for his business and community partnership involvement in San Diego.

A native of Danville, Illinois, Randall received a bachelor of science degree in business administration from San Diego State University. He and his wife, Terri, have three sons, John, Bryson and Cameron.

Randall March
First Vice President
Regional Manager
Washington Mutual Bank

The Honorable Harold Melton
Justice
Georgia Supreme Court

On July 1, 2005, Harold Melton was appointed to the Georgia Supreme Court by Governor Sonny Perdue. Previously, Melton served as executive counsel to Governor Perdue.

Melton spent 11 years in the Georgia Department of Law. He dealt with issues ranging from the creation of the Georgia Lottery Corporation to the administration of Georgia's tobacco settlement. Prior to joining the Governor's Office, Melton served as section leader over the Consumer Interests Division.

Melton earned a bachelor's degree from Auburn University and a juris doctorate from the University of Georgia. He previously served as a volunteer leader of Young Life Ministries for 11 years. He is currently a member of Atlanta Youth Academies and director of the teen ministry at Southwest Christian Fellowship Church.

In 2005 Melton was named a Georgia Super Lawyer by *Atlanta Magazine*. He was also featured in *Georgia Trend* magazine's 40 Under 40 Rising Stars in Georgia.

A native of Washington, D.C., Melton grew up in East Point and Marietta. He lives in Atlanta with his wife, Kimberly, and their three children.

**The Honorable
Steen Miles**
Senator, District 43
Georgia Senate

The Honorable Steen Miles represents southeast DeKalb and Rockdale Counties in the Georgia Senate. A journalist-turned-lawmaker, Miles is an outspoken advocate for children, consumers and special needs citizens.

As a freshman legislator, Miles introduced legislation to curb abuses in the title pawn industry and to provide affordable health care for Georgia children. She also toured the state, educating rural and elderly Georgians about the state's repressive photo identification bill. In May of 2006, the Stennis Institute chose Miles among 25 southern female policymakers for its prestigious Pacesetter Award.

Miles is a three-time Emmy Award-winner and is known as a pioneer among African Americans in broadcast journalism. In 1999 she left WXIA-TV for public service, capping a 30-year broadcasting career, which began in her hometown of South Bend, Indiana. There, she was the first black female television news reporter. She currently hosts the award-winning cable television show, *Faith and the City Forum*, a faith-based discussion of current events and public policy.

Miles attended Ball State University. She is the mother of two adult daughters and has two grandchildren.

The Honorable Yvette Miller is the first African-American woman on the Court of Appeals of Georgia. In 2006 she was reelected statewide by the people of Georgia to a second six-year term.

Miller serves on the board of visitors of Mercer Law School and the board of directors of the judicial section of the Atlanta Bar Association. She is a member of the Azalea City Chapter of The Links, Inc., a board member of the Georgia Association of Women Lawyers, and an honorary member on the advisory board of the Girl Scout Council of Northwest Georgia.

Miller served as chair of the Georgia Student Finance Commission, which regulates the HOPE Scholarship; a trustee of Leadership Georgia; and vice president of the Georgia Association of Black Women Attorneys. She was selected to attend the 2006 Sir Richard May Seminar on International Law in The Hague, Netherlands.

Miller is a member of Cascade United Methodist Church and a lifelong member of Steward Chapel AME. She is the daughter of Mr. and Mrs. Conrad Miller, and has one sibling, Dr. Conrad Miller Jr.

**The Honorable
M. Yvette Miller**
Judge
Court of Appeals of Georgia

Mercedes Miller is the assistant executive director for the second-largest convention center in Georgia, the Georgia International Convention Center (GICC).

A native of Atlanta, Mercedes began her hospitality career in sales, working for the Stouffer Waverly Hotel. She was part of the opening team for the Stouffer Concourse Hotel at Hartsfield-Jackson Atlanta International Airport. She started with the GICC as a national sales manager, advancing to director of sales and then to her current position.

Mercedes attributes her success in large part to her community involvement. She is the president of the Draper Boys & Girls Club of Metro Atlanta. Mercedes serves on the board of directors for the Clayton County Convention and Visitors Bureau and the Old National Merchants' Association. She also sits on the Georgia American Red Cross Minority Recruitment advisory board.

Mercedes is a member of the International Association of Assembly Managers and the American Society of Association Executives. She has been honored as one of Atlanta's most interesting personalities and a leader in her community by her inclusion in *Who's Who in Black Atlanta®*.

Mercedes Miller
Assistant Executive Director
Georgia International
Convention Center

MOST INFLUENTIAL

The Honorable Billy Mitchell
Representative, District 88
Georgia House of Representatives

Billy Mitchell was elected to the Georgia House of Representatives in 2002. He sponsored more legislation signed into law during his first term then any other freshman legislator, including the landmark advanced voting law. His colleagues selected him to receive the Georgia Legislative Black Caucus Freshman Legislator of the Year award.

Billy's rise in the legislature was recognized in his second term when his colleagues awarded him their highest honor, the Georgia Legislative Black Caucus Legislator of the Year award.

Professionally, Billy presently serves as vice president of government affairs for cable television operator, KLIP Communications. His responsibilities include franchise negotiation, which brings in nearly $100 million in annual revenue, and representing the company's community interests. Billy also hosts the radio talk show, *Community Forum*, on 91.9 FM WCLK, which is heard by a growing audience of more than 120,000 listeners.

A public speaker and writer, Billy is also a contributor to the best-selling book, *Keeping the Faith* by radio and television personality Tavis Smiley. The book was named the Best Literary Work for Non-Fiction at the NAACP Image Awards.

The Honorable
Ceasar C. Mitchell
Councilmember, Post One At Large
Atlanta City Council

Atlanta city councilmember Ceasar C. Mitchell practices real estate with the law firm of Thomas, Kennedy, Sampson & Patterson. On the Atlanta City Council, Ceasar has chaired the influential public safety and community development committees. He also sits on the budget commission, which sets the city's annual revenue levels. In 2004 Ceasar served as acting president of the City Council during a vacancy in the position.

Ceasar is actively engaged in civic, legal and community affairs, having served as board chairman of Hands On Atlanta and as a past president of the Gate City Bar Association. In 2003 he became the inaugural recipient of Leadership Atlanta's Rising Star Award, and he is a graduate of its 2005 class. Ceasar has been named one of the state's best and brightest in *Georgia Trend* magazine's 2005 feature of "Forty Under 40."

Ceasar is an Atlanta native and a product of its public schools. He received his bachelor's degree in economics and English from Morehouse College and his law degree from the University of Georgia.

The Honorable Felicia A. Moore was elected to the Atlanta City Council in 1997. Now in her third term, she serves as chair of the committee on council and sits on the finance/executive and transportation committees. During her tenure on council, she has served as the chair of the community development/human resources committee, the finance/executive committee and the transportation committee.

In December of 2005, Felicia was sworn in as president of the National Black Caucus of Local Elected Officials. As an active National League of Cities member, she serves on several committees and is the vice chair of the finance administration and the intergovernmental relations committee.

Moore is an active member of the Georgia Association of Black Elected Officials and the Georgia Municipal Association.

A licensed real estate broker with Keller Williams Realty, Moore is a member of the Atlanta and National Boards of Realtors. She graduated cum laude from Central State University in Wilberforce, Ohio with a bachelor of arts degree in communications.

**The Honorable
Felicia A. Moore**
Councilmember, District 9
Atlanta City Council

Lawrence L. Nelson Jr. is the founder and president of Lang Custom Homes, a premier residential developer/builder in the Greater Atlanta area. Lang Custom Homes was the exclusive builder of the Greenridge subdivision, which was recognized in *The Atlanta Journal-Constitution* as one of the most affluent African-American communities in DeKalb County. Lang currently has several new developments under construction.

A premier builder, Lang Custom Homes is a member of the National Association of Home Builders; has been named an Elite Builder by Home Builders Warranty Corporation; and is a licensed certified professional homebuilder.

Lawrence is an avid supporter of his community. Through sponsorship, Lawrence Nelson and Lang Custom Homes have enabled students and organizations alike to take shorter strides toward their goals. The Lang Custom Home Scholarship Fund, founded by Lawrence and Vanessa Nelson in 2006, recognizes outstanding academic achievement with a $2,000 scholarship toward college expenses.

Lawrence and his wife of 17 years, Vanessa, are supportive members of the Smoke Rise Community along with their two sons, Lavondré, 12, and Lawrence III, 9.

Lawrence L. Nelson Jr.
Founder & Chief Executive Officer
Lang Custom Homes

Monica Pearson
Anchor, Action News
WSB-TV Channel 2

Monica Pearson is WSB-TV Channel 2's 5:00, 6:00 and 11:00 p.m. Action News anchor. She joined the staff in August of 1975.

Previously, the University of Louisville graduate was a reporter with the *Louisville Times* for four years. She worked in public relations for Brown-Forman Distillers before joining WHAS-TV in Louisville as a reporter and anchor for two years.

Monica is a member of various professional organizations, which include: the Society of Professional Journalists, Sigma Delta Chi, the National Association of Black Journalists, the Atlanta Association of Black Journalists and The Junior League of Atlanta.

Monica has won 23 local and Southern Regional Emmy Awards during her career including one in 2003 for "Closeups."

Monica is a life member of the NAACP, and she secured a life membership for her daughter, Claire Patrice, at age 9 months. Married to John E. Pearson Sr., she is also a member of Alpha Kappa Alpha Sorority, Inc. A native of Louisville, Kentucky, her church membership is with Our Lady of Lourdes Catholic Church.

Richard J. Pennington
Chief of Police
Atlanta Police Department

Richard J. Pennington became the 22nd chief of the Atlanta Police Department in 2002. His law enforcement career began with the Metropolitan Police Department in Washington, D.C., where he rose through the ranks to become assistant chief. In 1994 he became chief of the New Orleans Police Department.

Pennington is a graduate of American University, the University of the District of Columbia, the FBI Academy National Executive Institute, the George Washington University Executive Development Program, and the Harvard University Program for Senior Executives.

Pennington is the past president of the National Organization of Black Law Enforcement Executives, and a board member of the American Red Cross-Metropolitan Atlanta Chapter and the Brady Campaign to Prevent Gun Violence. He is a member of numerous organizations including the International Association of Chiefs of Police, the Major City Police Chiefs Association, the Georgia Association of Chiefs of Police, 100 Black Men of Atlanta, Alpha Kappa Psi Fraternity, Inc. and Cascade United Methodist Church.

He was listed in *Ebony* as one of the 100 Most Influential and in *Governing* as Public Official of the Year.

D ottie Peoples has had ten chart-topping albums since her 1993 AIRGospel debut. Continuing to create music that connects with people of nearly all ages and tastes, her latest release is *The Water I Give*. With numerous Grammy, Stellar, Dove, GMWA and Soul Train awards and nominations, she is one of gospel's premier artists.

Born and raised in Dayton, Ohio, Dottie is the oldest of seven sisters and two brothers. She grew up in a church-going family where the sounds of traditional gospel rang throughout the house. She started singing in high school and church choirs. Her talent eventually caught the attention of gospel legend Dorothy Norwood, who invited Dottie to travel with her as a back-up singer. Shirley Caesar later became Dottie's musical mentor and close personal friend.

Dottie's marriage brought her to Atlanta and Salem Baptist Church. There, she was instrumental in forming Salem Baptist's own label, Church Door Records. She released two solo albums with Church Door Records before signing with AIRGospel.

Dottie was recently selected as the national spokeswoman for Speaking of Women's Health and Universal Sisters.

Dottie Peoples
Gospel Artist
AIRGospel

T yler Perry and his talents as a playwright, director, producer and actor have taken urban theater to another level. This New Orleans native has had a stellar decade and shows no signs of letting up.

In 1992 Tyler wrote a series of letters to himself in an effort to find catharsis for his own childhood pain. Those letters became his first hit musical, *I Know I've Been Changed*. He collaborated with Bishop T.D. Jakes to produce *Woman Thou Art Loosed* and *Behind Closed Doors*. He then brought to life a portrayal of a 78-year-old grandmother, Mabel "Madea" Simmons, and the following four productions made history.

Tyler received the 2004 Black Business Professionals Entrepreneur of the Year award. In 2001 he received the prestigious Helen Hayes Award for Outstanding Lead Actor. Tyler has appeared on the covers of *Jet* and *Essence* and been featured in numerous other magazines.

Tyler completed and released his first major motion picture in 2005, *Diary of a Mad Black Woman*. His next film, *Madea's Family Reunion*, opened at number one in the box office.

Tyler Perry
President & Chief Executive Officer
The Tyler Perry Company

**The Honorable
Charles E. Phillips Sr.**
**Councilmember
City of College Park**

The Honorable Charles E. Phillips Sr. is a city councilman and attorney in College Park, Georgia. Originally from Oklahoma, Phillips is a devoted husband and father of four, with a distinguished career that has taken him all over the world.

A U.S. Air Force veteran, Phillips served in Southeast Asia, the Arctic and Europe. He served as a senior official in the Office of Economic Opportunity and the Community Service Administration, and he helped establish the Inspector General Office of the Department of Defense.

Recently, Phillips led the initiative to build the Georgia International Convention Center and the new Public Safety Building in College Park.

Phillips belongs to the American, Federal, National, Georgia and Atlanta Bar Associations, the Georgia Trial Lawyers Association, the Georgia Association of Criminal Defense Lawyers, the ACLU and the NAACP. He received his juris doctorate from the Woodrow Wilson College of Law.

Phillips is a member of Sigma Delta Kappa Law Fraternity and the Hampton University Alumni Association. He is a board member of the Delta Sigma Theta Sorority, Inc. Fortitude Educational and Culture Development Foundation.

**The Honorable
Patsy Y. Porter**
**Judge
State Court of Fulton County**

A native of Atlanta, the Honorable Patsy Y. Porter is a Fulton County State Court judge. She presides over cases involving medical malpractice, wrongful death, automobile accidents, and criminal misdemeanor offenses.

Porter is a member and past president of the Georgia Association of Black Women Attorneys (GABWA). She is a member of the Gate City Bar Association, the board of trustees of the Georgia Bar Foundation, the board of directors of the Southwest YMCA, and the Board to Determine Fitness of Bar Applicants. She is a past president of the Atlanta Legal Aid Society and a 1991 Leadership Atlanta alumna.

Porter has received numerous awards including the Jurist of the Year Award, the Judge With A Heart Award, a 30-Year Award of Distinction, the Spirit of GABWA Award, and the Millennium Award of Excellence In Law. The Atlanta Business League lists her as one of Atlanta's Top 100 Black Women of Influence.

A graduate of Georgia State University, Porter received her law degree from Woodrow College of Law.

Judge Porter is married and she has two sons.

Gregory G. Pridgeon serves as chief of staff to the Honorable Shirley Franklin, the 58th mayor of the City of Atlanta. Pridgeon graduated from North Carolina A&T State University with a bachelor's degree in political science in 1974. He furthered his education with graduate studies at Virginia Polytechnic Institute and State University in Blacksburg, Virginia.

Pridgeon also served the City of Atlanta under the administrations of Mayors Maynard Jackson and Bill Campbell.

Pridgeon is active in the Atlanta community and has served with numerous organizations throughout the city. He is a member of Omega Psi Phi Fraternity, Inc. and attends Christian Friendship Baptist Church.

A sports fan and avid golfer, Pridgeon has been married to the former Jeannen Michelle Billups for more than 25 years. They have three children and have lived in the Grant Park neighborhood of Atlanta for more than two decades.

Gregory G. Pridgeon
Mayor's Chief of Staff
City of Atlanta

Erica Qualls is general manager for the Atlanta Marriott Marquis. Qualls is responsible for guest and associate satisfaction, managing the hotel's finances and assets, owner relations, and fostering business alliances that promote Marriott International. The Atlanta Marriott Marquis is Marriott International's third-largest hotel with 1,675 hotel rooms and more than 120,000 square feet of meeting and convention space.

During her 13 years with Marriott International, Qualls has held a variety of key positions. Previously, she was hotel manager for the Atlanta Marriott Marquis, and director of human resources and general manager in Sunnyvale, California.

Qualls is involved in national and local community organizations including the Children's Miracle Network, Hands on Atlanta and the United Way. She is a member of the boards of the Atlanta Business League and the UNCF Atlanta Corporate Campaign.

Qualls is listed as one of Atlanta's Top 100 Black Women of Influence by the Atlanta Business League. This year they presented Qualls with their prestigious League Leadership Award for outstanding volunteerism.

She has been married to David Bascoe for 21 years and is the proud mother of four.

Erica Qualls
General Manager
Atlanta Marriot Marquis

**The Honorable
M. Kasim Reed**
Senator, District 35
Georgia Senate

The Honorable M. Kasim Reed is a partner with Holland & Knight, LLP and a member of the Georgia General Assembly. He was elected to the Georgia Senate after two terms as state representative for House District 52.

In January of 2003, Reed became one of the youngest members of the Georgia State Senate. He currently serves on the Senate Judiciary, Higher Education, Retirement, and State and Local Government Committees. Reed is a member of the American and National Bar Associations as well as the State Bar of Georgia. He was also campaign manager for Mayor Shirley Franklin's successful effort to become Atlanta's first female mayor.

Reed's civic and professional leadership has been nationally recognized in *The New York Times*, *The Washington Post*, *Black Enterprise* and *Ebony*. He was also the youngest elected general trustee of the Howard University board and the first member to serve the university's board as both an undergraduate and a graduate student.

He received his bachelor of arts and law degrees from Howard University in Washington, D.C.

**The Honorable
Penny Brown Reynolds**
Judge
State Court of Fulton County

The Honorable Penny Brown Reynolds is a trial court judge in the State Court of Fulton County, Atlanta, Georgia. Formerly, Reynolds served as executive counsel to Governor Barnes, making her the first African American in Georgia's history to hold that position. She is a former State of Georgia assistant attorney general and prosecutor.

Reynolds is the founding chair of the judicial section of the Gate City Bar Association, the only statewide judicial section in Georgia. She is a member of the American and Gate City Bar Associations, the National Bar Association Judicial Council, the Council of State Court Judges, the Georgia Association of Women Lawyers, the Georgia Association of Black Women Attorneys, the Lawyers Club of Atlanta, and Alpha Kappa Alpha Sorority, Inc.

A Georgia State University graduate, Reynolds received her bachelor's degree, cum laude, after only three years of study. She received her law degree from Georgia State's College of Law.

Reynolds is married to Reverend Edward S. Reynolds, pastor of Midway Missionary Baptist Church in College Park, and is the mother of two adult sons, Michael and Fela.

Lee Rhyant serves as executive vice president and general manager of Lockheed Martin Aeronautics Company in Marietta, Georgia. Rhyant has more than 30 years of aerospace and automotive industry experience, having also worked for Rolls-Royce Aerospace and General Motors.

Rhyant serves on numerous boards including Bethune-Cookman College, the SafeAmerica Foundation and the Cobb Chamber of Commerce. He is a member of Omega Psi Phi Fraternity, Inc.

Rhyant was recognized as the 2005 Citizen of the Year by the SafeAmerica Foundation and received the Justice Robert Benham Award from Blacks United for Youth-Cobb for leadership, dedication and commitment to Georgia's youth. He was honored for superior leadership by various organizations including Bethune-Cookman College, the Georgia Minority Supplier Council and 100 Black Men of America.

Rhyant graduated from Bethune-Cookman College and received his master of business administration degree from Indiana University. He also studied at the London School of Business, MIT, Harvard, General Motors Institute and the University of Michigan.

Rhyant and his wife, Evelyn, have twin sons, Roderick and Broderick. They live in Roswell and attend Zion Baptist Church in Marietta.

Lee Rhyant
Executive Vice President &
General Manager
Lockheed Martin
Aeronautics Company

J.W. Robinson Sr. is the first African-American architect from Georgia to be elevated to fellowship in the American Institute of Architects (AIA). Robinson has been a practicing architect for more than 36 years, as well as an educator and mentor to African-American architects and other professionals. His work has included the historic preservation in the Sweet Auburn and Martin Luther King Jr. historic districts of Atlanta. He is a charter member of the National Organization of Minority Architects.

Born in 1927 in Hartsville, South Carolina, Johnson attended public schools in Georgetown, South Carolina. He graduated from the Hampton Institute in Virginia in 1949 with a bachelor of science degree in architecture. During his 15-year tenure at Booker T. Washington High School, from 1953 to 1968, he introduced new subjects such as descriptive geometry and inspired his students to enter the field of architecture.

Robinson's early practice was in residential architecture, helping reshape communities in Atlanta during a time of segregation.

Robinson continues to provide direction to the work of his firm, which now includes his two sons.

Joseph W. Robinson Sr.
President & Chief Executive Officer
J.W. Robinson & Associates, Inc.

Atlanta's

MOST INFLUENTIAL

Lisa Robinson
Founder & Principal Broker
Robinson Realty Group

Lisa Robinson, an 18-year resident of Atlanta, is the founder and principal broker of The Robinson Realty Group. Based in Atlanta, there are also offices in Buckhead and Detroit, Michigan. These multiple locations allow the firm to facilitate real estate transactions and services to buyers, sellers, investors and builders in the Atlanta and Detroit metropolitan areas.

Lisa and her team have been successful in building a broad spectrum of clients with listings and sales from $100 thousand to $4.5 million. Robinson Realty Group is comprised of more than 95 licensed real estate professionals with total gross sales volume in real estate transactions that exceeded $104 million in 2005.

Before opening the Robinson Realty Group in Atlanta, she was an award-winning agent at a leading national residential real estate brokerage. During her tenure, Lisa's sales performance helped the company become Atlanta's number one real estate firm in gross sales. Lisa has earned many awards, including 2006 Atlanta Business League Woman of the Year and *Atlanta Business Journal*'s Real Estate Industry of the Year Award for 2006.

Ray M. Robinson
President
East Lake Golf Club

Ray Robinson is president of the East Lake Golf Club (ELGC) and chairman of the East Lake Community Foundation (ELCF). As chairman, Robinson's responsibilities include strategic business development, corporate governance, membership development and assisting the ELCF in spreading the message about its successful model of community redevelopment.

Previously, Robinson was president of AT&T's southern region, where he was responsible for marketing, sales and promotions for AT&T's business and consumer services. Additionally, he held several other senior management roles with AT&T in the Atlanta area.

Currently, Robinson serves on the boards of Avnet, Inc., Citizens Trust Bank, Mirant Corporation and Aaron Rents. He is also a board member of the Metro Atlanta Chamber of Commerce, the Commerce Club, *Atlanta Tribune: The Magazine*'s editorial advisory board, the Woodruff Arts Center of Atlanta, and the Georgia Aquarium.

A Dallas, Texas native, Robinson earned his bachelor of science degree in finance and economics, and his master of business administration degree in finance from the University of Denver.

Robinson is married and has two adult children and one granddaughter.

H. Jerome Russell is a native of Atlanta, Georgia. In July of 1994, he became president and chief operating officer of the newly reorganized and consolidated H.J. Russell & Company, a fully-integrated construction and real estate company.

Under Mr. Russell's leadership, H.J. Russell & Company's annual revenue exceeds $150 million. The company's involvement in construction extends into major cities and states such as Atlanta, Richmond, Washington, Dallas, and New York. In addition, the property management division has increased its portfolio from managing 4,000 to more than 11,000 units in Georgia, Florida and Illinois.

Russell is a board member for several organizations including Zoo Atlanta, Citizens Trust Bank, Kennesaw State College, the Atlanta Urban League, First Union Bank, GPR Aviation, and most notably, H.J. Russell & Company. Likewise, he is a member of the Atlanta Business League and the Young Presidents Organization.

Russell is married and has four children. In his spare time, he enjoys basketball, tennis, golf, travel and occasionally a good book.

H. Jerome Russell
President & Chief Operating Officer
H.J. Russell & Company

Beginning in the early civil rights movement, Herman J. Russell has built one of the greatest success stories in America. H.J. Russell & Company is the fourth-largest minority industrial service company in the U.S. Russell's portfolio includes construction, construction management, real estate development and property management.

A quiet but influential civic leader, Russell worked closely with Dr. Martin Luther King Jr. in the 1960s. He became the first black member and president of the Atlanta Chamber of Commerce. He has served as a board member for several civic and business organizations.

Russell has received many awards including the Dow Jones Entrepreneurial Excellence Award, the National and Georgia Black MBA Association, Inc.'s Entrepreneur of the Year Awards, and Ernst & Young's 2001 Entrepreneur of the Year Lifetime Achievement Award.

A graduate of Tuskegee University, Russell holds honorary degrees from Morehouse College, Georgia State University and Morris Brown College.

Herman resides in Atlanta with his wife of 50 years, Otelia Hackney Russell. Their children, Donata Russell Major, H. Jerome Russell and Michael Russell, are all executives in the Russell companies.

Herman J. Russell
Chairman
H.J. Russell & Company

Michael Russell
Chief Executive Officer
H.J. Russell & Company

Michael Russell became chief executive officer of H.J. Russell & Company in October of 2003. He succeeds his father, Herman Russell, who founded the company in 1952 and led it for 50 years. A 16-year veteran of the construction and real estate development industry, Michael is charged with leading the company as it embarks on another 50 years. He also serves as chief executive officer of Concessions International, another Russell company.

Michael spent most of his career with H.J. Russell in a variety of executive positions, most recently as executive vice president.

Michael received a bachelor of science degree in civil engineering from the University of Virginia and a master of business administration from Georgia State University.

Active in the community in various arenas, Michael serves on the executive committee of the Metro Atlanta Chamber of Commerce; Trinity School's board of directors; the Hands on Georgia board; the University of Virginia Engineering Foundation; Georgia State Athletic Association's board; and the Grady Hospital board of visitors.

An Atlanta native, Michael and his wife, Lovette, have two sons, Michael Jr. and Benjamin.

Rory W. Sanderson
President & Chief Executive Officer
Sanderson Industries, Inc.

Rory Sanderson is president and chief executive officer of Sanderson Industries, Inc., a nationally recognized automotive supplier ranked in the BE 100s and one of Georgia's Top 25 minority-owned companies. With 33 years of comprehensive metal stamping, manufacturing and administrative experience, his responsibilities include leadership of all company departments, activities and systems development.

Born and raised in Chicago, Rory is a graduate of Chicago State University with a bachelor of science degree in business administration and finance. He is also an alumnus of the Amos Tuck Graduate School of Business Minority Business Executive Program and Advanced Minority Business Executive Program.

Rory serves on the boards of the Georgia Industry Association, the Bankhead Boys Association and The Carter Center. Likewise, he serves on the advisory boards of the Metro Atlanta Chamber of Commerce and the Ford Partnership for Advanced Studies at J.M. Therrell High School. He is also a member of the Society of Manufacturing Engineers and Alpha Phi Alpha Fraternity, Inc.

Rory resides in Smyrna/Vinings with his wife, Anise, and their three children, Tai, Rory II and Sean.

The 16th U.S. surgeon general, David Satcher, M.D. recently completed his term as interim president of the Morehouse School of Medicine in June of 2006. As the present director of the Center of Excellence on Health Disparities at Morehouse School of Medicine, he was presented with the first Poussaint-Satcher-Cosby Chair in Mental Health.

Satcher served as U.S. surgeon general and assistant secretary for health from February of 1998 until he announced his retirement in February of 2002. Previously, he served as president of Meharry Medical College in Nashville, Tennessee from 1982 to 1993, and director of the Centers for Disease Control from 1993 to 1998.

Satcher graduated from Morehouse College in Atlanta in 1963. He earned his doctor of medicine and doctor of philosophy degrees from Case Western Reserve University in 1970. Satcher completed his residency and fellowship training at Strong Memorial Hospital at the University of Rochester and the King-Drew Medical Center at the University of California, Los Angeles.

Born in Anniston, Alabama, he and his wife, Nola, have four adult children.

David Satcher, M.D.
Director
Center of Excellence on
Health Disparities
Morehouse School of Medicine

The Honorable David Scott is the U.S. representative for the 13th District of Georgia, representing part of the city of Atlanta and portions of 11 metro counties. Scott is a member of the influential Financial Services Committee, the capital markets and housing subcommittees and the Agriculture Committee. He also co-chairs the Democratic Group on National Security, providing leadership in fighting terrorism, maintaining a strong national security and military, and improving our economy and health care.

Scott received his bachelor of arts degree with honors from Florida A&M University. He received his master of business administration degree with honors from the Wharton School of Finance at the University of Pennsylvania.

He served in the Georgia House of Representatives from 1974 to 1982, and in the Georgia Senate from 1983 until his election to Congress in 2002.

Scott's family includes his wife, Alfredia, two daughters, Dayna and Marcye, son-in-law, Kwame, and two grandchildren, Kimani and Kaylin. His family also includes close friend and brother-in-law "Home Run King" Hank Aaron. Scott is the son of a minister and a man of strong faith.

The Honorable David Scott
Representative
Georgia's 13th Congressional District
U.S. House of Representatives

MOST INFLUENTIAL

M. Alexis Scott
Publisher & Chief Executive Officer
Atlanta Daily World

M. Alexis Scott is publisher and chief executive officer of *Atlanta Daily World*, a newspaper founded by her grandfather. She is responsible for the overall editorial content and general management of the paper. In 1932 W. A. Scott II founded the paper and it became the nation's first black-owned daily newspaper in the 20th century. *Atlanta Daily World* now appears once a week and can be accessed daily online.

Scott joined the paper in 1997 after a 22-year career with *The Atlanta Journal-Constitution* and Cox Enterprises, Inc. She worked her way up from reporter to vice president of community affairs at *The Atlanta Journal-Constitution* and later became director of diversity at Cox.

Scott is also a panelist on the political week-in-review television show *The Georgia Gang* shown on FOX5. A member of the board of directors of Atlanta Life Financial Group, she sits on the advisory board of The Coleman Group, another family business.

Scott attended Barnard College in New York and Spelman College in Atlanta. She is the mother of two sons.

The Honorable
Mark Anthony Scott
Superior Court Judge
Stone Mountain Circuit, Division 9

Judge Mark Anthony Scott was elected as a superior court judge in the Stone Mountain Judicial Circuit in August of 2004. Scott presides over civil matters, domestic relations and criminal felonies.

Scott graduated from the Howard University School of Law in Washington, D.C. in 1984. During law school, he became a member of the Kappa Alpha Psi Fraternity, Inc. He excelled in fraternal life, reaching the position of a province polemarch only seven years after initiation.

Prior to his election as a superior court judge, Scott's primary legal concentration was criminal defense work throughout the U.S. He serves on the faculty of Gerry Spence's Trial Lawyers College in Jackson Hole, Wyoming.

Scott is the immediate past president of the DeKalb Bar Association, where his passion for the law serves as a voice for the DeKalb County legal community.

He and his wife, Joan, have been married for more than 30 years and have two adult sons.

Mary Shy Scott, motivational speaker and retired music specialist, shares with audiences in the U.S. and abroad. She is the 23rd national president of Alpha Kappa Alpha Sorority, Inc., the first elected from the south Atlantic region. As such, Scott completed a $4 million building project on the Chicago national headquarters, negotiated a $15.5 million contract with DOL to operate the Cleveland Job Corps, and capitalized $1 million for the sorority's education foundation.

She holds 57 citations, 42 keys to cities and 58 proclamations. Scott received the Ouida '92 Award from the Benin Republic of West Africa for her lifetime achievements. The Mary Shy Scott Collections for Public Use are housed at the Springarn Center at Howard University and at the Auburn Avenue Research Library on African American History.

Scott holds a bachelor's degree from Spelman College, a master's degree from New York University and an honorary doctorate of humane letters from Miles College.

A native Atlantan, Scott is married to Alfred Scott Sr., and is the mother of Alfredene Scott Benton, Arthur Scott and lieutenant colonel Alfred Scott Jr.

Mary Shy Scott, HHD
23rd National President
Alpha Kappa Alpha Sorority, Inc.

Presiding Justice Leah Ward Sears has achieved a distinguished position in Georgia's history. She is the youngest person and first black woman to serve as a Superior Court judge in Georgia and to be appointed to the Georgia Supreme Court. She also retained her appointed position as a Supreme Court justice, thus becoming the first woman to win a contested statewide election in Georgia.

Before joining the Georgia Supreme Court, Sears was an attorney with the law firm of Alston & Bird and was a trial judge on the Superior Court of Fulton County.

Sears received her undergraduate degree from Cornell University and then graduated from Emory University School of Law. She earned her master's degree in appellate judicial process from the University of Virginia.

In addition to her participation in a wide variety of professional and civic affiliations, Sears is the proud mother of Addison and Brennan, and the wife of Haskell Sears Ward.

The Honorable
Leah Ward Sears
Presiding Justice
Georgia Supreme Court

MOST INFLUENTIAL

The Honorable
Joyce Sheperd
Councilmember, District 12
Atlanta City Council

The Honorable Joyce Sheperd represents the 12th District on the Atlanta City Council. She is vice chair of the community development/human resources committee. She is dedicated to making better neighborhoods for families throughout her district and the city.

The foundation for Sheperd's success is derived from the principle of grassroots leadership. She leads residents to take their communities into their own hands. Through her initiatives, District 12 and Atlanta's neighborhoods are learning key tools to assist them in taking charge of their communities.

Sheperd has served in various leadership positions including chair of the Neighborhood Planning Unit X; vice chair of the Atlanta Planning Advisory Board; co-chair of Keep Atlanta Beautiful; chair of the Community Alliance of Metropolitan Parkway; board member of the advisory commission commemorating the late Mayors Maynard Jackson and Ivan Allen; and co-founder of the City of Atlanta Neighborhood Deputies Program.

Joyce is the recipient of numerous awards recognizing her dedication to Atlanta including the National Common Cause Public Service Achievement Award, the Atlanta City Council President's Community Service Award and the John C. Birdine Distinguished Leadership Award.

Frank Ski
Host, *Frank & Wanda in the Morning*
WVEE V-103 FM

Frank Ski came to Atlanta in November of 1998 with one mission in mind: to take the V-103 morning show to number one. He accomplished his goal shortly before his first anniversary celebration.

A veteran of radio, television, and music production, Frank's broadcasting career spans more than 23 years. With record-breaking numbers in every time slot he has ever hosted, he is one of the top radio personalities in the nation. In 1998 Frank ventured to build yet another award-winning team, this time in Atlanta. He credits his rise to number one in Atlanta to his morning team.

Dedicated to helping others, he founded the Frank Ski Kids Foundation, which "exposes our kids to their future" through science, technology, arts, and athletics.

Frank has been honored by many civic organizations and has received numerous community awards. He is a member of the Atlanta Chapter of 100 Black Men of America and the 2003 Class of Leadership Atlanta.

Frank is married to Tanya Parker Rodriguez and has four sons, Jarrett, Franklin, Blake and Harrison.

John B. Smith Sr. was born in LaGrange, Georgia, where he started selling the *Chicago Defender* at the age of 8. A graduate of Morehouse College, he earned a master's degree in administration and a master's degree in mathematics from Atlanta University.

John was selected by the Atlanta Board of Education in 1960 as a teacher of mathematics and rose to the position of administrator within the schools. He retired from education in 1990 and has since worked publishing *The Atlanta Inquirer*.

John serves as chairman of the National Newspaper Publishers Association (NNPA). Additionally, he is an active member of Omega Psi Fraternity, Inc. and the Atlanta Branch of the NAACP. He sits on the board of directors of the Boy Scouts of America and is the founding secretary of the Atlanta Chapter of the National Association of Market Developers.

John was named a City Shaper, one of 25 More Who Are Making Atlanta What It Is, by *Atlanta* magazine.

He is the husband of Frances and has three adult children, Pamela, Lori and John B. Jr.

John B. Smith Sr.
Publisher & Chief Executive Officer
The Atlanta Inquirer

Jesse J. Spikes was born on May 17, 1950 in McDonough, Georgia. His formal education began in 1968 at Dartmouth College, where he received the Dean's Prize and graduated magna cum laude. In 1972 he attended University College, Oxford University in England as a Rhodes scholar, and in 1977 he received his juris doctorate from Harvard Law School.

Jesse is a senior partner in the corporate group at McKenna Long & Aldridge LLP. Previously he was legal advisor for Al Bahrain Arab African Bank, general counsel at Atlanta Life Insurance Company, law clerk to the honorable Damon Keith of the U.S. Court of Appeals, and a law clerk at Alston, Miller & Gaines.

Some of Jesse's current and professional affiliations include 100 Black Men of Atlanta, Children's Healthcare of Atlanta, and First Congregational Church. Some of his past civic, professional and social affiliations include the Agnes Scott College board of trustees, Emory University board of visitors, The Alliance Theatre, the Atlanta Business League, the Atlanta Organizing Committee for the 1996 Olympic Games and Sigma Pi Phi Fraternity, Inc.

Jesse J. Spikes
Senior Partner
McKenna Long & Aldridge LLP

Greg Street
On-Air Personality
WVEE V-103 FM

Greg Street is an on-air personality, entrepreneur, marketing master, record mogul and community activist. He has been instrumental in the radio industry, launching the careers of several top hip-hop and rap artists.

On Atlanta's V-103, Greg attracts a large and loyal audience of all ages. His passion for the community, especially children, spills over into his daily life. A founder of the Street Academy, Greg works to provide opportunities for at-risk youth to achieve extraordinary things. He established the Greg Street Scholarship fund and donates his time and money to help make a difference. He is often found providing words of encouragement at elementary and high schools.

Hailing from Hattiesburg, Mississippi, Street began his radio career at WORV and WJMG in his hometown. His journey took him to Mobile, Houston, and Dallas before he returned to Atlanta after three years of commuting between Dallas's KKDA and V-103.

Coming from humble beginnings, Greg went from selling his mix tapes from the trunk of his car to being recognized as one of most celebrated and respected on-air personalities in the country.

Louis W. Sullivan, M.D.
President Emeritus
Morehouse School of Medicine

Louis W. Sullivan, M.D., returned to Morehouse School of Medicine (MSM) in 1993 after serving as secretary of the U.S. Department of Health and Human Services (HHS) in the Bush administration. He served one of the longest tenures, 47 months, of any HHS secretary in history. At HHS, Sullivan was responsible for the major health, welfare, food and drug safety, medical research and income security programs serving Americans.

Sullivan became the founding dean and director of the Medical Education Program at Morehouse College in 1975. On July 1, 1981, MSM became independent from Morehouse College with Sullivan as its dean and first president.

Sullivan graduated magna cum laude from Morehouse College and earned his medical degree cum laude from Boston University School of Medicine. He is a member of Phi Beta Kappa Society and Alpha Omega Alpha Medical Honor Society.

In addition, Sullivan serves on several boards including Bristol-Myers Squibb, Boy Scouts of America, 3M Corporation, United Way of America, Medical Education for South African Blacks, Africare and Georgia-Pacific. He also serves on the editorial board of *Minority Health Today*.

Geri Thomas is a corporate diversity executive for Bank of America. Since 2001, she has been a senior staffing executive, responsible for staffing activities in support of the consumer and small business bank business groups. She was named corporate diversity executive in 2002. Thomas oversees corporate-wide diversity results and serves as a diversity resource to business lines, working closely with the diversity advisory council. With Bank of America since 1970, she started her career in consumer banking support.

Thomas is currently the vice chair of the State of Georgia Personnel Board. The board is responsible for providing policy direction for the State Merit System of Personnel Administration. Additionally, Thomas serves on the advisory board of Great Schools Atlanta, a public policy group of citizens dedicated to use research and data to improve public education in Atlanta.

A member of Alpha Kappa Alpha Sorority, Inc. and Beulah Missionary Baptist Church, where she serves on the board of trustees, Thomas holds a bachelor's degree from Georgia State University.

She is married to Ronald Thomas, and they have two children, Erinn and Erich.

Geri P. Thomas
Senior Vice President
Bank of America

The Honorable "Able" Mable Thomas, an Atlanta native, is serving as a state representative in the Georgia House of Representatives for a second term; the first term was from 1985 to 1993. Prior to her return to the House, Thomas served on Atlanta City Council, Post One, citywide. During her tenure, she was a tireless advocate for the elderly, economic development, women and family issues. Thomas is also a veteran grassroots organizer and an internationally recognized communications and public policy specialist.

Thomas is the owner of Master Communications, Inc., a communications and leadership business that seeks to empower individuals and organizations to create and control their own unique vision. Her memberships are numerous and they include the Atlanta Business League, the National Congress of Black Women (NCBW), the National Organization for Black Elected Legislators (NOBEL), Women in Government, Leadership Atlanta's Class of 1987, the Regional Leadership Institute, the Center for Women Policy Studies' Foreign Policy Institute, and the National Honor Roll of State Legislators.

Thomas was named one of the 50 Most Influential Women in Georgia by *Georgia Informer*.

The Honorable
"Able" Mable Thomas
Representative, 55th District
Georgia House of Representatives

MOST INFLUENTIAL

The Honorable
A.L. Thompson
Chief Judge
State Court of Fulton County Georgia

The Honorable A.L. Thompson was elected chief judge for the State Court of Fulton County Georgia in November of 2000. Previously, he served as judge in the Magistrate Court of Fulton County. Thompson's legal experience includes serving as counsel for several firms and as staff assistant for the Jimmy Carter presidential campaign. Internationally, he was a consulting expert on the organization of the court system for the Slovak Republic and the Republic of Malawi.

Thompson received a bachelor of arts degree in political science and history from Morehouse College, and a juris doctorate from the Boston College Law School.

A past member of several boards and organizations, Thompson's professional affiliations include the Andrew J. Young International Center at Morehouse College, the Georgia Association of State Court Judges and the American Judges Association. He holds memberships with the Atlanta, Gate City, American and National Bar Associations.

A recipient of many honors and awards, Thompson was born in Atlanta and is married to Dr. Maria L. Walker-Thompson. They have five children, Mark, Brian, Trevor, Albert and H. Walker.

Jannet M. Thoms
Deputy General Manager
Metropolitan Atlanta Rapid
Transit Authority

Jannet Thoms is the deputy general manager for the Metropolitan Atlanta Rapid Transit Authority (MARTA), the ninth-largest transit system in North America. As deputy general manager, Thoms shares oversight of the Authority along with the general manager/CEO. Previously, Thoms served as MARTA's chief information officer.

Thoms serves on the board of advisors of the Metro Atlanta Chamber of Commerce and the Georgia CIO Leadership Association. She is president of the National Black MBA Association-Atlanta Chapter and was named the 2006 Outstanding MBA of the Year. She is a member of the Coalition of 100 Black Women, Metro Atlanta Chapter.

The Technology Association of Georgia's Women in Technology honored Thoms as the 2006 Woman of the Year. She was featured in the *Atlanta Business Journal* as one of Atlanta's Most Influential African-American Women. Thoms was also named to the Atlanta Business League's 2005 and 2006 list of Atlanta's Top 100 Black Women of Influence.

Thoms has been featured in numerous publications including the *Atlanta Business Chronicle*, *Black MBA Magazine*, the *Atlanta Business Journal* and *Shape* magazine.

In 1986 the Honorable Michael Thurmond became the first African American elected to the Georgia General Assembly from Clarke County since Reconstruction.

Following his tenure in the General Assembly, Thurmond was called upon to direct Georgia's historic transition from welfare to work. He created the Workfirst program, which helped more than 90,000 welfare-dependent Georgia families into the workforce.

In 1997 Thurmond became a distinguished practitioner at the University of Georgia's Carl Vinson Institute of Government, and soon after was elected Georgia labor commissioner. Under his leadership, the Department of Labor saw the transformation of unemployment offices into state-of-the-art Career Centers, and Georgia was recognized as being number one in the nation in helping unemployed residents find jobs.

Thurmond also completed his latest book, *Freedom: Georgia's Antislavery Heritage, 1733-1865.*

Thurmond graduated from Paine College and earned a juris doctorate from the University of South Carolina School of Law. In 1991 he completed the political executives program at the John F. Kennedy School of Government at Harvard University.

Thurmond and his wife, Zola, are the proud parents of a daughter, Mikaya.

**The Honorable
Michael Thurmond**
Commissioner
Georgia Department of Labor

Since 1992, Pat Upshaw-Monteith has gone from co-executive director to executive director, and finally to president and chief executive officer of Leadership Atlanta in 2005. She has actively participated in the growth of Atlanta by imparting to new generations of leaders the legacy of values that have been central to Atlanta's success.

Upshaw-Monteith serves on the boards of numerous organizations including the DeKalb County Board of Commissioners and the MARTA board. She also served on the board of the DeKalb County Department of Family and Children Services, the Georgia Chamber of Commerce and the Junior League of Atlanta. Recently, she was appointed to the St. Pius advisory board.

Upshaw-Monteith earned a master's degree from Bowling Green State University and a bachelor's degree from Albany State University. Her love for the arts has evolved into an acting career, as she has appeared in several national television commercials, industrial films and the well-noted television series, *In the Heat of the Night.*

She is married to Frank Monteith and is the proud mother of a wonderful 15-year-old son, Brandon.

Pat Upshaw-Monteith
President & Chief Executive Officer
Leadership Atlanta

**The Honorable
Horace T. Ward**
Judge
U.S. District Court
Northern District of Georgia

Appointed by President Jimmy Carter in 1979, the Honorable Horace T. Ward serves on the U.S. District Court in Atlanta. In 1974 Ward was appointed to the civil court, becoming the first black trial court judge in Georgia. He was elevated to the Fulton Superior Court in 1977.

Ward graduated from Morehouse College with a bachelor's degree. He earned a master's degree from Atlanta University and a juris doctorate from the Northwestern University School of Law. He was awarded honorary doctor of laws degrees by Morehouse College and LaGrange College.

Ward practiced law in the firm of Hollowell, Ward, Moore & Alexander and successors from 1960 to 1974. The law firm conducted a statewide law practice, handling several significant civil rights cases.

In 1964 Ward was elected to the Georgia State Senate. He was only the second black person to be elected to that body since the Reconstruction period.

He was married to Ruth LeFlore Ward and they had one son. His wife and his son are deceased. Ward has four grandchildren and is a member of Friendship Baptist Church.

Janis L. Ware
President & Chief Executive Officer
Essence Unlimited

Janis L. Ware is a publisher, community development practitioner, real estate broker, housing expert, employer, businesswoman, community activist and entrepreneur. She has practical, hands-on expertise in all of these areas and more. A native of Atlanta, Janis is a graduate of Washington High School and the prestigious University of Georgia Terry College of Business.

Janis has worn many hats in her professional and civic career including serving as the current chair of Southside Medical Center. Her board memberships have included the Atlanta Housing Authority, Habitat for Humanity, the Empire Real Estate Board, the Atlanta Business League and the National Newspaper Publishers Association.

Janis is an alumna of Leadership Atlanta and has been recognized previously by *Who's Who in Black Atlanta*®. She is a recipient of the Women Making a Mark Award from *Atlanta Magazine*.

Janis is president and chief executive officer of Essence Unlimited, her real estate corporation. She is the second-generation owner of *The Atlanta Voice* which is celebrating its 40th anniversary. She also serves as the executive director of SUMMECH Community Development Corporation.

D r. R. L. White Jr. is the pastor and founder of the 14,000-member Mount Ephraim Baptist Church. The church, which he started with 13 members, has experienced astronomical growth since then.

White is also president of the Atlanta Branch of the NAACP, and he has served in this capacity for several years.

He has received the Atlanta Gospel Choice Award, a Trumpet Award, the Benjamin L. Hooks Religious Leader Award from the S.E. Regional 51st Annual Civil Rights Advocacy Training Institute (NAACP), and many others.

White holds a doctorate of ministry degree from the Interdenominational Theological Center, a master of divinity degree from Morehouse School of Religion and a bachelor of ministry degree from Luther Rice Seminary. He also holds an associate of science degree from Atlanta Metropolitan College.

A self-taught musician who has many recordings to his credit, White is also a published author with several books.

Reared in Macon, Georgia, White is married to Lorraine Jacques White, who is a minister and radio personality. Dr. White has five adult children.

Dr. R. L. White Jr.
Pastor & Founder
Mount Ephraim Baptist Church

H . Lamar Willis has served the citizens of Atlanta as the Post 3 At-Large council member since 2001. Reelected without opposition in 2005, he currently serves as president pro-tempore on the transportation, finance/executive and public safety committees.

After graduating from Morehouse College, Willis entered Carnegie Mellon University as a Woodrow Wilson fellow. There, he received his master of science degree and went on to Boston College Law School for his jurist doctorate.

Recognized in 2006 as one of *Georgia Trend's* 100 Most Influential Georgians, Willis remains active in his community as a member of the boards of directors of Techbridge, Southwest YMCA, and the Emory Board of Visitors. He is founder and chairman of the H. Lamar Willis Foundation, which since 2002 has awarded $150,000-plus to Atlanta high school seniors.

He is married to Dr. Kamili Willis, a graduate of Spelman College and the University of Medicine & Dentistry of New Jersey. They are the proud parents of 7-year-old Kayla and 2-year-old Henry. He and his family have been active members of Cascade United Methodist Church for nearly 30 years.

The Honorable
H. Lamar Willis
Councilmember, Post 3 At-Large
Atlanta City Council

The Honorable Cleta Winslow
Councilmember, Fourth District
Atlanta City Council

The Honorable Cleta Winslow, a veteran community activist, is currently serving her second term on Atlanta City Council. Over the years, Winslow has played an integral role in the revitalization of the West End, a historic inner-city neighborhood. She has contributed significantly to a broad range of initiatives, including those involving zoning, crime, drug reduction, affordable housing and economic development.

During her tenure as president of the West End Neighborhood Development Organization, she initiated a youth scholarship program for college-bound students and a youth leadership project that focused on community service. She received the A.P.P.L.E. Corps Award, the highest honor bestowed by Atlanta Public Schools, for her extensive volunteer work.

Winslow received her bachelor's degree in social work from Tennessee State University.

Winslow's previous work experience includes serving as chief social worker at the Carrie-Steel-Pitts Children's Home, and as director of housing for the Atlanta Urban League. A former city employee, she was a human service planner and a neighborhood planning unit coordinator in the Bureau of Planning. Winslow also served as president of the National Association of Neighborhoods.

Christopher C. Womack
Senior Vice President
Georgia Power Company

Chris Womack, a senior vice president, is responsible for Georgia Power's coal- and gas-fired generating facilities. He is also an officer in Southern Company Generation and Energy Marketing, which manages and generates electricity for the company's retail markets. The company also sells energy in the competitive wholesale business.

Joining Alabama Power in 1988, he held positions including assistant to the vice president of public affairs, director of community relations and vice president of public relations. He also served as senior vice president of public relations and corporate services, senior vice president of human resources and chief people officer of Southern Company.

Previously, Womack was a congressional legislative aide and a subcommittee staff director.

Womack is on the boards of A.G. Gaston Enterprises, the Boy Scouts of America-Southern Regional Council and INROADS. He is a member of 100 Black Men of Atlanta and a national trustee for the Boys & Girls Clubs of America.

A Greenville, Alabama native, Womack holds a bachelor's degree from Western Michigan University and a master's degree from American University. He also attended the Stanford Executive Program.

Dr. Frederick T. Work, Jr. specializes in a wide array of aesthetic and reconstructive surgical procedures for the head, neck, breasts, trunk, and extremities. Other areas of expertise include liposuction for body contouring, microvascular surgery, pediatric surgery and the treatment of skin cancers. Work has a special interest in the prevention and management of hypertrophic and keloid scarring, which commonly affect African Americans.

An alumnus of Georgia Institute of Technology and Morehouse College, Work received his medical degree from Morehouse School of Medicine. He completed his internship at Letterman Army Medical Center in California and concluded his residencies at Tripler Army Medical Center in Hawaii and at Emory University.

Work, certified by the American Board of Surgery, is an assistant professor of plastic and reconstructive surgery at Emory University and Morehouse School of Medicine. He appears as a regular contributor to Fox 5's *Good Day Atlanta*.

Work has recently introduced mesotherapy, laser hair, vein therapies, and The Hammam, a medical spa, to his practice. His vision is to deliver a comprehensive approach to the well-being of his patients.

Dr. Frederick T. Work Jr.
Plastic Surgeon
Atlanta Plastic & Reconstruction
Surgery Consultants, PC

The Honorable Tracey Wyatt is a member of the College Park City Council where he represents Ward III. He is currently serving as College Park's mayor pro-tem. As a member of the council, along with the mayor, Tracey shares the responsibility for approval of the city's budget and the hiring of the city manager and all city department heads. This includes the police and fire chiefs and finance and personnel directors. His primary responsibility, however, is to set policy for the city.

Tracey serves on the board of directors for both the College Park Neighborhood Association and the Airport Area Kiwanis Club. He is also an active member of the Old National Merchants Association. As a member of Wings of Faith Family Life Church, he has received the Stewardship Award.

Born in East Point, Georgia to a family that includes nine siblings, Tracey is single and enjoys reading, swimming and roller-skating.

The Honorable Tracey Wyatt
Councilmember, Ward III
City of College Park

Andrea Harris Wynn
President & Chief Executive Officer
Wynn Works, Inc.

Andrea Wynn, a native of Chattanooga, Tennessee, is president and chief executive officer of Wynn Works, Inc. and A & W Realty, Inc., one of the largest African-American independently-owned and operated developer, builder and real estate marketing firms in the Atlanta area.

The Atlanta Business League and *Women Looking Ahead News Magazine* list Andrea as one of Atlanta's Most Influential Women. Actively involved in numerous organizations, she is the co-founder and first chairperson of the East Point Business Association, a founding member of the East Point Main Street Board and board president of the South Fulton Partnership For Tomorrow. In addition to serving on several other boards, Andrea is the co-publisher of the new magazine *Moving South*.

Andrea graduated with a bachelor's degree from the Medical College of Georgia after completing Grady School of Nursing. She worked as a nurse practitioner for more than 18 years.

Andrea is married to William Wynn and enjoys working with her daughters, Kim Wynn Lewis and Keisha Wynn in their most recent venture, Kids R Kids School of Quality Learning at Cascade.

Prentiss Yancey
Counsel, Attorney at Law
Smith, Gambrell & Russell, LLP

Prentiss Yancey is counsel at Smith, Gambrell & Russell, LLP where he specializes in international law.

Yancey was a member of the Atlanta City Charter Commission that rewrote the charter of the City of Atlanta. He has been a member of the board of directors of the United Way of Metropolitan Atlanta, the Atlanta Chamber of Commerce international business council, the Governor's Commission on Criminal Justice and the Governor's Commission on Higher Education.

Yancey has been involved in major financings and refinancing for MARTA, Hartsfield-Jackson Atlanta International Airport, the City of Atlanta, and Fulton and DeKalb Counties. He was general counsel for the American Basketball Association until its merger with the National Basketball Association.

Yancey was a founder of the Broadcast Corporation of Georgia. In 1994 he took a leave from Smith, Gambrell & Russell to serve as president and chief executive officer of Africom Telecommunications Ltd., which formed to develop a business plan for the development and deployment of a mobile satellite-based telecommunications system for Africa.

A graduate of Villanova University, Yancey received his juris doctorate from Emory University.

James E. Young joined Citizens Trust Bank of Atlanta on February 2, 1998 as president and chief executive officer. Previously, under his leadership, First Southern Bank grew from $22 million in assets to $58 million in assets at the time of the merger. The merger created a financial services company with $184 million in assets and 11 metropolitan Atlanta banking locations. It is one of the top five African-American-owned commercial banks in the country.

A Cleveland, Tennessee native, Young received his bachelor's degree from Tennessee State University in 1971.

Young is a member of the boards of the National Bankers Association, the Atlanta Chamber of Commerce, the Atlanta Action Forum and Central Atlanta Progress. He also serves the DeKalb Convention and Visitors Bureau, the DeKalb County Pension Board, DeKalb Medical Center and the Atlanta Neighborhood Development Partnership. Additionally, Young is a board member for the Metro Atlanta YMCA and the Boys & Girls Club of Metro Atlanta.

Young is married to Rebecca Young, a DeKalb County Public Schools teacher, and they have three sons and a daughter.

James E. Young
President & Chief Executive Officer
Citizens Trust Bank

Lynnette Young is chief operating officer for the City of Atlanta, where she is responsible for the day-to-day operation and management of city government. Mayor Franklin has charged Young with re-energizing and refocusing city government.

Prior to joining the City of Atlanta, Young was principal and senior consultant with Damespoint Partners, a strategy development consulting firm.

For ten years Young served under Baltimore Mayor Kurt L. Schmoke as chief of staff, functioning as the chief administrative and operational officer (deputy mayor) of the city.

Her memberships on charitable and nonprofit boards have included the Associated Black Charities, National Aquarium in Baltimore, the Caroline Center, the Baltimore Zoo, the City Kids Art Factory (Florida) and Friends of the Fernandina Beach Library (Florida). She also served as chair of the Housing Authority of Fernandina Beach, Florida.

Young graduated from the University of Maryland, Baltimore County with a degree in political science. She also completed the certificate program for senior executives in state and local government at the John F. Kennedy School of Government at Harvard University.

She currently resides in Midtown Atlanta.

Lynnette Young
Chief Operating Officer
City of Atlanta

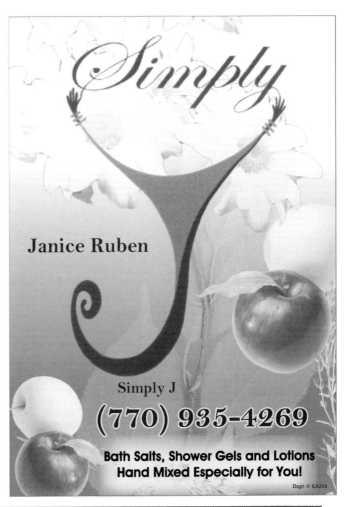

CORPORATE SPOTLIGHT

George Brooks
Vice President of Operations
Southeast Region
UPS

Gerard Gibbons
Vice President
Sales Strategy Worldwide Services
UPS

George Brooks is vice president of operations in the southeast region for UPS. Responsible for operations in Alabama, Tennessee, Georgia, North Carolina, South Carolina and Florida, he oversees 48,000 employees.

Brooks began his UPS career in 1983 as a part-time package handler in Carrollton, Georgia. In 1984 he was promoted to package car driver. He has held assignments in all facets of UPS operations. In 1999 Brooks was promoted to vice president of operations in the central Florida district, and was later named to the same position in Denver, Colorado. He joined UPS' southeast region in 2004.

Brooks received his bachelor's degree from the University of West Georgia in 1984. He received his master's degree in business administration with an emphasis in global management from the University of Phoenix. He is a graduate of the Columbia Senior Executive Program at the Columbia University Graduate School of Business.

Brooks actively supports Junior Achievement, the United Way and the National Urban League. He is a 26-year member of Omega Psi Phi Fraternity, Inc.

He and his wife, Gloria, have two daughters.

As vice president for corporate sales strategy at UPS, Gerard Gibbons is responsible for creating sales strategies on a global scale.

Gibbons joined UPS in 1989, starting as a driver in Los Angeles. In 1992 he was promoted to management and became a manager supporting consignee sales initiatives, working from the company's corporate headquarters in Atlanta. Gibbons headed west to Phoenix, Arizona in 1995 when he was promoted to director of sales. In 2001 he moved to Dallas after being named business development manager for UPS' southwest region. He stayed there until being promoted to his current position in Atlanta in October of 2005.

Gibbons holds a bachelor's degree in marketing from Howard University in Washington, D.C., and a master of business administration degree from Arizona State University.

Bill Gummer
National District Manager
UPS

Michael G. Johnson
Vice President of Human Resources
UPS

Bill Gummer has held a variety of roles in his career spanning more than a quarter century at UPS. Gummer started at UPS 26 years ago as a package car driver in Virginia.

Over the years, Gummer has risen through the ranks of the company, serving as an operations supervisor and division manager in the Laurel Mountain district, hub division manager in the metro Detroit district, and staff manager in the Pacific staff region. Gummer became a district manager with the national staff team in 2003.

Mike Johnson is vice president of human resources for UPS' domestic operations. He is responsible for the human resources components in communications, compliance, employee relations, employment, health and safety, public relations, training and development and workforce planning for more than 317,000 employees.

Johnson began his UPS career 30 years ago as a part-time package handler in Los Angeles. Johnson has held a variety of operations and human resources assignments in various parts of the country. In his previous assignment as a UPS human resources solutions manager, he researched and developed long-range planning projects for the human resources function.

Johnson attended DePaul University and earned a bachelor of arts degree in human resource management and organizational development.

Johnson is affiliated with several national organizations including the Society of Human Resource Professionals, the Employment Management Association and the Urban League. He serves on the board of the National Merit Scholarship Corporation and on the advisory board for the Executive Leadership Council. He also serves on the board of the National Black Child Development Institute.

James E. Mallard
Vice President, Procurement Services
UPS

Teri Plummer McClure
Senior Vice President,
Legal & Compliance, General Counsel
UPS

James E. Mallard is vice president of procurement services for UPS. Mallard is responsible for managing the company's annual global spending of approximately $15 billion. He is also responsible for the company's supplier diversity program.

A native of Mississippi, Mallard earned a bachelor of science degree in accounting from Jackson State University in Jackson, Mississippi, with continuing education at Nova University in Miami, Florida.

A UPS employee for 26 years, Mallard has vast experience in the company's international and domestic finance and accounting functions. During his career, Mallard has held positions including information services manager, accounting office manager, senior internal auditor, district controller, international finance manager, international controller and region controller.

In keeping with UPS' long-standing commitment to diversity and the community, Mallard serves on the board of directors for the National Minority Supplier Development Council (NMSDC), and is actively involved with the National Urban League's Black Executive Exchange Program (BEEP).

Mallard and his wife, Treece, have five children.

As senior vice president of legal and compliance and general counsel for UPS, Teri Plummer McClure oversees the company's legal and compliance activities worldwide.

McClure joined the UPS legal department as employment counsel in 1995. She is responsible for managing the relationships between the company and its Core Counsel Network, a group of law firms that represent UPS around the world. Prior to joining UPS, McClure practiced labor and employment law in Atlanta, where she handled all aspects of labor and employment-related state and federal civil litigation.

A native of Kansas City, McClure received a bachelor's degree in marketing and economics from Washington University in St. Louis, and a law degree from the Emory University School of Law.

In addition to her corporate responsibilities, McClure is a member of various bar associations and serves on the board of the Annie E. Casey Foundation, Junior Achievement of Georgia, the Atlanta Legal Aide Society and the Center for Working Families. She is active in many other civic and professional organizations.

Corporate Spotlight

Jim Winestock
Senior Vice President of Operations
UPS

Albert Wright
Vice President, Corporate Engineering
UPS

Jim Winestock is senior vice president of operations for UPS. He is responsible for all U.S. operations including the pick up and delivery of more than 14.1 million packages daily, and 407,000 employees. Winestock is also a manager of the UPS Management Committee which oversees the day-to-day management of the company.

A native of Greenville, South Carolina, Winestock joined UPS in 1969 as a part-time loader in Florida. He began his management career a year later after graduating from college. Since then, he has served in various functions including operations, finance/accounting and industrial engineering.

Winestock has served in several leadership positions including district manager in northeast Texas and Missouri, and vice president and region manager in the Midwest and North Central regions. He has been coordinator of UPS' Corporate Schools, the company's management training program, and he participated in the UPS Community Internship Program at the University of Tennessee-Chattanooga. He is a graduate of the Executive Management Program at the Wharton School of the University of Pennsylvania.

Winestock serves on the board of trustees for the National Urban League.

Albert Wright is vice president of corporate engineering for UPS. He is responsible for all automotive engineering, plant engineering and industrial engineering worldwide.

Wright began his career in 1977 as a package car driver in Bend, Oregon, and has served in several management positions. Prior to his current position, he served as industrial engineering manager in several UPS districts and the Pacific region.

In 1999 Wright was promoted to Gulf South district manager where he was responsible for 5,000 employees and managed all aspects of operations, customer service, business development, loss prevention and information technology in Louisiana and Mississippi. In 2000 Wright was promoted to vice president of plant engineering, overseeing all buildings, facilities, housekeeping and environmental compliance prior to taking his current position in February of 2004.

A native of San Diego, California, Wright attended Southern Utah University and Marylhurst University.

Wright is a recipient of the National Eagle Leadership Award, and holds board positions with organizations including Big Brothers Big Sisters, the Family Connection Partnership and Kettering University.

Wright is married and has five daughters.

CORPORATE SPOTLIGHT

Willa Alston
Event Coordinator
Georgia International Convention Center

Delroy Bowen
Executive Chef
Proof of the Pudding
Georgia International Convention Center

Willa Alston is a certified meeting professional (CMP) with ten years of experience in the hospitality industry. She is an event coordinator at the Georgia International Convention Center (GICC) in College Park, Georgia. She began her career in hospitality at the Omni Hotel at the CNN Center.

Willa's career path has provided opportunities to work with notable dignitaries and personalities over the years. One of her many events included coordinating the 2004 presidential campaign rally held at the GICC for John Kerry and John Edwards.

Willa is a member of Meeting Professionals International (MPI) and the International Association of Assembly Managers (IAAM).

Prior to joining the hospitality industry, Willa worked in the nonprofit sector in several positions at the Muscular Dystrophy Association. Formerly, she served as an intern at the American Cancer Society while majoring in public relations at Clark Atlanta University.

A native of Savannah, Willa currently resides in Riverdale, Georgia.

Delroy Bowen is the executive chef of the Georgia International Convention Center (GICC), and a two-year employee of the Southeast's largest catering company, Proof of the Pudding. In this position, he manages the culinary staff, creates menus, refines recipes and completes all purchasing for events at the GICC, some as large as 20,000 people.

Delroy began his career in the country's culinary capital, New York City. He became one of the city's most applauded chefs, first as chef at Robert De Niro's Tribeca Grill, then moving on to open 2Seven7, rated one of New York's very best restaurants.

Delroy is a culinary graduate and nominated alumnus of the year at The French Culinary Institute in New York City. He has been favorably reviewed in *The New York Times*, the *New York Post*, *Zagat New York City Restaurants*, *Paper Magazine*, *Time Out New York*, the *Naples Daily News*, *The Atlanta Journal-Constitution* and the *Southeast National Restaurant Association Magazine*.

A native of Jamaica, Delroy now resides in Atlanta with his wife, who is also a chef, and their two sons.

E. Denise Cole
Director of Sales
Georgia International Convention Center

Greg Cole
Event Coordinator
Georgia International Convention Center

E.Denise Cole is director of sales at the Georgia International Convention Center. In this position, she is responsible for the day-to-day operations of the sales department.

A 16-year veteran of the hospitality industry, Cole came to the Georgia International Convention Center from the Georgia World Congress Center where she held positions of increased responsibility. As national sales manager at the Georgia World Congress Center, she was instrumental in building the corporate market. Her hospitality background includes hotel group sales and catering sales.

Cole is a member of the National Coalition of Black Meeting Planners (NCBMP), the Hospitality Sales and Marketing Association International (HSMAI) and the American Business Women's Association (ABWA).

Greg Cole is currently employed as an event coordinator for the Georgia International Convention Center (GICC). In this position, he plans, orchestrates, manages and executes all assigned events. His most recent event was the immensely successful Radio One 1st Annual 2005 Dirty Awards.

With more than 18 years of experience in the hospitality industry, Greg has had a very successful career and has received numerous certifications and awards including Manager of the Year from Starwood Hotels & Resorts.

Greg has volunteered with Habitat for Humanity, the Salvation Army and the Atlanta Food Bank. An active member of Live Oak Baptist Church, his hobbies include gourmet cooking. In his spare time, he is also an avid reader and loves to travel.

A native of Pensacola, Florida, Greg is the proud father of his 6-year-old son, Bryce.

Archie Cuthbert
Chef de Cuisine
Proof of the Pudding
Georgia International Convention Center

A talented chef, Archie Cuthbert is the chef de cuisine at the Georgia International Convention Center (GICC) in College Park. An employee of Proof of the Pudding, he oversees a team of 25 in both the kitchen and stewarding departments.

Archie and his team have created some of the most memorable dining experiences in metro Atlanta. Among his past clients are the Democratic and Republican Parties, the BellSouth Golf Classic, Microsoft, the NBA, the NFL, the MLB, former President Bush, former President Reagan and dignitaries from around the world.

Archie received his associate degree from Hudson County Community College in New Jersey where he graduated as the Student of the Year. He also received the Martin Luther King Humanitarian Award. Archie served as vice president of the Bacchus Society, president of the Video Mince Club, junior member of the American Culinary Federation and captain of several sports teams.

A native of the Bronx, New York, Archie has been married for more than 19 years to Susan Cuthbert. Together, they have four beautiful kids, Alicia, Archie Jr., Aaron and Acazia.

Alex Harris
General Manager
Proof of the Pudding
Georgia International Convention Center

A lex Harris defies the negative stereotype that police officers' children are "bad apples." An Atlanta native and graduate of H.M. Turner High School, he is a former member of the U.S. Army, serving as a radar operator for two years.

The loving father of two daughters, Alex began his professional career at age 9 with his first paper route. His grandfather introduced him to hospitality in the summer of 1971. During subsequent summers and in his free time, Alex worked various jobs from banquet server to setup and client services.

After returning from the Army, Alex continued to pursue his love of food, people and service in the Atlanta hotel community. His on-the-job training placed him in various positions including banquet manager, executive steward, banquet captain, assistant food and beverage director, and now general manager of Proof of the Pudding by MGR, Inc. at the new Georgia International Convention Center.

Alex climbed to the top while maintaining his belief that "whether an intimate dinner for five or a gathering of 5,000, every client is a VIP."

Corporate Spotlight

Darcel Y. Ivey
Sales Manager
Georgia International Convention Center

Tamara McLaurin
Conference Service Manager
Proof of the Pudding
Georgia International Convention Center

Darcel Ivey is a sales manager at the Georgia International Convention Center (GICC), the second-largest convention center in Georgia. In this position, she is a leading sales revenue generator in the corporate and associations markets, as well as the social, military, educational, religious and fraternal (SMERF) markets.

With more than 15 years of hospitality industry experience, Ivey is an active member of the Georgia Chapter for Meeting Professionals International and the Professional Convention Management Association.

A proud alumna, Ivey is an active member of the Southeast Georgia Chapter of the Berry College Alumni Association. She also serves on the board of directors for the Hospitality Center of Excellence and the Perfected Praise Ministries/Perfected Dance Studios. As a dedicated member of Seed Faith Christian Ministries in Forest Park, she also donates her services as an administrator in thanks for all her blessings.

Ivey was born in Minneapolis, Minnesota and graduated from high school in Annandale, Virginia. She and Antonio, her husband of 13 years, reside in Jonesboro, Georgia and are the proud parents of their 4-year-old daughter, Brianna Gabrielle.

Tamara McLaurin is a conference service manager for Proof of the Pudding at the Georgia International Convention Center. In this position, she is responsible for planning and coordinating all catering needs for conference-related activities and meeting planner packages.

Tamara is a member of the Association of Bridal Consultants, the International Special Events Society and Sigma Gamma Rho Sorority, Inc. She is an active member of the Wings of Gabriel dance ministry at Elizabeth Baptist Church. Tamara has served as a big sister with the Big Brothers Big Sisters program and received an award for Big Sister of the Year in DeKalb County.

Tamara received a bachelor of business degree from James Madison University and a master of business administration degree from DeVry University.

None

None

Iris Owens
Catering Sales Manager
Proof of the Pudding
Georgia International Convention Center

Andrea Smalls
Event Services Manager
Georgia International Convention Center

Iris D. Owens, certified meeting professional (CMP), is a catering sales manager for Proof of the Pudding at the Georgia International Convention Center (GICC). In this role, she is responsible for catering some of the premier events in the Atlanta area. She enjoys being the vessel that assists clients in creating memorable events.

A native New Yorker, Iris began her career in catering sales at the Doubletree Hotel Atlanta-Buckhead. Prior to joining Proof of the Pudding, she served as an event coordinator for the GICC.

Iris earned her bachelor of arts degree in 1988 from Pace University in New York. She received her CMP certification in 2003.

Iris is an active member of Delta Sigma Theta Sorority, Inc. and is a faithful member of Ray of Hope Christian Church. She enjoys serving on various committees and projects that give her the opportunity to encourage, empower and enlighten others.

Iris is married to Ron Owens and they have two wonderful blessings, Rondald and Isabella. Her motto is: "Life is all about servitude."

Andrea Smalls is the event services manager for the Georgia International Convention Center. In this position, she manages the event services department and is responsible for all event activity at the GICC. As the manager, trainer and supervisor of the facility managers and other operational personnel, she is charged with maintaining events while ensuring that clients, attendees and guests have a fabulous experience.

Among her honors and recognitions, Andrea was featured in *Who's Who in Black Atlanta*® in 2003. She also received the City Manager Commendation for outstanding service in 2000.

Andrea received a bachelor of arts degree from Trinity University and a master of divinity degree from the Interdenominational Theological Center in 2000.

A native of San Antonio, Texas, Andrea is the wife of Glenn Smalls and the very proud foster mother of 7-month-old twins, Maquel and Makiyah.

Corporate Spotlight

Cindy Sumter
Senior Event Coordinator
Georgia International Convention Center

Sonia Williams
Catering Sales Manager
Proof of the Pudding
Georgia International Convention Center

Cindy Sumter has spent more than 19 years in the hospitality industry. She began her career at the Rochester Riverside Convention Center in Rochester, New York.

In 1989 Cindy moved to Atlanta and worked at AmericasMart as an event coordinator. During her nine-year tenure, she planned and coordinated events such as the Bronner Brothers Hair Show, the Atlanta Dream Jamboree and the Gift Show.

In 1998 Cindy joined the GICC as senior event coordinator and immediately put her vast experience to work. Her attention to detail and can-do customer service attitude makes her a favorite with clients. She lays claim to a philosophy that states: "Make my planners look good with successful events."

Cindy received an associate of arts degree from Bauder College in Atlanta. In June of 2005, she completed the IAAM Public Assembly Facility Management School.

Currently a Georgia resident, Sumter was born in Brooklyn and grew up in Rochester, New York. She is the proud mother of an 8-year-old son, Torren Cobie.

Sonia Williams is the catering sales manager for Proof of the Pudding, the exclusive upscale caterer for the Georgia International Convention Center.

In her current position, Sonia focuses her attention on selling the largest ballroom in the state of Georgia to social and corporate groups. She works closely with planners to develop and coordinate galas and special events. Those who have worked with Sonia describe her as having great attention to detail, exceptional customer service and an eye for seeing the big picture.

Sonia is active in industry associations including the National Association of Catering Executives, the International Special Events Society and the Perfect Wedding Guild. She is a member of the South Fulton Chamber of Commerce Ambassador's Program. In her free time, she volunteers with Hands on Atlanta.

Sonia resides in Atlanta with her husband, Gene, who is employed with Georgia Pacific. She is an active member of Word of Faith Family Cathedral Center.

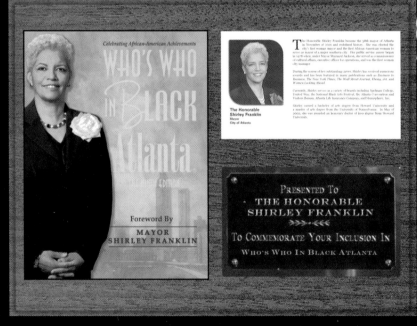

Atlanta's

CORPORATE BRASS

"Greatness is not measured by what a man or woman accomplishes, but by the opposition he or she has overcome to reach his goals."

DOROTHY HEIGHT

SOCIAL ACTIVIST, TEACHER & ADMINISTRATOR

Atlanta's

CORPORATE BRASS

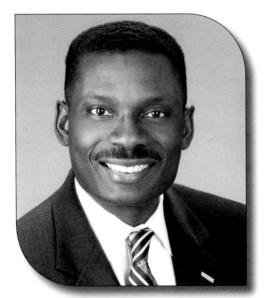

Leroy Abrahams
Retail Banking Executive
for Tennessee and Georgia
SunTrust Banks, Inc.

Leroy Abrahams is the central group retail line of business leader, a position he assumed in 2006. In this capacity, he oversees the retail and business banking activity of the SunTrust branches in Tennessee and Georgia.

Abrahams graduated from Texas Christian University with a bachelor of business administration degree and a major in finance in 1986.

Abrahams began his career in the Commercial Banking Training Program at a predecessor of Bank of America in Fort Worth, Texas. After spending the first five years of his career in commercial banking, he became community development officer at Bank One in Texas.

Prior to his present position, Abrahams was the consumer banking manager for AmSouth Bank in East Tennessee and served as the business banking group manager for Provident Bank in Cincinnati, Ohio.

Abrahams is new to Atlanta and recently joined the board of directors for Chris Kids. He has served on a variety of nonprofit boards including the East Tennessee Economic Development Association, the Knoxville Area Chamber Partnership, the Women's Haven, the Dogwood Arts Committee and the United Way allocations committee.

David Alpough
Community Manager
Brock Built Properties

Blazing the path of success in sales is a compliment that is easily attributed to David Alpough. An accomplished salesman with 18 successful years under his belt, David earned many accolades as a high performer. He is currently a real estate agent for Atlanta's Brock Built Properties.

Beginning his education at the University of Missouri in Columbia, David earned a bachelor of science degree in industrial management from Missouri State University. A natural athlete, he attended college on a football scholarship. David matriculated through Barney Fletcher School to become a real estate appraiser, an educational experience he uses as part of his real estate career. A native of Kansas City, Missouri, he is a founding member of Kappa Alpha Psi Fraternity, Inc., Mu Epsilon chapter at Missouri State.

Described by family and friends as a loving husband and father, he has been married to his college sweetheart, Nevienne, for 14 years. They are the proud parents of one daughter, Taylor. When he is not selling real estate, David still nurtures his love for athletics by enjoying bicycle riding and racquetball.

Joseph A. Arnold is senior vice president of SunTrust Bank Atlanta's institutional banking unit. Prior to his current position, he worked in treasury management as a technical sales representative, and from 1987 to 1995 he managed SunTrust's New York office.

In early 1995 Arnold relocated to Atlanta to manage the credit services division. Currently, as manager of the institutional banking group, his team is responsible for growing SunTrust Atlanta's relationships with not-for-profit clients.

Arnold currently serves on the boards and executive committees of the YMCA of Metropolitan Atlanta, the Boy Scouts of America-Atlanta Area Council, and Leadership Atlanta. He is also involved with the United Negro College Fund, Greater Atlanta Christian School and the American Cancer Society-South Atlantic Division. His past board service includes the One Ninety One Club and the Walter N. Ridley Scholarship Fund of the University of Virginia. He is an alumnus of Leadership Atlanta's Class of 2003.

Arnold is a native of Atlanta and is married to the former Renee Burton. They have three children, Joseph, Brittany and Jordan.

Joseph A. Arnold
Senior Vice President
Institutional Banking Unit
SunTrust Banks, Inc.

Arthur L. Bacon has been the director of finance and accounting for the Department of Aviation at Hartsfield-Jackson Atlanta International Airport since 1994. Bacon coordinates and supervises the accounts payable, accounts receivable, collections, financial analysis, fixed assets, general and project accounting divisions.

Prior to assuming his current position, Bacon served for four years as senior financial analyst in the City of Atlanta's Department of Finance, enterprise fund division. In that position, he supervised the work of financial analysts and accountants for the airport section of the enterprise fund division.

Earlier in his career, Bacon was a cost and properties accountant for General Motors Central Foundry Division in Saginaw, Michigan.

Bacon received a bachelor of science degree in accounting from Morris Brown College in 1976. He received a master's degree in business administration from Clark Atlanta University in 1980.

Arthur L. Bacon
Director of Finance & Accounting
Hartsfield-Jackson Atlanta
International Airport

CORPORATE BRASS

Kimberly Batten
Financial Consultant
AXA Advisors LLC

Kimberly Batten is a financial consultant with AXA Advisors. She seeks to guide clients toward financial security with strategic goal setting and customized financial planning. Kim's areas of focus are wealth accumulation, retirement planning, asset management, estate planning and wealth preservation.

Prior to joining the financial industry, Kim was a world-class professional track athlete for 12 years. She held the world record in the 400 hurdles for eight years and currently holds the American record. Kim won a silver medal in her premier event in the 1996 Olympics in Atlanta, and continued to acquire other outstanding achievements throughout her career. She is a recipient of ESPN's prestigious award, the ESPY.

Kim earned a bachelor's degree in social work from Florida State University. While in Tallahassee, she spent time speaking to local youth about a variety of topics including fitness, leadership, goal setting and athleticism. She is hoping to broaden these topics to include financial literacy in Atlanta.

A native of Rochester, New York, Kim is committed to educating youth and empowering women in the areas of finance and life.

Jamese Beauford
Group Vice President
SunTrust Bank, Atlanta

Jamese Beauford is a vice president/area manager in the retail banking division at SunTrust Bank, Atlanta. In this position, Jamese manages nine branch locations and is responsible for ensuring growth, profitability and consistent client expansion, attraction and retention.

She is the proud recipient of the 2002 Outstanding Atlanta Award, as well as the Special Act Award, awarded by the IRS to honor volunteers throughout metro Atlanta who contribute tireless efforts to volunteer, train and prepare taxes during tax season.

Jamese is a member of Delta Sigma Theta Sorority, Inc. and a member of the board of directors for the National Coalition of 100 Black Women. A faithful member of the Antioch East Baptist Church, she sings in the choir and is a member of the Steppers for Christ Ministry.

In 1994 she received her bachelor's degree in business economics from Florida Agricultural & Mechanical University.

An Atlanta native, Jamese is the devoted wife of Darryl Beauford and mother of Jaivyn Beauford. She resides in Fayetteville, Georgia and her motto is, "to whom much is given, much is required!"

Atlanta's
CORPORATE BRASS

C harles Bell is the budget management chief of Hartsfield-Jackson Atlanta International Airport. He is responsible for overseeing the development of the budget for the City of Atlanta's Department of Aviation. Charles and his staff, the Office of Management and Budget, monitor the department's budget and are responsible for airport management and performance analysis.

Bell is quite active in the community. He has served the past nine years on the board of directors for the Atlanta City Employees Credit Union and is chair of its supervisory committee. Additionally, he is a devoted member of the Atlanta Alumni Chapter of Kappa Alpha Psi Fraternity, Inc. His fraternal contributions include being a past chapter president, treasurer and secretary. Additionally, he serves as chair of the chapter's youth mentoring program and the fraternity's regional treasurer for Georgia and South Carolina.

Bell holds a bachelor's degree from Morehouse College and a master of business administration degree from Clark Atlanta University.

As a budget manager, Charles loves to say: "If you have no one to count the beans, you'll soon have no beans to count."

Charles E. Bell
Budget Management Chief
Department of Aviation
Hartsfield-Jackson Atlanta
International Airport

J ason Biske is the director of sales and retention for Comcast Cable in Atlanta. In this position, he is responsible for strategy formation and implementation for all inbound sales and retention activities. Since taking over the inbound sales responsibilities in 2003, Jason has been instrumental in growing Comcast Atlanta's subscriber base from 250,000 to more than 800,000. Additionally, his sales staff has grown from 50 to more than 240.

Jason received a master of science degree in management from the Georgia Institute of Technology in 1995. He completed his undergraduate work at Tulane University and received a bachelor of arts degree in economics.

A native of St. Thomas, U.S. Virgin Islands, Jason is married to Sheraunda Biske and is the proud father of his two sons and best friends, Michael and David.

Jason Biske
Director of Sales and Retention
Comcast Cable, Atlanta Region

Atlanta's

CORPORATE BRASS

**Retired Colonel
Courtland C. Bivens III**
Chief Engineer of Flight Testing
ARINC

Courtland Bivens III attended the U.S. Military Academy at West Point, where he acquired a bachelor of science degree in mechanical engineering. He obtained his master's degree in aerospace engineering from the Naval Postgraduate School. Next, he was selected to participate in the U.S. Naval Test Pilot School. Accepted in the U.S. Army War College at historic Carlisle Barracks, Pennsylvania, Bivens joined an esteemed list of graduates that includes General Colin Powell.

During 18 years at NASA Ames Research Center, Bivens obtained patents on two aeronautical inventions. In 2001 he retired as chief engineer of flight testing at the U.S. Army Aviation Technical Test Center. In 2003 he retired as a colonel in the U.S. Army Reserves. In a third career, he serves as deputy chief engineer of flight testing for Aeronautical Radio, Incorporated (ARINC).

A pilot and avid fencer, Bivens is a member of the Atlanta Fencing Club. He is married to Regina Lynch-Hudson and spends his spare time working on his wife's "honey-do" list, which includes building a wine cellar in their home.

Michol A. Brandon
Southeast Regional Sales Manager
***Essence* Magazine**

Michol A. Brandon is the Southeast regional sales manager for *Essence* magazine. Prior to joining *Essence* in October of 2004, Michol was known for her savvy sales and marketing prowess. Currently, she is responsible for the entire Southeast region, targeting its Fortune 100 companies for print advertising initiatives and objectives. Michol has increased revenue for the region to $4.8 million and continues to make a name for herself and this incredible brand. She has a bright future in the industry of advertising and marketing sales.

A native of Cincinnati, Ohio, Michol received a bachelor of science degree in fashion merchandising and marketing from Hampton University. She also attended The Ohio State University where she received a master's degree in clothing and textiles studies.

Michol is an active member of Alpha Kappa Alpha Sorority, Inc. and Hopewell Missionary Baptist Church. She is the proud mother of three little kings, Nadir, 7, and 3-year-old twin boys, Kahari and Kahir.

Moses Brown Jr. is vice president of corporate administration for the Alpharetta-based ChoicePoint, Inc. He directs administrative affairs, corporate purchasing, corporate travel and property management. He is also chairman of the ChoicePoint Foundation.

Brown earned a degree in business administration from Morehouse College and is a graduate of Leadership Atlanta. He serves on the board of directors of Prevent Child Abuse Georgia, the Excel Federal Credit Union, Zoo Atlanta, the Atlanta Sports Council, INROADS Atlanta, the Windward Business Association and the Greater North Fulton Chamber of Commerce. Brown also serves on the board of advisors of the Metropolitan Atlanta Chamber of Commerce and the Atlanta Braves.

Brown participates in the Morehouse College Executive Mentoring Program and is a member of 100 Black Men of America. A two-time recipient of the Equifax W. Lee Burge Community Service Award, Brown served as venue technology manager at the Georgia Dome during the 1996 Olympic Games. He also received the National Eagle Leadership Institute Award from *CareerFocus* magazine.

A Ft. Lauderdale, Florida native, Brown resides in Alpharetta with his two children, Maranie and Harrison.

Moses Brown Jr.
Vice President
ChoicePoint, Inc.

A native Atlantan, Wendell Brown is chief structural/electrical engineering inspector for Delon Hampton & Associates, the primary project management team for the City of Atlanta's Combined Sewer Overflow project.

Previously, Brown spent 20 years with MARTA (Metropolitan Atlanta Rapid Transit Authority) as chief inspector and quality assurance engineer, responsible for building the Kensington, Chamblee and Brookhaven stations. While at MARTA, Brown received OSHA safety certification from the Georgia Institute of Technology and construction management certification from the University of Wisconsin.

After returning from the U.S. Navy in 1974, Brown entered the International Brotherhood of Electrical Workers and earned his journeyman's electrical license. He earned his master electrical license in 1979.

As a member of 100 Black Men of America, Brown received the Man of the Year and the Outstanding Community Service Award. He received the Outstanding Georgia Citizen Award from the secretary of state. Brown served as an envoy team leader for the South African delegation during the 1996 Olympics. He and his wife, Scarlet, received the Excellence in Transportation and Leadership Award presented by the Atlanta Urban League.

Wendell H. Brown
Chief Structural & Electrical
Engineering Inspector
Delon Hampton & Associates

Audra Brown-Cooper
Senior Principal
Brown Group of Companies

Audra Brown-Cooper is senior principal of the Brown Group of Companies which consists of Brown Design Group, Inc., architecture and engineering; and Autaco Development, development and construction. The firm performs services including architecture, engineering, property management, development, construction and energy efficient consulting.

Audra's responsibilities include operations management and business development. She is responsible for the expansion of services to include development, construction and property management from the firm's initial core business of commercial architecture. She has 16 years of experience in the design and construction industry and six years of experience in property management and development.

Audra holds a master of business administration degree in finance from Georgia State University and a bachelor of science degree from Tuskegee University. She is also a certified erosion control inspector in the state of Georgia by the Georgia Department of Transportation.

Audra and Coy Cooper have three sons who are 19, 18 and 3 years old. Her hobby, whenever time permits, is reading novels.

Katherine Bryant
Vice President of Consumer Advocacy
ChoicePoint Inc.

Katherine Bryant is the vice president of consumer advocacy for ChoicePoint Inc. There, she is responsible for the company's consumer outreach, affected consumer and consumer advocacy functions. Before that, Katherine served as ChoicePoint's assistant vice president and general counsel.

Katherine currently provides leadership related to consumer outreach, consumer advocacy and consumer policy. In this capacity, she must build and maintain relationships with consumer advocates to create awareness of ChoicePoint consumer policies and practices, lead the operations teams responsible for assisting affected and curious consumers, and develop and evaluate policies regarding curious and affected customers.

Before ChoicePoint, Katherine was an associate with Morris, Manning and Martin, LLP in Atlanta and Rothgerber Johnson & Lyons LLP in Denver. Her practice consisted of mergers and acquisitions, employment law and general corporate matters.

Katherine is a former board member of the National Association of Professional Background Screeners. She graduated from Boston University with a bachelor of arts in history and has a juris doctorate from the University of Denver. She lives in Atlanta, Georgia.

Patricia M. Burrows
Behavioral Health Administrator
Kaiser Permanente of Georgia

P atricia Burrows has been with Kaiser Permanente of Georgia for more than 12 years. A clinical nurse by trade, Burrows has held several administrative posts of increasing responsibility in health care operations and currently serves as the health plan's behavioral health administrator. This past year, the behavioral health department made great accomplishments and was named Specialty Team of the Year.

Burrows is board certified in health care management and a fellow in the American College of Healthcare Executives. She was also a member of the faculty for the Institute of Healthcare Improvement and the Picker Institute.

A staunch community advocate, Burrows has worked closely with community organizations including the Clayton County Chamber of Commerce, March of Dimes and her church, Green Forest Community Baptist Church in Decatur, Georgia.

A native of New Jersey, Burrows received a bachelor of science degree and her master's degree in public administration from Rutgers University. She and her husband, Randy, have four children, Dorian, Randi, and twins Kalima and Karima. Her motto for life is "If it's going to be, it's up to me!"

T ina Capers-Hall is director of human resources for the metro Atlanta system of Comcast Cable. She implements various organizational initiatives through the management of a wide array of human resources functions including recruitment, employee relations, compliance, compensation and benefits, safety and employee development.

Prior to joining the cable industry, Tina worked in a variety of industries, including such organizations as TRW, Bristol-Myers, NEC Technologies, Prudential and Concessions International. She also served as an adjunct professor in the academic arena, and is a former assistant to the editor of the *Journal of Black Psychology*.

Tina served on the Georgia CASA board of directors. She is a Georgia 100 alumna, and a member of the Great Gals Network and the Cable Television Human Resources Association. She attends Cascade United Methodist Church.

Tina holds a bachelor's degree from Cornell University and a master of business administration degree from Clark Atlanta University.

Tina is married to John Hall, owner of Hall's of Fine Wines. They have two children, Ian, a freshman at Hampton University, and Gabrielle, a middle-schooler at Woodward Academy.

Tina A. Capers-Hall
Director, Human Resources
Comcast Cable

CORPORATE BRASS

Reginald Carson
Regional Operations Manager
Center for Disease Control and Prevention
Georgia Department of Human Resources

Reginald Carson is regional operations manager for the prevention services branch of the Georgia Department of Human Resources, specializing in the sexually transmitted disease control program. On assignment for the Centers for Disease Control and Prevention, he manages public service program policy throughout metro Atlanta and southern regions of Georgia in regards to STD prevention. Reginald has been with the CDC since 1992, and has received several outstanding yearly reviews for his work.

While working with the CDC, Reginald freelanced in sports broadcasting on the award-winning program *The Sports Vibe*. He received an award from the Delaware Press Association for his outstanding broadcast journalism. Likewise, he was featured in *Delaware Today* magazine as an emerging presence in sports broadcasting.

Reginald received a bachelor of science degree from Elizabeth City State University.

Reginald is a member of Omega Psi Phi Fraternity, Inc., Big Brothers Big Sisters of America, the Urban League of America, and a charter member of the Buckhead Cigar Club. The husband of Simone Silva-Carson, Reginald is the proud father of one daughter, Phoenix.

Ralph Cleveland
Senior Vice President
Engineering & Operations
AGL Resources

Ralph Cleveland became senior vice president, engineering and operations of AGL Resources in November of 2004. Primary among his responsibilities is executive oversight of the policy direction for the technical services and centralized operations of the company. Cleveland previously served as vice president of operations for Virginia Natural Gas. Prior to his work in local gas distribution, he worked in oil and gas production, research and development, natural gas processing and petrochemicals.

Cleveland is a member of the board of directors of the North American Energy Standards Board and a member of the national board of directors and public policy committee of the American Association of Blacks in Energy. He was a commissioner of the City of Virginia Beach Human Rights Commission.

Cleveland is a member of 100 Black Men and a life member of the National Society of Black Engineers, the National Black MBA Association and Kappa Alpha Psi Fraternity, Inc.

A Macon, Georgia native, Cleveland earned his undergraduate degree in mechanical engineering from Georgia Tech, and his master's degree in business administration from Tulane University in New Orleans.

Stacy Cole
Director, Government Affairs
Comcast Cable Communications, Inc.

Stacy Cole is the director of government affairs with the Atlanta region for Comcast Cable Communications, Inc., the largest provider of cable television and broadband services in the United States. As director of government affairs, Cole is responsible for maintaining relationships with elected officials and ensuring compliance of the cable franchise agreements in the Atlanta region.

Prior to joining Comcast, she served as director of government relations with Charter Communications. Additionally, Cole served as a law clerk for the Honorable Vernon R. Pearson, former chief justice of the Washington State Supreme Court, and was a senior assistant city attorney with the City of Atlanta Law Department, representing the Mayor's Office of Communications on cable and telecommunication matters. She is active in professional and community organizations and is a member of GABWA and NAMIC. She also serves on the boards of directors for Cool Girls, Inc., Literacy Action, Inc., and the Dogwood City Chapter of The Links, Inc.

Cole received a bachelor of arts degree from Washington State University and a juris doctorate from Gonzaga University School of Law.

Lauren-Elizabeth Colley
Director of Design
John Wieland Homes and Neighborhoods

Lauren-Elizabeth Colley is the director of design for John Wieland Homes and Neighborhoods of Atlanta, Georgia. As director, she provides leadership to the in-house staff of designers, and support to design managers in the company's Charlotte, Raleigh, Charleston and Nashville design centers. She is responsible for implementing business initiatives to produce monthly revenues of $1 million, as well as establishing practices to maximize the customer design experience.

Lauren-Elizabeth began her career at John Wieland Homes and Neighborhoods as a design consultant in 2000 and was soon promoted to design manager. In 2006 she assumed her current role as director of design. She was selected to participate in the company's Committed Leadership program, designed to further cultivate company members who demonstrate promising leadership potential.

Lauren-Elizabeth received a bachelor's degree in architecture with a minor in construction technology from the University of Virginia. A member of Alpha Kappa Alpha Sorority, Inc., she attends Ebenezer Baptist Church.

A native of Hampton, Virginia, Lauren-Elizabeth is the wife of Justin Colley and the mother of two daughters, Madison and Olivia.

Atlanta's
CORPORATE BRASS

Coy Cooper
Senior Architect
Brown Group of Companies

Coy Cooper is a senior architect with the Brown Group of Companies and a founding principal of Autaco Development. A registered architect with 19 years of experience, he specializes in designing commercial projects. Cooper is a licensed architect in Washington, D.C., Georgia and Alabama. He is certified by the National Council of Architectural Registration Boards (NCARB). Some of his projects include the 2,000-seat Bethune Cookman Performing Arts Theatre, several libraries and community centers, high-tech laboratories and multi-family housing.

Cooper holds a bachelor of architecture degree from Howard University in Washington, D.C.

In his free time, Cooper enjoys experimenting with electronics and working on home improvement projects. He is married to Audra Cooper, and enjoys spending time with their three sons, Vincent, Johnthan and Coy Jr.

Bill Davenport
Area Distribution Manager
Georgia Power Company

As area distribution manager for Georgia Power Company, Bill Davenport is responsible for the distribution and customer service operation in South Fulton. He manages four offices that serve 50,000 customers. He divides his time between addressing employee concerns, customer concerns and external issues such as community and economic development.

Davenport has worked for Georgia Power for 27 years as an engineering supervisor, a lead coordinator and as assistant to the regional manager. He developed a lighting plan that successfully tripled the yearly lighting sales.

Davenport is presently active on several boards in the South Fulton area. He is the vice president of programs for Partnership for Tomorrow, and the past president of the South Fulton Chamber of Commerce. He is also a board member of the Jesse Draper Boys & Girls Club, the South Fulton United Way, South Fulton Senior Services, and National Scholarship Services.

Davenport holds a bachelor's degree in engineering technology from Fort Valley State College, and a certificate in biblical studies from Ambassador Bible College. He is studying for a master's degree in religion from Liberty University.

Sadie Dennard joined Georgia Power in 1980, and has held various positions in communications and corporate relations. She is currently assistant region manager for Georgia Power's Metro East Region. In this role, Sadie works to ensure quality electric service for 300,000 customers in her area. Her external affairs work is focused on providing strategic support for education, economic development and civic and community initiatives.

Sadie is in her third term as an elected member of the Atlanta Board of Education. She has served as president of the board, and currently chairs the board's audit commission. As president of the Georgia School Board Association, she serves on several state and national education and public policy boards.

Sadie serves as a member on several boards, including Project GRAD Atlanta, Georgia Partnership for Excellence in Education and Community Education Partners. She is a member of the State Bar of Georgia Disciplinary Review Panel, The Links, Inc., and Smart Set.

Sadie holds a bachelor's degree in public communications from American University in Washington, D.C.

Her daughter, Brook, attends Vanderbilt University in Nashville, Tennessee.

Sadie Jo Dennard
Assistant Region Manager
Georgia Power

ReShon L. Dixon is the spa director of The Hammam Medical Day Spa. Her duties as a leader consist of medical product knowledge and training, payroll, promotion and marketing, and most importantly, responding to the needs of Hammam's clients and patients.

Her specialties are providing corrective skin care regimens, such as medical chemical peels, Microdermabrasion, laser hair removal, laser vein therapy, IPL for the removal of tattoos, laser genesis to produce collagen for younger looking skin, and Titan for maintaining elasticity of the skin. She is currently supervised by Dr. Frederick T. Work.

ReShon, a native of Omaha, Nebraska, moved to Atlanta in 1993 where she was trained at the International School of Skin, obtaining her license as a medical aesthetician in 1995. In 1998 ReShon attended Ultrasound Diagnostics and completed her externship at Saint Joseph Hospital and GBI. With this extensive training, she went on to perform echo studies on cadavers, graduating at the top of her class as a cardiovascular sonographer.

ReShon L. Dixon
Spa Director
The Hammam Medical Day Spa

Atlanta's
CORPORATE BRASS

Richard L. Duncan
Aviation Security Director
Hartsfield-Jackson Atlanta
International Airport

Richard L. Duncan, a certified protection professional (CPP), directs the airport security program at the world's busiest airport. He is charged with maintaining a safe and secure environment for more than 84 million passengers and 55,000 employees annually.

A retired U.S. Army major, Richard performed law enforcement and security management duties internationally. During Operation Desert Storm, he served the Chief Enemy Prisoner of War Branch and the U.S. Army Central Command. He received a Bronze Star for his outstanding service.

Richard is a past chairman of the Greater Atlanta Chapter of the American Society for Industrial Security. He also served as chairman of the public safety and security committee of the Airport Council International (ACI)-North America. A member of the ACI world security committee, Richard was named Security Director of the Year by *Access Control & Security Systems* magazine in 2004.

Richard received his bachelor's degree in criminal justice from the University of Florida, and his master's degree in education from the University of Southern California.

Richard is the husband of RaRhee and the proud father of three adult children.

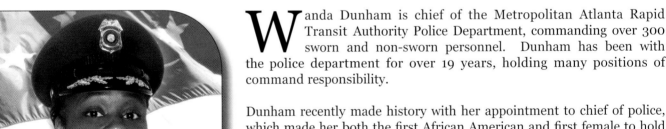

Wanda Dunham
Assistant General Manager
Police Chief
MARTA

Wanda Dunham is chief of the Metropolitan Atlanta Rapid Transit Authority Police Department, commanding over 300 sworn and non-sworn personnel. Dunham has been with the police department for over 19 years, holding many positions of command responsibility.

Dunham recently made history with her appointment to chief of police, which made her both the first African American and first female to hold this position.

Dunham received the Breaking the Glass Ceiling Award for leadership, a celebration of women's accomplishments in law enforcement, and the Chief Willie Smoot Community Service Award in appreciation for her outstanding service to the community. Dunham was also featured in the *Ebony* magazine for her historical accomplishments.

Dunham holds a bachelor of science degree from Jacksonville State University and received a master's degree in public administration with honors from Columbus State University.

A native of Atlanta, Dunham is married to Dwight Dunham and the couple has one son, Jordan.

Kellye Blackburn Eccles is a graduate of Spelman College, Clark Atlanta University and Fordham University. She is currently director of career planning and placement for non-business majors at Morehouse College. In the past three years, Kellye has increased the number of customers served by 117 percent. Recently, she was invited to present about best practices in career services programming at the 2006 Black Executive Exchange Program's national conference.

Kellye is the former assistant dean of campus life for Morehouse College, where she managed all chartered organizations on campus. She was invited to participate in Morehouse Leadership: A Management Development Program 2001-2002.

Kellye previously worked for the State of Georgia as acting director of the Violence Against Women Program, which provides funding and technical assistance to 21 rape crisis centers and 19 health districts in Georgia. She was recently invited to serve on the Morehouse-Spelman Task Force on Gender Relations, Violence and Campus Safety.

A native and current resident of Southwest Atlanta, Kellye is the wife of George Eccles and is the proud mother of two sons, Emerson and George Todd.

Kellye Blackburn Eccles
Director, Career Planning & Placement for Non-Business Majors
Morehouse College

An educator, editor, administrator, J. William Fulbright fellow, consultant, and the recipient of several faculty development grants, Dr. Hazel Arnett Ervin is an associate professor of English and the director of general education at Morehouse College. Trained in the teacher preparation program at Guilford College in the late 1970s and in African-American literature at Howard University in the early 1990s, Ervin promotes higher education that is outcome-based and measurable.

At Morehouse, Ervin serves in the role of director, overseeing the redesign of the college's core curriculum. She is a consultant to national testing services, a member of numerous educational organizations, and editor of the bestselling *African American Literary Criticism, 1773 to 2000*; *The Handbook of African American Literature*; and *The Critical Response to Ann Petry*. Ervin speaks frequently at colleges, universities, churches and libraries on pedagogy and assessment, the acclaimed 1940s writer Ann Petry, and the African-American oral tradition.

Her favorite quote is: "I am only one, but I am one. And I will not let what I cannot do prevent me from doing what I can."

Dr. Hazel Arnett Ervin
Director of General Education
Morehouse College

Atlanta's
CORPORATE BRASS

Valencia D. Evans
Director of Childcare Center
Southern Regional Medical Center

Valencia D. Evans is director of the childcare center at Southern Regional Medical Center. In this position, she manages the day-to-day operations of the center, is responsible for 13 team members and up to 75 enrolled children. Valencia cooperates with rules and regulations required by the State of Georgia as well as standards recommended by the National Association for the Education of Young Children.

She received a bachelor of arts degree from Georgia State University, and is scheduled to begin work on a master of arts degree in school leadership in January of 2007. Valencia received a national administrator credential in 2005 and trained as a child development associate in 2004. She is a member of the Georgia Association of Young Children, National Association for the Education of Young Children, Southern Early Childhood Association and the Association for the Advancement of Curriculum Development.

A native of Atlanta, Georgia, Valencia is a divorced mother of four daughters.

Lillie Farmer
Clinical Manager
Wound, Ostomy and Continence
Southern Regional Medical Center

Lillie Farmer is the clinical manager for the wound and ostomy department at Southern Regional Medical Center in Riverdale, Georgia, where she has been a part of the Southern Regional family for 29 years.

The care delivered to her patients involves a team approach in the development of protocols to manage simple and complicated wounds (vascular, dermal, and surgical), fistulas and minor skin disorders. Additionally, care and teaching is provided to ostomates and their families. Her other responsibilities include active participation on quality improvement teams, a professional development council and products standards and evaluations.

Lillie was the recipient of the Georgia Nurses Association's Nurse of the Year award for 2004 and was Clayton State University's Distinguished Health Science Alumni in 2005. She was one of 12 Legends in her workplace in 2004.

In 1985 Lillie received an associate degree in nursing, and a bachelor's degree in nursing in 1994 from Clayton State University. In 2003 she received a master's in education from Central Michigan University.

Lillie has three adult children and three grandchildren. Her hobbies include fishing and bowling.

Nedra Farrar-Luten is the director of human resources and organizational development of the Hartsfield-Jackson Atlanta International Airport. In this capacity, she directs the human resources, customer service, training and safety activities for the City of Atlanta's Department of Aviation.

Nedra is well-respected in the area of airport and public personnel management, having come to Hartsfield-Jackson after 14 years with the Raleigh-Durham Airport Authority in North Carolina. In her capacity as assistant airport director, she was responsible for human resources, customer service, training and the minority/female-owned business enterprise programs.

Nedra received a bachelor of arts degree in communications from North Carolina State University. She received certification in public personnel administration from the University of North Carolina's Institute of Government. She attained certification from the International Public Management Association for Human Resources as a certified professional in 2000.

A native of Brooklyn, New York, Nedra is the mother of two adult sons, Thomas David (TD) and Christian.

Nedra Farrar-Luten
Director of Human Resources
Hartsfield-Jackson Atlanta International Airport

Inspiring and energizing by action and example, Dr. Florence Ferguson is the dean of the School of Criminal Justice at American InterContinental University, Dunwoody Campus. She has seen enrollment increase from 64 students when the department first opened in May of 2004 to more than 300 today. Additionally, Ferguson was instrumental in adding a forensics concentration to the program.

Ferguson is a member of the American Society of Criminal Justice Studies, the Academy of Criminal Justice Studies and the Southern Criminal Justice Association. She regularly contributes chapters to criminal justice-related books and writes articles on the subject for magazines.

A native of Detroit, Ferguson earned her associate degree in law enforcement and a bachelor's degree in sociology from Mercy College of Detroit. She continued her education at the University of Detroit where she received her master's degree in criminal justice. She received a doctorate in social sciences from Michigan State University.

Dr. Florence Ferguson
Dean, School of Criminal Justice
American InterContinental University
Dunwoody Campus

Karissa Easley George
Director, Diversity &
Community Relations
John Wieland Homes and Neighborhoods

Karissa E. George is director of diversity and community relations for John Wieland Homes and Neighborhoods. She provides strategic direction to the company's diversity initiatives in addition to managing its philanthropic efforts. She is responsible for enhancing recruitment and retention, overseeing the diversity council and ethics review committee, and conducting ongoing cultural awareness and diversity training. Karissa also manages annual company charitable contributions as well as a 20-person grant committee responsible for annual employee contributions.

Karissa serves on the board of directors of Literacy Action and the Andrew & Walter Young YMCA. She also volunteers with the Girl Scouts and is a member of Providence Missionary Baptist Church and Delta Sigma Theta Sorority, Inc.

A member of Leadership Atlanta Class of 2005, Karissa was recognized as the 2005 Urban Influencer by the Atlanta Urban League Young Professionals.

Karissa received a bachelor of arts degree from Emory University. She was awarded a master's degree from the Andrew Young School of Policy Studies at Georgia State University.

A native of Atlanta, Karissa is the wife of Kwaku (KC) and the mother of Bakari.

Angela Gray
Vice President of Human Resources
Comcast Cable, Atlanta Region

As vice president of human resources for Comcast Cable's Atlanta region, Angela Gray provides strategic direction for human resources.

Angela is a fellow of the Betsy Magness Leadership Program. She has certifications in finance and HR strategy from the Society of Human Resources Academy. She supports her community through volunteering with the Children's Restoration Network, Comcast Cares, Cable Positive, Pathbuilders, Inc., and the American Heart Association. Previously, she served as the director of learning and development for Comcast's Southern division.

Angela holds a bachelor of science degree in education from Southern University and A&M College in Baton Rouge. She holds certifications from the Institute for Applied Management and Law, the DOL and the Equal Employment Opportunity Commission. Recently, she received the 2006 Red Letter Award for mentoring. She is a member of the Society for Human Resource Management, Women in Cable & Telecommunications, the National Association for Multi-Ethnicity in Communications and the National Association for Female Executives.

Angela has been married for 16 years and has three children, Alex, 13, Jordan, 11 and Addison, 9.

Mary Magee Gullatte has over 28 years of nursing experience, including hematology/oncology, blood and marrow stem cell transplant and solid organ transplant. She is presently inpatient director of oncology nursing at Winship Cancer Institute and Oncology Data Center of Emory University, and the director of nursing for oncology and transplant services at Emory University Hospitals in Atlanta.

She received her bachelor's degree from the University of Southern Mississippi, and her master's degree from the Emory University School of Nursing in Atlanta. A doctoral candidate at the University of Utah College of Nursing in Salt Lake City, Mary has various published works including two edited books, one of which was acclaimed Book of the Year in January of 2006 by the *American Journal of Nursing*.

An international presenter on cancer nursing topics, Mary recently spoke in Sydney, Australia and Oslo, Norway. She teaches youth Sunday school at Turner Chapel AME Church in Marietta.

She enjoys mentoring other professionals, writing, sewing, and cooking. Among her many accomplishments, Mary is a wife and mother of two children, Rodney Jr. and Ronda.

Mary Magee Gullatte
Inpatient Director of Oncology Nursing
Winship Cancer Institute
Oncology Data Center
Emory University

Moses A. Hardie Jr. serves as chief people officer of the insurance division for ChoicePoint, Inc. in Alpharetta, Georgia. Having served in this role since August of 2005, he is responsible for all strategic, advisory and operational human resources services for ChoicePoint's flagship operation. There are locations in Alpharetta, Georgia; Hartford, Connecticut; Orem, Utah; Dallas, Texas; San Ramon, California; and Chicago, Illinois.

Prior to his appointment at ChoicePoint, Moses was assistant vice president of human resources shared services for Allstate Insurance Company in Northbrook, Illinois.

Moses received his undergraduate degree from Hampton University and a master of business administration degree from the University of Illinois at Chicago.

Moses has served on the board of directors for the Hampton University School of Business, as well as several charitable organizations. He is a member of Kappa Alpha Psi Fraternity, Inc.

Moses and his wife, Joanne, have two adult children.

Moses A. Hardie Jr.
Chief People Officer, Insurance Division
ChoicePoint, Inc.

Lillian Harding
Director of Marketing
Comcast Cable Communications, Inc.

Lillian Harding is the director of marketing for the Atlanta system of Comcast Cable Communications and has more than 16 years of experience in the cable industry. In this role, Lillian oversees the marketing and sales responsibilities, including product marketing and messaging to ensure strategic, consistent positioning and proactive communications to targeted audiences.

Prior to joining Comcast, Lillian was with Wometco Cable and was instrumental in the branding and name change to Media One.

Lillian has served on the boards of the Tennessee Cable Television Association and the Cable Television Association of Georgia. She is a member of the National Association of Multi-Ethnicity of Atlanta. Recently, the Cable Association awarded Lillian with two first-place awards for Excellence in Multi-Cultural Marketing.

Lillian is a member of Global Destiny International Center in Duluth. In her spare time, she likes to golf, play the flute and piano, and travel.

Lillian holds a bachelor of arts degree in communication and advertising from Rutgers University.

Inga Harmon
Vice President
Harmon & Harmon Realtors, Inc.

Inga Harmon is vice president of Harmon & Harmon Realtors, Inc., a family-owned and operated business founded by her mother, Delois. Harmon is a second-generation realtor specializing in selling commercial and investment properties in both the middle Georgia and metro Atlanta areas. She possesses extensive field experience in residential and commercial construction thanks to the close tutelage of her father, Paul Harmon, founder of Harmon Construction, Inc. Her vast experience in the real estate arena coupled with her construction background of residential facilities gives Harmon versatility that puts her in demand.

Harmon is a multi-million dollar producer in both the Macon and the metro Atlanta areas. She is a life member of the Million Dollar Club. She successfully locates and negotiates transactions between many out-of-state investors and developers.

Harmon received her bachelor's degree from Clark Atlanta University in 1997. She holds a GRI (Graduate Realtor Institute) designation and is currently pursing the designation of CCIM (certified commercial investment member).

Michael Hewitt
Regional Vice President of Operations
Comcast Cable, Atlanta Region

M ichael Hewitt is the regional vice president of operations for Comcast Cable's Atlanta region. Hewitt's primary focus is on strengthening the region's field operations. He works directly with the leadership of Atlanta's four systems and the call centers to align processes, thus ensuring customer satisfaction throughout the service process.

Throughout his career, Hewitt has been credited for consistently delivering results that demonstrate growth in Comcast's video and high-speed Internet business. He was instrumental in launching new products like high definition television (HDTV), ON DEMAND and Comcast Digital Voice.

Hewitt began his career in the cable industry in 1995 as area director for TCI's Baltimore/Washington D.C. market. In 1999 he joined AT&T Broadband as the director of technical operations in Atlanta.

Following the acquisition by Comcast, Hewitt was named vice president and general manager, overseeing operations in Atlanta, and the counties of South Fulton, Gwinnett and DeKalb. He was promoted to his current position in May of 2006.

Hewitt holds an undergraduate degree in mechanical engineering from Stony Brook University and a master of business administration degree from Hofstra University.

D oug Hooker is vice president for PBS&J, a national engineering consulting firm. He coordinates development efforts throughout the Mid-Atlantic and Southeastern states. Previously, he held leadership positions with other engineering firms and was executive director of the Georgia State Road and Tollway Authority. He also served as commissioner of the Department of Public Works for Atlanta, leading the department through the 1996 Olympic Games.

Doug is deeply involved in the community, chairing the Regional Atlanta Civic League and the Emory University board of visitors. He serves on the board of the Metro Atlanta Chamber of Commerce, the Georgia Conservancy, the Institute for Georgia Environmental Leadership and the Regional Business Coalition. He has participated in Leadership Georgia, Leadership Atlanta and the Regional Leadership Institute.

Doug holds a bachelor's degree and master's degree in technology and science policy from the Georgia Institute of Technology, as well as a master of business administration degree from Emory University.

He is married to Patrise Perkins-Hooker, with whom he has two children. In his spare time, he enjoys reading and composing music.

Douglas Randolf Hooker
Vice President & East Director
PBS & J

CORPORATE BRASS

Joe Jackson
Supplier Diversity Director
Hartsfield-Jackson
Development Program

Joe Jackson is supplier diversity director for the $6.2 billion Hartsfield-Jackson Development Program. He is president and chief executive officer of the Greater Atlanta Economic Alliance, a 501(c)(3) organization endorsed by the Atlanta Department of Aviation.

Joe manages diversity initiatives involving inclusion and increasing the capacity and capabilities of small, female and minority-owned businesses interested in doing business with the airport. He has received several awards in the industry. Joe oversees all ongoing business development and technical assistance programs and has administered economic model research papers on behalf of the U.S. Department of Transportation.

With more than 20 years of experience in business development and diversity management, Joe's skills have led to growth and profitability for Fortune 500 companies in the automotive and transportation industries.

Joe received a bachelor's degree from the University of Southern Mississippi. He completed executive and leadership programs from Harvard Business School, Tuck Executive Education at Dartmouth and the American Management Association.

A native of New Orleans, Joe is married to Angela and they are the proud parents of Samantha, Joseph (Trey) and Brandon.

Cynthia Jenkins
Director
Corporate & Foundation Development
Southern Regional Health Systems

Cynthia Jenkins is the director of corporate and foundation development at Southern Regional Medical Center Foundation. In this capacity, she oversees the foundation of a 410-bed nonprofit medical center. Additionally, she is responsible for volunteer services and the First Steps Program, which is geared toward preventing child abuse.

Cynthia has spent more than 20 years in the private and public sectors working throughout the country in higher education, human resources, social services, economic development and customer services. She has held executive positions in the State of Maryland Department of Social Services and in The Toledo Hospital in northwest Ohio, which was once the largest hospital in the state.

Cynthia earned a bachelor's degree in education from Bowling Green State University and a juris doctorate from the University of Toledo. She volunteers for the Clayton County Juvenile Court Division and is very active in causes geared toward helping those in need.

Cynthia is married to Dr. Marcus Jenkins. Cynthia and Marcus are the owners of Onyxx Jazz Restaurant in Fayetteville. They reside in Fayetteville with their two wonderful daughters, Camille and Cymone.

With a vast knowledge of the organization, Sabrina Jenkins is the director of special events for the Atlanta Braves/ Turner Field. Her duties include negotiating contracts, managing budgets and overall marketing strategies, while supervising and executing event logistics. Additionally, she oversees the Atlanta Braves Supplier Diversity Program. Since joining the Braves, she has worked in the ticket sales and special events departments.

In 2004 Sabrina was awarded Supplier Diversity Champion of the Year for Turner Broadcasting, Inc. In 2005 she was nominated for the Heiskell Award, which highlights employees for their community service. Sabrina is also a two-time nominee for the Georgia Minority Supplier Development Council's Advocate of the Year Award. In October of 2006, Sabrina was nominated as one of the Top 25 Most Influential Women in Atlanta by *rolling out*.

Receiving a full scholarship, Sabrina graduated from Augusta State University with a bachelor's degree in business administration. A native of Atlanta, she resides in Douglasville and is a member of Salem Bible Church in Lithonia. Sabrina loves to read, horseback ride, golf and attend sporting events.

Sabrina Jenkins
Director, Special Events
Atlanta Braves/Turner Field

K. Michelle Sourie Johnson is The Home Depot's director of supplier diversity. As director, she created the company's first formalized supplier diversity strategy and supporting processes. Michelle's primary responsibilities include the sourcing and development of women-owned, minority-owned and small businesses; the training and support of more than 350 product and service buyers; and directing multi-level outreach activities on behalf of the entire Home Depot enterprise. Her efforts have won the company notable industry recognition.

In addition, Michelle oversees the varied administrative functions in support of the company's multi-billion dollar Government Services Administration contract. Previously, Michelle was employed by Wal-Mart Stores, Inc., where she was the first and youngest African-American attorney to serve as corporate counsel.

Michelle serves on several boards including the Georgia Minority Supplier Development Council, Girls Inc., SafeHouse and the National Center for American Indian Enterprise Development. Active within her church and community, she serves on the Vida Nueva Leadership Council and Leadership Atlanta.

An Oklahoma native, she earned a bachelor's degree in organizational administration from Oklahoma State University and a juris doctorate from the University of Kansas.

K. Michelle Sourie Johnson
Director, Supplier Diversity
The Home Depot

Atlanta's
CORPORATE BRASS

Kimberly D. Jones
Vice President of Student Affairs
American InterContinental University
Dunwoody Campus

Kimberly Jones is vice president of student affairs at American InterContinental University, Dunwoody Campus where she has worked for the last four years. As the vice president, Jones is responsible for activities directly impacting student success such as retention and career services.

Prior to her employment with AIU Dunwoody, Jones was employed with the University of Phoenix-Metro Detroit Campus. She had a very successful career there, working her way up from financial aid advisor to the associate director of finance.

Jones graduated with her associate degree from Lansing Community College. She received a bachelor of arts and a bachelor of science degree from Wayne State University. She graduated from the University of Phoenix with a master of arts degree.

A native of Michigan, she is married with three children. Jones is also the owner and operator of Unforgettable Cheesecake.

Rosemary Jones
Director, Supplier Diversity Program
Turner Broadcasting System, Inc.

Rosemary Jones joined TBS (Turner Broadcasting System), Inc. in May of 2002 after more than three decades with IBM. As director of the TBS Supplier Diversity Program, she develops and executes supplier diversity strategies and program initiatives for the company and works with appropriate networks and diversity organizations that promote inclusion.

A nationally known supplier diversity champion, Rosemary also provides diversity consulting to Turner's prime business partners, minority and women enterprises, and government agencies. Rosemary assisted Governor Roy Barnes and the State of Georgia with the development and implementation of the first Governor's Mentor Protégé Program.

Rosemary serves on the boards of directors for the Georgia Women Business Council, the Asian-American Chamber of Commerce, Cobb Micro Enterprise Center, and the American Hotel Lodging Association multicultural advisory council.

A recipient of numerous awards and honors, Rosemary was named one of Georgia's 100 Most Powerful and Influential Women in Corporate America from 2002 to 2005 by the Atlanta Business League and *Women Looking Ahead*.

An Atlanta native, Rosemary earned her bachelor's degree in business administration from the State University of New York.

Linda Jordan is senior vice president of institutional sales and marketing for Mesirow Financial. Linda is in charge of the Atlanta office of Mesirow Financial and is responsible for developing the firm's institutional relationships and marketing its investment management capabilities to plan sponsors and other institutional investors.

Linda received her master of business administration degree from the Fuqua School of Business at Duke University. She earned bachelor's and master's degrees in electrical engineering from the Georgia Institute of Technology, as well as a bachelor's degree in mathematics from Clark Atlanta University. She was recently selected for membership in the 2006 Academy of Distinguished Engineering Alumni at Georgia Tech.

Linda serves on the board of the National Association of Securities Professionals. She chairs the governmental relations committee for the Atlanta chapter of the National Black MBA Association and sits on the executive committee for the Atlanta chapter of the National Forum for Black Public Administrators. She is also a member of the Atlanta alumnae chapter of Delta Sigma Theta Sorority, Inc.

Linda Jordan
Senior Vice President
Mesirow Financial

John Kelley is manager of external affairs for Georgia Power's Atlanta region. A native of Augusta, he earned his bachelor of business administration degree from Savannah State University and his master of public administration degree from Georgia Southern University.

John manages and develops external strategies for the metro Atlanta area. In addition, he provides work direction to the region's external team. He has built and maintained strong professional and personal relationships with elected officials, statewide leaders, the Georgia Public Service Commission and leaderships of both local and national organizations.

His positions held with Georgia Power include manager of skills training, region comptroller, senior urban advisor and senior regulatory advisor. John is also chairman of the Atlanta Business League, and a past chair of the Committee for a Better Atlanta and the Savannah State University Foundation. He also served as chairman of the South DeKalb Business Incubator.

Currently he serves on several community organization boards, and along with his wife, Michelle, he is an active member of the New Life Presbyterian Church in College Park. They reside in Peachtree City.

John Kelley
Manager, External Affairs
Georgia Power

Marcus C. Kellum
Chief of Code Enforcement
City of Sandy Springs

Marcus Kellum is chief of code enforcement for Georgia's seventh-largest city, Sandy Springs. His main responsibility is to lead the effort in maintaining compliance with all city codes, ordinances and regulations.

Marcus was selected as one of *Georgia Trend* magazine's 2006 40 Under 40. In 2005 Marcus was elected vice president of the Georgia Association of Code Enforcement, and chairman of the certification committee. A graduate of the Gwinnett Neighborhood Leadership Institute, he helped organize the Harness the Power Gala, which brought together community leaders from different ethnic backgrounds to discuss diversity in Gwinnett County.

Marcus holds certifications as a building official, code enforcement administrator, and property maintenance and housing inspector. He received a certificate of achievement from the Federal Emergency Management Agency for leadership and influence.

A native of New York City, Marcus resides in Gwinnett County with his wife. He firmly believes: "For everyone to whom much is given, of him shall much be required."

Christopher Kunney
Director of Information Systems
Piedmont Healthcare

A certified professional in health care information technology, Christopher currently serves as director of information systems support for Kunney Piedmont Healthcare. He is responsible for help desk, telecommunications, applications and field support services for Piedmont's three hospitals and 19 affiliated clinics.

A Fort Valley State University graduate, he holds a bachelor's degree and an executive master's degree from The Georgia Institute of Technology. Christopher's civic activities include a position as an adjunct professor at DeVry University and DeVry's industry advisory roundtable. He was a member of the Former Black Business Professionals, an Entrepreneur's Conference presenter and commencement speaker for ITT Institute, and a volunteer for The Metro Atlanta Neurosurgery Foundation's Adopt-A-Village Project.

Christopher is the first recipient of the College of Healthcare Information Management Executives (CHIME) Minority Scholarship Award and a participant of CHIME's CIO boot camp. He recently appeared in an *Atlanta Hospital News* article entitled "Salute to Minorities in Healthcare."

His organizational involvement includes the National Black MBA Association Atlanta Chapter, Georgia Association of Healthcare Executives, Kappa Alpha Psi Fraternity and New Birth Missionary Baptist Church in Lithonia.

Chris Lyons is the deputy director of Sanofi Pasteur and is responsible for all of Blue Cross/Blue Shield and Humana Managed Care Organizations across the country. His mission is to protect and improve human health worldwide by providing innovative vaccines for the prevention and treatment of disease. He also plays an active role in the immunization community to maximize vaccinations. Sanofi Pasteur's vision is of a world in which no one suffers or dies from a vaccine-preventable disease.

Chris has 24 years of experience in the medical marketplace and has had a distinguished career with other medical companies such as Johnson & Johnson and Smith & Nephew Inc.

Chris received a bachelor of science degree from Central State University in Wilberforce, Ohio, and a master's degree in business administration from Shorter College in Rome, Georgia. He is a life member of Kappa Alpha Psi Fraternity, Inc. and a member of Prince Hall F&AM, St. Mark's Lodge #7 in Columbus, Ohio.

Chris and his wife, Linda, were both born in Pennsylvania. They have three sons, Christopher, Cameron and Cory.

A. Christopher Lyons
Deputy Director, National Accounts
Sanofi Pasteur, Inc.

Lance Lyttle is the chief information officer for the Department of Aviation, Hartsfield-Jackson Atlanta International Airport. In this position, he supports the organization's strategic objectives and assures the successful implementation and integration of technologies across the airport. He is responsible for leading all technology efforts related to the airport's voice and data infrastructure.

Lance sits on the editorial board of the publication, *Airport Technology International,* and the IT committee of the Wireless Airport Association (WAA). He is also a founding member of Emoquad Internet Services.

Lance received a bachelor of science degree with a double major in physics and computer science. In 1996 he was awarded a master's degree in management information systems from the University of the West Indies.

A native of Jamaica, Lance enjoys jet skiing and soccer. He is also an avid writer of poetry and quotes.

His favorite quote is: "Seek ye happiness with vigor and purpose, but break not the chains that bind thee in times of sorrow."

Lance Lyttle
Chief Information Officer
Department of Aviation
Hartsfield-Jackson Atlanta
International Airport

Atlanta's
CORPORATE BRASS

Celebrating African-American Achievements

Derrell Martin
Regional Human Resources Director
North America Southeast Region
Johnson Controls, Inc.

Derrell Martin leads the human resource function for the building efficiency group in the Southeast region of Johnson Controls, Inc., a leading supplier of building management systems and controls for quality building environments.

Derrell's responsibilities include ensuring the profitable growth of a $10 billion service business through his participation in the development of business plans, strategies and actions that ensure organizational performance, and positive employee and customer relations. He recently received two merit awards for exceeding customer expectations.

Prior to Johnson Controls, Derrell spent 12 years at Honeywell International Inc. and seven years with General Motors, holding various supervisory and managerial positions in production, quality control, internal audit and human resources.

Derrell has represented corporations on several cluster boards for historically black colleges and universities, the NAACP and the National Urban League. He received awards for his service to black employee self-help networks and employee service organizations.

A native of Saginaw, Michigan, Derrell holds a bachelor of arts degree in sociology and business administration from Saginaw Valley State University. He is a member of Zion Missionary Baptist Church in

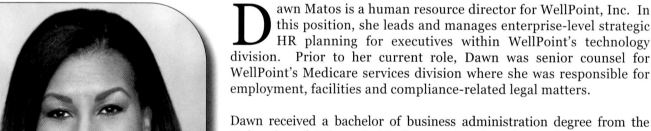

Dawn Matos
Human Resource Director
WellPoint, Inc.

Dawn Matos is a human resource director for WellPoint, Inc. In this position, she leads and manages enterprise-level strategic HR planning for executives within WellPoint's technology division. Prior to her current role, Dawn was senior counsel for WellPoint's Medicare services division where she was responsible for employment, facilities and compliance-related legal matters.

Dawn received a bachelor of business administration degree from the University of Wisconsin-Madison and a law degree from Marquette University.

Dawn is a member of the American Bar Association, the State Bar of Wisconsin, the Association of Corporate Counsel, the Society of Human Resource Professionals and Alpha Kappa Alpha Sorority, Inc.

Dawn is an active member of Community of Faith Family Church where she volunteers for the children's ministry and is a member of the praise dance team. She and her husband, Antonio, live in the metro Atlanta area with their 9-year-old daughter, Imani.

D r. Gary S. May, Steve W. Chaddick chair of the School of Electrical and Computer Engineering at the Georgia Institute of Technology, is the department's chief academic officer. He provides leadership to more than 100 faculty members and 2,300 students in the nation's seventh ranked program.

May performs research in computer-aided manufacturing of integrated circuits and has authored more than 240 publications. He was Georgia Tech's Outstanding Young Alumnus in 1993 and ASEE's Outstanding Minority Engineer in 2004. He received Georgia Tech's Outstanding Service Award in 1999, and two Best Paper Awards from IEEE.

May has created programs to increase participation among underrepresented students in science and engineering. Since 1998, 167 minorities have received doctorates in those fields at Georgia Tech, the most in the nation.

A St. Louis native, May received a bachelor's degree in electrical engineering from Georgia Tech and a master's degree and doctorate in electrical engineering and computer science from the University of California, Berkeley.

May and his wife, LeShelle, have two daughters, Simone and Jordan. He is a member of Cascade United Methodist Church.

Gary S. May, Ph.D.
Steve W. Chaddick School Chair
School of Electrical &
Computer Engineering
Georgia Institute of Technology

L isa A. Menzies is director of business development for Johnson Controls, Inc. In this position, Lisa builds partnerships with the historically black colleges and universities and other minority businesses. Building these relationships allows Johnson Controls to create partnerships that better serve the needs of the schools and the community.

Lisa has been featured in numerous magazines including the 2004 deans' edition of *US Black Engineer and Information Technology* and *BLACK COLLEGIAN Magazine*. In 2004 she was named one of the Nation's Most Powerful and Influential Women in *Women Looking Ahead News Magazine*.

Lisa serves on the boards of the National Black College Alumni Hall of Fame and the Georgia Association of Minority Entrepreneurs. She chairs the board of Opportunities Industrialization Center of New Orleans, and co-chairs the Bowie State University School of Business board of advisors and the Southern University College of Business MBA national board of advisors.

Lisa is a founding member of the HBCU Chiefs and Directors Association.

A native of New Orleans, Lisa attended Southern University at New Orleans and received a degree from Delgado College.

Lisa A. Menzies
Director of Business Development
Historically Black Colleges & Universities
Johnson Controls, Inc.

CORPORATE BRASS

Marsha I. Middleton
Director, Public Relations
Four Seasons Hotel Atlanta

Marsha Middleton is the public relations director at Four Seasons Hotel Atlanta, the city's only five-star, five-diamond hotel. She is responsible for managing the hotel's brand amongst the media and public as well as creating partnership opportunities that attract new business to the hotel and its four-star restaurant, Park 75.

After graduating cum laude with a degree in journalism from Florida A&M University, she began her career as a public relations manager with Habitat for Humanity International. Marsha then made the switch to corporate America when she joined The Home Depot as public relations manager, where she organized store grand opening events in the company's southeast division, including Home Depot's first store in Puerto Rico.

Marsha has been active in the Public Relations Society of America's Georgia chapter and its travel and tourism section. She is also a board member of the Atlanta Community Food Bank, Starlight Starbright of Atlanta and public relations chair for Flavor of Atlanta.

Marsha resides in Brookhaven with her husband, Will, and son, Trey.

Patricia A. Middleton
Managing Director, Surgical Services
Southern Regional Medical Center

Patricia Middleton is the managing director of surgical services at Southern Regional Medical Center. She is responsible for providing clinical and administrative direction to multiple services which support the care of patients in the perioperative area. These include pre-op, inpatient and outpatient surgery, post anesthesia recovery units, endoscopy and sterile processing.

Patricia was featured in the *Empire Who's Who Among Executive Professionals* for 2005-2006. She is a member of New Birth South Metropolitan Church, Delta Sigma Theta Sorority, Inc., the Association of Operating Room Nurses and the Georgia Organization of Nurse Leaders.

Patricia received her nursing degree from New Mexico State University. She earned her master's degree in health services administration from St. Francis University and recently completed her second master's degree in business administration.

A native of Alamogordo, New Mexico, Patricia is the wife of Tony Middleton and the proud mother of a daughter, Kelani, and a son, Xavier.

Chanda Moran is a business banking director in Wachovia Mortgage Corporation's business banking group, where she is responsible for building relationships that will position Wachovia as the premier provider of financial services to the southwest Atlanta business market. She works diligently leading a team of business bankers who are committed to meeting and exceeding the customers' financial needs.

Chanda joined Wachovia in 2002 from Bank of America, where she served as vice president of client management. In this role, she was responsible for managing commercial banking relationships and conducting industry research on existing and prospective customers.

Chanda has worked as a business consultant for more than 15 years. She began her career with Exxon/Mobil, where she advised independent dealers on the operations of their businesses. She transitioned that experience into advising entrepreneurs across various industry segments when she began her banking career in Atlanta.

Chanda holds a master's degree in general administration from Central Michigan University and an undergraduate degree in industrial administration from Mercer University.

She and her husband are the proud parents of two children, Keyra Jai and Jason II.

Chanda H. Moran
Business Banking Director
Wachovia Mortgage Corporation

Lynette Bell-Ndiaye is first vice president at SunTrust Bank in Atlanta, Georgia, where she manages the bank's community development program for the southeastern region of Georgia, Tennessee and portions of Alabama. She is a 16-year veteran of SunTrust, having worked for SunBank in Florida before relocating to Atlanta.

Her community service is extensive and she has served as a board or committee member for the DeKalb advisory council for the United Way of Metro Atlanta, the United Way Women's Legacy Regional Council, the Emergency Shelter Initiative, the Georgia Black Chamber of Commerce and the Georgia Community Development Roundtable.

Her other accomplishments include the 2006 Pioneer Award from the Metro Atlanta Chapter of 100 Black Women, the You Make A Difference Award from United Way DeKalb, and the Leadership award from United Way. She is a member of Delta Sigma Theta Sorority, Inc., and married to Mam-Ahmedou Ndiaye of Senegal, West Africa.

A Florida native, Bell-Ndiaye received her degree from Florida State University and received her certification as a compliance manager from the University of Georgia and the Georgia Bankers Association.

Lynette Bell Ndiaye
First Vice President
SunTrust Bank, Atlanta

Atlanta's
CORPORATE BRASS

Celebrating African-American Achievements

Ewa Ife Omo Oba
Manager
Shrine of the Black Madonna
Cultural Center & Bookstore

Ewa Ife Omo Oba is the manager of the Shrine of the Black Madonna Cultural Center & Bookstore in Atlanta.

Returning to the store after a five-year absence, Ewa hit the ground running, bringing a community friendly vibe along with her. A quirky blend of earth mother and African diva, Ewa brings more than 25 years of management experience to the bookstore. An avid reader, she continues her search for the big thing in black literature and her efforts have helped launch the early careers of many of today's African-American literary stars.

Ewa is currently creating venues to showcase the creative gifts of the black community in metro Atlanta. Using her role as the Kwanzaa coordinator at the Shrine, she is bringing those creative genres to the seven-day festival.

A published author and poet, Ewa began her career in broadcast journalism and public relations. A formally trained actor and director, she provides guided tours of the Cultural Centers and Bookstores, Karamu Galleries I and II, and the nationally acclaimed Black Holocaust Museum.

Dwight Pullen
Director for Runway 10-28
Hartsfield-Jackson
Development Program

Dwight Pullen served as director for the fifth runway project at Hartsfield-Jackson Atlanta International Airport. He is a program management consultant for the City of Atlanta and an employee of H.J. Russell & Company. He oversaw the execution of the $1.28 billion runway expansion, which culminated in the commissioning of "the most important runway in America" in May of 2006.

The runway project was completed tens of millions of dollars under budget and opened on time. Dwight was recognized in *Fortune* magazine and *Southeast Construction* for his stellar leadership and work. He was also spotlighted in *The Atlanta Journal-Constitution*.

Dwight received his bachelor of science degree in civil engineering. He serves on several nonprofit boards including the homeless prevention center, Caring For Others; marriage and family counseling with New Beginnings; and the Christian business leaders, Kings & Priests. His other memberships include the Project Management Institute, the National Society of Black Engineers and the Georgia Tech Alumni Association.

A native of Pittsburgh, Dwight is the husband of Eleanore and the proud father of four sons, Dwight III, Blake, Grant and Devontae.

368 WHO'S *Who*

A l Richardson is the regional supplier diversity manager for the controls group of Johnson Controls. In this position, he is responsible for implementing initiatives of the Controls Group's supplier diversity program. His responsibilities include developing diversity best practices, strengthening relationships with customers, minority organizations and the National Minority Supplier Development Council (NMSDC).

A two-time Johnson Controls Merit Award winner, Al has received Supplier Diversity Advocate of the Year nominations from the Georgia Minority Supplier Development Council. In 2003 Johnson Controls was awarded Corporation of the Year and inducted to the Billion Dollar Round Table from the NMSDC. Al currently serves on the board of directors for the Georgia, Virginia and Florida Minority Supplier Development Councils.

Before joining Johnson Controls, Al held project management positions for Raytheon Service Company and Cygna Energy Services Company. He started his career as an electrical engineer for Fluor Daniel International.

Al earned his bachelor of science degree in electrical engineering from Tuskegee University in Tuskegee, Alabama. Al has a daughter and resides in Conyers, Georgia.

Al Richardson
Regional Supplier Diversity Manager
Controls Group
Johnson Controls, Inc.

M elanie J. Richburg is the Southeast region human resources manager for the service and systems businesses of Johnson Controls, Inc., building efficiency group. Johnson Controls is a leading supplier of building management systems and controls for quality building environments. She serves as a key support to business leaders and regional management.

Before joining Johnson Controls in 2003, Melanie was an assistant professor in the department of counseling and psychological studies at Clark Atlanta University. Previously, she held positions as coordinator of the graduate program in counseling at Hampton University in Virginia and therapist for the National Basketball Association/National Basketball Players Association Aftercare Network.

A native of Montgomery, Alabama, Melanie is a licensed professional counselor, a national certified counselor and a certified sports counselor. She received a doctorate in counseling and human development from Clark Atlanta University. She has published several articles and presented at conferences on the local and national levels.

A member of Antioch Baptist Church-North and Alpha Kappa Alpha Sorority, Inc., Melanie completed her first marathon in 2002 with the American Stroke Association's Train to End Stroke program.

Melanie J. Richburg, Ph.D.
Southeast Human Resources Manager
Johnson Controls, Inc.

CORPORATE BRASS

Hugh Rowden
Mortgage Banking Director
& Vice President
Wachovia Mortgage Corporation

Hugh Rowden is a mortgage banking director and vice president for Wachovia Mortgage Corporation. In this position, he manages the general bank relationship while supporting the Atlanta central area, mortgage banking leaders.

Rowden is a member of the Southside Medical Center board of directors where he serves as finance chairperson, and he sits on the DeKalb Fulton Housing board of directors. One of his favorite volunteer jobs has been serving as scholarship chairperson for the Empire Board of Realtist for the last six years. He also participated in the Wachovia Retail Credit and Business Products Diversity Council.

Rowden attended the University of Northern Colorado and majored in business marketing. He also earned management certificates from the University of Arkansas and the University of Maryland in Europe.

A native of Mexia, Texas but raised in Colorado Springs, Colorado, Rowden and his wife, Michelle, are the proud parents of Sierra, 11 years old, and Cheyanne, 6 years of age. They are all active members of Decatur AME Zion Church in Decatur, Georgia.

John Scipio
Eastern U.S. Sales Manager
Team Division
NIKE, Inc.

John Scipio is responsible for the NIKE team business in the Eastern United States. In this position, he manages the sales and grassroots marketing efforts for the brand. Focusing on colleges, universities, high schools and youth organizations, John and his team are making the brand accessible to all levels of athletes.

John is an avid sports enthusiast who is fortunate to work in a field that he loves. A graduate of the University of Memphis, John is a member of Pi Sigma Epsilon business fraternity and the National Sales Network.

John is a native of Pickens, South Carolina. A proud father, he is the husband of Sarah Scipio.

Barney Simms
Senior Vice President, Community
Governmental & External Affairs
Atlanta Housing Authority

B arney Simms joined the senior staff of the Atlanta Housing Authority in August of 2002. As the agency's senior vice president for community, governmental and external affairs, he oversees management and maintenance of strong partnerships between the Atlanta Housing Authority, other intergovernmental agencies, and Atlanta's corporate, civic, community and faith-based organizations.

Through organizational involvement, Simms has actively served Atlanta's children and neighborhoods for more than three decades. He currently serves as chairman of the advisory board for the Fulton County Department of Family and Children Services, chairman of the board for the Scottsdale Child Development Center, chairman of the City of Atlanta's License Review Board, and secretary of the board for the Atlanta Development Authority.

Simms holds a bachelor's degree from Knoxville College and a master's degree from Clark Atlanta University. He is a graduate of Leadership Atlanta, the Academy for Community Leadership, and Advancement, Innovation and Modeling at North Carolina State University.

Simms, a trustee at Antioch Baptist Church North, is the father of two adult children, Justin and Natalie. He dotes excessively on his only grandchild, Jeremiah.

Ramon M. Singer
Director of Programs
100 Black Men of Atlanta, Inc.

R amon M. Singer is director of programs for 100 Black Men of Atlanta, Inc. In this capacity, he is responsible for administering and growing all of the service programs offered by the organization, as well as managing the program staff. Under his direction, the organization's programs have grown to reach more of Atlanta's underserved than ever before, with more services available to program participants.

During Singer's tenure, 100's flagship program has begun its fourth phase, an unprecedented $16 million commitment to provide mentoring, academic support and scholarships to 224 Atlanta Public Schools (APS) students. They have also opened a state-of-the-art computer lab available to all APS students, as well as a homeownership initiative for parents of program participants.

Singer is a member of the Southern Regional Education Board's policy campaign advisory committee and is the chairman of the APS Council of Southside High School. In addition, he received the Director's Community Leadership Award in 2001 from the U.S. Department of Justice and was recognized as Executive of the Year by the Boys & Girls Club of Metro Atlanta.

Atlanta's
CORPORATE BRASS

Maceo S. Sloan
Financial Advisor
Smith Barney

Maceo S. Sloan believes that helping clients achieve their financial goals begins with completely understanding their needs. Only then does he provide the comprehensive guidance to help them grow and manage their wealth. His clients have a financial partner who shares their vision, earns their trust, and works diligently to help them address their aspirations and create a legacy for future generations.

Building on his on own legacy, he has continued his family's history of five generations in financial services. He is a descendant of the founders of North Carolina Mutual Life Insurance Company, an investment management legacy established in 1898. His parents are Maceo K. Sloan, chairman, CEO and CIO of NCM Capital Management Group, one of the largest minority-owned investment management firms in the country, and Melva Wilder Sloan, retired university professor and entrepreneur.

Maceo earned his degree from Morehouse College. He joined Smith Barney in 2004 as a financial advisor. He is a member of the board of directors at Economic Empowerment Initiative and Corvettes Serving America Foundation. He enjoys family, church, civic activities and sports.

Tracy Renee Smith
Southeast Government
Account Manager
Ford Motor Company

Tracy Renee Smith joined Ford Motor Company in 1995 and has held a variety of marketing and sales assignments in Detroit, Michigan, Washington, D.C., Chicago, Illinois, and Atlanta, Georgia. She is currently the southeast government account manager specializing in the sale of motor vehicles to city, county and state governments in Alabama, Florida, Georgia, North Carolina, South Carolina and Virginia.

Smith is a graduate of Winthrop University where she received her bachelor of science degree in business with a minor in marketing. While attending Winthrop, she participated in an international exchange program and studied at Brighton Polytechnic in Brighton, England. She received her master of business administration degree from Georgia State University.

Smith is a member of the National Coalition of 100 Black Women, Metro Atlanta Chapter and the National Black MBA Association. A native of Greenville, South Carolina, she enjoys the arts, fitness and travel.

G. Brady Stringer is chief operating officer of QSG International, Inc., a management consulting firm providing services to colleges and universities, private sector, governmental and nonprofit organizations. In this position, he manages day-to-day operations, client development and service delivery.

Brady is a certified management consultant (CMC) by the Institute of Management Consulting and a certified business manager (CBM) by the Association of Professionals in Business Management. He is an honored member of Who's Who Worldwide, a registry of global business leaders, and Who's Who Among Successful African Americans. He is also a member of Cascade United Methodist Church, the Academy of Management, Standard and Poor's Society of Industry Leaders, Alpha Phi Alpha Fraternity, Inc., the Atlanta Tuskegee Alumni Club, 100 Black Men of Atlanta and Leadership Atlanta.

Brady attended undergraduate school at Troy State and Tuskegee Universities. He earned an executive certificate in international management from Thunderbird-The Garvin School of International Management and a doctor of philosophy degree from Columbus University.

A native of Troy, Alabama, Brady is divorced and the very proud father of Jasmine Brett Stringer.

G. Brady Stringer, Ph.D.
Executive Vice President &
Chief Operating Officer
QSG International, Inc.

Beverly D. Thomas is vice president of communications and public affairs for Kaiser Permanente of Georgia. She has been with the organization for 13 years and is the executive staff member responsible for government relations, advertising, member and marketing communications, public and media relations, and corporate giving and community benefit programs. Prior to joining Kaiser Permanente, she was vice president of public and community relations for the Grady Health System.

An active community volunteer, Beverly is chair of the board of AID Atlanta and a board member of the Atlanta Women's Foundation. She is a past chair of the Leadership Atlanta board of trustees and past chair of the Georgia Center for Nonprofits. She is also a member of the YWCA Academy of Women Achievers.

A native of Columbus, Georgia, Beverly holds a master's degree in public administration and a bachelor of arts degree in journalism from the University of Georgia. She also attended the Kaiser Permanente Executive Program at Stanford University.

In her spare time, Beverly enjoys reading, collecting books, and growing a variety of outdoor flowers and plants.

Beverly D. Thomas
Vice President
Communications & Public Affairs
Kaiser Permanente of Georgia

CORPORATE BRASS

Norris L. Tolliver
Senior Vice President
SunTrust Bank, Inc.

Norris Tolliver assumed his current position of director of high performance management for SunTrust in sales and corporate administration in July of 2002. He is responsible for influencing the company's lines of businesses, geographies and functions to relentlessly monitor and improve sales, service and retention, excellence in execution, credit quality and financial performance.

Norris has served as a member of SunTrust's Corporate Diversity Council since its inception in 2000, helping to establish diversity representation. He was instrumental in developing the first diversity representation leader boards to help drive achievement of SunTrust's aspirations, as well as heading the subcommittee responsible for preparing the business case to establish diversity as a business imperative for SunTrust.

Norris graduated cum laude from Florida State University with a bachelor's degree and earned his master of business administration degree from Georgia State University in 1980.

Norris' wife of 21 years is Louise Tolliver, and together they have three children, a girl and two boys. Norris is a 24-year member of Ben Hill Methodist Church, where he sings in the Majestic gospel choir.

Adrian M. Washington
Director of Pharmacy & Therapeutics
Kaiser Permanente of Georgia

Adrian M. Washington is the director of pharmacy and therapeutics for Kaiser Permanente of Georgia. In this role, Washington has led Kaiser's pharmaceutical program into state-of-the-art automation by implementing the first centralized, automated refill center in the Southeast.

At Kaiser Permanente, Washington has developed affiliated agreements with three schools of pharmacy in Georgia. He has worked to establish a Kaiser Permanente-sponsored endowment scholarship at Mercer University.

Washington also oversees ambulatory and clinical pharmacy services, purchasing and inventory management, formulary development and management, and coordination with the Georgia State Board of Pharmacy and the Georgia Drugs and Narcotic Agency. He supervises more than 215 licensed and non-licensed staff members.

A graduate of the Mercer University School of Pharmacy, Washington is a member of the National Pharmaceutical Association, the Academy of Managed Care Pharmacy, the Georgia Pharmaceutical Association, and the Mercer University College of Pharmacy and Health Sciences board of visitors.

Washington resides in Fayetteville with his wife, Ptosha, and three children.

Since 2002, Janulyn Lennon Washington has served as the first female aviation security manager for Hartsfield-Jackson Atlanta International Airport, the busiest airport in the world. She is responsible for managing the airport security program which serves more than 240,000 passengers and 55,000 employees daily.

Previously, Washington was deputy superintendent of a certified direct supervision jail in Virginia. She was the first African-American female in the region to hold this position.

Washington is a first-degree black belt and a former Alvin Ailey dance scholarship recipient. A community service leader, Jan taught complimentary karate and dance lessons to children who live in the inner city. She is also an active member of Delta Sigma Theta Sorority, Inc.

A graduate of North Carolina Central University, Washington received a bachelor of science degree in pre-law. She earned her master of science degree, summa cum laude, in criminal justice and security administration from Coppin State University.

A woman with a purpose and a plan, Washington is a native of Baltimore, Maryland. She is the wife of Kenneth and mother to two sons, Khyle and Khris.

Janulyn Lennon Washington
Aviation Security Manager
Hartsfield-Jackson Atlanta
International Airport

With the outstanding ability to produce quantitative outcomes through quality professional relationships, Diane D. Waugh is manager of community relations and business development for Coca-Cola Enterprises Inc. (CCE). In this position, she manages the Southeast market unit's community relations and business development initiatives to expand and implement strategic customer and community leadership programs that enhance the image and reputation of CCE. Additionally, Diane is responsible for developing and managing local relationships among community leaders and organizations. She also serves as a visible liaison on all related community and grassroots activities.

Diane is a member of the Metropolitan Atlanta Chapter of the National Coalition of 100 Black Women, the Association of Fundraising Professionals, the African American Development Officers network and the National Grant Writers Association. A graduate of Morris Brown College, she holds a bachelor of science degree in organizational management and is currently pursuing her master of science administration degree from Central Michigan University in Atlanta.

A native of Harlem, New York, Diane is the wife of Clifford J. Waugh and the proud mother of a daughter, J'Cora L. Davis.

Diane Davis Waugh
Manager, Community Relations
& Business Development
Coca-Cola Enterprises, Inc.

CORPORATE BRASS

Carlis V. Williams
Regional Administrator
Administration for Children & Families

Carlis V. Williams serves as the southeast regional administrator for the federal Department of Health and Human Services/ Administration for Children and Families (ACF) in Atlanta. She has oversight for ACF human service programs including Head Start, child welfare, foster care, adoption, childcare, developmental disabilities, Temporary Assistance to Needy Families, child support enforcement, and runaway and homeless youth.

Before coming to Atlanta, Carlis was the executive assistant for Health and Human Services to the governor in the State of Indiana.

Carlis has served in various capacities in Georgia including the Governor's Task Force on a New Georgia; the United Way's Smart Start board; and the Georgia Supreme Court Commission on Children, Marriage and Family Law advisory group. A member of Leadership Atlanta Class of 2007, she works in the community as a volunteer in the areas of early education, mental health and the elderly.

Carlis graduated from Ball State University with a bachelor's degree in psychology and master's degrees in social psychology and counseling and guidance. Her philosophy of life is: "Giving is better than receiving...if we all give, everyone wins!"

Denise E. Williams
Director, Information Technology
Southern Regional Health System

Denise Williams is director of the information technology division for Southern Regional Health System in Riverdale, Georgia. In this position, she is responsible for planning and designing, and implementation and support activities for all applications including intranet and Internet. Denise has worked in health care for nearly 20 years in various delivery organizations.

Denise received her bachelor of science degree from Albany State University and her master of science degree from Mercer University. She is currently pursuing a doctor of health administration degree through the University of Phoenix where she is also an associate faculty member. She maintains certifications in project management, software development and health care law.

Denise is a resident of Fayetteville, Georgia and enjoys watching movies, playing basketball, cooking, sewing, interior decorating and spending time with her family.

Dr. Victor Williams
Dean, School of Information Technology
American InterContinental University
Dunwoody Campus

With more than 25 years in information technology (IT), Dr. Victor Williams is dean of the School of Information Technology at American InterContinental University, Dunwoody Campus. There, he oversees the day-to-day operations of the IT school, in addition to teaching bachelor's and master's level courses in information technology. Williams also conducts academic IT research, publishes papers and presents his findings at conferences nationally and internationally.

Williams graduated from Regents College of the University of the State of New York (now Excelsior College) with a liberal arts degree. He then attended Golden Gate University where he received his master's degree in human resources. Williams received his doctorate in information systems from Nova Southeastern University.

In addition to his work in the world of academia, Williams knows the business world well. He is a former employee of IBM, CTI and the Georgia Institute of Technology.

Evonne Yancey
Director, Government &
Community Affairs
Kaiser Permanente of Georgia

Evonne Yancey is director of government and community affairs for Kaiser Permanente of Georgia. A Georgia groundbreaker, she is one of the health plan's original staff members. She oversees government and community relations, the Community Benefit Program and the Educational Theatre Program.

Prior to joining Kaiser Permanente, Yancey held leadership positions in program development and planning with the Atlanta Regional Commission, the State of Delaware, and Senior Citizen Services of Metropolitan Atlanta.

A staunch community advocate, Yancey served as chair of the board of trustees for the Atlanta-Fulton County Public Library. She is a member of the board of advisors at the Emory University Rollins School of Public Health, the YWCA Academy of Women Achievers, the CDC Foundation, the Georgia Women's Forum and the Atlanta Regional Health Forum. Additionally, Yancey is a member of the Leadership Atlanta Alumni Association.

Yancey received her bachelor's degree from Fisk University and her master of education degree in rehabilitation counseling from Boston University. She holds a certificate in corporate community relations from Boston College.

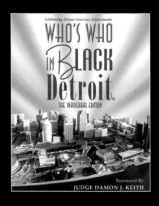
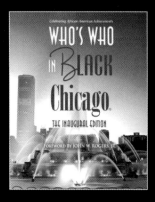
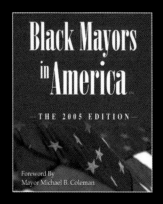
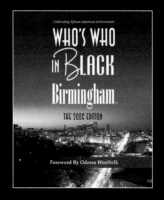
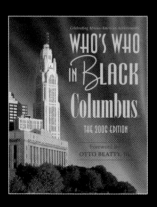

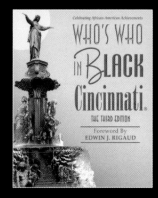
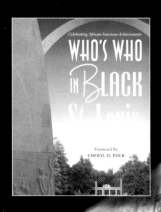
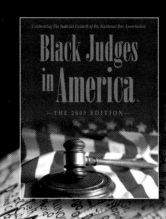

Atlanta's

MEDIA PROFESSIONALS

"The key to realizing a dream is to focus not on success but on significance - and then even the small steps and little victories along your path will take on greater meaning."

OPRAH WINFREY

TELEVISION PIONEER AND PHILANTHROPIST

Silas Alexander III
Morning Show Host
WR&B 102.5

Tanjuria Anderson
Owner & Chief Executive Officer
The Catering Consultants, Inc.

Silas Alexander III, also known as "Si-Man Bayebaay," is a native of Eatonton, Georgia. He has been in the field of broadcasting, both in radio and television, for 25 years.

Former weatherman and news director for the NBC TV station in Macon, Georgia, Si-Man also worked as a videotape editor and field host for WXIA-TV 11Alive in Atlanta. He has worked many formats of radio including country, heavy metal, jazz, gospel, top 40 and urban music.

To date, he is with Radio One Atlanta as the host of the morning show, *Wakin' Up Atlanta from Five Till Ten*, on the new WR&B 102.5. Si-Man is very active in the community and is committed to making a difference in Atlanta.

Si-Man and his wife, Sandra, have one son, Silas IV.

Tanjuria Anderson is the owner and chief executive officer of The Catering Consultants Inc., TCC Publications and *CONNECT Magazine*. The Catering Consultants provides consulting services to many businesses.

In 2004 Tanjuria expanded The Catering Consultants by creating TCC Publications under which she publishes Atlanta's fastest-growing premier services guide, *CONNECT Magazine*. *CONNECT* is a premier services resource guide offering information on dining, accommodations, events and entertainment.

Tanjuria has been featured in the *Atlanta Tribune*. Additionally, she has been a guest on *The Rude Awakening* on 680 The Fan and *Crosstalk* morning show with Jean Ross on WAOK 1380 AM.

Tanjuria's professional affiliations include the Metro Atlanta Chamber of Commerce and the Georgia Minority Supplier Development Council. In 2005 she received the Champion Award from the Atlanta Women's Power Caucus. She was recently named a finalist for the Atlanta Business League Super Tuesday Award in the category of Success Against the Odds.

A native of Chicago, Illinois, Tanjuria is an active member in the media ministry at Victory Church in Stone Mountain. She enjoys sports, exercise, traveling and riding her motorcycle.

Carl Anthony
Host
A Gypsy Life...Productions

Rojene Bailey
President
Golden Communications, Inc.

Carl Anthony joined the award-winning television company, A Gypsy Life...Productions in early 2005 as co-host of the popular weekly television series *In My Opinion...* His natural charm, knowledge and professionalism made him a popular host on many red carpets. He recently served as an *In My Opinion...* and *IMO Reveals...* red carpet host for the Annual Trumpet Awards, the International Civil Rights Walk of Fame and the 78th Annual Academy Awards®. His exclusive interview with Academy of Motion Picture Arts and Sciences president Sid Ganis was a 2006 highlight.

Carl is also an Atlanta radio disc jockey and host of *Serenade to the City.* Over the past 18 years he has dedicated himself to the preservation and promotion of the African-American art form, jazz.

Carl began his communications career in 1971 as an associate for a public relations firm in Washington, D.C., which eventually led him to become a promoter, producer, disc jockey and television personality.

Carl volunteers his time mentoring students and spends countless hours advocating good health, the protection of the environment, and support for live jazz performances.

Rojene Bailey is best known as host of *BluesTime in the City* on KISS 104.1, Sundays from 4 to 7 p.m. He is also known for his many years as a multi-Emmy-winning television producer and director. He is currently the executive director of The Beulah Rucker Museum and Educational Foundation.

He was educated at Columbus College in Columbus, Georgia (now Columbus University) and got his start in television there. Over the years, Rojene has produced, directed, written and edited many programs for Georgia Public Television and other organizations, including the Georgia Music Hall of Fame, where he is the only producer/director to win an Emmy for a live production.

He has received numerous awards for his work, including 18 Emmy nominations, six of which he won, and he was inducted into the National Academy of Television Arts & Sciences Silver Circle for lifetime achievement in November of 2002.

Rojene now spends much of his time working with the Beulah Rucker Museum and Educational Foundation, playing with his precious granddaughter, listening to the blues, and of course, perfecting his golf game.

Vince Bailey
Producer & Host
Outreach with Vince Bailey

Tracey Baker-Simmons
President & Executive Producer
B2 Entertainment, LLC

Vince Bailey is the producer and host of the television program *Outreach with Vince Bailey*, which spotlights small businesses, corporate professionals and nonprofit organizations. A 25-year media veteran, Vince owns and operates Vince Bailey Productions, a full service audio/video production and consulting company. He is heard in Atlanta and nationally as he provides voice talent for many commercial clients such as the Centers for Disease Control, Tropical Smoothie Café, the Association of Black Cardiologists, and various sporting and special events.

Vince has served on many boards and committees including Atlanta Job Corps' community advisory council, Fulton County Schools' career and technical education advisory council, and the Fulton County Workforce Investment Board. He currently serves on the board of directors for the Atlanta Business League and is a member of the Atlanta Black Agenda Resource Center, the Concerned Black Clergy, and the Georgia Association of Latin Elected Officials.

A native of Gary, Indiana, Vince and his wife of 19 years, Tracy, live in Lawrenceville, Georgia and are the proud parents of two sons, Vincent Jr. and Victor.

Tracey Baker-Simmons is president and executive producer for B2 Entertainment, LLC. A seasoned film and television producer, she has more than ten years of experience in production. Tracey was an executive producer and creator of the reality series, *Being Bobby Brown*, which aired on the Bravo television network in the summer of 2005.

Tracey began her career in marketing and promotions with Warner Brothers Music and later made the transition into film production. In 1998 she launched Strange Fruit Films (SFF). As executive producer at SFF, she oversaw the production of the feature film, *Book Of Love*. Tracey worked as a freelance producer in television production. Her clients included distributor Pearson Television, and ABC and CBS networks.

She has also been named one of *Atlanta Woman* magazine's Top 25 Women to Watch in 2006 and a Youth Vibe 2006 Media Mogul.

Tracey holds a bachelor's degree in marketing and finance from the University of Memphis.

Her professional affiliations include the Independent Feature Project, the National Association of Television Professional Executives, the National Association for Female Executives, and Women in Film.

Atlanta's
MEDIA PROFESSIONALS

Morris Baxter
Host, Morning Jazz
Jazz 91.9 WCLK

Felicia J. Browder
Media Relations Manager
Hartsfield-Jackson Atlanta
International Airport

Originally from Detroit, Morris Baxter is a graduate of Norfolk State University. He started his career in radio at WOWI in Norfolk, Virginia. Moving up in the radio world, he worked at WMYK as a program director for ten years.

After several job opportunities at WNBZ, WSVY and WKYS, and a position as an entertainment reporter at WAVY (CBS), Baxter moved to Atlanta as a regional manager for Loud Records/Sony. He was promoted to senior director of national promotion, working projects for platinum artists including Wu Tang Clan, Mobb Deep and Big Pun.

Baxter held the title of southeast regional director of promotions for ArtistDirect/BMG and later national director of promotions, working with such artists as Slum Village and Eightball. His voice was featured on the multi-platinum-selling BlackStreet album, *Another Level.*

Baxter's love for radio continues to live on by guest hosting sports radio programs during his travels to various markets. His last stint was co-hosting *Inside the Hawks* for the Atlanta Hawks. Currently, he is the morning show host of *Morris in the Morning* on Jazz 91.9 WCLK.

Felicia J. Browder is the media relations manager and chief spokesperson for Hartsfield-Jackson Atlanta International Airport. In her 20s, she is the youngest chief spokesperson ever to serve at the world's busiest airport, and among the youngest of her counterparts worldwide.

Felicia was honored by the *Atlanta Business Chronicle* in October of 2006 as one of the city's top 40 Up & Comers. Additionally, she is Mayor Shirley Franklin's nominee for the 2007 class of the Forum of Young Global Leaders. This organization connects innovative young leaders from around the world to create solutions for global issues such as poverty, environmental degradation and the AIDS epidemic.

Felicia teaches at Emory University's Institute for Professional Learning. A youth mentor, she also serves on the board of directors for the Atlanta chapter of Dress for Success, an international nonprofit organization that empowers disadvantaged women.

A native Peach and graduate of the University of Georgia, Felicia enjoys writing and publishing, dancing, traveling, volunteering, public speaking, entrepreneurial ventures and extreme sports. She is working on several creative projects to be introduced in 2007.

MEDIA PROFESSIONALS

Wayne K. Brown
Vice President & Regional Manager
Radio One, Inc.

Charisma Cannon
Public Relations Assistant Manager
Hartsfield-Jackson
Atlanta International Airport

In June of 2000, Wayne K. Brown joined Radio One, Inc. as vice president and regional manager of its Charlotte, North Carolina (WQNC-FM), and Atlanta, Georgia (WJZZ-FM, WHTA-FM, WPZE-FM and WAMJ-FM) markets. He oversees the operations of the Charlotte station and assumes the responsibilities of vice president/general manager for the Atlanta stations.

A Washington, D.C. native, Wayne graduated from Syracuse University's Newhouse School of Communications. He started his career with CBS in 1978 and was soon promoted to sales analyst for the CBS Television Network. After three-and-a-half years in network television, he was hired as an account executive for CBS flagship radio station WCBS News Radio 88.

Wayne continues to be very active with the Syracuse University Newhouse School of Communications. He is most proud of the Wayne K. Brown Scholarship established for minority students at Newhouse. His primary goal is to assist talented minorities in joining the communications industry. Wayne serves on the board of directors for the Radio Advertising Bureau and the North Carolina Association of Broadcasters.

Wayne and his wife, Neysa, have two sons, Dylan and Drew.

Charisma Cannon is the public relations assistant manager for Hartsfield-Jackson Atlanta International Airport. She is responsible for assisting the media relations manager in disseminating accurate, timely information about Hartsfield-Jackson, establishing relationships with key local and national media outlets, creating crisis communications plans and managing their implementation. Charisma is also project manager for the airport's travel magazine, *Hartsfield-Jackson Connections*, overseeing content and ensuring Hartsfield-Jackson's key messages are conveyed to the traveling public in a lively and entertaining format. She is also a contributing writer for *Hartsfield-Jackson News* (HJN), the airport's online publication.

Prior to her current position, Charisma was employed with Boys & Girls Clubs of America where she oversaw the organization's $100 million Club Tech program, a technology-driven initiative in partnership with Microsoft Corporation.

In her 13-year career, Charisma has also created public relations and marketing campaigns for Planned Parenthood of New York City and several other corporate and nonprofit organizations. A native of Chicago, Charisma holds a bachelor of arts degree from Columbia College in Chicago.

Jamie Carlington
Senior Public Relations Coordinator
Southern Regional Health Systems

Velva Carter
Owner
A Gypsy Life...Productions

Jamie Carlington, senior public relations coordinator for Southern Regional Health System, oversees all aspects of media relations for the medical facility. She manages the hospital's community magazine, *Prism*, as well as the employee newsletter, "Connections," and media/community Web site postings. Jamie is also an active member on several hospital committees.

Jamie has more than 15 years of experience in the public relations arena, including positions as a public affairs captain for the U.S. Army, a government affairs assistant and environmental lobbyist in the Washington, D.C. area, the curator/director for the oldest art gallery in Bermuda, a communications officer for the consul general of Bermuda and finally, a publicist in the cable industry.

A native of Gary, Indiana and a graduate of Indiana University (Bloomington), Jaime is a member of the Indiana University Alumni Association and the Atlanta Association of Black Journalists. She is active within her local community and her church, College Park C.M.E. Church, where she serves on the board of trustees and various other committees including the children's ministry department. Jaime and her daughter, Taylor, reside in Riverdale.

Velva Carter is an award-winning television producer, director and owner of the Atlanta-based television company A Gypsy Life... Productions. A Gypsy Life...Productions currently produces the nationally aired television programs *Dr. Tates: Adventures In Good Health, In My Opinion...* and *IMO Reveals*. This year's special television coverage included the 78th Annual Academy Awards where Carter highlighted the foreign language film nominees. This year, Carter expanded her production company to include a new production studio, Studio V.

Carter also serves as founder and chief executive officer of A Gypsy Life...Foundation, a nonprofit foundation dedicated to transforming student filmmakers into legitimate filmmakers.

President and chief executive officer of Carter-Tates Enterprises, Inc., she and her business partner, Dr. Stephen Tates, launched the all natural herbal product line Dr. Tates™ Herbal Tinctures & Tonics™. The product can be found in many health food stores, fitness centers and doctor's offices in more than 41 states and nine foreign countries.

Carter's greatest joy is time spent with her business partner and husband, Dr. Stephen Tates.

MEDIA PROFESSIONALS

Cari Champion
Anchor & Reporter
WGCY-TV CBS 46 News

Ray C. Cobb
Corporate Sales Underwriter
Jazz 91.9 WCLK

Cari Champion joined CBS 46 as a weekend anchor and weekday reporter in April of 2006. She began her career in journalism while in college as an assignment editor at KCOP in Los Angeles.

Armed with an English degree from UCLA and an indefatigable spirit, Cari began her career in West Virginia. Always aspiring for the bigger and the better, she moved on to Orange County, California and then to West Palm Beach, Florida. From the beginning, Cari has been getting to the heart of stories and touching the hearts of those who listen to and watch her. From hurricanes to election scandals, Donald Trump to Rush Limbaugh, Cari is always shoulder-to-shoulder with the best in the business.

Moving to Atlanta was an easy choice. Cari knows Atlanta was and still is the heart of the civil rights movement. She believes living in the city is an opportunity to learn more about that time in history and perhaps become involved in future plans.

Outside of work, Cari is the inveterate yoga enthusiast. She also volunteers time with the elderly and disabled.

Ray C. Cobb, corporate sales underwriter for Clark Atlanta University, is responsible for identifying prospective clients and generating sales revenue for Jazz 91.9 WCLK and the division of communication arts.

Ray entered the advertising industry as an intern for the classified advertising department at *The Atlanta Journal-Constitution* (AJC) in the summer of 1997. After graduating college, Cobb returned to AJC where he served as an advertising assistant and inside sales representative from 1998-2002. In 2001 he was the recipient of the Inside Sales Person of the Year for classified advertising callbacks division.

As an associate producer on *ATL Insider*, a collaborative effort between Clark Atlanta University Television and WATL, he helped the "edutainment" program receive a 2006 Southeast Emmy for its second season.

Cobb holds a bachelor's degree in mass communication from the University of South Florida and lives in downtown Atlanta. In his spare time, he enjoys acting and the performing arts. One of Ray's greatest accomplishments was a 2001 trip to South Africa where he developed a passion for HIV/AIDS awareness and advocacy.

Keely L. Collins
Director of Sales
Radio One Atlanta

Amanda Davis
Co-Anchor
WAGA-TV/FOX5

Keely L. Collins is the director of sales for Radio One Atlanta, with 19 years of radio sales experience in the Atlanta market. In her current role, she is responsible for the sales operations of Radio One Atlanta's four radio stations, WHTA Hot 107.9, WJZZ Smooth Jazz, WPZE Praise 97.5 and WAMJ Classic Soul. Radio One is recognized as one of the fastest growing radio groups in Atlanta.

Collins' sales career started at WZGC-FM Z93, where she was an account executive for five years. She joined WALR Kiss FM, then Ring Radio, in 1991. Later that year, Collins moved to WVEE-FM/WAOK-AM, the number one station in the market, as an account executive.

In 1994 Keely was promoted to local sales manager. From there, she was promoted to sales manager, then general sales manager. During her 13 years at V-103/WAOK, she helped develop and oversee For Sisters Only, V-103's signature event, which grew into a million dollar event.

Keely left V-103/WAOK in 2004 to accept the position of director of sales for Radio One Atlanta.

Amanda Davis is the Emmy-winning co-anchor for the top-rated *FOX NEWS* at 6 p.m. and 10 p.m. Davis came to FOX5 in 1986 from WSB-TV Atlanta where she was an anchor and reporter.

At FOX5, Davis has reported on various issues and served as anchor of the noon news. She launched the highly successful *Good Day Atlanta* before taking over the main anchor chair.

Throughout her career, Davis has received numerous honors and awards, including five Emmys from the National Academy of Television Arts and Sciences, including the Best Newscast honors for anchoring *FOX5 NEWS* in 1999 and 2000. Likewise, she has received five awards from the Atlanta Association of Black Journalists, including Best Anchor in 2000.

Davis' work to place Georgia's children in permanent homes is truly her labor of love. She began this project in 1997 with a series of stories called "A Place to Call Home." The Freddie Mac Foundation then came to FOX5 with the idea of presenting weekly profiles of children available for adoption and *Wednesday's Child* was launched in November of 2000.

Jocelyn Dorsey
Director, Editorials & Public Affairs
WSB-TV Channel 2

J. Crystal Edmonson
Broadcast Editor
Atlanta Business Chronicle

Jocelyn Dorsey has been with WSB-TV for 30 years, and has served as director of editorials and public affairs at Channel 2 since 1983. From 1973 to 1983, Jocelyn was an anchor, reporter, producer and assignment editor for WSB-TV's *Channel 2 Action News*. She was the first African-American anchor of a Channel 2 newscast as well as the first African-American news anchor in the Atlanta market.

Jocelyn supervises the selection, creation and marketing efforts for all special events and community outreach programs of the Family 2 Family Project, WSB-TV public service projects, WSB-TV's Speaker's Bureau and WSB-TV Tours. She is also a producer, writer and narrator for various corporate and nonprofit organization videos.

Among her personal honors, Jocelyn was the first African American inducted into the NATAS Silver Circle for her more than 25 years in the field of journalism. She was also the first woman and first African American to receive the Broadcaster's Citizen of the Year Award, a lifetime-achievement award for her work in broadcasting and in the community, presented by the Georgia Association of Broadcasters.

Crystal Edmonson is the broadcast editor for the *Atlanta Business Chronicle*, where she contributes local, in-depth stories about business and the economy to WABE 90.1 FM, the local NPR affiliate. You can also catch her on the radio each morning on Smooth Jazz 107.5 FM, and Sports Radio 790 The Zone. In addition, Crystal produces business features for the Atlanta television program *TBS StoryLine*, which airs on Saturday mornings. As a media professional, Crystal often speaks to groups about Atlanta's business landscape or serves as an emcee for business events.

Crystal has a bachelor's degree from Emory University and a master's degree from the Medill School of Journalism at Northwestern University.

Crystal is a member of the Emory alumni board and vice chair of programming for the Atlanta chapter of the Caucus of Emory Black Alumni.

She also chairs the Summer Minority Internship Program committee for the *Atlanta Business Chronicle*'s parent company, American City Business Journals. In its first year, the program placed eight college students in newspaper internships from San Francisco to Washington, D.C.

Connie Flint
Program Director & Host
WPZE FM, Praise 97.5 FM

Jolene Butts Freeman
Chief Press Officer
Fulton County

A native of Decatur, Georgia, pastor Connie Flint was called as an evangelist in 1987 and was ordained in 1989. She has gained much notoriety throughout the United States due to extensive travel and spreading the gospel of Jesus Christ.

Flint has had the honor of preaching in Jerusalem, in the Garden of Gethsemane, the Upper Room, Egypt and Ghana, West Africa. For 14 years, Flint was the program director and morning show host at the gospel radio station WAOK until December of 2001. She was then given the vision of Truth Evangelistic Ministries, Inc. and the position of organizer and pastor.

Her dream of a 24-hour FM gospel radio station came to fruition in December of 2002 when she became part of the Praise 97.5 family. As a result, she presently works as program director and host of the *Praise Party* in the afternoons.

Jolene Butts Freeman is the chief press officer for the Fulton County Press Office. In this position, she manages the media and public relations activities for the Office of the County Manager and the Board of Commissioners. She also serves as chief media spokesperson and information liaison to all local, national and international news media.

Jolene is an Emmy-winning journalist and former reporter for Atlanta's WSB-TV. She is a 1998 recipient of the Atlanta Association of Black Journalists' Pioneer Black Journalist Award. Jolene is also a photographer and owns Infinite Exposure Photography. Her photographs have graced the cover of *Investor's Digest* and have been featured in the promotional materials of local artists and actors.

Jolene received her bachelor of arts degree from Clark Atlanta University and her master's degree in broadcast journalism from Northwestern University in 1991.

A native of Atlanta, Jolene is a member of Alpha Kappa Alpha Sorority, Inc. and the volunteer cheerleader coach for Cascade Youth Organization. She is the wife of Jerry E. Freeman Jr. and is the proud mother of Jazmine and Jerry Freeman.

Atlanta's
MEDIA PROFESSIONALS

Reggie Gay
Radio Personality
The Reggie Gay Gospel Show

Cheryl Renee Gooch, Ph.D.
Associate Dean
Division of Communication Arts
Clark Atlanta University

Reggie Gay is Atlanta's premiere gospel radio/ television personality. His name became synonymous with gospel music on KISS 104.1.

Gay's program has been syndicated via Cumulus Radio Network on 92Q FM in Nashville, Tennessee and KISS 94.1 in Wilmington, North Carolina. He has worked in a variety of roles for radio stations including program manager for GLORY 1340 from April of 1998 to June of 2001; KISS 104.1 from 1996 to 2004; program manager for WYZE AM 1480 from November of 2003 to January of 2005; and currently as assistant general manager of WTJH 1260 AM. Reggie also hosts a show on AIB TV.

A native of Lexington, Kentucky, Gay is a licensed and ordained minister. He serves on the advisory board of the Stellar Awards and is a member of Kappa Alpha Psi Fraternity, Inc. His charitable organization, Suitcases for Kids, raises money to buy luggage for foster children.

Gay played the role of band announcer for Morris Brown College in the movie *Drumline*. *The Reggie Gay Gospel Show* is simulcast weekdays on 91.9 FM WCLK and WTJH 1260 AM.

Dr. Cheryl Renee Gooch is associate dean of Clark Atlanta University's division of communication arts, which includes the departments of mass media arts, speech communication and theatre arts, WCLK 91.9 and CAU-TV.

She holds a bachelor's degree from Howard University, a master's degree from Northwestern University and a doctorate degree from Florida State University.

A seasoned educator, Gooch also worked as a professional journalist for print and broadcast media. She is an active member of the Association for Education in Journalism and Mass Communication, the Broadcast Education Association and the National Association of Black Journalists.

Her professional interests include media and the advancement of civil and human rights agendas. Her published research covers press freedom issues in post-apartheid South Africa, popular culture representations of African Americans in music videos and television programming policy in the English-speaking Caribbean. She is a former freedom forum teaching fellow and recipient of grants for investigative journalism and scholarly research.

A native of Waterbury, Connecticut, Gooch is an avid genealogist who can recite her African ancestry, both maternal and paternal, back five generations.

Karyn Greer
Anchor & Reporter
WXIA-TV 11Alive

Sheryl Riley Gripper
Vice President of Community Relations
WXIA-TV 11Alive

Karyn Greer joined *11Alive News* in 1999. She serves as a reporter for 11Alive's special projects unit as well as an 11Alive News anchor for *11Alive Weekend* at 6 p.m. and 11 p.m. Karyn came to 11Alive from WGNX-TV, where she completed a ten-year tenure in the primary co-anchor position for that station's weeknight newscasts.

Greer began her broadcast career in 1983 at WCIA-TV in Champaign, Illinois. She moved to WICD-TV the following year where she worked as a weekend anchor and reporter. She then spent three years in Charleston, South Carolina, where she was the solo anchor for the highest-rated newscast in the market.

A long-time Atlanta resident, Karyn has a history of hands-on community involvement. She is the past president of the Atlanta Press Club and currently serves on the board of governors for the National Academy of Television Arts & Sciences. She is the recipient of numerous awards honoring both her professional work and her community contributions.

Karyn is a native of Chicago, Illinois. She and her husband, Tony, have two sons, Kyle and Tyler.

Sheryl Riley Gripper is the vice president of community relations for WXIA-TV 11Alive, Atlanta's NBC affiliate. In this position, she manages public service events and cause-related marketing campaigns for the station. Sheryl is the executive producer of the Emmy-winning *11Alive Holiday Can-a-Thon*, Georgia's largest televised food-raising event.

Sheryl is a winner of multiple Emmys and the founder of the Black Women Film Preservation Project, an organization that has celebrated the history of women in film since 1996.

Sheryl was named WXIA's first female vice president in 1982 and was featured in *USA Today* as an Ortho 21st Century Woman.

In 1972 Sheryl received her bachelor of arts degree from Spelman College, and in 1977 she received her master's degree in education from Georgia State University. In 2000 she was awarded a master of arts degree in film and video from Georgia State University.

A native of Waco, Texas, Sheryl is married to Jeff Gripper, Atlanta's first world karate champion, and is the proud mother of three sons, Edward, Jefferey and Ellis.

MEDIA PROFESSIONALS

Lori I. Hall
Creative Marketing Director
Radio One Atlanta

Sonya Hamm
Radio Show Host
WPZE, Praise 97.5 FM

Lori I. Hall is the creative marketing director of Radio One Atlanta. In her current role, she is responsible for the overall marketing of stations WHTA, WJZZ, WAMJ and WPZE.

Lori graduated from Fisk University in Nashville, Tennessee with a bachelor of arts degree in English. Additionally, she received her master's degree in mass communication from the Walter Cronkite School of Journalism and Telecommunications in Tempe, Arizona.

Lori began her radio career in Phoenix, Arizona, where she worked in promotions for four different stations. In 1999 she was named promotions assistant for V-103 and WAOK in Atlanta. She was then promoted to promotions director at a start-up station in West Palm Beach, Florida. After a successful year, she headed further south to Miami, Florida, where she was named promotions director at yet another start-up station. During her tenure in Miami, *Radio & Records* nominated her for Promotions and Marketing Director of the Year.

In her spare time, she enjoys reading, scrapbooking and photography. She is also a member of Alpha Kappa Alpha Sorority, Inc.

Sonya Hamm is the host of *The Breakfast Club* on WPZE, Praise 97.5 FM. A native of Durham, North Carolina, Sonya was one of the top morning show personalities at Radio One Raleigh's WNNL "The Light" 103.9 FM. She also hosted a weekly television program at Raleigh's CBS and Fox affiliate stations.

Sonya holds a bachelor of arts degree in speech communications and theater from Fayetteville State University, and she attended graduate school at North Carolina Central University.

She has received two awards for Gospel Announcer of the Year from UJAM and WALJO, was nominated for *Black Radio Exclusive*'s Breaking the Glass Ceiling award, and Gospel Music Workshop of America's (GMWA) Gospel Announcer of the Year.

Sonya is a licensed and ordained minister and has served as chaplain of the North Carolina, South Carolina and Virginia chapters of GMWA. She is the founder of Christian Career & Business Women of America, Inc., and the author of *Kick Your Life Into Overdrive*.

She now resides in Atlanta with her husband, Gary Hamm. They have been happily married for 20 years.

Aileen Harris
Publisher & Cofounder
GoDeKalb.com

Brandon P. Johnson
Managing Member
LC3 Media Group, LLC

Aileen Harris is the publisher and cofounder of GoDeKalb.com, an innovative and interactive news Web site covering the news, events and people of DeKalb County, Georgia. Aileen oversees the content, sales and marketing for the Web site, which was founded in 2004.

GoDeKalb.com also produces a business breakfast series, business seminars, networking mixers and other special events. In September of 2006, GoDeKalb.com was named a finalist in the DeKalb County Office of Economic Development's first annual Innovative Concepts in Business Award.

Aileen has been covering DeKalb County for more than ten years and has interviewed leading newsmakers in the political, entertainment and business fields. She worked first as a reporter with *The Champion Newspaper* and later as the editor of the *Community Review*, *DeKalb Journal* and *The Story-Central DeKalb* newspapers.

She is a 1993 summa cum laude graduate of Stillman College in Tuscaloosa, Alabama, with a degree in communications. A native of Buffalo, New York, Aileen has lived in DeKalb County since 1993.

Brandon Johnson owns BlackAtlanta.com and several other sites specializing in diversity, Internet marketing and e-commerce. BlackAtlanta.com is destined to be one of the premiere metropolitan African-American community, news, entertainment and business sites for Atlanta. Honoring the rich heritage of Atlanta, while staying on the cutting edge of the best events, news and more, the Web site is an Internet trendsetter.

Johnson graduated Phi Beta Kappa from Atlanta's Morehouse College. Morehouse introduced him to the immense cultural, business and educational opportunities for African Americans in Atlanta. This introduction, coupled with corporate information technology experience, has allowed Johnson to build a great foundation for BlackAtlanta.com's role as a major force in diversity advertising initiatives.

Johnson's past promotions and site clients have included Akademiks Clothing line, TV One, Honda, Warner Brothers Records, Comcast, Full Gospel Baptist Church and numerous local promoters and businesses. He has also created strategies for utilizing multiple streams of virtual incomes through co-branded partnerships with Hotels.com, Mamma.com and Match.com.

Brandon lives in Lithonia with his wife, Kimberly, and their four children, Lewis, Chazmyn, Chandler and Chase.

MEDIA PROFESSIONALS

Joyce Littel
Host, *The Quiet Storm*
WVEE V-103 FM

Tosha Love
Assistant Program Director
WVEE V-103 FM

Joyce Littel is host of V-103's popular evening show *The Quiet Storm*, the ever-popular *Love and Relationships* show, and the nationally syndicated *AutoScoop* with Adam Goldfein.

Joyce's experience in radio spans more than 22 years. She is the president and chief executive officer of Littel Concepts, LLC, a marketing, promotions and consulting firm based in Atlanta and Decatur. She is also president and founder of the Joyce Littel - Sista For Sisters Foundation.

Joyce finds time to contribute to her community. She successfully produced and created the First Word Youth Poetry Slam, a citywide poetry competition for youth.

She is the renowned author of *Poetic Moments - A Collection of Poetry & Affirmations from V103's Quiet Storm*. Joyce is the creator and producer of a stage production called *Passion & Poetry*. She is a member of Black Women's Investment Club, the National Coalition of 100 Black Women of Metro Atlanta, Alpha Kappa Alpha Sorority, Inc. and the National Council of Negro Women.

Joyce is married to James H. Jackson, and they have two sons, one daughter and three grandchildren.

A native of White Plains, New York, Tosha Love began her career in radio in Atlanta, Georgia. Her first radio gig was at WRFG 89.3 FM in Atlanta. This led to her career at WVEE V-103 in 1998 as an on-air weekend personality. From that point on, her career took off. She became the music director in 1999, and in 2002, Love was promoted to assistant program director of V-103.

Tosha received a variety of awards and nominations. She was awarded Music Director of the Year in 1999-2000 by the NBPC for her first year as a music director. Her other awards include being honored as one of the Top Ten Most Influential Women in the music industry by NABFEME; an award from the Million Dollar Record Pool; a nomination by Gavin in 2000; Music Director of the Year 2001-2002 by Gavin; and nominations by *R&R* for Music Director of the Year in 2001, 2002, and 2003.

Previously, Love taught radio broadcasting at the Connecticut School of Broadcasting. She is currently teaching for the Broadcasters Training Network.

Shawn D. Lovings
General Manager
Uptown Magazine

Donna Lowry
Kids & Schools Reporter
WXIA-TV 11Alive News

Shawn D. Lovings is general manager of *Uptown Magazine*. He is responsible for the advertising, marketing, special events and distribution of the publication in the Southeast United States.

Before joining *Uptown Magazine*, Lovings worked as an advertising executive for *Upscale Magazine*, a lifestyle publication. Since moving "Uptown," Lovings now has the creative reach and media vehicle to inspire the African-American male community.

Lovings serves in various capacities with many different civic and professional organizations. He is a board member of the Kingstreet.com Management Group, Mothers Rebuilding Atlanta and the National Black Arts Festival. Lovings also takes time to substitute teach and mentor at Martin Luther King Elementary School in Clayton County, Georgia.

A native of St. Louis, Missouri, Lovings graduated from Jackson State University with a bachelor's degree in advertising, and he is knowledge management certified through Day Wheel Inc.

Lovings currently resides in Atlanta, Georgia with his beautiful daughter Sierra.

Donna Lowry joined WXIA-TV 11Alive News in 1986. During her tenure, she has covered the entire spectrum of news stories. In the past several years, she has received recognition (including Emmy awards) for her coverage of everything from child abuse and domestic violence to daycare and educational issues.

Lowry's career in broadcast journalism began while attending Chatham College in Pittsburgh, Pennsylvania, where she received a bachelor of arts degree. After a short stint in radio, she obtained a master's degree in journalism from Northwestern University. She has five years of previous experience at television stations in Florida and Illinois.

Lowry serves on the boards of several organizations including the Old National Christian Academy. She is a member of the Education Writers Association, the National Academy of Television Arts & Sciences, the Magnolia Chapter of The Links, Inc. and the Atlanta and National Associations of Black Journalists. She is also a member of Friendship Baptist Church in College Park and serves on the courtesy guild.

Donna and her husband, Bennet Reid Jr., have three daughters, Lakisha, Nicole and Analla.

Marsha D. Meadows
Vice President of Marketing
Radio One Atlanta

René Miller
Chief Executive Officer
Omega Media, LLC

Marsha D. Meadows, from Albany, Georgia, started her broadcasting career in 1997 with Radio One as an intern with Hot 97.5, now Hot 107.9, in Atlanta. Throughout her years at Radio One, she has held several positions in the Atlanta market, including special events coordinator, music director, promotions director and on-air personality (formerly M&M).

In 2002 Marsha was promoted to work in the corporate office as the executive assistant to chief operating officer Mary Catherine Sneed and as national director of urban marketing. In March of 2005, she was promoted to the position of vice president of marketing, where she organizes national promotions and events for all Radio One stations, including the *Russ Parr Morning Show*.

Marsha has also established two businesses, M2 Travel and M2 Media, a mass media marketing and event planning business. She is working on establishing her nonprofit organization, Marsha's Angels Foundation.

René Miller is the chief executive officer of Omega Media, LLC in Atlanta. Under her leadership, the company has grown over the past five years. She manages the business of Omega Media from contract negotiation to marketing strategies for corporations.

René wears several hats. She owns Omega Media, and she is the midday host for WSB-TV's *Georgia Lottery, Cash 3*. A multi-faceted woman, René also serves as the afternoon on-air personality for Radio One's Smooth Jazz 107.5-FM. With more than 23 years of radio experience, she has served as a radio host and a director of marketing and promotions.

René has been featured in several magazines, including *Atlanta Woman*, *Atlanta Tribune: The Magazine* and *Rolling Out* magazine. She received the Atlanta Business League's 2004 Creative Style Award and V-103's 2004 Community Achievement Award.

A native of Nuremburg, Germany, René is a member of Antioch Baptist Church. She also serves on the advisory board of *Atlanta Woman* magazine.

René is married to Kevin Alston, and she enjoys roller-skating in her house while cooking and cleaning.

Jovita Moore
Anchor
WSB-TV Channel 2

Parquita Nassau
Senior Account Manager
Cox Radio Atlanta

Jovita Moore anchors weekdays on *Channel 2 Action News* and files news reports during the week. She is a member of the National Association of Black Journalists and the Atlanta Association of Black Journalists, where she was vice president from 2003 to 2005. She is also an active member of the Junior League of Atlanta.

A New York native, Jovita earned a master's degree from Columbia University Graduate School of Journalism. She holds a bachelor's degree, with a major in literature, from Bennington College in Bennington, Vermont.

A member of the 2004 class of Outstanding Atlanta, Jovita has also been featured in *JEZEBEL* as of one Atlanta's 50 Most Beautiful. In 2001 she received an Emmy for Outstanding Medical Reporting for her two-part series *Women and Fibroids*, which also received Best Hard Feature by the Atlanta Association of Black Journalists.

Jovita donates countless hours speaking to school groups, visiting with civic associations, hosting events for community agencies and mentoring students. She and her husband, Sean, also run a nonprofit youth organization, Live to Prosper.

Jovita and Sean have three children.

Perhaps best known as radio personality "Marie Stevens," Parquita Nassau is a talented individual within the media industry. She is the founder and president of the Black Radio Hall of Fame.

A former Miss Black Georgia and Spelman College graduate, Nassau began her radio career at age 19. She was known for many years as Marie Stevens, hostess of the popular *Kiss Classic Café* on KISS 104. She later worked at V-103 as "Nikki Nassau."

A native of Liberia, West Africa, Nassau was raised in Atlanta. Her professional achievements include co-anchoring the cable newsmagazine *Upbeat Atlanta* and hosting her own syndicated hip-hop radio program. She has been featured on *The Joan Rivers Show* and in *Ebony* and *Jet* magazines.

Nassau has served on the board of the National Black Programmers Coalition, and has been involved with several organizations including Big Brothers and Big Sisters, the National Association of Black Journalists and the National Association of 100 Black Women.

Nassau is presently an award-winning senior account manager with Cox Radio Atlanta, and often volunteers for charitable causes.

MEDIA PROFESSIONALS

Tammy Nobles
Assistant Station Manager
Jazz 91.9 WCLK

Gene Norman
Chief Meteorologist
WGCY-TV CBS 46 News

Tammy Nobles serves as assistant station manager for Jazz 91.9 WCLK, a public radio station licensed to Clark Atlanta University in Atlanta. She is responsible for general supervision of the station's membership fund-raising, community affairs production and administrative support.

Prior to WCLK, Nobles served for 13 years as membership director for KLON FM 88.1, the country's largest jazz format public radio station serving Los Angeles and Orange Counties in California. Nobles also served as foundation director for the Evander Holyfield Youth Foundation in Atlanta.

Nobles attended the Art Institute of Atlanta, where she studied in the culinary arts program. She also wrote, created and launched the business plan for Annie Laura's Kitchen Soul Food restaurant, now operating in its fifth year in Riverdale, Georgia.

Nobles received a bachelor of science degree in business administration and finance from California State University, Long Beach. She likes studying personalities and is a member of World Changers Church International.

Gene Norman is the chief meteorologist at the CBS affiliate in Atlanta. His weekday broadcasts at 4, 6 and 11 p.m. have been twice-honored with Emmys for Best Weathercast and Best Weathercaster by the Georgia Associated Press. Gene serves as the station captain for the annual March of Dimes WalkAmerica campaign.

Before January 2000 Gene was the weekend meteorologist at KTRK-TV in Houston, Texas. Television is a second career for Gene, who originally developed weather software for NASA's space shuttle program.

Gene serves as chair of the broadcast board of the American Meteorological Society and is on the board of governors of the Southeast chapter of the National Academy of Television Arts & Sciences.

Gene holds a bachelor of science in earth and planetary sciences from the Massachusets Institute of Technology and a master of science in meteorology from the University of Maryland. He lives in southwest Atlanta with his wife Elaine. Between them, they have four children.

Condace Pressley
Assistant Program Director
News/Talk 750 WSB

Corey A. Punzi
Promotions Manager
Radio One Atlanta

Condace Pressley is assistant program director for News/Talk 750 WSB, Atlanta's news, weather and traffic station. In this position, she manages one of America's most respected news/talk radio stations. Condace is also producer and host of the award-winning public affairs program, *Perspectives*.

An award-winning journalist, Condace has been recognized by the Associated Press, the University of Georgia, American Women in Radio and Television, and Outstanding Atlanta, among others.

Condace serves on the advisory board for the Henry W. Grady College of Journalism and Mass Communication at the University of Georgia, and sits on the board of directors for the Atlanta Press Club. She is a past president of the National Association of Black Journalists and served on the board of the Radio-Television News Directors Association. She has appeared on CNN, C-SPAN, MSNBC and *Nightline*.

Condace received a bachelor of arts degree in journalism from the University of Georgia and is active in her church and community.

Corey A. Punzi is the promotions manager for Smooth Jazz 107.5 and Grown Folks Radio 102.5. He is responsible for all of the station's promotions.

In college, Corey had his own radio show which segued into a bachelor of arts degree in television and radio broadcasting. His radio career then began in Atlanta with V-103 during the 1996 Summer Olympics. Later he became promotions assistant and gospel morning show producer for then KISS 104.7 and GLORY 1340. After a stint at Cox Radio (KISS 104.1), he was named director of marketing for WALR-AM, former sister station to WALR- FM.

In his spare time, Corey sits on the board of governors for the March of Dimes A.I.R. Awards, volunteers as a media consultant for *In The Life Atlanta*, a LGBT nonprofit organization, and encourages young people to set magnanimous goals in life. He is also founder of *the affaire, inc.*, a boutique marketing and publicity firm, and is penning his first literary piece.

Brenda Reid
Media & Community Relations Manager
Publix Super Markets, Inc.

Clarence Reynolds
Co-Anchor
WXIA-TV 11Alive

Brenda Reid is the media and community relations manager for Publix Super Markets, Inc. She is responsible for corporate giving, media and public relations, having served as the company spokesperson since 2000.

Previously, Reid served as the public relations and communications manager for *The Atlanta Journal-Constitution* where she spent 20 years in the newspaper business.

A graduate of Leadership Atlanta's Class of 2003, Reid sits on the campaign committee for the United Negro College Fund. She is a member of various committees and organizational boards including the Metro Atlanta YWCA, the Safe America Foundation and the Metro Atlanta Chamber of Commerce's education committee. She is also a trustee for the Birmingham Chamber of Commerce.

Reid holds a bachelor of arts degree in mass communications and journalism from Clark Atlanta University.

Brenda and her two sons, Horace Jr. and Brendan, live in Lithonia, Georgia. They are members of St. Philip AME Church in Decatur.

Clarence Reynolds joined the 11Alive team in October of 2005 as co-anchor of the weekday morning and noon newscasts.

He graduated from American University in Washington, D.C. with a bachelor of arts degree in communication and went to work for cable shopping giant QVC. Later, as the executive producer and host of *BET Shop*, Clarence led the creation of the nation's first African-American-themed shopping program on Black Entertainment Television (BET).

Clarence earned a master of science degree in counseling psychology from Troy State University, and he used that training to produce and host award-winning public affairs programs for PBS affiliates in Indianapolis and Orlando.

Clarence has also worked as chief correspondent on *Antiques Roadshow FYI*, a spin-off of the popular PBS series, and he helped launch the morning show on the Indianapolis FOX affiliate, WXIN.

He is a member of Alpha Phi Alpha Fraternity, Inc., the National Association of Black Journalists and the 2007 Class of Leadership Atlanta.

Angela Robinson
Host & Executive Producer
In Contact

Jean Ross
News Director
1380 WAOK AM & WVEE V-103 FM

Veteran and esteemed broadcast journalist Angela Robinson is the host and executive producer of *In Contact*, an award-winning news and public affairs talk show. She is also the president of A. Robinson Communications, LLC.

From 1994-1997, Angela was primary news anchor for the NBC affiliate in Atlanta. Prior to NBC, she spent 10 years at WTTG, FOX television's award-winning newscast in Washington, D.C., as a reporter, talk show host and primary news anchor. From 1978-1983, she worked as an editor and general assignment reporter for the CBS affiliate in Atlanta.

Angela is a Telly Award winner and has received multiple awards from the Southern Regional Emmys, the National Association of Black Journalists, and the Atlanta Association of Black Journalists. In 2005 she was honored as Journalist of the Year by the RainbowPush Coalition.

A graduate of Syracuse University, Angela was awarded the Chancellor's Citation from Syracuse University for distinguished achievement in journalism.

Angela is a member of the National Association of Black Journalists' Region 4 Hall of Fame. She holds membership and affiliation with several professional and community organizations.

Jean Ross is co-host of *The Morning Show* on Atlanta's talk radio station, 1380 WAOK AM, and she serves as news director of both WAOK and WVEE V-103 FM. Excited to be part of the rebirth of the historic WAOK, Ross has worked to make 1380 WAOK Talk Radio as popular and important to the community as its predecessor.

Ross began her career in radio as a volunteer before becoming a reporter, anchor, and assistant news director at WEAA-FM, Morgan State University Radio. In 1978 she became one of the first voices on Baltimore's V-103 FM (WXYV). Over the course of the next 19 years, she worked as news anchor, public affairs director, morning show co-host and even host of her own morning show, *Jean Ross and Co.* Ross was also host and producer of the nationally syndicated program *Focus on Women*, which aired in 50 cities in the United States and the Caribbean in 1990 and 1991.

MEDIA PROFESSIONALS

Jerry Rupert
Program Director
Hot 107.9/WHTA FM

Wanda Shelley
Vice President & Head of Production
B2 Entertainment, LLC

Jerry "Smokin' B" Rupert is heating up the airwaves on Hot 107.9 in Atlanta. A Milwaukee, Wisconsin native, Jerry has worked at eight radio stations nationwide, including WAWA, WNOV, KYOK, WLUM, KHYS, WVEE, WHXT and WHTA. His extensive experience includes extraordinary editing and detailing as a mixer, production manager, on-air personality, engineer and program director.

Jerry is a renaissance man who loves music, meeting people and building careers. As the creator of the "Hot Car Phone Check-In" on Hot 97.5 in Atlanta, Jerry encouraged listeners to call into his show during the "Five O' Clock Traffic Jam." This segment became the hottest feature on the station. As owner of Smokin' B Productions, he introduced the syndicated radio show *The Car Phone Mega Mix*, which aired in various cities throughout the U.S.

Jerry is sending up positive smoke signals throughout the radio industry as he steps out on faith, commitment and a wealth of experience to take radio to the next level. He continues to create innovative programming features for Hot 107.9 in Atlanta as program director of the station.

Wanda Shelley serves as vice president and head of production for B2 Entertainment, LLC. As head of production she oversees all aspects of the projects that are placed into production. She was also an executive producer and held a majority of the production duties for the reality series, *Being Bobby Brown*, which aired on the Bravo television network in the summer of 2005.

With more than ten years of marketing and sales experience, Wanda has managed sales territories with budgets in excess of $5 million. She also served as an executive producer for the independent film, *Book of Love*. She brings a wealth of marketing experience, passion and entrepreneurial spirit to the company.

Wanda was named one of *Atlanta Woman* magazine's Top 25 Women to Watch in 2006 and a Youth Vibe 2006 Media Mogul.

Wanda holds a bachelor's degree in marketing from Georgia State University.

Her professional affiliations include the Independent Feature Project, the National Association of Television Programming Executives, the National Association of Female Executives, and Women in Film.

Cynné Simpson
Evening News Anchor
WGCY-TV CBS 46 News

Dena J. Smith
Press Secretary
Director of Communications
Georgia Department of Human Resources

Cynné Simpson is an award-winning journalist who anchors the evening editions of CBS 46 News. She joined the news team in 2004 from sister station KCTV in Kansas City, Missouri.

Cynné was featured in *Ebony* magazine's article, "Young Leaders: 30 for 2006." She has also received an Emmy nomination, two William Randolph Hearst Writing Awards, a Poynter Institute fellowship and a Congressional Award for Community Service.

At 27, Cynné is one of the youngest major market evening news anchors in the country. She graduated magna cum laude from Howard University in Washington, D.C., where she majored in broadcast journalism and minored in Spanish. While studying, Ted Koppel was so impressed with her ability to report in English and Spanish that he selected her for a semester fellowship with ABC News: *Nightline*.

Cynné is a native of West Bloomfield, Michigan, but grew up in Sacramento, California. She has also lived in Spain and Costa Rica as an exchange student.

Dena J. Smith is press secretary for the Georgia Department of Human Resources and director of its office of communications. There she is responsible for media and public relations for the state's public health, child welfare, aging, mental health and other social services.

Smith formerly headed her own strategic consulting firm, Smith Communications, specializing in media relations and crisis management. Her previous experience also includes serving as director of media relations for the Alisias Group, an Atlanta-based public relations company, and as spokesperson for the City of Detroit's housing commission under the administration of former Mayor Dennis Archer. Smith started her professional career as a reporter for *The Atlanta Journal–Constitution*. She is a member of the National Association of Black Journalists and the Black Public Relations Society of Atlanta.

Originally from Chicago, Smith is an avid golfer.

Atlanta's
MEDIA PROFESSIONALS

Celebrating African-American Achievements

Shelice M. Smith
Director of Marketing and Promotions
Infinity Broadcasting Atlanta

Hank Stewart
Poet, Motivational Speaker, Author

Shelice M. Smith is the director of marketing for Infinity Broadcasting Atlanta which includes radio stations WVEE V-103 and WAOK. She is leading the companies' initiatives in developing innovative new programs and station promotions, and generating non-traditional revenue. She joined WAOK/WVEE in 1999 as the director of promotions before leading the business development department, which includes event marketing, promotions, Web site marketing and client driven campaigns.

Smith began her career in media 17 years ago in her hometown of Buffalo, New York, at the heritage urban radio station WBLK, where she established the promotions and marketing department. She joined Atlanta's WALR-FM in 1995 as the marketing director, then the Atlanta Urban Radio Alliance and Kicks 101.5 as a sales account executive.

Smith has the honor of serving on the advisory board for the American Red Cross minority recruitment campaign. The Atlanta Business League selected her as one of the 100 Women of Influence, and *Women Looking Ahead News Magazine* voted her one of the most Powerful & Influential Women in Media for the past three years.

Hank Stewart is a noted poet, motivational speaker and author. Widely recognized from performances on FOX5 Atlanta during Black History Month, Stewart, who has been called a messenger of hope, considers spirituality, history and love as his major influences for delving into the world of literature.

Stewart has worked on programs with former Vice President Al Gore, Tavis Smiley, the late Rev. Hosea Williams and the late Johnny Cochran. He has performed for McDonald's Heritage television commercials, the Essence Music Festival and *Quiet Storm*, a weekly radio broadcasting show highlighting talented poetry and jazz artists on Atlanta's V-103.

Stewart is the founding member of Five Men On A Stool and the president of the Hank Stewart Foundation, which promotes literacy for delinquent teens. His first mainstream published novel, *Three Fifty-Seven AM*, co-authored with Kendra Norman-Bellamy, will be released early 2007.

A devoted Christian and father of one son, Austin, Stewart believes that firm spiritual guidance can help an individual remain true to the mission of life and success.

Joe Taylor "Miss Sophia"
Host, "Girl Talk"
WVEE V-103 FM

Chandra Thomas
Writer
Atlanta Magazine

"Miss Sophia" was born Joe Taylor in Calvert, Texas and grew up in Houston. He attended Texas Southern University as a theatre major. A comedian for quite some time, Miss Sophia enjoys making people laugh. Miss Sophia is the entertainment reporter on *Frank & Wanda in the Morning*, and she travels and host pageants on a national level. Her hobbies are reading, traveling, singing, telling jokes, eating, watching the news and sports and eating.

Moving to Atlanta with dreams of taking his comedy career to the next level, Taylor had not thought about radio, but it was in God's plans. Being part of *Frank & Wanda in the Morning* is a dream someone else conjured up, but he is grateful for the blessing.

Miss Sophia still hosts club parties and performs regularly throughout the country including regular appearances in New York, Texas, Florida and Tennessee. Her quote is: "The whole world is a stage for me to share my God-given talent with everyone, so smile, because God loves you and laughter is good for you."

Chandra Thomas is an award-winning journalist and the only African-American writer on staff at *Atlanta Magazine*. She has used her platform to write stories that highlight important issues facing women and people of color. Chandra was invited to share the details of her in-depth feature highlighting racial disparities within Georgia's judicial system in a national appearance on the MSNBC network. Her story prompted segments on *ABC Prime Time* and *Good Morning America*.

In 2005 the Atlanta Association of Black Journalists honored Chandra with a feature-writing award for her introspective piece about tracing her African roots.

Chandra served as an associate producer for Fox 5's *Good Day Atlanta*. After graduating with a bachelor's degree in journalism from Clark Atlanta University, she worked as a reporter/fashion columnist for the *Birmingham Post-Herald* newspaper in Alabama and as co-host of the radio program, *Talkback Live*. Chandra also served as a morning show producer for Birmingham's ABC affiliate.

A New Orleans native, Chandra has worked as a stringer for *Essence* and *Newsweek* magazines. She is the co-founder of the African-American discussion group, TalkBLACK Atlanta.

MEDIA PROFESSIONALS

Tara Thomas
Event Marketing Coordinator
WVEE V-103 FM & 1380 WAOK AM

Shawneen C. Thompson
General Sales Manager
CBS Radio, WVEE FM, WAOK AM

Tara Thomas is the event marketing coordinator for The People's Station, V-103 and News Talk WAOK.

Thomas came to Atlanta from Seat Pleasant, Maryland. She began her career in 1994 as an intern for *The Frank and Jean Morning Show* at WXYV/ V-103 in Baltimore while attending Towson State University. After graduating with a bachelor of science degree in mass communications, Thomas performed a short stint at WUST-AM, a foreign language station in Virginia. She rejoined Frank Ski as producer of his morning show on Baltimore's 92Q Jams FM. When *The Frank Ski Morning Show* moved to Atlanta, she became the entertainment reporter and fill-in morning show host. After nine years in broadcasting, Thomas stepped down as morning show producer to pursue a personal goal, event marketing. In 2003 she was named V-103 and WAOK's event marketing coordinator, a position created for her by CBS Radio Atlanta's vice president and general manager, Rick Caffey.

Thomas has been profiled in *Ebony* and she has been honored by *Women Looking Ahead News Magazine* as one of the 100 Most Influential Women in Media.

Shawneen C. Thompson is the general sales manager for CBS Radio, WVEE FM and WAOK AM. Her 17-year radio career includes a myriad of formats including classic rock, oldies, sports, adult contemporary and urban radio. Shawneen began her career in Columbus, Ohio at the top-rated CHR station WNCI-FM. Various promotions within Nationwide Communications led her to KDMX-FM in Dallas, Texas as the marketing director, then back to her hometown to launch sister station WCOL FM. Shawneen's experience also included Radio One properties WCKX FM, WXMG FM and WJYD FM as local sales manager before arriving in Atlanta.

Shawneen's personal mentors, who are among the most influential women in radio, have influenced her to provide leadership and improve the quality of advocating the advancement of women to senior positions. Previously, she was president for the American Women in Radio and Television, Buckeye Chapter. In addition, Shawneen has been recognized by Nationwide Communications as an up-and-coming young African American in radio.

Linda Torrence
**Community Relations &
Public Service Director
WAGA-TV/FOX5**

Shelley Trotter
**Director, Communications & Marketing
Jazz 91.0 WCLK**

As FOX5's director of community relations and public service, Linda Torrence is the primary liaison between the television station and the Atlanta community. She manages projects dealing with community issues and sponsorship activities with nonprofit organizations. She is also managing director of FOX5 editorials and producer of the *Georgia Gang*.

Prior to FOX5, Linda was vice president of marketing and communications with the Private Industry Council in Portland, Oregon. She was also regional director of human resources for Rogers Cable Television, where she hosted her own talk show, *Women in Focus*.

The American Academy of Pediatrics presented Linda the Friend of Children Award, and Atlanta Business League named her one of Atlanta's Most Influential African-American Women. She has been profiled in several magazines including *Southern Flair, Face to Face* and *Atlanta Woman*.

She serves on several boards of directors including DeKalb County Chamber of Commerce, the Boys & Girls Club of Metro Atlanta and the American Heart Association.

A graduate of Arkansas Baptist College, Linda is married to Joe Phillips, general manager of the DeKalb County Schools television system.

Shelley Trotter serves as director of communications and marketing for Jazz 91.9 WCLK. She develops and markets image pieces for external/internal communications and oversees logistics for special events and signature activities. Additionally, Shelley lends talent to promotional, voice-over and copywriting efforts.

Shelley's debut in public radio came nearly 20 years ago as a student news anchor for WEAA-FM in Baltimore, Maryland. Her former positions include director of human resources at WITF-TV/FM in Harrisburg, Pennsylvania and employment outreach project coordinator for the Corporation for Public Broadcasting in Washington, D.C. She also served three other commercial radio and television stations.

Seven years ago, Shelley's passion for promoting traditional musical art forms among youth helped spawn the Atlanta Jazz Festival Youth Jazz Band Competition, which showcases middle and high school jazz bands. Since its inception, she has served as the competition's Atlanta Jazz Festival consultant.

Shelley holds a bachelor's degree in communications from Morgan State University. An active member of Word of Love Christian Church in Fairburn and a board member of For The Children, Inc., Shelley credits all opportunities to Jesus Christ.

MEDIA PROFESSIONALS

Osei Tuffour
Radio Host
WVEE V-103 FM

James H. Welcome
Chief Executive Officer
Group Americus Business
and Entertainment Services

An aspiring actor and model, Osei (pronounced O-say) studied with the renowned Freedom Theater repertory company. More than 64 million people regularly listened to Osei's polished baritone voice on various television spots, as he was the primary male voice-over talent for the Black Entertainment Television (BET) network.

While working toward becoming a sports medicine physician, Osei's first brush with the airwaves happened at WHOV 88.1FM, Hampton University's jazz station. While interning, he worked at WPGC-FM with the legendary Donnie Simpson and his morning crew, then moved up to overnights and weekends for that station. Soon, he was hosting the coveted, sexy night show, *Love, Talk & Slow Jamz.*

Born in Kitchner, Ontario, Osei has lived in many places including Cleveland, Detroit, Virginia, New York and Ghana, West Africa, the native country of his parents.

Osei most admires his parents, James Earl Jones, Oprah Winfrey, Kofi Anann, Quincy Jones, Shawn Carter, Kevin Liles and Queen Latifah. His favorite pastimes are exercising, traveling, swimming, cooking, playing sports and reading.

James H. Welcome is the chief executive officer of Group Americus Business and Entertainment Services in Atlanta. Group Americus and its wholly-owned subsidiaries, *NEWSMAKERS Live!* and the *NEWSMAKERS Journal*, provide streamlined business and marketing consulting services to a variety of clients in business and entertainment. Since 1971, Welcome has been recognized as being among the nation's most renowned concert producers, club impresarios and advisors in the music field. This experience lends itself to Mr. Welcome in his position as executive producer and publisher of Atlanta's premier live political black forum, *NEWSMAKERS Live!*, which hosts such guests as Minister Louis Farrakhan, Cynthia McKinney, Jesse Jackson and Shirley Franklin.

The Group Americus family of companies forms a consulting firm where the focus is black business development, fund-raising for nonprofits and entertainment events.

Welcome received his undergraduate degree from St. Francis College and attended Columbia University's Executive School of Business. He is a member of the Association of Fund Developers, as well as the MBA Association.

Lorraine Jacques White
Host, *PowerTalk*
1380 WAOK AM

JaQuitta Williams
Reporter
WSB-TV Channel 2

Lorraine Jacques White currently hosts *PowerTalk* on 1380 WAOK AM. Breaking news, politics, racial issues, entertainment, community concerns, relationships and more are the morning order for *PowerTalk,* where Lorraine and her guests provide knowledge and the community gains power.

A woman of substance, she has organized, promoted and conducted seminars, workshops and church retreats across the country. She also serves as director of Christian education at Mount Ephraim Baptist Church, where her husband, Dr. R. L. White Jr., is pastor. Lorraine hosted the popular radio talk show *Ministerial Insight*, which featured some of the nation's most recognized public figures including Kweisi Mfume, Reverend Jesse Jackson, and Reverend Al Sharpton.

She was one of 23 women leaders selected to participate in a special video at the Smithsonian Institute in Washington, D.C. The Atlanta Business League named her among the 100 Most Influential Women in Atlanta. She also co-authored the inspirational book *Sister-to-Sister*.

Lorraine is an honors graduate of the Interdenominational Theological Center with a master of divinity degree.

Together, Lorraine and Dr. White have traveled the globe with their complimentary ministries.

JaQuitta Williams has been a reporter for WSB-TV, Channel 2 since 2004. She came to Atlanta after serving as a morning anchor and reporter at KSHB-TV/NBC Action News in Kansas City, Missouri. While there, she hosted *Lifetime Moments*, a weekday program that featured inspirational stories about women and their families.

Prior to joining KSHB-TV, JaQuitta worked as an anchor and reporter at WLFL-TV in Raleigh, North Carolina; WBIR-TV in Knoxville, Tennessee; and WRDW-TV in North Augusta, South Carolina.

JaQuitta's introduction into the world of broadcasting began when she was in college at Savannah State College. Throughout her life, she sang in church, school, college choirs, pageants and fairs, so she initially enrolled as a music student. Then, following the advice of a close friend, JaQuitta enrolled in a broadcast journalism class. She loved the course so much she changed majors.

JaQuitta is a member of Alpha Kappa Alpha Sorority, Inc. along with the National Association of Black Journalists and the Atlanta Association of Black Journalists. A native of Augusta, she is a Southerner at heart.

MEDIA PROFESSIONALS

Wendy Williams
General Manager
Jazz 91.9 WCLK

Christine Willis
General Manager
WTJH 1260 AM Radio

Wendy Williams enters her 13th year as general manager of Jazz 91.9 WCLK-FM, a National Public Radio (NPR) member station licensed to Clark Atlanta University. Williams also served as general manager of NPR member station WEAA-FM, licensed to Morgan State University in Baltimore, Maryland. She began honing her broadcasting skills in the 80s in commercial television and radio.

Williams currently serves as chair of the African-American Public Radio Consortium Inc., a national organization that develops national programming for diverse public radio audiences, including *The Tavis Smiley Show* from NPR and *News & Notes* with host Farai Chideya. Currently under development is a program with host Michel Martin, formerly of ABC News *Nightline*. She served on the board of directors for Public Radio Development and Marketing, Inc., a national organization offering fund-raising and marketing services for public radio.

Williams received her communications degree from Bowling Green State University in Ohio and holds a master's of business administration from Clark Atlanta University. A member of Alpha Kappa Alpha Sorority, Inc., Williams loves traveling, cooking and meeting people.

Christine Willis began her early broadcasting career under the guiding hand of her father, assisting him in the day-to-day operation of corporate responsibilities in the chain's numerous radio stations. Her broadcasting skills include sales, collections and management. In August of 2001, Christine moved to Atlanta to assume management of WTJH 1260 Radio, a 5,000 watt AM gospel music/ministry station. Under her guidance, WTJH radio was relocated from East Point to more modern studio facilities in Southwest Atlanta. The new complex includes three separate broadcast studios and state-of-the-art equipment.

Her current plans include the acquisition of several FM stations. Her mission is to better serve metro Atlanta with great music, ministries, and fresh and vital information in every capacity.

Christine is the mother of two handsome sons, Steven G. Felton Jr. and Alexander "Alex" Lashawn Felton. She is the daughter of media mogul Bishop Levi and Mrs. Hortense Willis Sr. of Norfolk, Virginia.

Cie Cie Wilson
Promotions Manager
Praise 97.5 FM
Radio One Atlanta

Rob Wilson
Executive Producer & Talk Show Host
1380 WAOK AM

Atlanta native Cie Cie Wilson is the promotions manager for Praise 97.5 FM. She is responsible for creating on-air promotions for the FM gospel format. Co-producing The Stone Mountain Gospel Celebration for the past two years, which has featured Donnie McClurkin, Dorinda Clark Cole and Hezekiah Walker, has been a personal achievement in making her mark in the gospel music community. With over 20 years in the entertainment industry, her mission is to connect the community with issues that matter. She has a passion for working with women and children's organizations and creating opportunities to support the Hosea Feed The Hungry food campaigns and donations toward the Atlanta Union Mission.

Wilson recognized her niche for grassroots promotion working with UniverSoul Circus as media production/ promotion manager creating sizzling advertising campaigns marketed to millions in major cities.

Her music career achievements include ten years with Warner Bros. Records, assisting in the early career development of artists on the music charts today, and at Intersound, promoting the resurgence of live music projects featuring artists George Clinton, The Dazz Band, Lakeside and more.

Rob Wilson is executive producer and talk show host of *Solution and Remedies* on 1380 WAOK AM. A master of teaching credit- and wealth-building concepts, he is the best-selling author of *Unlocking Wealth, Working Out Credit*, and the self-help book *Ordered Steps*. As a motivational speaker, Wilson encourages all people to look inside themselves for their worth. He delivers his Mastering Your Credit and Unlocking Wealth seminars series to standing-room-only crowds across the nation. His debut book, *Unlocking Wealth,* takes a candid look at how people need to learn the foundation to financial independence, right here, right now.

Wilson has appeared on CBN's *The Money Club* as well as ABC Network Radio's *The John Arnold Show* and *The Tom Pope Show.* He has been a guest speaker for Partners in Education, with Wachovia Bank of Georgia, and he is chairman of G.I.V.E.B.A.C.K., a nonprofit outreach program.

Wilson is also founder and general manager of Wealth Accumulation Concepts, where he has devoted his efforts to educating the public. He is a credit consultant for numerous mortgage and financial services companies.

WellPoint, Inc. would like to congratulate everyone highlighted in the *Who's Who in Black Atlanta*. We honor you and the diversity of talent within our great community.

As the largest publicly traded commercial health benefits company in America, formed through the merger of Anthem, Inc. and WellPoint Health Networks Inc. in 2004, WellPoint, Inc. now serves approximately 34 million members nationwide.

While WellPoint operates on a national scale, its focus remains local. Its mission is to "improve the lives of the people we serve and the health of our communities." To carry out this mission, WellPoint currently has a force of approximately 42,000 associates, all focused on balancing its "one company, one team" core value and its national scope with a strong local presence. And WellPoint has made managing diversity a central component of its corporate culture.

Today, Diversity Management at WellPoint means actively cultivating opportunities for women and minorities to advance through the company ranks. In 2005, 60 percent of its management positions were held by women, 18 percent by minorities, and five of the sixteen Board of Director members are women.

The company's focus on managing diversity has not gone unnoticed by external organizations, with recognition coming from a wide range of sources including *Working Mother* magazine's *Top Companies for Women of Color, Profiles in Diversity Journal 2006 International in Diversity Award, DiversityInc's Top 50 Companies for Diversity, Black Equal Opportunity Employment Journal*, the National Association of Female Executives, *FORTUNE*, and *CAREERS & the disABLED* magazine.

To support their diversity efforts at the leadership level WellPoint has a dedicated Diversity Workforce and Development (DWD) team led by their vice president of Diversity and Workforce Development, David Casey. Casey works closely with executive vice president of Human Resources, Randy Brown, chairman, president, and CEO, Larry C. Glasscock, and the Executive Leadership Team to determine diversity strategies, measures, and approaches.

One of the most visible indicators of WellPoint's commitment to cultivating leadership diversity – within and outside its own corporate environment – is the pivotal role it played in establishing the Diversity Leadership Academy of Greater Indianapolis (DLAGI) in 2003. The company committed more than half a million dollars to the academy's initial development, creating an innovative, hands-on learning program for building diversity-management leadership skills within the Indianapolis community. In the three years since the launch of the program, over 130 leaders from business, government, faith-based, non-profit, and education have graduated. This represents 109 businesses resulting in alumni taking their newfound awareness and skills back to the decision-making tables in their communities.

What seems clear from the company's experience to date is that the best way to implement diversity strategies is to fully and fundamentally internalize them: to treat diversity management as a standard business practice. The individuals featured in this journal are exemplary models of living WellPoint's core values each and every day.

For more information about our company and our commitment to diversity and culture, please visit us at **wellpoint.com**.

Atlanta's

COUNSELORS AT LAW

"The only way to make sure people you agree with can speak is to support the rights of people you don't agree with."

ELEANOR HOLMES NORTON

LAWYER & ACTIVIST

COUNSELORS AT LAW

Gordon R. Alphonso
Partner, Attorney at Law
McGuireWoods LLP

Precious Anderson
Founding Partner
Chief Executive Officer
The Anderson Firm, LLC

Gordon R. Alphonso is a partner in the Atlanta office of McGuireWoods LLP. He provides environmental representation, counseling and litigation services to corporations on legislative, regulatory and judicial matters under state and federal environmental laws, with an emphasis on air, solid and hazardous waste issues. His practice covers day-to-day compliance matters, enforcement defense, environmental litigation, and assessment of potential environmental liabilities in connection with corporate transactions.

Prior to joining McGuireWoods, Alphonso was a partner in the Atlanta office of Troutman Sanders. From 1997 to 1999, he worked in-house at Georgia-Pacific Corporation as chief division counsel for communication paper and tissue, and from 1990 to 1997 as chief counsel for environmental matters. Prior to joining Georgia-Pacific, Alphonso served as an assistant attorney general for the State of Georgia.

Alphonso received his bachelor's degree from Clemson University in 1977 and his juris doctorate from the Mercer University School of Law in 1983.

Alphonso received an "AV" rating from Martindale-Hubbell. He was recognized as a Super Lawyer in *Law & Politics* and *Atlanta Magazine* for his environmental law excellence.

Precious Anderson is a partner with The Anderson Firm, LLC, a legal and business boutique in downtown Atlanta. Precious represents and advises clients in a myriad of business and entertainment matters such as business and strategic planning; contract drafting, review and negotiation; and dispute resolution.

Precious' clients include small to mid-sized businesses, entertainers, entrepreneurs, developers, high net worth investors, start-ups and nonprofits. She also represents companies in the entertainment, technology, food service, apparel, marketing and holistic living industries.

Precious received her juris doctorate in 1998 from Harvard Law School. She graduated summa cum laude with a bachelor of science degree in broadcast journalism and a bachelor of arts degree in political science from Florida A&M University in 1994.

Precious is a member of the State Bar of Georgia, the United Way V.I.P., Delta Sigma Theta Sorority, Inc. and the steering committee for the Arthritis Foundation-Georgia Chapter. She is a board member of the Atlanta Community Food Bank, Investing in Our Youth, the Spelman College Museum of Fine Art and the distinguished host committee for the GotJazz Series.

Lecora Bowen
Attorney at Law
Lecora Bowen & Associates

Terence G. Clark
Member, Attorney at Law
Miller & Martin PLLC

Lecora Bowen, of Lecora Bowen & Associates, has represented multinational, nonprofit corporations, and handled extensive construction and civil litigation.

Previously, Bowen was an expert for *11Alive News* on the Buckhead murders and a religious freedom expert on Trinity Broadcasting Network. A favored speaker, she has delivered speeches to the Army Corps of Engineers, Metro Upward Bound programs, high schools and religious functions.

Bowen has appeared in several nationwide registers such as *Who's Who in Executives and Businesses, Who's Who Among Outstanding Americans, Who's Who Among Outstanding Young Women of America* and *Who's Who Among American Junior Colleges.*

In 1979 Bowen received her bachelor of business administration degree from Memphis State University. In 1984 she received her juris doctorate degree from the Cecil C. Humphreys School of Law of Memphis State University.

A native of Holly Springs, Mississippi and an ordained minister, Bowen has a love for children and has served as a private child intervention source.

Terry Clark concentrates his practice on commercial real estate leasing, representing developers and lenders. He has represented institutional investors, real estate investment trusts and major local and national real estate and management companies in office, retail and industrial lease transactions. Terry has represented lenders and borrowers in conduit and securitized loan transactions, and has represented banks and institutional lenders in making construction and term loans. He has also represented developers of residential subdivisions, retail shopping centers and office developments.

Terry is the head of the real estate practice group, comprised of approximately 25 attorneys firm wide. He also serves on the firm's hiring committee and diversity committee.

He is a member of the State Bar of Georgia, the National Bar Association, the Gate City Bar Association, ACRE Net and CoreNet Global.

Terry received a bachelor of arts degree from Baruch College, City University of New York, cum laude in 1988, and a juris doctorate from New York University School of Law in 1991. He was a senior editorial staff member of the *New York University Law Review.*

COUNSELORS AT LAW

Denise Cleveland-Leggett
Legal Consultant

Thomas A. Cox Jr.
Member, Attorney at Law
Miller & Martin PLLC

Denise Cleveland-Leggett is an accomplished attorney as well as a community leader in Atlanta. She jointly received her bachelor of arts degree and associate of science degree from Oakwood College in 1981. She subsequently received her juris doctor degree from Boston University School of Law in 1984.

Leggett currently serves as a legal consultant to major companies and on issues relating to Title VII and other employment-related matters. She serves as president of the board of trustees for Literacy Action, Inc., and president of the board of councilors for the Margaret Mitchell House and Museum. She was recently selected as a member of the board of trustees for the Atlanta History Center. In 2001 she was appointed by the lieutenant governor and commissioned by the governor to serve as a member of the Georgia Commission for Women. She has also served as a member of the Georgia State Ethics Commission.

Leggett has been married to her loving husband for over 20 years, Dr. Christopher Leggett, an interventional cardiologist. She has two beautiful children, Alexandria, 17, and Christopher, 10.

Thomas A. Cox Jr. is an experienced litigator who concentrates his practice in the areas of labor and employment and litigation defense. He serves as vice chairman of the firm's labor and employment department. Cox is rated "AV," the highest rating attainable, by the *Martindale-Hubbell Law Directory* and has been selected as a Georgia Super Lawyer. He defends multiple private sector corporate clients in all types of employment-related litigation, arbitration, and mediation, including claims of discrimination and sexual harassment, claims under the ADA, FMLA, Title VII and the intentional infliction of emotional distress. His practice is conducted primarily in federal courts throughout the United States.

Cox has been a featured panelist in a Daily Report expert's roundtable involving age discrimination claim avoidance. His cases have also been featured in *Ohio Lawyers Weekly*. Cox previously practiced in the Georgia Attorney General's Office, the Fulton County Attorney's Office and the United States Department of Justice in Washington, D.C. He graduated with a bachelor of arts degree, cum laude, from Morehouse College and with a juris doctorate from Boston College Law School.

Alexandrina Douglass
Chief Counsel
Latin American Operations
ING Americas

Donald P. Edwards
Attorney at Law
The Law Offices of Donald P. Edwards

Alexandrina (Alex) Douglass is chief counsel for intellectual property and information technology as well as chief counsel for Latin American operations for ING North America Insurance Corporation, the Americas' regional headquarters for ING Groep NV. Previously, Alex was an associate at Troutman Sanders, LLP. She also practiced at The Red Hot Law Group of Ashley LLC and was director of network licensing for the Latin America division of Turner Broadcasting System.

A graduate of Northwestern University, she went on to attend Howard University School of Law. While practicing as a Fulton County public defender, Alex was awarded a Ford Foundation Fellowship to attend the Fletcher School of International Law and Diplomacy. Subsequently, she was an intern for Governor Zell Miller.

Alex is a board member of the Center for Black Women's Wellness and The Partnership Against Domestic Violence. Additionally, she is a member of the Atlanta Women's Foundation law day committee, and the advisory council for the National Association of Minority and Women Law Firms.

A New York native, Alex has resided in Atlanta for 16 years.

In private legal practice since 1973, Don Edwards specializes as a trial lawyer in the areas of personal injury, wrongful death and medical malpractice.

A devoted community servant, Don chairs the Fulton County Board of Ethics. He serves on the boards of Boy Scouts of America-South Atlanta Sankofa District and the Christian Council of Metropolitan Atlanta.

A 2004 Gate City Bar Association Hall of Fame inductee, Don received the Chief Justice Award for community service, the State Bar of Georgia's highest community service award. He received the Silver Beaver Award from the Boy Scouts of America Atlanta Area Council.

Since September of 2001, Don has hosted, produced and sponsored an award-winning cable television program, *Every Church A Peace Church*. His peacekeeping efforts garnered the 2005 World Council of Churches Blessed Are The Peacemakers Award.

Don graduated cum laude from Morehouse College and earned a juris doctorate degree from Boston University School of Law.

A Buffalo, New York native, he is the husband of Jo Roberson Edwards, and the grateful father of Nia, Domia and Dawnalisa Edwards.

COUNSELORS AT LAW

Ronald J. Freeman Sr.
Managing Member
Johnson & Freeman, LLC

Karen D. Fultz
Partner, Attorney at Law
Cozen O'Connor

Ronald J. Freeman Sr. is co-founder of the law firm of Johnson & Freeman, LLC. His primary focus is in the areas of construction law and business litigation.

Freeman earned a bachelor of arts degree in political science, graduating with high honors in 1982 from Morehouse College. A Regent's Opportunity Scholar, he received his juris doctor degree from Georgia State University College of Law in 1985.

Freeman's professional appointments include judge (pro hac) of the Magistrate Court of Fulton County and chief judge of the Municipal Court of Riverdale. In 2004 and 2006 he was named a Georgia Super Lawyer in Business Litigation by *Atlanta Magazine* and *Law & Politics*. He is the 2006 recipient of the A.T. Walden Outstanding Lawyer Award.

Born in Stuttgart, Germany, Freeman is very passionate about the practice of law, a talent and gift given to him by God, enabling him to fulfill his purpose as a servant leader. He is married to the former Gwendolyn Hood and is the proud father of two children, Chelsea and Ronnie.

A partner with Cozen O'Connor, Karen D. Fultz was admitted to practice in Georgia in 1998. Her area of concentration is subrogation and recovery, and domestic relations.

Her professional experience includes serving as a judicial intern to the Honorable Denise Page Hood of the U.S. District Court for the Eastern District of Michigan; assistant vice president of estate settlement at Bank of America; and as an associate with The Zweifel Law Firm and Lackland & Associates, LLC.

Karen has served as president of the Gate City Bar Association and a board member of the Atlanta Legal Diversity Consortium and the Atlanta Bar Association. A member of the Georgia Association of Black Women Attorneys and the Georgia Association of Women Lawyers, she was appointed to the local bar activities committee for the State Bar of Georgia. Additionally, Karen is a volunteer for the Atlanta Volunteer Lawyers Foundation and Georgia Legal Services.

Karen holds a bachelor of arts degree from Michigan State University and a juris doctorate from Thomas M. Cooley Law School.

Latoicha Phillips Givens, Esq.
Attorney At Law
Phillips Givens, LLC

Nicol J. Hanyard
Attorney at Law
Hanyard Law Office, P.C.

Latoicha Phillips Givens is the founding member of Phillips Givens, LLC. Her practice includes representing clients before governmental entities; representing nonprofit organizations; and business legal matters including incorporations, business reorganizations and business asset purchases.

Prior to starting the firm, Givens worked for a mid-sized New York firm. She then went on to have an illustrious career in politics. She served as chief of staff for a Florida representative and as legislative counsel to the Georgia Senate majority leader's office.

Givens has been featured in *Atlanta Tribune: The Magazine,* where she was recognized for her commitment to educating individuals on effective business development. She serves on the board of The Witness Project of Greater Atlanta and is a member of the American Bar Association and the Georgia Association of Black Women Attorneys.

Givens graduated cum laude with a bachelor's degree in political science and English from Florida A&M University. She received her juris doctorate from The Catholic University of America.

She is married to Shawn J. Givens and has one son, Shawn J. Givens II.

In 1995 attorney Nicol J. Hanyard established her personal injury and family law practice, Hanyard Law Office, P.C. Since her practice began, Hanyard has successfully provided attentive and aggressive legal representation for numerous individuals with personal injury, child support, divorce, custody and adoption.

Hanyard is a member of the American Bar Association and the State Bar of Georgia. She has been featured on the WPBA television program *Layman's Lawyer.* Additionally, Hanyard has been invited to speak at various schools and organizations, including Spelman College, the Grandparents Association of Atlanta, Waldon Middle School and Georgia State University School of Law. She is also a member of Alpha Kappa Alpha Sorority, Inc. and volunteers time to several organizations.

Hanyard came to the great city of Atlanta in 1987 to attend Spelman College, where she earned her bachelor of arts degree in 1995. She earned her juris doctorate from Georgia State University School of Law.

Originally from Dallas, Texas, Nicol is the proud daughter of Bernard and Sally Hanyard.

COUNSELORS AT LAW

James T. Harris
Intellectual Property Counsel
UPS

H. Eric Hilton
General Counsel and Corporate Secretary
H.J. Russell & Company
Concessions International, LLC

James Harris is intellectual property counsel for UPS. In this position, he manages the legal aspects of UPS' worldwide patent, trademark and copyright portfolios, as well as UPS' advertising and sponsorship matters.

Previously, James practiced with law firms in Chicago and Atlanta and taught at Columbia College in Chicago. He was a commissioner on the Illinois Supreme Court Committee on Character and Fitness. Before practicing law, James was a project engineer for General Motors.

He received a bachelor of science degree in mechanical engineering from Tennessee State University and a law degree from the Chicago-Kent College of Law. In 2003 he received a master of business administration degree from Emory University.

James is a board member of Zoo Atlanta and the Guilford Forest Homeowners Association, as well as president of the Twelve Atlantic Station Residential Condo Association. He is also a member of the 100 Black Men of America and Kappa Alpha Psi Fraternity, Inc.

A Chicago native, James is the husband of Cheryl Love-Harris and is the proud father of two sons and two daughters, Kendall, DeGreer, Jakari and Chanel.

H. Eric Hilton is general counsel and corporate secretary of H.J. Russell & Company, the nation's largest minority-owned construction firm, and Concessions International, LLC, a national hospitality management company focusing on the operation of airport concessions. In his dual role, Hilton is responsible for overseeing all aspects of the legal function for both companies.

Hilton holds memberships in a number of professional and civic organizations including the American Bar Association, the Association of Corporate Counsel, the Minority Corporate Counsel Association and Kappa Alpha Psi Fraternity, Inc. He has been a featured speaker and is quoted in a number of legal publications including *GC South Magazine* and the *Daily Report*.

Hilton earned his bachelor of science degree in economics from Hampton University and his juris doctorate from the George Washington University Law School.

Hilton serves as a volunteer on-air reader for the Georgia Radio Reading Service, providing audio broadcasts for the visually impaired. A native of Washington, D.C., Hilton and his wife, Marla, are the proud parents of two children, Hunter and Juliana.

Allegra Lawrence-Hardy
Litigation Partner
Sutherland Asbill & Brennan LLP

Bernie Lawrence-Watkins
Attorney at Law
B. Lawrence Watkins & Associates, PC

Allegra Lawrence-Hardy is a litigation partner in the national law firm of Sutherland Asbill & Brennan LLP, focusing on labor and employment law. She has litigated cases in federal and state courts for Fortune 100 companies across the country. Allegra regularly advises employers on compliance with the various employment laws and often speaks to management, lawyers, and human resources professionals on labor and employment law issues.

She has been recognized as one of the top litigators in the state by *Georgia Trend*, *Atlanta Magazine* and the *Fulton County Daily Report*. Allegra chairs Sutherland's diversity committee and is a member of the firm's hiring committee. She is also a founding member of the Atlanta Legal Diversity Consortium, a past president of the Georgia Association of Black Women Attorneys, and a member of the board of directors for the Justice Center of Atlanta. She also chairs the Georgia Bar's women and minorities in the profession committee.

Allegra graduated magna cum laude from Spelman College and holds a law degree from Yale University.

An Atlanta native, Allegra is married to Timothy Hardy.

Bernie Lawrence-Watkins specializes in the area of transactional entertainment law. Additionally, she provides consultation to small businesses relating to legal formation, corporate law and government-related programs/contracting.

Lawrence-Watkins has frequently appeared as a guest speaker and panelist at seminars and conferences across the country, including the 2005 Harvard University Black Law Student Association's spring conference.

Lawrence-Watkins is licensed to practice law in the state of Georgia. She is an active member of the Black Entertainment and Sports Law Association, Alpha Kappa Alpha Sorority, Inc. and the Atlanta Chapter of Jack and Jill of America, Inc. A board member of the Smyrna Athletic Association, she also volunteers for the Minority Business Development Agency MED Week committee.

Born in Dominica, West Indies, Lawrence-Watkins was raised in New York City. She earned a bachelor of business administration degree in marketing from Howard University in 1990 and a juris doctorate from the University of Baltimore School of Law in 1995.

She is married to Dana S. Watkins and has two sons, Pryce and Reign.

COUNSELORS AT LAW

Corliss Scroggins Lawson
Founding Partner
Corliss & Associates, P.C.

Tracie J. Maurer
Partner, Attorney at Law
Smith, Gambrell & Russell, LLP

Corliss Scroggins Lawson is the founding partner of Corliss & Associates, P.C. located in the historical downtown district of Fayetteville, Georgia. Prior to opening her own firm on June 1, 2006, she was a complex commercial litigator and managing partner of the Atlanta office of Lord, Bissell & Brook, LLP.

Lawson's practice covers a broad array of legal areas, including products liability, environmental, construction defect, unfair and deceptive trade practices, toxic torts, complex insurance defense, premises liability, railroad and aviation defense as well as other general tort and breach of contract cases. She is also experienced in handling employment discrimination and sexual harassment cases. A seasoned litigator, her experience includes trying cases, heavy motion practice, arbitration, mediation and administrative hearings.

Lawson has been selected as a Georgia Super Lawyer for the years 2005, 2006 and 2007. She also recently joined Henning Mediation and Arbitration Service as a mediator and is a registered mediator with the Georgia Office of Dispute Resolution.

Tracie J. Maurer is a partner in the litigation section of Smith, Gambrell & Russell, LLP. She focuses her practice in the area of employment law, exclusively representing employers.

Maurer graduated in 1986 with a degree in psychology from the University of Michigan. She pursued post-baccalaureate studies in middle grades education at Clark Atlanta University and Georgia State University, maintaining a place on both dean's lists. In 1996 Maurer received her juris doctorate from the University of Georgia where she served as executive chairperson of the Moot Court Board and president of the Black Law Students Association. Additionally, she was elected to the Order of the Barristers and the Lumpkin Inn of Court.

Prior to entering law school, Maurer worked for several years as an educator in the Atlanta and Charlotte, North Carolina public school systems.

Maurer is a member of the State Bar of Georgia.

P. Andrew Patterson
Senior Partner, Attorney at Law
Thomas, Kennedy, Sampson & Patterson

Patrise Perkins-Hooker
Partner, Attorney at Law
Hollowell, Foster & Gepp, PC

P. Andrew Patterson is senior partner in the law firm of Thomas, Kennedy, Sampson & Patterson. He is responsible for the corporate section of the firm. He specializes in real estate and municipal bond law. Patterson's law firm is the largest minority-owned firm in the state of Georgia.

Patterson has served as chairman of the Georgia State Board of Bar Examiners, and is a former trustee of the Louisville Presbyterian Theological Seminary in Louisville, Kentucky. He is a member of Alpha Phi Alpha Fraternity, Inc., Sigma Pi Phi Fraternity, Inc., the Guardsmen, and Cascade United Methodist Church. In addition to his many honors, Patterson was awarded the key to the City of Atlanta.

Patterson received a bachelor of arts degree from Fisk University and a law degree from Harvard Law School.

He is married to Dr. Gloria P. Patterson, and is the father of Pickens A. Patterson III, M.D. and Staci E. Rucker, Esq.

Patrise Perkins-Hooker is a partner in the commercial transactions group of Hollowell, Foster & Gepp, PC, one of the city's oldest and largest minority-owned law firms. She specializes in serving clients in the areas of commercial real estate, development services, zoning, general corporate services and probate law.

Patrise has been a recognized leader in the legal arena. She is a past president of the Gate City Bar Association, an active member of GABWA, a member of the real property law section's executive committee, and a member of the State Bar of Georgia's board of governors.

Patrise is also an active community volunteer who serves as the founding chair of the Juvenile Justice Fund and treasurer of the Georgia WIN List. She is a former trustee of the Georgia Tech Alumni Association and a former chair of the Emory Goizueta Business School Alumni Association's board of directors.

Patrise is married to Douglas R. Hooker and they have two children and three grandchildren. She is a native Atlantan and an active member of Alpha Kappa Alpha Sorority, Inc. and Radcliffe Presbyterian Church.

Leron E. Rogers
Partner, Attorney at Law
Hewitt & Rogers

Tacita A. Mikel Scott
Partner, Attorney at Law
Morris, Manning & Martin, LLP

Leron E. Rogers is a partner at the firm of Hewitt & Rogers. The firm's practice areas include business transactions, entertainment law and business litigation, among other services.

Leron heads the firm's entertainment law practice group and is known throughout the country for representing high-profile entertainers and athletes in their professional and business ventures. In addition to negotiating contracts for professional athletes, Leron represents successful artists, producers, management companies, songwriters, record labels and publishing companies.

Leron maintains a sense of balance by associating himself with worthy causes and nonprofit organizations including the Divots Fore Dreamers Golf Tournament and the High Museum of Art. He is also a member of the National Academy of Recording Arts and Sciences and Kappa Alpha Psi Fraternity, Inc. He is a frequent speaker and featured panelist at conferences and workshops, and has been featured in local and national publications.

Leron received his bachelor of business administration in finance degree at Southwest Texas State University and his juris doctorate from the Florida State University College of Law.

Tacita Scott is a partner with Morris, Manning & Martin, LLP. Her law practice involves representation of management in all areas of employment law as well as handling complex commercial litigation matters.

Atlanta Woman magazine named Tacita one of Atlanta's 25 Power Women to Watch in 2006. Also in 2006, *Atlanta Magazine* named her a Georgia Rising Star SuperLawyer. Furthermore, Tacita is a member of the esteemed Leadership Atlanta Class of 2007.

In addition to serving on the board of directors for Goodwill Industries of North Georgia, she serves on the boards of trustees for the Lawyers' Committee for Civil Rights Under Law and the William Baker Choral Foundation. An advocate for diversity, Tacita chairs her firm's diversity committee and serves on the advisory board for the Atlanta Large Law Firm Diversity Alliance.

A graduate of Spelman College and Vanderbilt University School of Law, Tacita is the proud wife of professional actor Thom Scott II.

Douglass P. Selby
Partner, Attorney at Law
Hunton & Williams LLP

Jeffrey E. Tompkins
Partner, Attorney at Law
Thomas, Kennedy, Sampson & Patterson

Douglass P. Selby's practice focuses on public finance, including serving as bond and underwriters' counsel for government and private activity bonds, and corporate representation of governmental authorities as outside general counsel. His experience includes advising, negotiating and documenting transactions in connection with the issuance of tax-exempt bonds and providing general corporate advice to governmental authorities.

Doug is a member of the State of Bar Georgia, the National Association of Bond Lawyers and the Gate City Bar Association. He is a former chair and member of the City of Atlanta Government Board of Ethics and a graduate of the Regional Leadership Institute and Leadership Atlanta. Also a director of the Herndon Foundation, Doug was named a Georgia Super Lawyer Rising Star in 2005.

Doug received a juris doctorate degree from the University of Chicago Law School in 1995. He received a master of business administration degree in finance from Harvard University in 1990, and a bachelor of business administration degree in marketing, cum laude, from Howard University in 1986.

Jeff Tompkins is a partner with Thomas, Kennedy, Sampson & Patterson, Georgia's oldest minority-owned law firm. A trial lawyer, Jeff regularly represents Fortune 500 companies in various types of complex legal matters.

Jeff serves on the National Conference of Bar Examiners' special committee on the test of legal research knowledge and skills. He also serves on the Atlanta Judicial Commission and the advisory board of the Atlanta Volunteer Lawyers Foundation. Previously, he served as chairman of the South Atlanta District of the Boy Scouts, on the editorial board of the *Georgia Bar Journal,* and as a barrister in the American Inns of Court.

Jeff is a Phi Beta Kappa graduate of Morehouse College and holds a doctor of laws degree from Emory University. At Emory, he served as director-in-chief of the Moot Court Society. He was awarded the D. Robert Owen Memorial Award, the James C. Pratt Memorial Award, and was elected by the faculty to the National Order of Barristers.

A native of Atlanta, Jeff resides in northwest Atlanta with his wife, Tania, and daughter, Emeri.

COUNSELORS AT LAW

Michael W. Tyler
Partner, Attorney at Law
Kilpatrick Stockton LLP

Michael Tyler is a partner with Kilpatrick Stockton LLP where he practices commercial litigation and land use law.

Tyler earned his juris doctorate from Harvard Law School. He received a master of public administration degree from Harvard University and a bachelor's degree from Morehouse College.

Tyler serves on the board of trustees for the Piedmont Park Conservancy, The Children's School, the National Black Arts Festival, Providence Missionary Baptist Church and the Lawyers' Committee for Civil Rights Under Law. He previously served on the board of the Georgia Regional Transportation Authority, the State Disciplinary Board of the State Bar of Georgia, the Atlanta Zoning Review Board, the Atlanta Urban League, and as vice president of the Gate City Bar Association.

Tyler has twice received the Gate City Bar Association's A.T. Walden Outstanding Lawyer Award. He was featured in the *Atlanta Business Chronicle*'s Who's Who in Atlanta, *Georgia Trend* magazine's Legal Elite, and *James Magazine*'s Georgia's Super Lawyers.

He is married to Cathy Clark Tyler and has three children, Michael, Malcolm and Matthew.

Lisa A. Wade
Partner, Attorney at Law
Swift, Currie,
McGhee & Hiers, LLP

Lisa A. Wade joined Swift, Currie, McGhee & Hiers, LLP as a partner in 2000. Her defense practice focuses on workers' compensation claims and general insurance litigation. She is also a member of the firm's employment practices section. In the area of workers' compensation, she represents self-insured and commercially-insured companies, defending claims of all types. As approved counsel for the Atlanta Board of Education since 1991, Lisa has responded to various employment practice issues and has defended several of the board's workers' compensation claims.

Lisa is a member of the American, Gate City and Atlanta Bar Associations, as well as the State Bar of Georgia, the Georgia Association of Black Women Attorneys and the Atlanta Claims Association. She became a member of the City of Atlanta's board of zoning adjustment in 1992 and served as chairperson from 1996 to 1998.

A graduate of Leadership Atlanta, Class of 2002, Lisa is a 2005 and 2006 Georgia Rising Stars Super Lawyer. She received her undergraduate degree from Brown University and her law degree from the University of Georgia School of Law.

Brent Wilson
Partner, Attorney at Law
Elarbee Thompson

A partner at Elarbee Thompson, Brent Wilson represents management clients in labor relations and employment matters. He is a frequent speaker on employment litigation and was an adjunct professor of labor relations at the Emory University School of Law.

Brent is a past chair of the labor and employment section of the Atlanta Bar Association and a past co-chair of the State Bar of Georgia's diversity program. A fellow of the College of Labor and Employment Law, he was featured in *Black Enterprise* as a Leading Black Lawyer and a Georgia Super Lawyer. He was also featured in *Georgia Trend* magazine's Georgia Legal Elite.

Brent serves on the board of directors of the Boys & Girls Clubs of Metro Atlanta, St. Jude's Recovery Center, the YMCA policy council, the United Way homelessness task force, 100 Black Men of Atlanta and Omega Psi Phi Fraternity, Inc.

Brent graduated with honors from Morehouse College and received his juris doctorate from the State University of New York at Buffalo. He is married to the former Trojanell Bordenave. They have one daughter, Terrahney.

Atlanta's

ENTREPRENEURS

*"There is no royal flower-strewn path to success.
And if there is, I have not found it - for if I have accomplished anything in life it is
because I have been willing to work hard."*

Madame CJ Walker

Entrepreneur & Millionaire

Atlanta's
ENTREPRENEURS

**Tracey Moss, Tamika Dixon
& Deaundra Metzger**
Owners
360° Salon

Tracey Moss, Tamika Dixon and Deaundra Metzger are the owners of Atlanta's renowned 360° Salon. Artistry, commitment to community service and craftsmanship are the essential elements that make up this partnership.

Tracey Moss began her career in 1997. Her creative eye, reputation for cutting-edge detail and attention to creative direction and detail has solidified Tracey as a respected celebrity stylist and trendsetter. Her vast knowledge and extensive training is exemplified in her styling versatility.

Tamika Dixon, a true visionary, strives to maximize creative expression through hairstyling. Tamika has landed positions as a chemical and product tester with some of the industry's leading companies, gaining her notoriety for her extensive knowledge and an acute eye for detail.

Deaundra Metzger is a 16-year veteran in the beauty industry. Steadfast in her devotion to share the knowledge that was bestowed upon her, she has trained stylists for ten years. Deaundra has produced and directed her very own haircutting video. Her creativity and high standards result in flawless styling and artistic expression.

Dwan Abrams
Founder & President
Nevaeh Publishing, LLC

A resident of Atlanta, Dwan Abrams is a writer, publisher and professional speaker. She is the author of *The Scream Within* and *Only True Love Waits*. In addition to writing full-time, she is the founder and president of Nevaeh Publishing, LLC, a full-service, self-publishing company.

Originally from St. Petersburg, Florida, Abrams has lived throughout the United States and Europe. After graduating with honors from King's Academy High School, she enlisted in the United States Air Force where she served honorably for four years. While in the military, Abrams was promoted six months early to the rank of senior airman. In recognition of her outstanding service, she was awarded Airman of the Month and Personnel Specialist of the Quarter.

Abrams graduated from the University of Alabama in Huntsville with a bachelor's degree and master's degree in marketing.

She has been featured in *Booking Matters* magazine, taped a 30-second public service announcement to support "Feed the Hungry," and appeared on the television show *Atlanta Live*. Her next project is a Christian anthology entitled, "The Midnight Clear: Stories of Love, Hope and Inspiration."

Millie Allie is broker and chief executive officer of Platinum 500 Realty, Inc., which she founded in 2001. Platinum 500 Realty is a full-service company specializing in new construction, re-sales, property management and bank foreclosures. She is responsible for overseeing the day-to-day activities of the office, reviewing contracts and monitoring the training for her agents, all while pursuing her designation for commercial real estate.

Millie graduated high school with honors in 1977 at the age of 16. She joined the Army in 1978 at 17 with her parents' written permission and served on active duty until 1994. The majority of her time spent on active duty was served at the Pentagon in Washington, D.C. as an administrative specialist with departments such as the Army Discharge Review Board, the Congressional Correspondence Agency and the National Guard Bureau.

A native of Pittsburgh, Pennsylvania, Millie is divorced with no children. She enjoys golfing and is a member of World Changers Church International. She gives all credit for her peace and joy to her faith in God and God's grace and mercy.

Millie Allie
Founder & Broker
Platinum 500 Realty, Inc.

Carolyn Anderson is president and chief executive officer of SECCES Productions, LLC, an international special events and promotional planning company. This 14-year-old Atlanta and Dallas-based company started in 1994.

Carolyn has organized special events and promotions in Jamaica, Ireland, England, Barbados, Mexico and Brazil. She recently completed a very successful visit to Bangkok, Thailand and Florence, Italy. She is especially proud of her 14-year relationships with Air Jamaica, Jamaica and The Bahamas Tourist Board Offices.

SECCES Productions is not limited to overseas special events. On a local and national level, they also plan everything from wedding events to the popular Atlanta Falcons/New Orleans Saints game.

Carolyn has been interviewed by numerous publications including *Atlanta Tribune: The Magazine*, *The Good Life*, *Ebony*, *Essence*, *Upscale* and *Sisters INC.*

A proud Army brat, Carolyn believes that God alone carved out her wonderful life, and she accepts no credit for the many blessings she has enjoyed. She is the mother of two adults, Loren Jr. and Lyne'ya. She recently became the joyful grandmother to Shawn Christopher Lowe Jr.

Carolyn Anderson
President & Chief Executive Officer
SECCES Productions, LLC

ENTREPRENEURS

Ron S. Baker
President & Chief Executive Officer
Intouch Communications, Inc.

Ron S. Baker is president and chief executive officer of Intouch Telecommunications, Inc., a communications technology company. His direct responsibilities include business development, finance, operations and community relations.

Some of Baker's client portfolio includes the City of Atlanta, IBM, Southern Company, Fulton County, Verizon, Georgia Power, BellSouth and the Association of Black Cardiologists.

Formerly a board member of the Georgia Minority Supplier Development Council and Atlanta Business League, he also served as minority business enterprise input committee chair and vice chair of business opportunities. Under Baker's leadership, the focus was to build better relationships with corporate, government and institutional entities and secure business opportunities for member business enterprises.

Before forming Intouch, Baker worked as general manager for Georgia Cabinets, where he implemented strategies and programs to build market share among architects, general contractors and corporations. As senior sales representative for Lanier Corporation, he increased sales more than 200 percent, winning 20 top sales awards.

A St. Louis native, Ron Baker received a bachelor's degree from Saint Louis University and attended master of business administration studies at the University of Wisconsin.

Djana Bell
Director
Norma's Academy of Dance

Atlanta native Djana Bell began her training with her late mother, Norma Bell-Mitchell, founder of Norma's Academy of Dance. She continued her training at the Atlanta Ballet, Southern Ballet Company, Terpsichore Dance and Florida State University. She feels that her strengths lay in training young children to perform with professional companies.

As director of Norma's Academy of Dance for more than 20 years, Bell's greatest reward has been for her students to obtain scholarships to the Alvin Ailey American Dance Theatre, Dance Theatre of Harlem, The American Ballet Theatre, The Joffrey Ballet Company and Debbie Allen's Imagination Celebration. Likewise, her students have obtained scholarships to the University of the Arts in Philadelphia, Florida State University and New York University.

Bell's students perform throughout Atlanta and the state of Georgia. Additionally, they have performed for the Children's Healthcare of Atlanta parade, the WSB Fourth of July Parade, the 100 Black Men parade, the Festival of Trees, Marietta-Roswell Delta Sigma Theta Alumnae Cotillions and numerous church, civic and social functions.

The proud mother of Elyse and Erin, they reside in Fairburn, Georgia.

ichael J. Bohannon is chairman and president of Bovanti Corporation, the Atlanta-based, multi-divisional products and services company. In business for 23 years, Bovanti Corporation is comprised of Bovanti Cosmetic Stores and Spas and Bovanti Elite Agency, amongst numerous other ventures.

One of the company's key programs is the Bovanti Awards Program, which raises funds and awards scholarships to outstanding college-bound students. The Bovanti Awards also recognize community leaders of Atlanta who are making a difference. Bovanti has also enjoyed a 15-year business relationship with the Bahamian government.

Michael's vision for the future of Bovanti includes meeting the national demand of Bovanti Cosmetics' distributorship and franchising opportunities in the U.S. and abroad.

A native of Lexington, North Carolina, Michael graduated from Lexington Senior High School. He gives back to his community through T-shirt donations, his scholarship program and his Feed the Needy Program. Michael graduated from North Carolina Central University in Durham, North Carolina, and he currently serves as president of the Greater Atlanta North Carolina Central University Alumni.

Michael and his wife, Anita, have two daughters, Marquis and Marquel.

Michael J. Bohannon
Chairman & President
Bovanti Corporation

lorence Branch began her colon therapy practice in 1973 in Brooklyn, New York before moving to Atlanta and opening Healing Waters in 1986, recognizing her services as a "God-given gift."

A graduate of Australian Naturopathic School in Portage, Indiana, she studied under Robert A. Wood, considered the father of colon therapy. Branch also attended The Health Maintenance Institute where she completed courses in massage therapy and medicinal herbs. She has conducted services in colon health and fasting at some of Atlanta's largest churches, including Hillside International Truth Center, her church home since 1986.

Branch has received numerous awards from various humanitarian organizations. She has been featured in *Upscale*, *Essence* magazine, *Sister 2 Sister*, *The Atlanta Metro* and on numerous radio and television programs.

Semi-retired since 2003, she is a member of The International Association for Colon Hydrotherapy.

Florence Branch
Owner
Healing Waters Colon Hygiene

ENTREPRENEURS

Tyler Briant
Celebrity Airbrush Makeup Artist

Tyler Briant has created fabulous faces in Atlanta, Miami, New York and Paris, France. As a real makeup artist, she has invested more than $50,000 for her professional training and business development. She has never depended on the limited training of a makeup counter. Instead, she obtained a state license with a background in esthetics, sanitation and sterilization in 1995, and has trained with world famous makeup artist Sam Fine of New York.

Tyler does professional makeup artistry for photography headshots, commercial ads, editorials, television, record labels and weddings. Her clients include international companies such as CNN, WATL 36, UPN 69, HBO, The Trumpet Awards, Paul Mitchell, CoverGirl, Revlon, Vidal Sasson and Purple Ribbon (Virgin Records).

She was a makeup artistry instructor for the Georgia State Board Continuing Education Program in 2001. Today, she practices expert airbrush makeup artistry that is popular amongst Hollywood stars. She is also applauded as the premiere celebrity eyebrow stylist of Atlanta.

Percy A. and
Jenice V. Brinkley
Real Estate Agents
RE/MAX of Atlanta

Percy Brinkley was the past vice president and emerging market manager for the home loans group at Washington Mutual. After 20 years in the mortgage industry, Percy has joined his wife of 26 years as an associate broker with RE/MAX of Atlanta.

Jenice Brinkley has been a member of the DeKalb County Association of Realtors and the Empire Board of Realtists Million Dollar Club for the past five years. Jenice has also made the President's Club of RE/MAX International for the past two years. In 2006 Jenice was named Realtor of the Year for the DeKalb County Housing Authority.

DeKalb County residents for more than 20 years, the Brinkleys are active members of Beulah Missionary Baptist Church where their pastor is Rev. Jerry D. Black.

Percy is a native of Durham, and Jenice is a native of Murfreesboro, North Carolina. They are both graduates of North Carolina Central University.

Their son, Rashad, is a freshman at Bethune Cookman College and will join the team once he graduates.

Deidre F. Brown is a founding managing member of Brown & Pipkins, LLC where she serves as chief executive officer for the Ascential, Acsential Technologies, Acsential Services and Acsential Construction divisions. With ten-plus years of professional experience, she oversees contracted projects for the City of Augusta, Hartsfield-Jackson Atlanta International Airport, the Georgia Department of Human Resources, the Transportation Security Administration and the United States Department of Housing and Urban Development.

A participant in the Women Flying High Initiative, she is the recipient of the 2000 Female Business Enterprise Phoenix Trail Blazer Award presented by Ben DeCosta.

Deidre holds bachelor's and master's degrees from Clark Atlanta University. She has served on the board of the Georgia Coalition for the Peoples' Agenda. An alumna of United Way Volunteer Improvement Leadership Program, she is a member of the Marvin C. Goldstein Project Understanding with the Atlanta American Jewish Committee, the Women's Initiative Next Generation Women's Legacy, the Order of the Eastern Star, and a life member of the National Council of Negro Women.

Deidre F. Brown
Chief Executive Officer
Brown & Pipkins, LLC

Dolores Bundy is an award-winning journalist, author and editor who spearheads her own international firm, DB Networks Corporation. As chief executive officer, she has an exemplary track record in developing, organizing, training, consulting and implementing programs in the political arena, as well as in the entertainment field.

Bundy is a much sought after travel writer with published materials on East Asia, South America, Tahiti, the British Virgin Islands, as well as many African countries including South Africa, Ethiopia, Uganda, Tanzania, Kenya and Cape Verde.

On the domestic scene, the native New Yorker has been recognized and rewarded for her work in the entertainment genre. Bundy is one of the first African-American women to form a company managing the careers of great artists including Ali Woodson, lead singer of the Temptations, and Reggae superstar Bob Marley, among others.

In 2001 Bundy solidified her role as a literary virtuoso by authoring a smash line of romance books entitled *Brown Sugar Diaries®*. She currently owns the trademark and is developing the series for stage, television and film.

Dolores Bundy
Chief Executive Officer
DB Networks Corporation

Milton J. Burns
President & Chief Executive Officer
All Professional Insurance Group

Milton J. Burns is president and chief executive officer of All Professional Insurance Group. All Professional Insurance Group is a full-service business/commercial and nonprofit insurance brokerage.

In this position, Milton's primary responsibilities to the firm include growing revenues, enhancing profitability, retention of the client base and managing the firm's day-to-day operations. He lives by the motto "all things are possible backed by faith and action," evidenced by the firm's explosive growth during his three years at the helm.

Milton has won several awards for his sales and customer service performance, including No. 1 Producer, Top Salesman, No. 1 Franchise Salesman, and President's Club Member. He is also an active member of the Omega Psi Phi Fraternity, Inc., Mentors for Our Future and the Atlanta Business League.

A graduate of Clark Atlanta University with a bachelor's degree in finance, Milton was awarded a master of business administration degree in finance and marketing from Clark Atlanta University.

Staci Y. Bush
Principal
SYB Consulting, LLC

Staci Y. Bush is principal of SYB Consulting, LLC, a charitable foundation and public relations management firm with integrity. SYB's clients span the political, nonprofit and corporate sectors, including H.E.A.T., Inc., Darryl Hicks' campaign for secretary of state and the AGL Resources Private Foundation.

Bush received a bachelor of science degree in biology from Georgia Southern College. Upon graduation, she was hired by Southern Company. During her tenure with Southern, she worked in nuclear generation, external and governmental affairs (Washington, D.C.) and corporate charitable contributions. She joined AGL Resources, Inc. in 2001, where she was manager of community affairs and served on the board of directors for the AGL Resources Private Foundation.

Bush is a Hull fellow for the Southeastern Council of Foundations and serves on the board of directors for the Heating Energy Assistance Team, Inc., the Atlanta Business League Foundation and the advisory board of the AGL Fund of the CSRA (Augusta). Additionally, she serves on the Georgia Energy Assistance Task Force and the American Gas Association's Community and Public Affairs Task Force.

Paul Cheeks
Principal
Paul Cheeks Architects

Paul Cheeks heads his own Atlanta-based architectural firm. For more than 37 years, Paul has conceived and executed projects for federal, state and local governments in Ohio, Pennsylvania and Georgia.

A few of his achievements include directing the rehabilitation of City Hall East, and the implementation of a variety of works for the Hartsfield-Jackson International Airport Projects. Paul has also accepted a large number of private commissions including Parkland Development Corp. for the rehabilitation of Parklane Villa Apartments in Cleveland, and for the rehabilitation of the University Towers in Atlanta.

Paul is a former director of the Cleveland Design Center, a nonprofit organization providing architectural services to those who could not afford them. He has also been a recipient of awards from the Pre-Cast Concrete Company for his innovative use of their product.

Paul received a bachelor of arts degree in architecture from Kent State University in 1966, and is a registered architect in Georgia, Ohio, Pennsylvania and North Carolina.

An Atlanta native, Paul is married and has two sons and a grandson.

Walter Cleveland
Owner
National Mail Center

Walter Cleveland is the owner of National Mail Center, which is a subsidiary post office. He also heads the Future Leaders Nonprofit Youth Organization, which employs, trains and assists youths. As president of the Greenbriar/Campbellton Road Business Coalition, Walter is responsible for bringing the coalition together to focus on the development and redevelopment of the Campbellton/Greenbriar Corridor.

Walter retired from Lucent Technologies after 30 years of service. He trained labor leaders, served as the affirmative action committee coordinator, assisted Junior Achievement in marketing, and negotiated employee contracts. He also served as the program administrator for United Way.

A strong strategic thinker and team builder, Walter was president of the A. Phillip Randolph Institute, vice president of AFL-CIO District 10, executive vice president of CWA, and co-coordinator of the Winnie Mandela U.S. Fundraising Tour. In addition, he served as committee member and coordinator of the Martin Luther King Jr. Holiday March celebration committee.

A Savannah, Georgia native, Walter is the son of Maxine Cleveland. He is the proud father of three sons, Antonio, Broderick and Walter III, and one daughter, April.

ENTREPRENEURS

Rhonda A. Crockett
Realtor & Owner
CENTURY 21 Premier Realty

Rhonda Crockett of CENTURY 21 Premier Realty is a woman on the move. Not only does she specialize in luxury residential and commercial real estate, she also assists and trains others in the buying and selling process of real estate worldwide.

A graduate of The Institute of Luxury Home Marketing, Rhonda's professionalism and knowledge of real estate has made her a multi-million dollar producer with CENTURY 21, the Empire Board of Realtist, Inc. and the National Association of Realtors. Likewise, she has been featured in *The Atlanta Journal-Constitution*, *Atlanta Woman* magazine, *Unique Home Elite 2006*, *Distinctive Homes* and *KNOWAtlanta*.

Additionally, Rhonda is the president and owner of D.E.C. Pallet Logistics located in Fayetteville, Georgia. She has used her 18 years of combined corporate and real estate experience to educate and train others in computer technology and marketing.

A native of Reidsville, North Carolina, Rhonda is the very proud mother of two handsome young men, David Jr. and Daniel Crockett, who are both honor roll students.

Tabitha Daniel
Broker & Owner
RE/MAX Marketplace

Tabitha Daniel is the broker and owner of RE/MAX Marketplace, the premier real estate agency in South Fulton County's hottest-developing area, Camp Creek. She has been a real estate professional and broker for nearly a decade and has special designations to better serve her customers: ABR (accredited buyer representative) and CAPS (certified aging placement specialist).

Tabitha leads a dynamic team of real estate professionals who live up to their mission of providing the highest level of customer service, loyalty and integrity. They are committed to working for the betterment of the community through new construction, re-sales, commercial real estate and special community activities.

Tabitha is a Georgia native. She received her bachelor of arts degree in management and human resources from Georgia State University. She won the Success Against The Odds Award from the Atlanta Business League. Tabitha is also a member of the Million Dollar Club, the Atlanta Board of Realtors and the National Association of Realtors.

Anthony Myles Davis is owner of Anthony Davis Designs, a couture fashion and image design service. His approach to design is sophisticated, sensual and incredibly personal. The objective of enhancing a client's personal style and effectively defining it to project their character is paramount. His priority is to make every client feel unique.

Anthony is a seasoned professional with 25 years of valuable knowledge from the retail and hospitality industry. He served as a style and wardrobe consultant for numerous university and college pageants, as well as a wardrobe advisor for pageants. In 2005 and 2006 he assisted with the Pink Ribbon Fashion Show, benefiting the Georgia Breast Cancer Coalition Fund. In 2005 he assisted with the Tea at the Ritz fashion show presented by Parisian Phipps Plaza.

A native of Birmingham, Alabama, Anthony studied fashion merchandising and wardrobe construction at the University of Montevallo. He has received awards for his creative abilities and was a featured designer on *Good Day Alabama*.

Anthony is a member of Alpha Phi Alpha Fraternity, Inc. He attends Our Lady of Lourdes Catholic Church.

Anthony M. Davis
Owner, Couturier & Stylist
Anthony Davis Designs

Alexis Day is founder and top-producing Realtor for Star Realtor Group, proudly affiliated with Keller Williams Realty-Buckhead. She specializes in luxury homes, opulent estates and golf communities, and is the Realtor of choice to many high-profile individuals.

Raised in Palos Verdes Estates, California, a suburb of Los Angeles, Day now resides in Atlanta where she has found the city's diversity and progressiveness to be the reasons she considers Atlanta her city of choice to call home.

She loves her profession as a Realtor and is also involved in Atlanta community fund-raising. Day is a member of the Crohn's & Colitis Foundation, serving on the committee for the Children's Legacy Luncheon. She is also a member of the Arthritis Foundation, and she serves on the committee for the Atlanta Policeman's Ball.

Day earned her degree in visual communications from the American InterContinental University, London, England, and she is a licensed Realtor in the states of Georgia and Oklahoma.

Alexis Day
Founder, Star Realtor Group
Keller Williams Realty-Buckhead

ENTREPRENEURS

Jea Delsarte
President
Jedel Beaux-Arts

Jea Delsarte has a unique passion for people, and her philanthropic work is as hectic as her pharmacy practice. Her passion for art stems from her 17 years as the wife and business partner of Louis Delsarte and mother of Rachel who is also a visual and performing artist. As president of Jedel Beaux-Arts, she coordinates exhibitions and special projects for artists and manages the Delsarte Printmaking Studio.

The Delsartes have donated time and art to numerous organizations including Habitat for Humanity, the Atlanta Youth Academy, Hammonds House Museum, the United Negro College Fund, the Faculty Resource Network at New York University, Jack and Jill of America and Seven Stages Theatre in Atlanta. Her other philanthropic projects include the Health Careers Program at Spelman College and Morehouse College. In 2005 she received a Distinguished Service Award from Spelman College.

Delsarte's affiliations include Alpha Kappa Alpha Sorority, Inc., the National Coalition of 100 Black Women, Inc.—MECCA Chapter, the National Pharmacy Association, The Carats Inc. and the Hammonds House Museum, where she serves on the board of trustees.

Ivory Dorsey
Author & Trainer

As a professional speaker, trainer, facilitator and author, Ivory Dorsey has informed and inspired audiences since 1984. Ivory has an extensive background in corporate America in the areas of field sales, field sales management and other results-oriented assignments. She has spoken at all levels to the finest corporations, cruise lines and organizations worldwide.

While knowledge is growing at an alarming rate, Ivory believes it is time to perform beyond the knowledge. It is time to bring God to work in a way that reveals the excellence, ethics and results of the authentic believer.

Ivory believes that all of the skill, pain and pleasure she has experienced in life and at work, prepared her for the ultimate assignment: to address the tandem nature of business and biblical principles. Her book, *Soft Skills for Hard Times*, focuses on soft skills. The greatest soft skill of all to master is faith/risk.

anquinetta Dover is chief executive officer, president and founder of DoverStaffing and the Dover Training Institute. Celebrating its tenth year, DoverStaffing is a full-service, 8(a) certified staffing agency and GSA contractor whose extensive list of clients includes AGL Resources, Kawasaki, FEMA, Spelman College, USDA, Manpower and Grady Hospital. Dover Training Institute is a 501(c)(3) training and life enhancement organization offering unique programs for youth and adults.

A humanitarian, Dover was awarded a resolution by the Georgia State Senate and was presented the Success Against the Odds award by the Atlanta Business League. Georgia Labor Commissioner Michael Thurmond presented Dover, as chair of the Atlanta Employer Committee, with the Project of the Year Award. She was also featured in *Atlanta Business Chronicle*'s special edition of "CEO University."

Dover serves on the board of the Georgia Breast Cancer Coalition Fund and is active in numerous professional and community service organizations including The National Coalition of 100 Black Women, Inc.

A native of Greenwood, South Carolina, she received an economics degree from Spelman College and is a member of Delta Sigma Theta Sorority, Inc.

Sanquinetta Dover
President & Chief Executive Officer
DoverStaffing

aren I. Duckett is the president and chief executive officer of Duckett Design Group, Inc. (DDG), an architectural and interior design firm. Established in 1985, DDG has provided comprehensive services in the disciplines of architecture, interior design, facility planning and programming, urban planning and construction management.

As president of DDG for the past 21 years, Duckett directs the administration, marketing and contracting activities of the firm, and she is involved in all major aspects of projects. These include facility programming, site analysis, space allocation planning, growth projections, operations analysis, budget control and client liaisons.

Duckett built DDG upon a perceptive understanding of her clients' needs and a responsive and consistent execution of service delivery. Some of her clients include the City of Atlanta, Hartsfield-Jackson International Airport, the City of Savannah, DeKalb Medical Center and Fulton County.

Duckett has a bachelor of arts degree in architecture, a master of arts degree in urban planning, and a juris doctorate from Woodrow Wilson School of Law.

A native of Rochester, New York, Karen and her husband, Wardell, make their home in Atlanta.

Karen I. Duckett
President & Chief Executive Officer
Duckett Design Group, Inc.

Peggy Duncan
Personal Productivity Expert
PSC Press & Productivity

Peggy Duncan is a personal productivity expert and trains nationally on organization, time management and technology.

Peggy is the author of several books: *Conquer Email Overload with Outlook*, *Put Time Management to Work*, and *Just Show Me Which Button to Click! in PowerPoint 2003*. She is also a media spokesperson, editor of an online magazine and a writer for business publications. She has appeared on national television shows including the *Today Show*, *Black Enterprise Report*, and the U.S. Virgin Islands PBS affiliate. Her advice has also appeared in *O, The Oprah Magazine*, *Essence*, *Real Simple*, *Federal Computer Week*, *Black Enterprise* and more.

Peggy is a SCORE Atlanta volunteer and produces a series of highly successful conferences for small business owners. She received her bachelor's degree in marketing and a train-the-trainer certification from Georgia State University.

A native of Durham, North Carolina, Peggy is the proud mother of Steven and grandmother of Christopher. Her computer is her hobby, and her favorite quote is: "A closed mouth does not get fed."

Damali Edwards
Chief Executive Officer
Edwards Consulting Firm, Inc.

Damali Edwards founded Edwards Consulting Firm, Inc. in 2002 and serves as chief executive officer. The company recruits mid- to senior-level management in a wide range of industries, and functional and diversity search assignments. In this role, she is responsible for business development, operations and search execution.

Edwards is a member of industry organizations such as the Atlanta Executive Search Roundtable, the Georgia Association of Personnel Services and the International Association for Corporate and Professional Recruitment. She currently serves on the Small to Mid-Size Business Council and the regional education policy committee for the Metro Atlanta Chamber of Commerce. Additionally, she is a member of Delta Sigma Theta Sorority, Inc.

Edwards is a graduate of the University of Virginia where she received her bachelor of arts degree. She is also a graduate of the *FastTrac* business development program hosted by Georgia State University, as well as the United Way VIP program for nonprofit board development.

Barbara Elliott and Jennifer Ward-Woods have more than 17 combined years of decorating experience. They have won several Dream Room Awards and have ranked number one in retail sales in past years. They have also had their work published in major magazines such as *Good Housekeeping*, *Window Fashions*, *Decorating Solutions* and others.

Together, the sister team has transformed hundreds of residential and commercial spaces. Their work ranges from designing one room to designing large commercial jobs with many spaces. They have completed commercial products from small offices for dentists, doctors and attorneys to more specialized businesses such as hotel, daycare and a megachurch.

Established in 1969, Interiors by Decorating Den has more than 500 franchisees and decorators worldwide.

Interiors by Decorating Den is a sponsor of Decorating for a Difference. Decorators worldwide have raised more than $200,000 to support breast cancer research, education and screening treatment. During 2003, Barbara and Jennifer hosted a Dream Homes of Color Tour and raised $8,000-plus for the fund-raising cause.

**Barbara Elliott
& Jennifer Ward-Woods**
Franchise Partners
Interiors by Decorating Den

Morris Finley is president and chief executive officer of Morris Finley & Associates, Inc., an enterprise consisting of printing, property investment and consultation services. His offices are located in the Sweet Auburn/Martin Luther King Historic District.

A retired public servant and Atlanta city councilman, Morris has been an advocate of entrepreneurship. Presently, in addition to his part-time print shop obligations, he acts as a consulting partner with Gateway Project Developers, Intl., LLC, a company specializing in the strategic partnering of innovative concepts with results-oriented financiers and developers.

After attending D. T. Howard High School and Clark College, Morris, a native Atlantan, heeded Uncle Sam's call in 1958, attending the Boston School of Lithography during his enlistment. Following an honorable discharge, he returned home to a promising career as a printer.

Morris' many career achievements include authorship of the famed "Finley Ordinance," the framework for Atlanta's Affirmative Action legislation.

Married to Ingé, Morris is the proud father of six, including "Lil" Morris.

Morris Finley
President & Chief Executive Officer
Morris Finley & Associates, Inc.

ENTREPRENEURS

Angelia Gay-Northern
Founder
Angel's Paradise
Higher Learning Academy

Angelia Gay-Northern is the founder of Angel's Paradise Higher Learning Academy. Angel's Paradise Higher Learning Academy I and II have received the highest national accreditation from the National Association for the Education of Young Children. The academy offers specialized learning programs in an environment customized so that each child will encounter a balance of activities designed to help them achieve goals for social, emotional, physical, intellectual and creative development.

A graduate of Georgia State University, Angelia holds a bachelor of arts degree in public relations and journalism. She is active in the community and has affiliations with several educational organizations. Additionally, she has served as the vice president for the Georgia United Child Care Consortium and Associates.

Angelia is a member of the Georgia Child Care Association, the National Black Child Development Institute, and the Atlanta Business League. To her credit, she has won the Atlanta Business League's Success Against the Odds Award and the Georgia Minority Business Neophyte Award.

A native of Atlanta, Angelia is married to Stephen Northern and is the mother of three beautiful children.

Denise Gray
Owner
Denise Gray Photography

The skill of photography is one taken quite seriously by Denise Gray, owner of Denise Gray Photography. She focuses on location photography and specializes in event services such as corporate, portraiture and special events. Her distinguished clientele includes such Fortune 500 companies and metropolitan Atlanta businesses as Turner Broadcasting System, AGL Resources and the Atlanta Marriott.

A highly sought-after professional, Denise has been tapped as the official photographer for *Who's Who In Black Atlanta*® and the Atlanta Business League, just to name a few.

A community servant, Denise is a mentor with Big Brothers Big Sisters of Metro Atlanta. She is also an American Red Cross Minority Recruitment Advisory Board member, and a board member of Integrity Networking Group, Camp Girlfriends and the Sisters Empowerment Network. She has also been affiliated with Sistagraphy, an organization of her professional peers.

Denise received formal photography training at the Southeastern Center of Arts in Atlanta. A native of Chicago, Illinois, she has made Atlanta her home.

Herbert W. Greene Jr. is the visionary behind Urban Suburban, Inc., a real estate development company. Herbert is a second-generation Morehouse man graduating in 1991. He began his career working in the construction business and bail bond company his father started.

His venture into development began in 1981 with his purchase and renovation of boarding houses. Since 1985, Urban Suburban's portfolio has grown to $22 million. His premier properties are the Urban Suburban corporate headquarters on Peachtree and The Atlanta Executive Center, an 85,000-square-foot mid-rise on Martin Luther King.

Herbert has diversified his holdings. His other businesses include an art gallery, restaurant, bail bonding, importing and debt collection.

Herbert was born in Atlanta in 1963 to Herbert and Naomi Greene. He is a member of Antioch Baptist Church, the Urban Christian Network and Deities Charities International. He is also a board member of the Atlanta Black Chamber of Commerce and vice chair of The Benedita da Silva Foundation.

Herbert is an extensive traveler and frequently visits foreign countries. He, his wife Cynthia, and their three children reside in Atlanta.

Herbert W. Greene Jr.
President
Urban Suburban, Inc.

Michael Hightower is the founder and managing partner of The Collaborative Firm, LLC, a real estate and strategic planning firm based in Atlanta. The Collaborative Firm provides targeted economic development and public policy guidance to local governments, developers, nonprofit entities and governmental agencies. The Collaborative Firm offers a unique blend of expertise involving both public and private land use development services.

Hightower has more than 25 years of experience in the public, private and educational arenas. Under his leadership, more than $1.3 billion of new private-sector development was secured for South Fulton County located in Atlanta. Hightower has received nearly 300 awards and honors during his professional career. He was the youngest individual ever to serve as president of the National Association of Counties (NACo).

A native of College Park, Georgia, Hightower graduated from Clark Atlanta University with honors. He and his wife, Sandra, reside in Atlanta with their daughter, Evie.

Michael Hightower
Founder & Managing Partner
The Collaborative Firm, LLC

Denise Troutman Holden
President & Chief Executive Officer
Professional Empowerment
Network, Inc.

Denise Holden, president and chief executive officer of Professional Empowerment Network, Inc. (PENI), is a certified professional image and empowerment consultant. She has more than 22 combined years of experience in image consultation, Web design, personal empowerment and business brand development.

Denise has a practical eye for the real life application of image management and brand development. She enjoys sharing her knowledge to empower and motivate her clients and audiences.

Denise's professional affiliations include president of the Atlanta Chapter of the Association of Image Consultants International (2007-2009), the National Association of Black Female Executives in Music and Entertainment, and the American Society of Training and Development.

Denise is the founder of Success Suits You©, a nonprofit program that provides donated professional business suits, accessories and personal mentoring to low-income women in the metro Atlanta area.

A Columbus, Georgia native, Denise currently resides in Lovejoy with her daughter, Brittany. A successful real estate investor, she enjoys traveling, motorcycle riding and being involved in community charitable programs.

Kristal Alise Holmes
Attorney at Law

Kristal Alise Holmes is an attorney licensed in the state of Georgia. She began her legal career as a staff attorney for the late Honorable Lenwood A. Jackson of the City Court of Atlanta. After serving as Jackson's staff attorney, Kristal became a prosecuting attorney for the City of Atlanta, followed by DeKalb County and finally in Gwinnett County.

In October of 2006, Kristal started her own law practice. Her practice areas primarily involve criminal defense and family law.

Kristal is an active member of the Gwinnett County Bar Association, Georgia Lawyers for the Arts and the Georgia Association of Criminal Defense Lawyers.

Kristal received a bachelor of arts degree from Spelman College and her juris doctorate from the Emory University School of Law. While in law school, Kristal studied abroad at the International Law Institute at Macquarie University in Sydney, Australia.

A native of Gary, Indiana, Kristal enjoys painting, drawing and attending art exhibits.

Harold Jackson, Ph.D., is founder, president and chief executive officer of The JacksonHeath Group. JacksonHeath is an Atlanta-based consulting firm launched in 1990 to provide strategic counsel, diversity communication, development programs and marketing to businesses, nonprofits and academic institutions.

A former public relations executive with Monsanto, Hill & Knowlton and The Coca-Cola Company, Jackson has directed several college communications programs, and he was vice president of institutional advancement at Howard University. His career includes positions as an assistant editor at *Ebony* and as a television show host. He has received awards from the International Association of Business Communicators, the Public Relations Society of America and the Council for the Advancement and Support of Education (CASE).

Jackson serves on boards and counsels civic organizations, including the Georgia Hispanic Chamber of Commerce, the Rainbow/PUSH Coalition and the Asian American Resource Center.

He holds a bachelor's degree from Savannah State University, and a master's degree in journalism and a doctorate from the University of Michigan.

A Savannah, Georgia native, Jackson and his wife, Lillian, have three daughters and a son.

Harold Jackson, Ph.D.
Founder, President, &
Chief Executive Officer
The JacksonHeath Group

Samuel T. Jackson is president and chief executive officer of the Economic Empowerment Initiative, Inc. (EEI). Founded in 2001, the EEI's mission is to help students on high school and college campuses understand how to manage their financial resources.

Samuel is a native of Timmonsville, South Carolina. He graduated from Emory University with a bachelor's degree in economics. In 2006 Samuel was honored with the Martin Luther King Jr. Community Service Award for excellence in community innovation and change from Emory's Goizueta Business School and the Rollins School of Public Health.

Samuel is a member of the Commerce Club, the United Way's Alexis de Tocqueville Society, and the leadership council for the United Way's African American Partnership. He serves on numerous advisory boards and councils for nonprofit agencies across the country. Samuel is a member of the board of directors for the Southern Regional Council, the Ryan Cameron Foundation and the Terrance Mathis Foundation. In his spare time, he enjoys golf, cooking, chess and classical music. He frequently participates in charity events.

Samuel T. Jackson
President & Chief Executive Officer
Economic Empowerment Initiative, Inc.

Ira Jackson Jr.
President
Perfect Image

Ira Jackson Jr. is president of Perfect Image, a commercial printing business headquartered in Marietta, Georgia. Under his leadership, Perfect Image has been named the Georgia Minority Supplier Development Council of the Year and the National Minority Supplier Development Council Regional Supplier of the Year. The company specializes in producing a variety of marketing collateral including brochures, training manuals, posters, pocket folders and newsletters.

An active member of the community, Jackson is involved with the Salvation Army Boys & Girls Club board, the East Lake Junior Golf Academy board, the Alexis de Tocqueville Society and the United Way.

Jackson is a graduate of Leadership Georgia and Leadership Atlanta. Previously, he served on the board of directors for the Metro Atlanta Super Bowl Host Committee, the Georgia Minority Supplier Development Council, the Atlanta Chamber of Commerce and the National Urban League, Atlanta office.

Jackson received a bachelor's degree from Rhodes College. He completed the Advanced Management Program at Dartmouth University and the Executive Management Program at the Kellogg Business School.

A native of Atlanta, Jackson is married with two daughters.

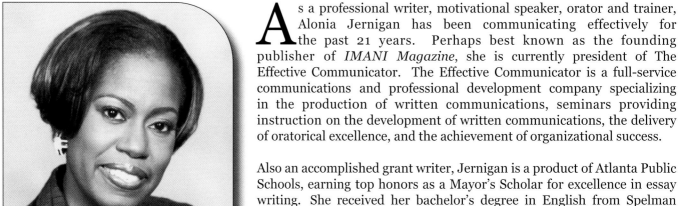

Alonia Jernigan
President
The Effective Communicator

As a professional writer, motivational speaker, orator and trainer, Alonia Jernigan has been communicating effectively for the past 21 years. Perhaps best known as the founding publisher of *IMANI Magazine*, she is currently president of The Effective Communicator. The Effective Communicator is a full-service communications and professional development company specializing in the production of written communications, seminars providing instruction on the development of written communications, the delivery of oratorical excellence, and the achievement of organizational success.

Also an accomplished grant writer, Jernigan is a product of Atlanta Public Schools, earning top honors as a Mayor's Scholar for excellence in essay writing. She received her bachelor's degree in English from Spelman College, and she earned credits toward her master's degree from Luther Rice Seminary.

She is a licensed and ordained minister of the gospel, and she serves on the boards of directors for Achieve Academy of Atlanta and the Vine City Community Outreach Community Development Corporation.

Jernigan is the wife of Elder James Jernigan, the mother of James Jr., Kori and Emmanuel, and the guardian of her niece, Laquita.

Yvonne Bryant Johnson is chief executive officer of Bryant & Associates, LLC, an executive coaching and training company. Johnson has skillfully utilized the business acumen gained from a 25-plus year career in corporate America to help executives and organizations achieve their goals in sales, leadership, diversity and customer service.

She has served as director of the Educational Opportunity Program at George Washington University and branch manager of AT&T's Atlanta Customer Care Organization and global sales team.

Johnson is board chair of the Youth Ensemble of Atlanta and Sickle Cell Empowerment for a Liberated Life. She is past board president of Partnership Against Domestic Violence, board member of the Georgia Center for Children, and a graduate of Leadership America and Leadership Atlanta.

Johnson graduated with honors from Spelman College, where she was later recognized as one of the first alumnae to receive the Alumnae Achievement Award in the area of business. She received a master of business administration degree from Emory University and also attended Johns Hopkins University and the Universities of London and Ghana.

Yvonne Bryant Johnson
Chief Executive Officer
Bryant & Associates, LLC

Simone Joye is chief executive officer of AllWrite Communications, a grant-writing and promotional firm founded in 2002. AllWrite was the first minority-owned grant-writing firm in New Jersey. In 2005, AllWrite relocated to Atlanta.

An avid Motown fan, Simone created 30 Plus Classics, an AllWrite subsidiary that produces the monthly event A Soulful Affair. AllWrite also publishes *Atlanta 24/7*.

Simone's career has included positions at Dow Jones & Company, *The City Sun* and service on the boards of the National Association of Black Journalists (NABJ) and the Federation for the Preservation of Hip-Hop Culture.

During executive-level positions at the YWCA and as chief executive officer of the Boys & Girls Club of Newark, Simone raised over $3 million in contributions for youth and families. Her experiences have appeared in *The New York Times*, the *Star Ledger* and *Black Enterprise*. In 2002 Simone was recognized as Woman of the Year by the Delta Mu Zeta chapter of Zeta Phi Beta Sorority, Inc.

A New York City native, Simone received a bachelor of arts degree from Hunter College.

Simone Joye
Chief Executive Officer
AllWrite Communications

ENTREPRENEURS

Steve Julal
President/Owner
VAAS Professionals, LLC

Steve Julal is president of VAAS Professionals, LLC, a certified public accounting firm founded in 2002. The firm offers services in the real estate, sports and entertainment, and small business industries. The core area of focus includes financial reporting, taxes, audit, consulting and business management.

Before becoming a business owner, Steve worked for a "Big Four" CPA firm. His diverse experience in accounting encompasses privately-owned businesses, financial services companies, real estate, telecommunications and government entities.

Steve was also an adjunct professor where he lectured courses in accounting and auditing. He is currently a columnist on tax issues with various publications and conducts seminars.

A graduate of Oral Roberts University, he holds a bachelor of science degree in accounting and a master of business administration degree. Steve is a member of the American Institute of Certified Public Accountants (AICPA) and the Georgia Society of CPAs. He is a registered certified public accountant in the state of Georgia.

Originally from Jamaica, Steve now calls Atlanta home. The proud father of a daughter, Shaneen Julal, he enjoys running, weight lifting and mentoring.

Jamahl L. King
Founder & Chief Executive Officer
S.T.E.P.S. Event Planning Firm, Inc.

As founder and chief executive officer of S.T.E.P.S. (Striving Towards Excellence with Perfection in Sight) Event Planning and Marketing Firm, Jamahl L. King has established a solid reputation for conceptualizing and actualizing events with a profound level of quality. Since graduating from Morehouse College with a degree in mass communications in 1993 and launching S.T.E.P.S. in 1996, King has remained in constant demand.

King's clients include SWI Consulting, Groundrush Media, Keith Sweat, Infiniti Broadcasting Corporation, WVEE-FM, The Cochran Firm of Atlanta, Time Warner, *OverTime Magazine*, Rainforest Films and Sony Urban Music. S.T.E.P.S. was featured in *Upscale* magazine, *Sister 2 Sister* magazine, *Atlanta Tribune: The Magazine* and *The Atlanta Journal-Constitution*. The Atlanta Urban League Young Professionals presented King with the 2004 Dream Catchers Award.

A native of Hammond, Indiana, King sits on the board of directors for America SCORES Atlanta, Black Males With Initiative of West Georgia University, and the Miss Black Georgia USA Foundation. He has been featured for six consecutive years in *Who's Who in Black Atlanta*® and is a member of Victory Church in Stone Mountain.

Atlanta native Kimberly Wynn Lewis completed Woodward Academy and matriculated at West Georgia College. Afterwards, she completed nursing school and worked for ten years in geriatric and pediatric nursing. Kim is a seasoned nurse with a strong interest in seniors and babies. She worked with Dr. Winton King, a well-known pediatrician, and was also employed by Kaiser Permanente and Wesley Woods Geriatric Center.

Kim is a licensed Realtor and Realtist and is a Million Dollar Club member. She has been very instrumental in marketing several developments throughout Atlanta, including selling more than 100 new homes in the Summerhill community. Her major emphasis continues to be marketing new construction and the resale of residential property.

As co-owner of Kids R Kids @ Cascade, she is actively involved in the operation of the family-owned business.

Kim is married to Terence Lewis, an executive vice president at Main Street Bank, and they are the proud parents of Brandon and Taylor. Both Kim and Terence are members of the 2004 Leadership Georgia class. Their family worships at Providence Baptist Church in College Park.

Kimberly Wynn Lewis
Co-Owner
Kids R Kids @ Cascade

Regina Lynch-Hudson, a publicist and luxury lifestyles writer, is the owner of The Write Publicist & Co. Lynch-Hudson maintains an exclusive clientele that primarily consists of leaders in the medical, travel, architectural and legal industries.

As a home renovation enthusiast, she has developed her love for restoration into an active second career. Her home design articles have appeared in national publications, including *Ebony* magazine. Her own home renovation appeared before 89 million viewers on four episodes of *HGTV*, and a segment on TV One's *Living With Soul*, which was voted for a Best Lifestyle Award at Hollywood's 12th Annual NAMIC Vision Awards.

Regina has traveled extensively, visiting exotic locales around the world that often provide her with inspiration for travel articles. She has penned destination catalogs and articles for companies such as Vacation Express, AirTran Airways and North American Airlines. She also handles destination marketing for resorts, bed and breakfasts, and tourism boards. When she is not traveling with her husband, aerospace engineer and pilot, Col. Courtland Bivens III, the avid gardener can be found playing in the dirt.

Regina Lynch-Hudson
Owner
The Write Publicist & Co.

Dionne Mahaffey-Muhammad
President & Chief Executive Officer
The CPAI Group, Inc.

Dionne Mahaffey-Muhammad is the president and chief executive officer of The CPAI Group, Inc. (CPAI), whose staffing division provides college-educated personal assistants to celebrities, and has become known in Hollywood circles as the "Staffing Agency to the Stars™." CPAI was named the official concierge for the NFL Players Association during the 2004-05 NFL season. From a state-of-the-art call center, CPAI provided lifestyle management services to 1,896 active NFL players and 5,000-plus retired members. This historical appointment was the first time that such a contract was awarded to a minority- or female-owned company.

Dionne is also the author of *Beyond the Red Carpet*, a career guide focusing on behind the scenes careers in entertainment. Her agency has been featured as a Hollywood insider on *Oprah*, MTV and E! Networks.

Dionne received her bachelor's degree from Auburn University. She is an active member of Alpha Kappa Alpha Sorority, Inc., the United Way Volunteer Involvement Program and the Motorcycle Alliance of Georgia.

In her spare time, she enjoys spending time with her children, Ashanti, 9, and Nasir, 7.

Joseph Malbrough
Owner/Operator
The UPS Store

Joseph Malbrough is owner/operator of The UPS Store in Smyrna, Georgia. He oversees the day-to-day operations of the packing, shipping and business services center.

Prior to becoming an entrepreneur, Malbrough was assistant vice president of new business development for United Way of Metropolitan Atlanta. In that role, he launched the new business initiative that targeted small- to medium-sized Atlanta-based companies for United Way's annual employee campaign.

Previously, Malbrough was manager of key accounts at the Metro Atlanta Chamber of Commerce for ten years, where he was the top revenue producer for nine consecutive years.

Currently, he serves on the board of directors for the U.S. Fund for UNICEF, and he is a member of Antioch Baptist Church North.

A native of Beaumont, Texas, Malbrough is a graduate of Lamar University with a bachelor of arts degree in communications.

He resides in Smyrna with his wife, Cara, and his two sons, Evan and Jared.

Cepada Martin
Owner & Chief Executive Officer
Vases With Faces

Cepada Martin is owner and chief executive officer of Vases With Faces and the wife of nationally renowned, award-winning artist Lydell Martin. Cepada has successfully managed and marketed Vases With Faces since 1996.

Vases With Faces is reputable for designing corporate awards/gifts for events such as Turner Broadcasting's Trumpet Awards, WVEE V-103's For Sisters Only, Arista Records (Aretha Franklin) and the Atlanta Business League, to name a few.

Cepada has traveled extensively throughout the United States developing new markets for the one-of-a-kind art pieces designed in her Atlanta-based studio. She believes that art is one of the best investments that an individual or corporation can make and that buying original art is the way to go.

An Atlanta native, Cepada is the mother of two daughters, Bakisa and Baceka, and the proud grandmother of one, Kalize.

Visionary artist Lydell Martin has been impressing audiences with his artwork for more than 30 years.

Lydell began his professional career in 1991 with the formation of Vases With Faces. In addition to his art, Vases With Faces also provides original graphic designs, CD covers and screen-printing services for a number of promotional items.

In 1995 Lydell began an innovative use of ceramics that enraptures viewers, with work that has been commissioned by Turner Broadcasting, the United Negro College Fund, High Museum of Art Atlanta, the Atlanta Business League and the NAACP, just to name a few.

Born in Macon, Georgia, Lydell's formal training came from basic art classes. His God-given talent was formed and nurtured through the school of trial and error. His experimentation in numerous mediums led to his diverse and unique style, which reflects an inner passion created from life experiences, personal inspirations and a strong spiritual foundation.

Vases With Faces is family-owned by Lydell, Cepada and daughters, Bakisa and Baceka.

Lydell Martin
Artist
Vases With Faces

ENTREPRENEURS

Yolanda Martin
Owner & Broker
Martin Prosperity, Inc.

Yolanda Martin is the owner/broker of Martin Prosperity, Inc., a full service real estate firm where she trains her agents to "go that extra mile." She has made a commitment to client satisfaction, and her goal is to earn clients' trust through business professionalism.

Martin is a member of the Atlanta Board of Realtors and the Empire Board of Realtists. As such, she is also an active member of the Million Dollar Club. She has also been named Agent of the Year and Agent of the Month.

Martin attended Atlanta Area Tech, where she received a certificate of completion for computer processing. She also attended Bible college and received her evangelistic license, subsequently serving as a Sunday school teacher and a Sunshine Band leader/teacher for several years.

A native of Queens, New York, she and her husband have been blessed to see 24 years and three children together; a daughter, 14, and two sons, 27 and 28.

Corey "Coco" McDonald
Chief Executive Officer
Senior Executive Baker
Cakes By Coco, Inc.

Corey McDonald has been mixing up cakes since birth, on the hip of his mother and at the hem of his grandmother's apron. Affectionately named "Coco" by his grandmother, he has spent the last 15 years perfecting the recipes his mother passed on to him. At 10 years old, his brother, Yuric, baked and decorated Coco's 5th birthday cake.

Coco began baking in 1991 to pay for his final year at Lincoln University. He took a trade that had been passed down generations in his family and developed it into a thriving Atlanta business and an absolute metropolitan must-have. He moved to Atlanta upon the urging of his fraternity brother, Joe Torry. Actor, comedian and philanthropist, Torry extended his support, home and kitchen to the beginnings of Cakes By Coco.

Coco is the proud father of Mariama McDonald, "Baby Cakes." He is a member of Omega Psi Phi Fraternity, Inc. A St. Louis native, Coco is a natural philosopher.

India Miller began her career as an event planner in 2000 after attending Clayton State College where she majored in communication. She specializes in social events in Atlanta, with movers and shakers from Chris Tucker to Jermaine Dupree. She eventually joined radio personalities Ryan and Kysha Cameron in planning events for their foundation, which is the source for a great deal of charitable work.

Miller joined Martin, Yolanda and Bernice King in the remembrance of their mother, the late Coretta Scott King, on her birthday at the Martin Luther King Center where she was interviewed about Mrs. King's legacy. Currently, she is an active member of the RainbowPUSH Coalition, where she marched beside Rev. Jesse Jackson, Mayor Shirley Franklin, actor Harry Belafonte and singer Willie Nelson for voter's rights in Atlanta.

She currently resides in Atlanta with her children, Clairissia, Diamond and Reginald. A favorite quote by her late mother and grandmother (Willie Mae and Clara Miller Perdue) is, "Always strive to be someone of importance."

India Miller
Event Planner

Joel Miller is the founder and chief financial strategist of Wall Street Capital Funding, Inc., one of the nation's highest-ranked mortgage originators.

At 18, Miller began his career in finance, working under some of Wall Street's most influential financial strategists. Three years later, his ambition led him to Atlanta where he founded Wall Street Capital Funding, a private mortgage bank. By age 28, Miller had become one of the youngest mortgage bankers in the history of the United States.

Today, Miller continues to expand his scope of influence in the world of finance as an investor, developer, public speaker and author. He maintains professional affiliations that include the Real Estate Executive Council, Rapport Leadership International and The Core Training, Inc. His true passion, however, remains creating opportunities for black men and women by helping them to realize their financial goals through strategic planning, wealth building and money management.

When not working, Miller enjoys spending time with his wife of 15 years and his two sons. His personal motto is "different is not always better, but better will always be different."

Joel Miller
Founder & Chief Financial Strategist
Wall Street Capital Funding, Inc.

ENTREPRENEURS

Melvin Maurice Miller
Musician

Melvin Maurice Miller was born and raised in Chicago, one of the largest cities historically known for great jazz. He recently returned from a nationwide tour with the UniverSoul Circus that began in January of 2002.

He has performed across the globe at a variety of venues including Orlando, Florida for the opening of Epcot Center; Tokyo, Japan for the Mirage Bowl; and Switzerland for the Montreaux Jazz Festival. Melvin has traveled and/or performed with such artists as The Temptations, Lou Rawls, The Dells, The O'Jays, James Brown, Wynton Marsalis, Dizzy Gillespie, Roy Hargrove and Miles Davis.

A well-rounded musician, Melvin also held the position of principal trumpet with the African American Philharmonic Orchestra of Atlanta.

He regularly performs the national anthem for Atlanta Falcons and Atlanta Hawks games, and he recently appeared on *Atlanta Tonight*. Melvin wrote and performed the opening fanfare for the 2001, 2002, 2004 and 2005 Trumpet Awards, and he was musical director for the 2006 Trumpet Awards.

He is affectionately called "young man with a horn," a title bestowed on him by his mother.

Jacquee Minor
President
J. Minorlogues, LLC

Jacquee Minor is president of J. Minorlogues, LLC, a marketing enterprise specializing in speechwriting, event scripting and writing narrative biographical profiles. She creates words that speak volumes for corporate executives, executive directors, business owners and elected officials.

Minor's work is featured as the official Atlanta Female Powerhouse writer for the ninth edition of *Who's Who In Black Atlanta®*. She previously worked in marketing and public relations for the Southern Christian Leadership Conference, West End Medical Center and First Class, Inc., and in journalism as a radio news editor and program director. Minor currently serves as secretary on the Atlanta City Board of Ethics, which interprets, monitors and enforces the city's code of ethics.

She is an Atlanta Junior League member, and a reader for the Georgia Radio Reading Service. She recently completed the Leadership Development University program. Minor earned her bachelor of arts degree in broadcast journalism at Louisiana State University.

Yonelle Andrea Moore is the president and chief executive officer of The Moore Mediation Group, providing mediation and arbitration services.

Moore earned a bachelor of arts degree in political science from the University of the District of Columbia and a juris doctorate from the Pepperdine University School of Law. She is the recipient of several leadership awards, and is fluent in Spanish.

A member of Leadership Cobb Class of 2007, Moore is a dedicated community servant. She serves as the vice president of membership for Speaking With Power Toastmasters Club and is a volunteer mentor with Another Way Out, Inc. She is also a member of the South Cobb Arts Alliance, a diamond life member of Delta Sigma Theta Sorority, Inc. and a silver life member of the NAACP. Professionally, she is a member of the West Cobb and the Cobb County Chambers of Commerce, as well as the South Cobb Business Association.

A native of Guyana, South America, Moore is the proud mother of one child, Gabrielle. They attend Word of Faith Family Worship Cathedral.

Yonelle Andrea Moore
President & Chief Executive Officer
The Moore Mediation Group, Inc.

Award-winning chef Tony Morrow is the founder, chief executive officer and executive chef of The Pecan, Inc. and Flavours Gourmet Catering, Inc. Born in St. Albans, New York, Morrow was raised in southwest Atlanta.

He earned a bachelor of science degree in marketing from Tuskegee University. He was then commissioned into the Air Force as a second lieutenant. During his eight-year tour of duty, Morrow was promoted to the rank of captain and served as chief financial officer for the Titan Missile System. He received his master of business administration degree in management from The University of South Dakota in Vermillion in 1991. He is also a cum laude graduate of the Art Institute of Atlanta School of Culinary Arts.

He is a member of Kappa Alpha Psi Fraternity, Inc. and Elizabeth Baptist Church. Morrow has been a resident of southwest Atlanta for over 25 years. He and his wife of 17 years, Caiphia, have one son, DeVaughn.

Tony Morrow
Founder & Chief Executive Officer
The Pecan, Inc.

ENTREPRENEURS

Virginia L. Parham
Co-Owner & Vice President
Your Sales Up, Inc.

Virginia L. Parham is the co-owner and vice president of Your Sales Up Inc. She sells advertising for several clients, including Who's Who Publishing Company, *Atlanta Tribune: The Magazine*, *Cultured Living Atlanta Magazine*, *Gwinnett Parents*, and *Johns Creek Magazine*.

Virginia's sales career began with employment at Hutzler's Department Store in downtown Baltimore, Maryland as the first black sales supervisor. For many years, she worked as a part-time interviewer for her mother's company, Lottier/Nixon Interviewing Service, a marketing research company. She was the first black female to sell advertising for Rueben Donnelly Yellow Pages, and the first female employed by *Ebony* magazine as the merchandising and sales promotion manager for the Baltimore market. She was responsible for introducing black mannequins for display in the Baltimore downtown area.

Virginia relocated to Georgia to work in the advertising department at *Atlanta Tribune:The Magazine*. She attended Morgan and Coppin State College majoring in English and elementary education.

A native of Baltimore, Virginia resides in Alpharetta, Georgia with her husband. She has one daughter, two sons, and five grandchildren.

Cynthia Jones Parks
President
Jones Worley

Cynthia Jones Parks founded Jones Worley in 1990. Under her leadership, Jones Worley has provided wayfinding and signage consultation to such organizations as Charlotte Transit, Spelman College, The Coca-Cola Company, Turner Properties and Jacksonville Public Library. In 2006 the firm was awarded such projects as the donor program for Morehouse College, master plan for Virginia State University, and signage and wayfinding for both UNC Chapel Hill and Georgia State University Library.

Parks' accomplishments have been recognized in *Black Enterprise*, *Georgia Trend*'s 40 Under 40 – Georgia's Rising Stars; *Business to Business*, *Ebony* and CNBC News' *How to Succeed in Business*.

Parks holds a bachelor of visual arts degree from Georgia State University and is an alumna of the Minority Business Executive Program (Amos Tuck School of Business Administration, Dartmouth College).

She is a member of the Federal Reserve Bank of Atlanta, the American Public Transportation Association, the Society of Marketing Professional Services, the American Institute of Graphic Arts, and the Society for Environmental Graphic Design. She is also a member of the 1997 class of Leadership Atlanta.

R one' Y. Paulding is a woman of merit with diverse specialties in business management, marketing and real estate. She is co-founder of Global Money and co-owner of Keller Williams Realty, Atlanta Classic.

Consistent with the founder's philosophy, Keller Williams Realty, Atlanta Classic seeks to provide aid to first time homebuyers, repeat buyers, sellers and investors as well as new construction and commercial gurus.

Paulding has the added advantage and the commensurate leverage of a team that has focused on multi-pronged approaches to a variety of real estate ventures, allowing them through the years to acquire, reengineer and maintain properties within the U.S. and internationally.

Rone' is co-owner and contributor of three Keller Williams offices. She was recognized as the top team for Keller Williams in the southeast region with $37 million in closed sales, the No.1 team for the Metro South Board of Realtors, and designated one of the top 100 for the state of Georgia.

Rone' Y. Paulding
Co-Owner
Keller Williams Realty, Atlanta Classic

D on Rivers is founder and president of Rivers Productions, Inc. (RPI), an entertainment production company based in Atlanta since 1981. He is also founder of the R.E.A.C.H. Complex, Inc., a nonprofit 501(c)(3) organization created to teach young people about the music entertainment business.

RPI provides a diverse team of industry professionals and entertainment production services, national and international artists, concert productions, event management, consulting services, and events throughout the United States and abroad.

RPI donates annual entertainment services for the fund-raising events of several nonprofit organizations such as the Trumpet Awards, Prevent Child Abuse of Georgia, 100 Black Men, the Center for the Visually Impaired, 100 Black Women, Breast Cancer Survivors, the Mayor's Seniors Ball, and the United Negro College Fund.

Rivers is a member of the American Society of Composers, Authors and Publishers, the National Academy of Recording Arts & Sciences and the High Museum.

Prior to establishing RPI, Rivers was director of audio education at Shaw University and producer at WBT radio.

He received his bachelor of arts degree in radio, television and film production from Shaw University.

Don Rivers
Founder & President
Rivers Productions, Inc.

Thomasene Blount Roberts
Chief Executive Officer & Owner
Dream Catcher Events

Thomasene Blount Roberts is chief executive officer and owner of Dream Catcher Events, which specializes in the design, planning and coordination of meetings, special events and occasions. She uses the best multi-disciplinary teams to consistently guarantee professional results.

Thomasene is the recipient of the 2006 Twinkie Award for the Best Marketing Idea on a Shoe String Budget. She has been featured in numerous publications including *Who's Who in America*.

Thomasene is a founding member of 100 Black Women, Metropolitan Atlanta Chapter. She is a former adjunct professor of events and wedding planning for Georgia Perimeter College. Previously, she served as vice president of programs for the International Special Events Society and co-chaired the Atlanta AIDS Partnership Fund volunteer advisory committee. She is a member of Delta Sigma Theta Sorority, Inc.

Thomasene attended Fisk University and received her bachelor's degree from Morris Brown College. She was awarded a master's degree in educational psychology and pursued further study toward a doctorate in psychological services at Clark Atlanta University.

She is the proud mother of one daughter, Asha Rashad, and grandmother to Jelani Rashad.

Donna Robinson
President, Affirmative Defense
Response System Program
R. L. Robinson

Donna Robinson is president of R.L. Robinson's Affirmative Defense Response System Program. Donna provides free evaluations for companies to determine whether they are in compliance with federal, state and legislative laws that deal with safeguarding non-public information. Since civil, criminal and class action lawsuits can be lodged against companies if they are not in compliance, she assists with compliance and affirmative defense preparation.

Donna received a bachelor's degree from Washington University in St. Louis and a business degree from Riverside University in California. This year she completed her training with the Institute of Fraud Risk Management and became a certified identity theft risk management specialist.

Donna was featured in *The Absolute Best Way in the World for Women to Make Money*, a book of inspiration for women. She was also featured in the Cambridge *Who's Who Among Executive and Professional Women, Honors Edition*.

Donna is a volunteer member of the literacy group at Praise Academy. She is married to Ronnie Robinson, and is the proud mother of Ronnie Jr., Lavor, Stephen, Demerra, Bryana and Kayla.

Earnestine Shuemake
Founder
OBA's Atlanta

Earnestine Shuemake, a décor consultant and visual artist, is founder of OBA's Atlanta. Taking God-inspired ideas, her father Ernest's creative wisdom and her mother Mary's heart, Earnestine creates fantasy and function in her designs. Her out-of-the-box style has been honored by several awards.

She has been featured in such publications as *Newsweek*, *Essence by Mail*, *Women's Wear Daily*, *GoodLife*, *The South Fulton Neighbor*, *Onyx Woman* and *The Atlanta Journal-Constitution*.

Earnestine's client list includes the City of Atlanta, Hyatt Regency, the DoubleTree Club Hotel, the City of East Point, North American Properties, *Who's Who In Black Atlanta*®, the High Museum of Art, Camp Creek MarketPlace, The Shops of Cascade, the Brown Design Group, the Atlanta Public Library and private individuals.

She is also founder of Camp Girlfriend, an organization for spiritually motivated sisters. Earnestine is a member of Rakes and Hoes Gardening Club, the High Museum of Art and the City of East Point business and industrial development board.

"Ms. E" is happily married to Robert Wayne Stokes and has an adult son, Oba, the company's namesake.

Julietta Boyd Smith
President & Owner
Your Missing Link

Julietta Boyd Smith is president and owner of one of the most dynamic, sought-after companies, Your Missing Link. Her virtual assistant business is the reason many of today's executives and businesses have been able to reach a higher level of efficiency and financial goals. Julietta has been called on to provide services throughout the Southeast region of the U.S. due to her ability to always be one step ahead and manage the details of business.

Julietta belongs to Ray of Hope Christian Church and is an active board member of the West DeKalb Chapter of Mocha Moms, Inc., where a priority is to close the gap in minority achievement. She believes higher education is not an option; it is a *must*, with emphasis in educating young people about entrepreneurship.

Julietta currently holds a bachelor of science degree in biology from South Carolina State University, and she will soon complete the Keller Graduate School of Management. A Columbia, South Carolina native, she is the wife of Henry and the mother of three beautiful children Raven, Danielle and Henry III.

DeShawn Snow
Owner
EDJ Realty, LLC

DeShawn Snow is the owner of EDJ Realty, LLC, a full-service boutique real estate firm. DeShawn has a unique appreciation for the necessities associated with luxury living and has structured EDJ to provide service and conveniences, such as a full-service concierge program and a corporate condo, that are unparalleled in the real estate realm.

DeShawn is a member of the Institute of Luxury Home Marketing and is recognized by *Who's Who in Luxury Real Estate*.

She received a bachelor of arts degree in marketing from Michigan State University, is currently an active member of Behind the Bench and serves on the boards for Literacy Action and the Shoot 4 the Moon Foundation. Additionally, she founded the DeShawn Snow Foundation to empower teenage girls with self-esteem issues. Building a future for others through the success of her own business endeavors, DeShawn contributes a percentage of EDJ Realty profits to the foundation.

A native of Detroit, Michigan, DeShawn is the wife of Eric Snow and the proud mother of three sons, Eric, Darius and Jarren.

Norma F. Stanley
President
NFS Communications, Inc.

Norma F. Stanley is an award-winning marketing communications consultant, providing public relations and diversity marketing services to various industries including business, government, entertainment, banking, food service and many more. Among her past clients are General Motors, AFC Enterprises, Gladys Knight, Bank of America and the City of Atlanta.

In addition to her strategic public relations services, Norma has worked as a freelance writer and editor for local and national newspapers and business and gospel magazines including *The Atlanta Journal-Constitution*, the *Atlanta Business Journal*, *Forecast* and *Gospel Truth Magazine*.

The mother of a special needs child and an avid community supporter, Norma lends her professional and personal time to organizations that support the disability community, including All Children Are Special, Inc.

A journalism graduate of Long Island University in New York, Norma is the author of two books with two more scheduled for release in 2007, all dealing with issues of parenting a special needs child. A singer/songwriter, Norma has sung background vocals and written a number of songs for rising Atlanta R&B, gospel and inspirational jazz recording artists.

Jacqui Steele is founder and president of Steele Program Managers, LLC in Stone Mountain, Georgia. She started the construction management firm just over a year ago and is now managing more than $60 million in projects. With more than 16 years of experience in the construction industry, Jacqui has worked on projects for MARTA, Spelman College, the Georgia Board of Regents, Hartsfield-Jackson Atlanta International Airport, the DeKalb County Board of Education and DeKalb County. Having managed more than $1.2 billion worth of projects, Jacqui has truly been a part of the growth of Atlanta over the years.

Jacqui has served in various community and professional organizations. She has traveled the world for business and leisure but always returns to the Atlanta area which is dear to her heart.

With a passion for life and a drive to challenge herself beyond what others believe possible, Jacqui sets high standards for all that she does.

A native of Atlanta, Jacqui has three children, Martez, Joseph and Amber. She is married to the love of her life, Larry.

Jacqui Steele
Founder & President
Steele Program Managers, LLC

Teague Stradford-Stovall is president and designer of Teague Stradford Enterprises, International. Since 1994 her firm has manufactured custom designed academic, choir, judicial, pulpit and wedding clothing.

Teague is a professor and mentor at American InterContinental University (AIU) in the fashion design/marketing department and has developed a training video for her students. She is a member of Fashion Group International, is listed in several Who's Who in America and international editions, and was recognized by *Women Looking Ahead News Magazine* as a Creative Style Award finalist in 1996.

As a designer, stories featuring her have run in *The Atlanta Journal-Constitution*, *The Korean Times* and others. Her designs have shown in Air Tran Airlines' magazine, *The New York Times*, and *Women's Wear Daily*. Currently, her artistic works, including wall art and photographs of murals she designed and painted, are on display at AIU/Buckhead and the New Orleans/French Quarters home gallery.

Teague holds associate and bachelor's degrees from Parson's School of Design and a master's degree from Goddard College.

Her immediate family includes her husband, Danny Dean Dow, daughter, Diane, and granddaughter, Jhania.

Teague Stradford-Stovall
President & Designer
Teague Stradford
Enterprises, International

Atlanta's
ENTREPRENEURS

Sonja Strayhand
President
Sonja Strayhand Interiors

Sonja Strayhand is an award-winning interior designer for both residential and commercial customers. President of Sonja Strayhand Interiors, she operates a full-service interior design firm that handles every aspect of a design project, from concept to final installation.

Sonja's designs have gained wide recognition. She is featured in *Atlanta Woman* magazine's 25 Power Women to Watch in 2006. She received the Atlanta Business League's 2005 Outstanding Achievement in Creative Style award, the 2004 Street of Dreams Luxury Home Tour, and was named one of *Women Looking Ahead* magazine's Ordinary Women with Extraordinary Talents in 2003.

A graduate of the Atlanta College of Art, Sonja is one of the premier showcase designers for the exclusive Brian Jordan Le Jardin community of South Fulton. Her high-profile client list includes celebrities, top corporate executives, dignitaries and major commercial developers around the country.

Sonja stays abreast of industry trends through professional affiliations such as the American Society of Interior Designers and the International Interior Design Association.

Sonja and husband, Ronald Strayhand, have one son, Ronald Jr.

Belinda Stubblefield
Proprietor
WineStyles Cascade

Belinda Stubblefield is proprietor of WineStyles Cascade, a unique wine store that brings a taste of wine country to her community. She and her husband, Ron Frieson, decided to pursue this entrepreneurial venture in May and celebrated their grand opening in November of 2006.

Before WineStyles, Stubblefield held several senior positions at Delta Air Lines, including vice president of global diversity, director of customer care and director of marketing planning.

Stubblefield began her career in sales with IBM. She then focused on marketing with Procter & Gamble and Nestle, leaving as director of marketing for cat food businesses Fancy Feast, Friskies, Chef's Blend, and Alpo cat food.

Active in the community, she has served on the boards of Leadership Atlanta, the Atlanta Convention and Visitors Bureau, the Piedmont Park Conservancy, and Women Looking Ahead. Stubblefield was recognized as Executive of the Year by the Georgia Minority Supplier Development Council and received a Laurel Award from *Aviation Week & Space Technology.*

Stubblefield received a bachelor's degree from UCLA and a master of business administration degree from Harvard Business School.

Frankie Thompson Enterprises, Inc. was founded by Frankie Thompson in 1982. His emerging company has international contracts specifically in the industrial supply of pipes, pumps, valves, generators, HVAC systems and lighting systems. His company is certified as an 8(a) minority business with the Small Business Administration, the Georgia Department of Administrative Services and the Georgia Department of Transportation. It is also recognized for exports by the United States Department of Commerce.

Frankie is a 1974 graduate from Savannah State College with a degree in business administration. He is also a graduate of the Georgia Governor's Mentor Protégé Program. Frankie is active in community affairs, showcased by his membership in the Georgia Utility Contractors Association, where he serves on the legislative committee and the community services committee.

Frankie Thompson
President & Chief Executive Officer
Frankie Thompson Enterprises, Inc.

Brenda J. Tolliver is managing broker for RE/MAX Executives, Inc. In this position, she manages an office of 50 Realtors and their day-to-day activities.

Brenda serves on the board of directors for the DeKalb Association of Realtors, as well as the professional standards and Million Dollar Club committees. An active life phoenix member of the Million Dollar Club, she belongs to the RE/MAX 100% Club and was inducted into the RE/MAX International Hall of Fame.

Brenda is the national president of the Clark Atlanta University Alumni Association. She is a member of the Clark Atlanta University Guild, the Clark Atlanta Athletic Booster Association and the CAU board of trustees. She is also a past president of the DeKalb Alumni Chapter.

A member of Friendship Baptist Church, Brenda serves as secretary to the board of trustees. She is a member of Alpha Kappa Alpha Sorority, Inc.

Brenda received her bachelor's degree from Clark College and her master's degree from Atlanta University. A certified residential specialist and accredited seller representative, she holds Graduate Realtor Institute designation. She is a native of Chattanooga, Tennessee.

Brenda J. Tolliver
Managing Broker
RE/MAX Executives, Inc.

Atlanta's
ENTREPRENEURS

Celebrating African-American Achievements

Ardra Tippett
Chief Financial Officer
Marketing Director
Cakes By Coco, Inc.

Ardra Tippett partnered with Corey McDonald in 2003 to expand the reach and depth of Cakes By Coco, Inc. She is responsible for sales, marketing, motivation and morale.

A dedicated entrepreneur, Tippett earned the privilege to drive the legendary Mary Kay pink Cadillac for four years. She owned a Sprint PCS dealership, several tax preparation offices around the city and a business consulting firm, all of which she gave up to share in the sweet dreams of expanding Cakes By Coco nationwide. Having built a small business on her own, she knows the value of cooperative economics (Ujamaa) and loyalty and believes that "together we are better."

Tippett is a graduate of the University of Kansas in Lawrence, Kansas. She is a nine-year member of New Birth Missionary Baptist Church. The eldest child of Myrian Nicholson and James Tippett, her proudest accomplishment is raising her multi-talented, bilingual 11-year-old daughter, Nia Tippett.

Her favorite quote is: "Excuses are monuments of nothingness, they build bridges that lead to nowhere, those who use these tools of incompetence are masters of nothingness."

Kya L. Walker
Founder & President
Writing Concepts Agency

Kya L. Walker is the founder and president of Writing Concepts Agency, based in Atlanta. The agency is becoming known as the premiere service provider for writing and graphic arts needs. While working as community relations manager for the world's largest bookseller, Kya was able to assemble some of the most talented writers and graphic artists from across the U.S.

Writing Concepts Agency has helped many other entrepreneurs, authors and entertainers take their projects to the next level by communicating their vision to the public.

Kya has been writing for the past ten years, first for television and then expanding her horizons to work as a freelance writer. She graduated summa cum laude from Universidad Interamericano de Puerto Rico with a bachelor of arts degree in business.

Kya resides in Metropolitan Atlanta and enjoys cooking, writing and public speaking.

464 WHO'S *Who*

Kevin Waller is chief executive officer of Ubiquity Enterprises and chief operating officer of Vision Marketing Group. He engages several industries including health/wellness, travel/tourism, multi-media production and real estate. Additionally, he is chief of managerial accounting at the U.S. Army Forces Command headquarters.

Kevin is a retired lieutenant colonel who served for 21 years as an Army finance officer. He is a member of Kappa Alpha Psi Fraternity, Inc., Rotary International and the Shiloh Baptist Church music ministry.

In 1982 he received a bachelor of arts degree from Lincoln University (Missouri) and was recognized by *Who's Who Among Students in American Universities and Colleges*. In 1984 he earned an MBA from The Ohio State University, and in 2001 he was awarded a master of arts degree in information systems from Webster University. He was recently inducted into the Lincoln University ROTC Hall of Fame.

Born in Chicago, Kevin is the husband of Priscilla Waller and is the proud father of three children, Christina, Kevin Jr. and Chrystle.

Kevin L. Waller Sr.
Chief Executive Officer
Ubiquity Enterprises

Charmaine Ward, chief officer of CW Marketing Consultants stimulates business success by consistently employing a 360-degree approach to marketing: create, execute and measure.

Georgia-Pacific, John H. Harland and Bank of America all entrusted Charmaine to skillfully manage marketing teams and budgets, successfully lead community relations programs and diversity initiatives, and flawlessly execute product introductions and branding campaigns.

Charmaine donates her time to the Atlanta chapters of the National Coalition of 100 Black Women and National Black MBA Association, as well as the West End Medical Center. The American Marketing Association, Atlanta Business League, Delta Sigma Theta Sorority, Inc. and Leadership Atlanta also value Charmaine's active participation.

Helping students and entrepreneurs replicate marketing success is another of Charmaine's passions. She frequently speaks at INROADS Atlanta and historically black colleges and universities. She also serves as a panelist, workshop presenter and keynote speaker utilizing her proprietary programs "Maximizing Your Marketing Dollars" and "Marketing YOU to Win."

Charmaine graduated, magna cum laude, with a bachelor's degree from Clark Atlanta University and earned a master of business administration degree from Kennesaw State University.

Charmaine Ward
Chief Executive Officer
Business Consultant
CW Marketing Consultants, Inc.

ENTREPRENEURS

Kimberly N. West
President & Chief Executive Officer
SpyderWeb Technologies, Inc.

Kimberly N. West is president and chief executive officer of SpyderWeb Technologies, Inc., a leading technology consulting firm in Atlanta. She and her staff provide technology consulting, disaster recovery and implementation services for business entities. A recognized small/medium business technology expert and public speaker, Kimberly has been quoted in *USA Today* and appeared in *Atlanta Tribune: The Magazine*. Likewise, she is regularly featured in *VARBusiness* and *CRN* magazines, providing commentary on the state of technology for small and medium businesses.

Kimberly is an alumna of the University of Miami (Florida) where she matriculated in business management. She holds several technical certifications and graduate credentials in e-commerce from St. Thomas University in Minneapolis, Minnesota. She was the first and only African-American female to take part in the inaugural IPED Channel Elite/ Babson College MBA program in 2004.

A native of New York now living in Atlanta, Kimberly enjoys preparing gourmet cuisine and gardening in her spare time, and she is an avid student of Middle Eastern dance.

Jason C. Williams
National Press Secretary
100 Black Men of America, Inc.

Jason C. Williams brings almost 15 years of marketing and public relations experience to his clients as a marketing and media consultant. He is currently the public relations agent for 100 Black Men of Atlanta, Inc. and serves as national press secretary for 100 Black Men of America, Inc. Williams is also public relations agent of record for Gourmet Services, Inc., the nation's largest minority-owned food services company.

Before becoming an independent consultant, Williams was chief executive officer of the marketing firm Gelignite Communications, Inc. There, he was responsible for managing the strategic direction and growth of the firm, whose marquis clients were GMAC, Cracker Barrel and NMotion.

Named to *PR Week*'s 30 Under 30, he has served as a vice president for Edelman Public Relations Worldwide (the world's largest independent public relations firm) and has worked at public relations (PR) firms Hill & Knowlton and Cohn and Wolfe. During his career in PR, Williams has managed programs for some of the world's largest and fastest-growing companies, including BellSouth, AT&T and COMPAQ.

Williams is a graduate of Dartmouth College.

Ms. Sherita Williams is the owner and founder of Atlanta-based hair salon chain Genesis Hair Art, Inc., as well as Evan-Nicole Cosmetics, Image Makers International and the nonprofit organization known as the U-Imagine Project.

Her experience goes beyond hair styling. Artistry and image consultation has made Williams a leader within her industry. A few of her world-renowned clients include Evangelists Creflo and Taffi Dollar, Grammy-winning artists Mary Mary and Vickie Winans, supermodel Mi Mi Roche and Miss Georgia 2004, Danica Tisdale.

In recognition of her talents, Williams was awarded the title of Best Hair Color Salon in the South, and she received the Phoenix Award for outstanding achievement and service within the community. Her designs have been admired in national publications such as *Ebony* and *Essence*, and honored in *Atlanta Tribune: The Magazine* and *Sophisticated Black Hair* magazine.

A graduate of Clark Atlanta University, Sherita Williams recognizes that her duties as a faithful Christian and mother are the more important pieces of her accomplishments. She is blessed with her most precious gift from God, her daughter, Evan-Nicole.

Sherita Williams
Owner & Founder
Genesis Hair Art, Inc.

Yvonne Wiltz is president and chief executive officer of VonCreations, Inc., a full-service event management and marketing company. The company provides a wide range of services to plan and execute meetings, conferences and special events.

The company has an extensive list of nonprofit, public and private sector clients. These include YMCA of Greater Atlanta, National Black Arts Festival, Hughes Spalding Children's Hospital/Grady Health Systems, Bank of America, MARTA, and the U.S. Department of Commerce Minority Business Development Agency.

Most recently, VonCreations, Inc. was tapped by Cubic Transportation Systems to implement a community outreach program for MARTA as it rolls out "Breeze," its new automated fare collection system.

Yvonne has received numerous awards and accolades for her volunteerism and business acumen. She has served as a national officer of the National Coalition of 100 Black Women and immediate past president of the Metro Atlanta Chapter.

A native of Atlanta, she attended Spelman College and Columbia University.

Yvonne Wiltz
President & Chief Executive Officer
VonCreations, Inc.

ENTREPRENEURS

Rolonda Wright
Owner
Oodlez Concierge

Utilizing combined skills of organization, creativity and event planning, Rolonda Wright is the proud owner of Oodlez Concierge, a full-service concierge company based in metro Atlanta. The Texas native started her business in 2004 after realizing that she had a knack for completing a wide array of tasks that were taking away from the daily lives of those whom she served. With various clientele, including attorneys, senior citizens and corporations, Oodlez Concierge is built upon a foundation of excellent customer service and integrity.

Wright attended Texas Southern University, majoring in communications. She is actively involved in her community, serving on the board of directors for the Gems and Jewels mentoring program, where she chaired a financial literacy program. She is also a board member of Social and Economic Development for Men, Women and Children (SEDMWC).

Members of Victory Church in Stone Mountain, Rolanda and her husband Leonard have a blended family consisting of four daughters. In her spare time, she enjoys reading, singing, shopping and organizing events.

Keisha Nicole Wynn
Co-Owner
Kids R Kids @ Cascade

Keisha Wynn is co-owner of Kids R Kids @ Cascade, a school of quality learning for children from six weeks to 12 years old. The school opened in 2003 and serves the Cascade area and surrounding communities. In 2004 the school was granted a Georgia pre-kindergarten program.

An Atlanta native, Keisha graduated from Woodward Academy and completed her bachelor of science degree in business administration at Florida A&M University School of Business. She completed the commercial lending training program at Bank of America, where she spent several years as a relationship manager in commercial, nonprofit and government lending.

A licensed real estate broker with A & W Realty, Inc., Keisha is also active in real estate. She has numerous affiliations, including the Atlanta Board of Realtors and the Empire Board of Realtists.

Keisha is a member of the East Point-College Park Chapter of Delta Sigma Theta Sorority, Inc. She is also a member of the board of directors for the Women's Employment Opportunity Project and a volunteer with several other organizations.

Keisha is the proud mother of Jacob and Jadelyn.

Jeanette Zakkee founded Zakkee and Associates after developing a strong interest in the printing industry while in high school. Her 27 years of experience as a typesetter, graphic designer, printer, instructor and manager enhance her ability to fulfill the needs of businesses in the private and public sectors.

Jeanette has been named among *IMANI Magazine*'s Most Admirable Entrepreneurs and among the 100 Most Influential and Powerful Women in Georgia by *Women Looking Ahead News Magazine.* She has been a finalist for several Atlanta Business League awards, along with the Georgia Minority Business Award. Concerned Black Clergy (CBC) named her Businesswoman of the Year, and she received the President's Award and a Service Award from the National Coalition of 100 Black Women (NCBM) MECCA Chapter.

Jeanette is a member of the Georgia Chamber of Commerce, Atlanta Business League, NAACP Atlanta Chapter, NCBM MECCA Chapter and CBC. She holds board positions with Gems & Jewels Family Resource Center, Giwayen Mata, Georgia Genealogy Researchers and Human Rediscovery.

A California native, Jeanette is married to Daleel and has two daughters and two granddaughters.

Jeanette Khalilah Zakkee
President
Zakkee and Associates

Chaka Zulu is co-chief executive officer of Disturbing Tha Peace Records and Ebony Son Entertainment Inc., both based in Atlanta. Zulu has been making his mark in the music and entertainment business for well over ten years, both as an instrumental figure in launching many careers in the industry, and as a mentor to several people.

A devoted father of two, he has been a leader in his community since childhood. He was a leading member of community-based youth groups that promoted self-pride and activism, as well as a tutor and peer counselor in his time at John F. Kennedy High School in New Orleans, Louisiana. Zulu also worked with many fraternal organizations while attending Clark Atlanta University.

He began his music career while attending college as an intern for various record labels and as an on-air personality for WRFG, a community-based radio station in Atlanta. He later became the music director and an on-air personality for Atlanta's Hot 97.5 radio station. Currently, he manages the multiplatinum, Grammy award-winning artist and actor, Ludacris.

Chaka Zulu
Co-Chief Executive Officer
Disturbing Tha Peace Records
Ebony Son Entertainment

Atlanta's

SPIRITUAL LEADERS

*"I am black, but comely, O daughters of Jerusalem,
like the tents of Kedar, like the curtains of Solomon."*

SONG OF SOLOMON 1:5 MKJV

SPIRITUAL LEADERS

Diana Branch
Senior Pastor
Pilgrim Church of Atlanta

Diana Branch is the senior pastor of the Pilgrim Church of Atlanta, a sister church of the Pilgrim Cathedral of Atlanta.

Branch completed studies at the Church of Christ Bible Institute in Washington, D.C. and New York City, and graduated with honors from The School of Prophets Institute for Leadership Empowerment. She has received countless awards and citations from local churches and community organizations. A member of the Decatur Chapter of the National Council of Negro Women, Branch has been featured in *Good News* and has been recognized for her leadership in the East Atlanta community.

Branch has an astonishing healing ministry that has drawn hurting hearts from all over the metro Atlanta area. She has two powerful messages, Matters of the Heart and Shattering Strongholds, which have empowered, enlightened and delivered many from bondage. She can be heard on Atlanta's Love WAEC 860 AM Monday through Friday.

She is married to Bishop Kent D. Branch who is also her spiritual leader, and is the proud mother of two daughters, Courtney and Chloe, and a son, Kent II.

Bishop Kent D. Branch
Bishop, Southern Jurisdiction
Pilgrim Assemblies
International, Inc.

Founder and leader of one of Atlanta's fastest growing ministries, Bishop Kent D. Branch has inspired a holistic and prophetic vision for the people of southeast Atlanta and Decatur. As bishop of the southern jurisdiction of the United States, Branch directs the spiritual development of affiliated churches within the Pilgrim Assemblies International, Inc.

A native of Harlem, New York, Branch received a doctor of ministry degree from Drew University, doctor and master of divinity degrees from Emory University, and a master and bachelor of business administration degree from Pace University.

With 25 years of ministerial leadership, Branch has birthed a myriad of organizations in Atlanta and Decatur. Pilgrim Church and Pilgrim Cathedral of Atlanta host several ministries including Pilgrim Christian Academy and Learning Center, the East Lake Adopt-a-Family Ministry, and his newly established Pilgrim Faith-Based collaboration with the Fulton Atlanta Community Action Authority.

Branch reserves family time with his beautiful children, Courtney LeNise, Chloe LeNae and Kent II. His wife, Diana, partners with him in ministry as pastor of Pilgrim Church of Atlanta.

Bishop Dale Carnegie Bronner
Founder & Senior Pastor
Word of Faith Family Worship Cathedral

Bishop Dale Bronner is the founder and senior pastor of Word of Faith Family Worship Cathedral, an interdenominational ministry founded in 1991. It now has more than 10,000 members.

Bronner is a conference speaker, leadership trainer and accomplished author. He has several titles in print, including *Get A Grip*, *Guard Your Gates*, *A Checkup from the Neck Up*, and *Treasure Your Silent Years*. He also contributed to *Man Power* and *Failure: The Womb of Success*.

The fourth son born to the late Nathaniel Hawthorne Bronner Sr. and Robbie Bronner, he is a graduate of Morehouse College, where he finished as the top student in religion. He earned his doctorate degree from Christian Life School of Theology in 2001 and was consecrated as bishop in 2003.

A member of the Martin Luther King Board of Preachers at Morehouse College, Bronner also serves on the board of directors and is a partial owner of Bronner Brothers Manufacturing Company, a multimillion dollar family-owned corporation.

Bronner resides in Atlanta with his wife Nina, four daughters, and one son.

D r. Gerald L. Durley is pastor of historic Providence Missionary Baptist Church in Atlanta. Providence Church is well known for its community outreach initiatives aimed at enhancing human welfare by providing food and housing referrals, involving fathers with their families, and offering alcohol and substance abuse counseling.

Gerald is a psychologist who in the 1960s became deeply involved in the civil rights movement. He was a member of the first U.S. Peace Corps to go to Nigeria, West Africa. He was also a university professor and administrator at Illinois University, Clark Atlanta University and Morehouse School of Medicine. A rare resource, people across the nation seek out his counsel.

Gerald has an undergraduate degree from Tennessee State University, a master of science degree from Northern Illinois University, a doctorate of psychology and urban education from the University of Massachusetts, and a master of divinity degree from Howard University.

Gerald was born in Wichita, Kansas but grew up in California and Colorado. He is the father of Nia and Hasan and is married to Muriel Durley. Together they have four grandchildren.

Dr. Gerald L. Durley
Pastor
Providence Missionary
Baptist Church

T he Reverend William E. Flippin Sr. is a native of Nashville, Tennessee. He received his education and earned a bachelor of arts degree in mathematics and business administration from Fisk University in Nashville. In addition, he holds a master of divinity degree from Candler School of Theology at Emory University in Atlanta, Georgia and a doctorate of ministry degree from McCormick Theological Seminary in Chicago, Illinois.

Faithfully serving as senior pastor of The Greater Piney Grove Baptist Church in Atlanta since 1990, Flippin has led Piney Grove to a unique sense of mission and outreach. He also serves as the founder and chief executive officer of The Pearl Initiative, Inc. and Pearls of Great Price Ministries, Inc.

Flippin has been married for over 30 years to Sylvia Taylor. They are the proud parents of three sons who continue the family legacy of preaching: Revs. William E. (Kedra S.), Richard C. and Joseph C. T. Flippin, and a daughter, Sylvia Joi.

Rev. William E. Flippin Sr.
Senior Pastor
The Greater Piney Grove
Baptist Church

P astor Benjamin Gaither serves as senior pastor of Stronghold Christian Church in Lithonia. His leadership and influence does not end with the Stronghold family; it extends to the DeKalb County community. As a law enforcement detective with the DeKalb County Division of Homeland Security, Gaither serves the community as a governmental official. In addition, he serves as an advisor to the DeKalb County Drug Court and Women Against Domestic Violence.

Gaither has received numerous accolades for his dedicated commitment to servant leadership. In 2006 he received the Atlanta Gospel Choice Award in recognition of his outstanding pastoral leadership.

His educational pursuits have resulted in a bachelor of arts degree in criminal justice and supplemental coursework in biblical studies and business management. With more than 25 years in criminal justice and ministry, Gaither's passion to empower people still burns brightly.

Benjamin Gaither
Senior Pastor
Stronghold Christian Church

Atlanta's

SPIRITUAL LEADERS

Rev. Dr. Cynthia L. Hale
Founder & Senior Pastor
Ray of Hope Christian Church

The Reverend Dr. Cynthia L. Hale is founder and senior pastor of Ray of Hope Christian Church in Decatur, Georgia. More than 8,500 persons have joined in the last 21 years, making Ray of Hope the fastest-growing Disciple church in the nation.

Hale is a native of Roanoke, Virginia. She received her bachelor of arts degree from Hollins College in Virginia, and her master of divinity degree from Duke University in North Carolina. Hale holds a doctor of ministry degree from United Theological Seminary in Ohio. She has also received three honorary doctorates of divinity.

Hale served as a chaplain for federal correctional facilities in Colorado and North Carolina, and was the first female chaplain to serve in an all-male institution.

Hale has been in the ministry for 28 years. She has received many honors and awards that mark her accomplishments and contributions to the state of Georgia and beyond. Her ministerial gifts have drawn thousands to witness the power of God upon a woman with a mission to impact and transform this world into the Kingdom of God.

Pastor Philip Igbinijesu
Senior Pastor
Word Assembly

Pastor Philip Igbinijesu is the apostolic set man and God's visionary for Word Assembly in Atlanta. Word Assembly is a mission oriented church ministry with outreaches in the nations of Belgium, South Africa, Zambia and Nigeria with a passion for Kingdom relevance and social impact.

An author, television host and conference speaker, Igbinijesu travels widely with a mandate to reach nations, raise leaders, revive ministries and restore marriage and family values. Aside from serving as the president of the board of trustees and central executive committee of Word Assembly, he is also the president of Philip Igbinijesu Ministries International, Proof Producers Bible College and Agape International. Additionally, he is chief executive officer of Havilah Inc. and Prevailing Word Publishers.

Igbinijesu earned a bachelor of laws degree from the University of Benin and a bachelor of literature degree from the Nigerian Law School. He is married to Deborah and together they have twins Joshua and Jochebed, a boy and girl.

Dr. Benson M. Karanja
President
Beulah Heights Bible College

Dr. Benson M. Karanja is president of Beulah Heights Bible College in Atlanta. He serves as the commissioner for the Transnational Association of Christian Colleges and Schools, and on the commission for accreditation for the Association for Biblical Higher Education. He is the only American serving on this type of dual commission.

Karanja was appointed as board member of Moi Africa Institute to represent the U.S. In 2005 he was recognized as Man of the Year by the secretary of state of Georgia. He was also honored as one of the Most Influential Leaders in Atlanta. As a mentor for migrant ethnic leaders, he is closing the gap of cultural thinking and introducing them to Christians and business leaders.

A native of Kenya, Karanja received his bachelor of arts degree from Beulah Heights Bible College. He received a master of business administration degree from Brenau University, and a master of library science and doctorate in education from Clark Atlanta University. An author, his latest book is *A Grain of Sand*.

He and his wife, Esther, have three children.

P astor André Landers is the senior pastor of New Birth South Metropolitan Church in Jonesboro, Georgia. Through God's awesome power, the membership has grown to over 11,000 members in five years, and in May of 2004 God enlarged the territory of the church with 43 acres of land in McDonough, Georgia. The new campus is slated for completion in 2007 and will serve as a community haven of Kingdom discipleship.

Landers has made his mark on the metropolitan area with the development of strategic programs and community partnerships designed to break the barriers of racial and economic divide. Through a new Community Impact Center, New Birth South will continue to fully equip the community with a holistic educational approach that places emphasis on partnering with schools, local businesses and government.

Landers is a native of Atlanta, Georgia. He has been married for 17 years to Kimberley Landers and they are the parents of twin daughters, Devin and Morgan. Landers received his bachelor's degree in administration and marketing at the State University of West Georgia in 1988.

Pastor André Landers
Senior Pastor
New Birth South
Metropolitan Church

B ishop Eddie L. Long is God's visionary for New Birth Missionary Baptist Church, located in Lithonia, Georgia. The membership has grown from 300 members in 1987 to a membership of more than 25,000 today. Through the years, Bishop Long's uncompromising and bold teaching of God's word has changed the lives of people both at New Birth and around the world.

Long has achieved many triumphs on local, national and international levels. He is the founder and chief executive officer of Faith Academy, New Birth's school of excellence. He serves as the vice chair of Morehouse School of Religion's board of directors, is a member of the board of visitors for Emory University, and is a trustee for North Carolina Central University and Morris Brown College. He also serves on the board of directors for Safehouse Outreach Ministries.

Through Long's ministry, people are discovering their destinies. Because of the favor on his life, he has close relationships with leaders in the religious, political and entertainment arenas. Consequently, this humble servant is advancing the Kingdom of God in a completely new way.

Bishop Eddie L. Long
Senior Pastor
New Birth Missionary
Baptist Church

R ev. Timothy McDonald III has served as senior pastor of First Iconium Baptist Church since 1984. He is also chair of African American Ministers In Action and founder of the African American Minister's Leadership Council. In addition, McDonald served several terms as president of the Concerned Black Clergy of Metro Atlanta, and he serves on the board of directors for the People for the American Way.

Previously, McDonald was director of Operation Breadbasket and special projects for the Southern Christian Leadership Conference. He has also spearheaded projects around drugs, economic empowerment, South Africa, Central America, the Middle East and homelessness.

McDonald has received The Presidential Award of Merit from the Concerned Black Clergy, the Phoenix Award from Atlanta's Gospel Choice, and induction into the Martin Luther King Jr. International Board of Preachers at Morehouse College.

McDonald became an ordained minister in 1975. He received a bachelor's degree from Berry College and a master of divinity from Emory University in 1978.

Rev. Timothy McDonald III
Senior Pastor
First Iconium Baptist Church

He is married to Shirley Ann Neal McDonald and has three children, Nikisha, Timothy IV and Ebony.

Atlanta's
SPIRITUAL LEADERS

Rev. Dr. James Allen Milner Sr.
Senior Pastor
Chapel of Christian Love
Baptist Church

Rev. Dr. James Allen Milner Sr. was ordained as a minister in 1973. In March of 1976, he organized the Chapel of Christian Love Baptist Church where he still serves as senior pastor.

Milner earned his doctor of ministry degree from the Morehouse School of Religion at the Interdenominational Theological Center (ITC) in 2006. He also earned his master of divinity degree from ITC. He has studied Christian counseling through the Christian Counseling and Education Foundation located in Philadelphia, Pennsylvania.

He is a member of the NAACP and Southern Christian Leadership Conference, as well serving on the Regional Commission for the Homeless. His awards include the Duran Cassan Award for theology students and the Concerned Black Clergy's Salute to Black Fathers Award.

Milner has been married for 41 years to his childhood sweetheart, the former Janice Hardaway, a retired educator. They were blessed with three children: Sherri Milner-Owens, 37, James A. Milner II, 31, and Tiffani D. Milner, 22, a graduate of Tennessee State University. They also have one granddaughter, Kelli Owens, 14, and one grandson, Brian Owens, 6.

Apostle Jamie T. Pleasant, Ph.D.
Chief Executive Pastor
Kingdom Builders
Christian Center

Apostle Jamie T. Pleasant is the chief executive pastor of Kingdom Builders Christian Center, a multicultural, discipleship and economic empowerment ministry. Pleasant's God-given vision for economic empowerment makes Kingdom Builders one of the most cutting-edge ministries in the Atlanta area.

He is a past recipient of Atlanta Gospel Choice's Chosen Award and one of the 100 Most Influential Pastors by the *Atlanta Business Journal*. He is featured in publications such as the *Atlanta Tribune* and *Imani* magazine. He has also met government officials such as President Clinton and Nelson Mandela.

Pleasant has two bachelor's degrees, one from Benedict College and one from Clemson University, as well as a master of business administration degree from Clark Atlanta University. He also attained a doctorate degree in business management from Georgia Tech University, the first African American in Georgia Tech's 111-year history to do so. He currently teaches marketing at Clark Atlanta University.

Pleasant is married to Kimberly Pleasant and is the proud father of two sons, Christian and Zion Pleasant and one daughter, Nacara Ross.

Dr. Joseph M. Ripley Sr.
Founder & Pastor
The Body of Christ Church
International, U.S.A.

Dr. Joseph M. Ripley Sr. is founder and pastor of The Body of Christ Church International, U.S.A., a nondenominational church located in College Park, Georgia. What began in 1983 with 50 people has grown to nearly 7,000.

The Body of Christ Church International, U.S.A., a multifaceted ministry, includes the School of Ministry, Healing School, Business By The Book, IMPACT Tutorial Program, Partners in Education, English As A Second Language Classes, Technology Learning Center, Big Brother/Big Sister, Prison and Youth Detention Center Ministries, StreetReach, Missions, and Success In Life Classes.

Regarded as an internationally known author, motivational and conference speaker, Ripley has traveled to such places as Hawaii, Central America, Australia and China. He can be seen and heard nationally and internationally on the *Living in Victory* broadcast via television and radio, teaching believers to "feed their faith and starve their doubts to death."

Ripley attended the University of Georgia, and holds a doctorate degree from the New Covenant International Bible College.

He and his wife, Marjanita, are the proud parents of April, Heather and Joseph Jr.

Dr. Kenneth L. Samuel, native of Darlington, South Carolina, received his doctor of ministry degree from the United Theological Seminary in Dayton, Ohio. He was licensed and ordained under the pastorates of Dr. Joseph Roberts and Dr. Martin Luther King Sr. at the historic Ebenezer Baptist Church in Atlanta, Georgia.

Samuel is the pastor of Victory for the World Church in Stone Mountain, Georgia and has served as an adjunct professor in religion and philosophy at Clark Atlanta University and as a teaching assistant in homiletics at Emory University's Candler School of Theology. His first publication, *Solomon's Success: Four Essential Keys to Leadership*, highlights vital components of King Solomon's effective and relevant leadership for contemporary times.

Samuel serves on numerous local and national boards, including president of the DeKalb County NAACP, and past president of the Georgia Council on Adult Literacy. He volunteers as a chaplain for the DeKalb County Jail and as the southern regional chaplain of the Alpha Phi Alpha Fraternity, Inc.

He is the father of one daughter and resides in Stone Mountain, Georgia.

Dr. Kenneth L. Samuel
Pastor
Victory for the World Church

"Son of Thunder" Jasper W. Williams Jr. has served as senior pastor of Salem Bible Church in Atlanta and Lithonia for 43 years. He involved the church in a variety of social action ministries, such as organizing a welfare assistance program, a temporary aid fund to assist the socially challenged, a scholarship fund and a national drug ministry. Williams is a founding partner of the Unity Coalition and chief executive officer of the Preaching Network. He also instituted the Jasper Williams Preaching & Pastoring Conference.

Williams is a graduate of Morehouse College majoring in sociology with a minor in religion. He is the recipient of many awards and honors, such as the Rev. C.L. Franklin Masters Award, the NAACP Award, the Award of Excellence given by the Gospel Music Workshop of America, and the Martin Luther King Humanitarian Award. He holds honorary doctorate of divinity degrees from Miller University and Temple Bible College and Seminary.

Jasper Williams Jr. is a father of two sons, Rev. Jasper Williams III and Rev. Joseph Williams.

Jasper W. Williams Jr.
Senior Pastor
Salem Bible Church

The Reverend Christopher A. Wimberly, was called by God to preach His Word at the age of 19. It became clear God's hand was upon the ministry of this young man's life, leading him to travel the United States from coast to coast, spreading the gospel of Jesus Christ.

In June of 2004, Wimberly was called to lead the Hunter Hill First Baptist Church in Atlanta, Georgia. As the congregation's youngest pastor, he is taking the church "beyond the walls" by providing a vision to evangelize, enlighten, embrace, encourage, equip, empower and exalt the people of God. Wimberly is truly a man of God, leading the people of God to do the will of God.

Wimberly attended Beulah Heights Bible College in Atlanta, Georgia where he was the recipient of the Paul A. Anderson Scholarship. To further his studies in ministry, he is presently enrolled at Liberty University in Lynchburg, Virginia.

Wimberly is a native of Winder, Georgia. He was born on April 19, 1977, to Deacon Robert and Mrs. Rachel Wimberly.

Rev. Christopher A. Wimberly
Pastor
Hunter Hill First Baptist Church

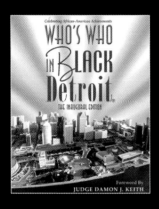
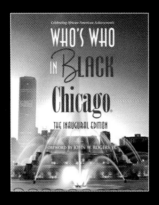
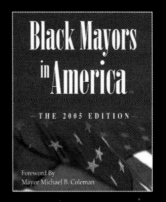
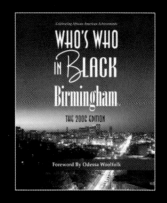
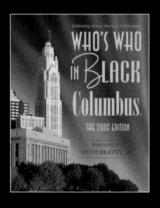
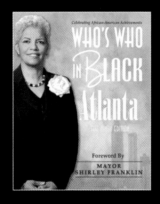

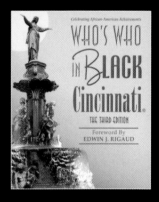
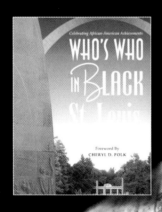
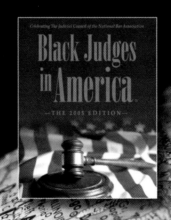

Atlanta's

COMMUNITY LEADERS

"There is one thing you have got to learn about our movement.
Three people are better than no people."

FANNIE LOU HAMER, 1917-1977

VOTING AND CIVIL RIGHTS ACTIVIST

Axel D. Adams
National Director
1K Churches Connected
RainbowPUSH Coalition

Axel Adams is national director for RainbowPUSH Coalition's (RPC) 1K Churches Connected financial literacy program based in Atlanta. He supervises the work of directors in New York, Los Angeles, Detroit and Chicago. Together they service 1,100 pastors/churches who collectively represent more than two million parishioners.

Adams was the chief operations officer for RPC in the Chicago headquarters office and the youngest chief operations officer ever hired. Prior to RPC, he was employed at Westinghouse Savannah River Company as a supervisor in the nuclear material processing division where he received the first Community Service Award. At the age of 22, Adams was elected to city council in New Ellenton, South Carolina. He served two four-year, elected terms and served as mayor and police commissioner. He was the first African American elected and appointed. Adams is also managing director of New Vision Financial.

Some of his affiliations include AAdams Group, Inc. (founder), the NAACP (former state advisor), RainbowPUSH Coalition; Knowl Tec & Associates; and Baafam Record Company (consultant). He attended Aiken Technical College where he studied chemistry.

Joseph H. Beasley
Executive Director
Antioch Urban Ministries

Joseph H. Beasley is the executive director of Antioch Urban Ministries in Atlanta, Georgia. He is also the southern regional director of the National RainbowPUSH Coalition, the organization led by the Reverend Jesse Jackson Sr.

Through his work with Antioch Urban Ministries, he facilitated a number of programs, including a national model for supporting homeless persons. Through his work with RainbowPUSH, he has actively fought discrimination and injustice regionally, nationally and internationally.

Beasley was born the son of a sharecropper in Fayetteville, Georgia. He served 21 years in the U.S. Air Force and retired in 1978 as a police superintendent. An appointee to the Atlanta Olympic Leadership Team, he was named one of the Most Influential People in Atlanta, and listed among the Top 50 African American Men in Georgia.

Beasley is a speaker and advocate for social justice and human dignity. He is the author of several articles and opinion pieces, and he hosts a news program on the most listened to station in Atlanta, WAOK Radio.

Beasley is married and has three children, nine grandchildren and one great-grandchild.

Kimberly Boykin
Founder &
Chief Executive Officer
boys who d.a.r.e., Inc.

Kimberly Boykin is founder and chief executive officer of boys who d.a.r.e., Inc., a program designed to promote literacy among young males ages 4 to 17. Designed to expand educational experiences and cultural learning, the program provides thematic literacy events created to offer early literacy intervention.

Kimberly developed the program to empower young boys and restore faith in the men of the community as they uplift and encourage young boys. The program demonstrates the importance of literacy within the community while encouraging them to dream.

Kimberly is the proud recipient of the 2004 National Coalition of 100 Black Women's Unsung Heroine Award and the 2005 Presidential Award for Volunteerism.

Kimberly received a bachelor of science degree in human resource development from Georgia State University and is currently working on a master of business administration degree from the University of Phoenix.

An Atlanta native, Kimberly has dedicated her life to the service of others, demonstrated by her active membership in Hunter Hill First Baptist Church. Her most treasured gift is her son, Evann-Lawrence. She is the proud daughter of Margaret Boykin.

Atlanta's
COMMUNITY LEADERS

D. Jean Brannan is president and chief operating officer of the Sickle Cell Foundation of Georgia, Inc. In this position, she manages the daily activities of the foundation throughout the state of Georgia.

She is an active member of her community, serving as a member of the state newborn screening advisory council, the advisory board of the Red Cross and the Atlanta Public Schools adult education advisory committee. She is also an active member of St. Anthony Catholic Church.

Jean has received numerous honors and awards, including the Atlanta Medical Association's Pillar of Strength Award and the National Coalition of 100 Black Women's Unsung Heroine Award. To her credit, she also received one of the Intergenerational Resource Center's 2005 Portraits of Sweet Success.

Jean received her bachelor of arts degree in business administration from Morris Brown College.

A native of Miami, Florida, Jean is the wife of Solomon Brannan, the mother of two sons and one daughter, and the grandmother of two.

D. Jean Brannan
President & Chief
Operating Officer
Sickle Cell Foundation
of Georgia, Inc.

Stephen Brown is the assistant director of admission at The Lovett School, an independent school in Atlanta for kindergarten through 12th grade. There, he interviews and evaluates prospective students and assists in hiring and mentoring faculty of color. He also serves as an upper school mathematics instructor and a track and field coach.

Previously, Stephen played professional football as a wide receiver for the Chicago Bears. An Olympic athlete, he competed in the 2000 Summer Olympics in Sydney, representing his late father's homeland of Trinidad and Tobago in the 110-meter high hurdles.

Stephen was awarded an athletic scholarship to Wake Forest University, where he earned a bachelor's degree in mathematics. He was the university's first All-American in track. In 2003 he received a master of business administration degree from the Duke University Fuqua School of Business. He joined Wachovia Capital Markets, LLC as an associate where he supported hedge and mutual fund accounts.

A native of Washington, D.C., Stephen is married to Lillian Johnson Brown. He has a stepson, Julian, and a baby daughter, Caitlyn.

Stephen Brown
Assistant Director
of Admission
The Lovett School

An Atlanta native, visual artist and professional fund-raiser, S.D. "Sam" Burston joined the staff of the United Negro College Fund in 1997 as assistant area development director. In his new role as regional director, he is responsible for corporate and municipal workplace initiatives. Burston holds a bachelor's degree in art education from Morris Brown College and has studied at the Atlanta College of Art.

In 2005 he was featured in special shows during Black History Month, the National Black Arts Festival, the Hammonds House and the 2005 Trumpet Awards' inaugural Meet the Artist.

Burston is a member of Iota Phi Theta Fraternity, Inc. and has been involved in various local, civic organizations and causes. He is a member of Ben Hill United Methodist Church.

Burston and his wife, Janet, are the proud parents of four, Samantha, Darrell, Chris and Len.

S.D. "Sam" Burston
Regional Director
Southeast Field Operations
United Negro College Fund, Inc.

COMMUNITY LEADERS

Dawn Robinson Butler
Development Director
100 Black Men of Atlanta, Inc.

Dawn Robinson Butler is the development director for 100 Black Men of Atlanta, Inc. There, she is responsible for managing and cultivating corporate, foundation and a variety of stakeholder relationships.

Before joining 100, Dawn served as regional director of resource development and communication for Mercy Housing, Inc. There, she was able to double the philanthropic budget and developed a comprehensive fund-raising and communications strategy.

Dawn has served in various leadership roles in Atlanta, including regional manager for the Fannie Mae Foundation and executive director for the Community Affairs Ministering Programs. She has had the opportunity to work at diverse organizations in Atlanta to bring about community change.

A Hull fellow of the Southeastern Council of Foundations, Presidential Management Intern finalist and a former board member of the Rockdale Foundation for Excellence in Education, Dawn earned a master of public administration degree from Georgia State University and a bachelor's degree from Fort Valley State University. While with Fannie Mae, Dawn participated in a summer program at Harvard University's Design School of Executive Management.

Dawn is married and the mother of three.

Monica Cabbler
Chief Executive Officer &
Founder
Cabbler & Associates

Monica Cabbler is a USA track and field athlete training for the 2008 Olympic Games. Off the field, Cabbler serves as a corporate spokesperson and keynote speaker representing national organizations such as the U.S. Drug Enforcement Administration, Organization of Black Airline Pilots, Women's Sports Foundation, and various school systems. She uses the stage of sports as a platform for community outreach.

Her professional background is in sports marketing, image branding and public relations with Cabbler & Associates. She aligns other athletes and corporations with opportunities to impact their communities and build legacies for upcoming youth leaders. Her personal initiative targets childhood obesity, promoting the importance of kids fitness and healthy lifestyles.

Cabbler received her bachelor of business administration degree in marketing from the University of Georgia, where she is currently an executive board member of Georgia's Athletic Alumni Association. Cabbler also plays an active role within the National Governing body of the USA Track and Field association, along with its local Georgia association.

Monica is a native of Roanoke, Virginia and a member of Ray of Hope Christian Church.

Gwendolyn Campbell
Executive Director
Atlanta Federal
Executive Board

Gwendolyn Campbell is the executive director of the Atlanta Federal Executive Board. She works directly with more than 100 federal agency heads in metropolitan Atlanta, representing 47,000 federal employees. Her responsibilities include promoting national initiatives of the president and responding to the needs of federal departments/agencies and the Atlanta community.

Campbell serves as a catalyst for enhancing intergovernmental partnerships; establishing and maintaining communication links that promote interagency cooperation along the business lines of homeland security, emergency preparedness, workforce development and community outreach; and enhancing training and human capital initiatives. Recently, she created a government-wide leadership program to address the issues of succession planning. Through the combined federal campaign, more than $4.5 million was raised for nonprofit organizations in 2005.

Campbell graduated from Fisk University with a degree in history. She completed graduate studies in public administration.

A member of Cascade United Methodist Church, Campbell's community activities include the United Negro College Fund, the Clark Atlanta University Guild, the Atlanta Fisk Club and Leadership Atlanta.

A prolific writer, her hobbies include reading, traveling, and creating games and puzzles.

Janice McKenzie-Crayton is president and chief executive officer of Big Brothers Big Sisters of Metro Atlanta, Inc. (BBBS), a position she has held since January of 1992. She has led BBBS through strategic growth, expanding its reach to ten metro Atlanta counties serving more than 2,700 children.

Janice is a member of the distinguished Atlanta Rotary Club. She serves on the boards of the American InterContinental University, Atlanta Partners for Excellence in Education and St. Joseph's Mercy Foundation. Additionally, she is on the community advisory board for The Junior League of Atlanta. An alumna of Leadership Atlanta and Leadership Georgia, Janice is a former member of the Georgia Commission for Service and Volunteerism.

In 2005 Janice was acknowledged as a Diva by *Business to Business* magazine. In 1999 she received the Women of Distinction award from the Crohn's and Colitis Foundation, as well as the Atlanta Business League's Women of Vision award.

Janice holds both a bachelor's and a master's degree from Howard University. She lives in Atlanta with her husband, Pernell, and two daughters, Janell and Carrie Rose.

Janice McKenzie-Crayton
President & Chief Executive Officer, Big Brothers Big Sisters of Metro Atlanta, Inc.

Ericka Brown Davis was elected to the Clayton County Board of Education in 2000, and reelected to the Board in 2002 and 2006. In 2005 Davis was unanimously elected to serve as chair of the board, making the her second African American to do so. Under her leadership, the school system maintained its accreditation and is now considered a local standards school board by the Georgia School Board Association.

Currently, Davis serves as the director of communication for the Georgia State Financing and Investment Commission, the Georgia Building Authority and the State Properties Commission. She is a graduate of the University of Georgia and holds a master of science degree in technical and professional communication from Southern Polytechnic State University.

Davis was selected for the 2003 Class of the Regional Leadership Institute by the Atlanta Regional Commission, and in 2004 she won the National Association of Government Communicators' Award of Excellence for Writing.

She attends Siloam Church International where she serves as coordinator of the scholarship fund.

Davis is the proud mother of one daughter, Jessica Leigh-Ann.

Ericka Brown Davis
Board Member
Clayton County Board of Education

Dr. Patricia Dixon is president of the National African American Relationships Institute (NAARI), a 501(c)(3) organization committed to relationships, marriage and family education and support.

She is associate professor in African-American studies at Georgia State University (GSU) where she was awarded a healthy marriage grant for five years to fund a collaboration between GSU and NAARI. This program provides relationship and marriage education to individuals and couples in the Atlanta metropolitan area, as well as ten to 15 other cities with the highest proportions of African Americans. She is author of the book, *African Relationships, Marriages and Families: An Introduction.*

Dixon is president of Georgia Residential Mortgage, Inc. and affiliate branch manager of the National Association of Real Estate Brokers—Investment Division Inc., Housing Counseling Agency, which provides housing counseling and education.

She received her doctorate in African-American studies from Temple University and her master of business administration degree from Howard University. She is the wife of Timothy Spear, executive vice president of NAARI.

Dr. Patricia Dixon
President
National African American Relationships Institute

COMMUNITY LEADERS

Hattie B. Dorsey
Founder &
Chief Executive Officer
Atlanta Neighborhood
Development Partnership, Inc.

Ellen N. Fleming
Chief Executive Officer &
Executive Director
Peoplestown
Revitalization Corp.

Melodee J. Ford
President &
Chief Executive Officer
Junior Academies, Inc.

A s founder and chief executive officer of the Atlanta Neighborhood Development Partnership, Hattie B. Dorsey is a leading advocate for housing issues. One of her most important accomplishments has been the shifting of perception about the importance of revitalized neighborhoods and the critical need for an affordable, mixed income housing approach that includes all segments of the population.

Dorsey has demonstrated how affordable housing, once thought only a problem for the poorest of the poor, affects a larger part of the economic population strata. She continues to make clear the connection between housing and quality of life issues, including air quality, transportation and the availability of clean water. Dorsey's organization, now in its 12th year, is leveraging housing development activities, a fully-accredited CDFI loan fund and policy advocacy to transform Atlanta's neighborhoods.

Dorsey participates in local and national dialogues on topics of community development, race relations, economic development, regional equity and public policy. She serves on committees/boards for the Federal Reserve, Central Atlanta Progress, Atlanta Streetcar, FannieMae, the Enterprise Foundation, Washington Mutual, the International Women's Forum and Spelman College.

E llen Fleming is chief executive officer and executive director of Peoplestown Revitalization Corp., a nonprofit community development corporation that represents the Peoplestown community of more than 2,700 residents. In this position, she manages the revitalization of the Peoplestown community through housing development, community development and economic development. As a former successful corporate executive, she is fostering change within the community-based organization and developing products and services to enhance sustainable economic growth in the community.

Ellen has received numerous awards and recognition for achievements as a leader throughout her diverse career. In 2002 she was honored with a doctor of divinity degree for her more than 15 years of demonstrated leadership in ministry. She is also a 2006 participant in the Georgia Center for Nonprofit's CEO Central 60 leadership program.

Ellen received both her bachelor's and master's degrees in mathematics from Miles College and the University of Alabama in Birmingham, respectively. She currently teaches mathematics at two universities.

M elodee J. Ford is the president and chief executive officer of Junior Academies, Inc., an African-American nonprofit educational organization which she founded in 2002.

Having 34 years of experience in education as a teacher and administrator in public, parochial and independent schools, Melodee has successfully designed and implemented many academic programs, trained numerous educators and actively promoted the involvement of parents and community in the schools.

She is leading Junior Academies in opening 85 independent pre-kindergarten through grade 12 schools across 17 states. The first of these schools, the Rosa Parks Leadership Academy, will open in Atlanta in the fall of 2007.

Melodee has received various leadership, principal and community awards. She is a member of the Georgia Chamber of Congress, the NAACP, the Atlanta Business League, the National Association of Independent Schools, and several educational organizations.

She holds a bachelor's degree from Howard University and a master's degree in administration and supervision from the University of the District of Columbia.

A Washington, D.C. native, Melodee and her husband George have six children and six grandchildren.

Joan P. Garner serves as president and chief executive officer of the Historic District Development Corporation, one of Atlanta's oldest and most successful community development organizations. A former HDDC board chair, Garner now heads up the organization's redevelopment efforts in Atlanta's Old Fourth Ward.

A lifetime activist and social justice advocate, Garner, who also resides in the community, takes the reigns of HDDC at a crucial period in Atlanta's development. With a reputation for coalition building, her focus is on forging strong partnerships in the redevelopment of the Auburn Avenue commercial district, with special attention paid to restoring the historic Herndon Plaza. She continues to build on the HDDC legacy of creating affordable in-town housing.

Previously, Garner served as executive director of Southern Partners Fund, a public foundation created by community leaders and activists in the South, organizing and advising community-based organizations on taking control of their communities. Garner completed Leadership Atlanta and served on the Fulton County Arts Council. She was appointed by Mayor Shirley Franklin to the commission to memorialize former Mayors Maynard Jackson and Ivan Allen.

Joan P. Garner
President & Chief Executive Officer
Historic District Development Corporation

Michael German is the national lead coordinator for the U.S. Department of Housing and Urban Development's (HUD) Interagency Council on Homelessness. There, he works to advance the development of state interagency councils on homelessness and ten-year plans to end chronic homelessness around the country. The council works to better coordinate the activities of 20 federal agencies currently involved in assisting the homeless.

German joined HUD's Atlanta Field Office as the Atlanta regional director's liaison in 1999. Previously, he served as district manager to U.S. Representative John Lewis. German was the first director of the Office of Grants Development for the City of Atlanta under Mayor Maynard Jackson. He also served as deputy executive director of the Atlanta Housing Authority and spent 15 years with the Federal Emergency Management Agency (FEMA).

His professional endeavors include international commerce and assignments in France, Germany, Spain, England, Scotland, Denmark, Canada, Mexico, the Republic of China and the Netherlands.

German graduated from Alabama State University and completed studies at the John F. Kennedy School of Government Executive Program at Harvard University.

Michael German
National Lead Coordinator Interagency Council on Homelessness, U.S. Dept. of Housing and Urban Development

Howard W. Grant, Ph.D., is executive director of the Atlanta Board of Education. He is responsible for the day-to-day administration of the board. Grant was previously employed by the Atlanta Regional Commission, where he developed civic and environmental justice strategies.

Grant is a graduate of Morehouse College, and he earned his master's and doctorate degrees from Clark Atlanta University. He is a scholar-practitioner in the fields of public policy, environmental justice and social capital. He has provided leadership training to immigrant communities in Metropolitan Atlanta, and is on faculty at Atlanta Metropolitan College.

Grant is a member of Omega Psi Phi Fraternity, Inc., the Charles Kettering Foundation, the Diversity Leadership Academy of Atlanta, Leadership Atlanta and the Regional Leadership Institute. He also serves on the boards of directors for VSA Art of Georgia, the Fulton Atlanta Community Action Authority, the League of Women Voters, the Regional Leadership Foundation, and the United Negro College Fund.

Grant, his daughter, Madison Veronica, and son, Carrington Winslow, are members of Cascade United Methodist Church and reside in the Cascades.

Dr. Howard W. Grant
Executive Director/ Administrator Atlanta Board of Education

Angela Henderson
Director of Administration
New Birth South
Metropolitan Church

Angela Henderson is the director of administration for New Birth South Metropolitan Church in Jonesboro, Georgia. Under the leadership of senior pastor Andrè Landers, Henderson's responsibilities include managing the business operations, human resources and a $7 million annual budget. She also provides strategic planning for a $25 million building project slated for completion in 2007. New Birth South is one of the fastest growing churches in the southeast region. With only four years in existence, New Birth South's membership has grown to over 11,000.

Before joining New Birth South, Henderson made corporate history as the first African-American woman to hold the positions of regional area manager and director of distribution operations for AGL Resources, Inc. In keeping with a long-standing commitment to community, she served on the board of directors for several organizations including the metro Atlanta chapter of the American Red Cross and Cool Girls, Inc.

A Griffin, Georgia native, Henderson graduated from Dillard University in New Orleans, Louisiana with a bachelor's degree. She is a member of Delta Sigma Theta Sorority, Inc. and resides in Stockbridge, Georgia.

Young T. Hughley Jr.
President
& Chief Executive Officer
Reynoldstown Revitalization
Corporation

As president and chief executive officer of Reynoldstown Revitalization Corporation, (RRC) Young T. Hughley Jr. is an innovator and creative leader in the area of community development and revitalization. To date, RRC has invested more than $18 million into the Reynoldstown community. His professional skills include housing development, community building, capacity building, partnership development, fund-raising/special events planning and program and staff management.

A native of Georgia, Hughley holds a bachelor of arts degree from Morehouse College. He is a founding member and president of the Atlanta Housing Association of Neighborhood Based Developers. He also served on the advisory council for the Federal Home Loan Bank of Atlanta.

As a Fannie Mae fellow and United Way/Casey fellow, he attended Harvard University's John F. Kennedy School of Government. Those experiences contributed to his knowledge of public policy and reinforced in him the drive to remain progressive and current in community building changes and theory. Despite his demanding schedule, Hughley finds time to serve as chair of the Fulton County advisory board for the United Way of Metropolitan Atlanta.

Dr. Leslie C.
Bentley-Jackson
Founder, Solid Foundation
Home-School Study Program, Inc.

Leslie C. Bentley-Jackson grew up in Maple Heights, Ohio and graduated from Maple Heights Senior High School in 1986. She continued her education at Wright State University in Dayton, Ohio. In June of 1991, she graduated with a bachelor of arts degree in English and was commissioned a second lieutenant through ROTC.

In August of 1995, Leslie graduated from Clark Atlanta University with her master of arts degree in education and became a certified teacher in Georgia. In 2004 she received her doctor of education degree in educational leadership from Clark Atlanta University.

Leslie is a graduate of the NxLevel Entrepreneur Training Program based out of New Birth Missionary Baptist Church. In August of 2004, she founded Solid Foundation Home-School Study Program, Inc. in Stone Mountain. With students ranging in age from 4 to 14, she is looking to expand her program to high school by spring of 2007, along with a host of other program additions.

Brenda B. James
City Clerk
City of East Point

Brenda B. James is a certified city clerk for the City of East Point. She has worked with the city for 20 years, and has served as customer service manager and acting city manager.

Brenda is a past matron of Ruth Chapter #102, Order of the Eastern Star, a Prince Hall affiliate. For her dedication and commitment to community service, she received the Outstanding Georgia Citizen Award from the secretary of state. She volunteers with the Sickle Cell Anemia Foundation and has adopted a Hurricane Katrina family.

Brenda is also a member of Nabbar Court #123, Daughters of Isis. Her training and dedication earned her the Deputy of the Oasis of Georgia Award in 2005. Likewise, she has been honored as one of Georgia's 100 Most Powerful and Influential Women by *Women Looking Ahead News Magazine*.

A native of Tuskegee, Alabama, Brenda is married to Primis T. James. They have two children and four grandchildren. Brenda is a member of Andrews United Methodist Church in Jonesboro.

Tharon L. Johnson
Deputy Chief of Staff
Office of Congressman
John Barrow

Tharon L. Johnson serves as deputy chief of staff for Congressman John Barrow from Georgia's 12th Congressional District. With several years of local and state government experience, Tharon plays a central role in running the district's day-to-day operations.

Previously, Tharon worked as a public relations specialist with Georgia Labor Commissioner Michael L. Thurmond, serving as the department's legislative liaison during the general session. He has also worked under former Atlanta Mayor Bill Campbell.

Over the years, Tharon has successfully worked on a number of political campaigns for local and statewide elected officials in various roles including campaign manager, political consultant, and political and field director.

In the past, Tharon served as president of the NAACP Metro Atlanta Young Adult Council, vice president of programs for the Young Democrats of Georgia and vice president of finance for the Young Democrats of Fulton County. He is also a member of Alpha Phi Alpha Fraternity, Inc.

Tharon grew up in Athens, Georgia and graduated from Clark Atlanta University with a bachelor of arts degree in history.

Samuel L. Lovett Sr.
District 3 President
National Alliance of Postal
and Federal Employees

Samuel Lovett is District 3 president of the National Alliance of Postal and Federal Employees. He is a member of Local 321 and has been affiliated with the organization for more than 40 years. Samuel held numerous positions in the union before being elected to District 3 president. As a union official, he represented many employees in the federal and postal services. He can be credited with saving many jobs and creating opportunities for people who may have otherwise been unrepresented.

A native of Atlanta, Samuel is a product of the Atlanta Public Schools and Clark College. He is a lifelong member of New Grant Chapel AME Church where he is a member of the steward board, a Sunday school teacher and president of the men's ministry. He also served as a scout leader, community activist and a member of the NAACP.

Samuel is the husband of Bernice and the proud father of eight children, LaBrian (deceased), Connie, Vicki, Gary, Patrice, Eric, Samuel and Sandra.

Atlanta's
COMMUNITY LEADERS

Celebrating African-American Achievements

Deborah Lum
Executive Director
Atlanta Workforce
Development Agency

Deborah Lum is a community leader with more than 35 years of experience. Currently, she is the executive director of the Atlanta Workforce Development Agency. Lum has formed a collaboration of partners encompassing state and local governments, local academia, nonprofits and private sector organizations through which the center can offer city residents a comprehensive array of services. Her impact on the community through employment training programs has been immeasurable in producing a ready pool of qualified workforce professionals to meet local employment needs.

Lum oversees Mayor Shirley Franklin's Next Step ... The Atlanta Promise initiative, a mission to adopt Atlanta public school seniors and assist them in their steps towards a college education, technical training and meaningful employment. To date, the initiative has raised over $2 million and assisted more than 1,500 Atlanta high school seniors.

Lum was married to the late Tony Patrick and is the daughter-in-law of Alley Patrick, known as one of the most prominent black radio announcers in Atlanta. She is the proud mother of two children, Tony Jr. and Briana.

David Manuel
Director of Community
Relations
Project Director
Woodruff Arts Center

David Manuel currently serves as the director of community relations and project director for the Woodruff Arts Center in Atlanta. There, he is responsible for promoting the Woodruff Arts Center and its divisions to the various communities of Atlanta.

David has been with the Center in various capacities since 1984. After graduating from the Atlanta College of Art with a bachelor's degree in advertising and a minor in graphic design, he has served at the Center as both the operations manager and the events supervisor.

Currently David is host of the Urban Film Review, a monthly screening of independent American films. The project director for The Montreux Jazz Festival in 2005, he also serves on the executive board of the Callonwolde Fine Arts Center, the Mexican Center of Atlanta and the Caribbean Chamber of Atlanta. Additionally, he serves on the board of the Atlanta Business League, The Boys & Girls Club of DeKalb County and the Bureau of Cultural Affairs advisory grant panel.

David resides in Lilburn, Georgia, with his wife, Lori, and sons, Branden and Blake.

Dan Moore Sr.
President & Chief
Executive Officer
APEX MUSEUM

Dan Moore Sr. is the founder and president of the APEX MUSEUM in Atlanta. In his role as president and chief executive officer, he is responsible for the development of a state-of-the-art African-American museum that allows visitors to walk through history from ancient African civilizations to contemporary times.

Dan is an accomplished producer, writer, editor and filmmaker. He has received a number of awards including the CEBA Award, the State of Georgia's Humanities Award and recognition from African World Museum.

Dan has successfully run several companies, including two film companies in his hometown of Philadelphia, Pennsylvania and in Atlanta. He has filmed Bill Cosby, Melba Moore, Maynard Jackson, Gale Sayers and the president of Liberia, West Africa. His clients have included BellSouth, the Prince Hall Masons, MARTA and the National Park Service.

While serving as a producer for ABC affiliate WPVI-TV in Philadelphia, Dan produced 26 half-hour shows and six one-hour specials.

Dan resides with his wife, Estella, in Stone Mountain and has two sons, three grandchildren and five great grandchildren.

A dedicated, multitalented individual, Helga J. Moore founded All Children Are Special, Inc. (ACAS) four years ago. This nonprofit organization fills the major void in educational therapeutic child and adult care services within the growing disability community, locally and nationally.

As founder and chief executive officer of ACAS, and the mother of a disabled young adult son, Helga has more than 20 years of experience as a caretaker, nurse and peer counselor. She developed the All Children Are Special Educational Child/Adult Care Center, assisting thousands of working mothers like herself, with physically and mentally challenged children, to find comfort in the care and development of their children.

Helga's diligence has helped secure corporate, governmental, civic, educational, entertainment and religious support from major entities like General Motors, Atlanta Life Financial Group, BellSouth and State Farm, but she is not resting on her laurels. Helga is using her musical talent as a rising inspirational jazz recording artist to build the facility. In the meantime, the Center's Atlanta headquarters and first operating facility are scheduled to open in early 2007.

Helga J. Moore
Founder &
Chief Executive Officer
All Children Are Special, Inc.

B renda Muhammad is a nationally certified victim advocate. She serves as the executive director of Atlanta Victim Assistance, Inc., a 22-year-old nonprofit which provides services to victims of crimes.

She is also the elected school board representative from District One for the Atlanta Board of Education and has the distinction of having served as its first African-American female president.

Channeling the loss of her first son to violence at age 16, Brenda founded Mothers of Murdered Sons & Daughters, a national organization dedicated to stopping the plague of violence. Her work in this area has afforded her the opportunity to meet and work with present and former United States Presidents, and address members of Congress regarding funding and policies related to violence prevention.

Brenda has been featured as a violence prevention spokesperson in local and national media and recognized by numerous organizations for her courageous commitment.

She is currently a candidate for a master's degree from Southern New Hampshire University where she is specializing in nonprofit management.

Brenda Muhammad
Executive Director
Atlanta Victim
Assistance, Inc.

E ricka D. Newsome is director of community affairs for the Atlanta Braves and executive director of the Atlanta Braves Foundation. In this capacity, Newsome directs the many corporate relations and community service initiatives of the Atlanta Braves, and implements the philanthropic programs of the Braves Foundation. Dedicated to strengthening communities and brightening the futures of children, Newsome is instrumental in furthering the Braves' long-standing commitment to being a strong community partner and giving back to organizations in need.

A native of Toledo, Ohio, Newsome earned a bachelor of science in exceptional education from the University of Central Florida, and a master of science in sports marketing from St. Thomas University in Miami, Florida.

Active in the community, Newsome currently serves on the board of the Andrew & Walter Young Family YMCA. She is a member of the Atlanta Partners for Education advisory council, the Atlanta Corporate Donors Forum, the Turner Broadcasting System's volunteer council and Delta Sigma Theta Sorority, Inc.

Ericka D. Newsome
Executive Director
Atlanta Braves Foundation

Atlanta's
COMMUNITY LEADERS

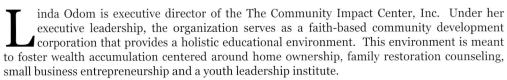

Celebrating African-American Achievements

Linda M. Odom
Executive Director
The Community Impact Center, Inc.

Linda Odom is executive director of the The Community Impact Center, Inc. Under her executive leadership, the organization serves as a faith-based community development corporation that provides a holistic educational environment. This environment is meant to foster wealth accumulation centered around home ownership, family restoration counseling, small business entrepreneurship and a youth leadership institute.

Before assuming her role at the center, she served as a senior vice president in the Wachovia Bank, Georgia banking division for 20 years. Additionally, Linda provides community leadership by serving on the boards of the Latin American Association, Southern Regional Medical Center Foundation and Women Looking Ahead (WLA).

Her awards include being selected as one of the Atlanta Business League's 100 Most Influential Women, WLA's 100 Most Influential Women and a 2003 Leadership Atlanta Alumni. In addition, she has been featured in numerous magazines regarding her accomplishments and commitment to community service.

Linda's philosophy on life is that we, who are prospering, are truly prosperous when we reach back and empower those who have lost hope or need direction to increase their quality of life.

Elisabeth Omilami
Chief Executive Officer
Hosea Feed the Hungry and Homeless Care Center

Elisabeth Omilami is chief executive officer of the largest African-American-owned human service organization in the Southeast. The Hosea Feed the Hungry and Homeless Care Center on Donnelly Avenue in Atlanta is a place of rescue and restoration for thousands of people around the globe.

Elisabeth created Summer Artscamp, providing classes in visual arts, drama, creative writing, dance and anger-management to at-risk youth. Hosea's outreach extends internationally to medical distribution and feeding programs in Haiti, Uganda and the Ivory Coast.

Elisabeth is an award-winning actor with more than 50 film, television and stage projects on her resume. Her film credits include *Glory Road*, *The List*, *MaDea's Family Reunion* and *The Ray Charles Story*. She is a recipient of the Phoenix Award from Mayor Shirley Franklin and the City of Atlanta.

Elisabeth and her husband, Afemo, are active members of Abundant Life Church in Lithonia. They participate in the prison, missions and drama ministries.

Born in Atlanta, Elisabeth is the daughter of late civil rights activists Reverend Hosea and Juanita T. Williams. She has two wonderful children, Awodele and Juanita.

Joyce E. Suber
President
College Options Foundation

Joyce Suber has spent her career teaching both elementary and high school, serving as a private school administrator and counseling students and families concerning the college selection process. Her work has spanned the full socioeconomic spectrum of families in the U.S., from the most prestigious universities and college-prep high schools to one of the largest urban school systems in America.

An expert in the fields of college counseling and student services, Joyce operates on a platform for success, assisting students and families at all stages of the college planning process. She recently completed a book for The Princeton Review on the topic of pre-college experiences, which high school students can use to enrich their lives and their college applications.

Joyce has served on numerous boards and committees for various organizations such as president of the College Options Foundation in Peachtree City. She is also a founding partner in Nextstep Associates, an educational consulting firm operating in metro Atlanta and Chicago. Nextstep specializes in college planning, school start-up, program development and evaluation and gifted student advocacy.

M. von Nkosi
Director of Research,
Policy & Information
Mixed Income
Communities Initiative

As director of research, policy and information at the Atlanta Neighborhood Development Partnership, M. von Nkosi has directed the Mixed Income Communities Initiative since 1998. He is dedicated to using mixed-income and mixed-use communities as a strategy to help those who struggle to pay for housing.

Nkosi is also the president and chief executive officer of The MXD Collaborative, Inc., a consulting firm established in 1992 to bring the best creative minds together and improve urban environments. He holds licenses to practice architecture in Georgia, Florida, and Illinois and is a member of the American Institute of Architects.

A graduate of Hampton University and Illinois Institute of Technology with his bachelor's and master's degrees in architecture, Nkosi has also completed doctorate course work in architecture at Georgia Institute of Technology. His knowledge of urban design, architecture, multimedia and academic research helps move smart growth forward in metropolitan Atlanta. He is also a Life fellow of the Graduate School of Business at the University of Cape Town, South Africa and the Terry Sanford Institute of Public Policy at Duke University.

Theresa Walker
Executive Director
Georgia Black Chamber
of Commerce

As executive director of the Georgia Black Chamber of Commerce (GBCC), Theresa Walker is continuing the legacy of her late husband, Lou Walker. He was founder and chairman of the GBCC, DeKalb County commissioner, business owner, and a film and television character actor.

Theresa has more than 30 years of experience in public relations, marketing, government relations, and special event design and production. She was co-owner with her husband of Paragon Productions and Blues in the Alley nightclub in Underground Atlanta.

Theresa is a charter/founding member of the Metropolitan Atlanta Chapter of 100 Black Women. She has received numerous honors including the Phoenix Award from the Public Relations Society of America-Georgia Chapter, and the Outstanding Georgia Citizen award from the secretary of state. She was featured in *Atlanta Tribune: The Magazine* in a story saluting women trailblazers. Additionally, she is a representative for the National Association of Women Highway Safety Leaders and the Georgia DUI Task Force.

A native of Chicago, Illinois, Theresa has four children and five grandchildren. She is a member of Saint Philip AME Church in Decatur.

Jason Warner
Director of Community
Relations
DeKalb County Government

Jason Warner is the director of community relations for DeKalb County Government and works directly with chief executive officer Vernon Jones as a part of his key administrative staff. As one of the youngest directors in one of the most culturally diverse counties in the country, he is responsible for maintaining effective relations among elected officials, the various communities and county employees through an array of internal and external communications and various countywide events.

He also serves as the executive director for the DeKalb County Community Relations Commission and a member of the veterans advisory board, the DeKalb Council on Literacy, and an advisor to the Lisa "Left Eye" Lopes Foundation.

Warner is a native of Miami, Florida and a graduate of Florida A&M University's School of Journalism and Graphic Communication. He brings leadership from his years in scouting, while earning the highest rank attainable, Eagle Scout. He has been married to his lovely wife Sybil for two years.